Walking the Talk
Pathways to Leadership

Walking the Talk
Pathways to Leadership

Michael J. Termini

Society of Manufacturing Engineers
Dearborn, Michigan

Copyright © 2007 Society of Manufacturing Engineers

987654321

All rights reserved, including those of translation. This book, or parts thereof, may not be reproduced by any means, including photocopying, scanning, digitizing, recording, or microfilming, or by any information storage and retrieval system, without permission in writing of the copyright owners. No liability is assumed by the publisher with respect to use of information contained herein. While every precaution has been taken in the preparation of this book, the publisher assumes no responsibility for errors or omissions. Publication of any data in this book does not constitute a recommendation or endorsement of any patent, proprietary right, or product that may be involved.

Library of Congress Catalog Card Number: 2007923855

International Standard Book Number (ISBN): 0-87263-851-0
ISBN 13: 978-087263851-8

Additional copies may be obtained by contacting:
Society of Manufacturing Engineers
Customer Service
One SME Drive, P.O. Box 930
Dearborn, Michigan 48121
1-800-733-4763
www.sme.org

SME staff who participated in producing this book:
Rosemary Csizmadia, Senior Production Editor
Steve Bollinger, Manager, Book & Video Publications
Christine Verdone, Cover Design
Frances Kania, Administrative Coordinator

Printed in the United States of America

Dedication

This book is dedicated to the thousands of technical professionals each year who undertake the transition from individual contributor to manager. Your journey will be filled with challenges, joys, and disappointments. Each day will require you to evaluate the actualities of your situation and make decisions to ensure the sustained momentum of your organization and career. Some of those decisions will be straightforward, some unpopular, others complex. Your career growth will depend upon the success of those decisions, the success of your organization, and the success of your employees. You must recognize and accept the fact that you cannot do it alone. You will need help—from your employees, from your peers, and from your superiors. Build your support network with great care.

The transition will take time and patience. Your skills as a manager and leader will be honed by experience. Even though you may be an excellent individual contributor with outstanding technical skills, the skill sets you will require to be an equally outstanding manager and leader are radically different. Challenge yourself, but be realistic in setting your goals. Learn every day from your mistakes and successes. Create a daily journal of "lessons learned" and take note of what worked, what did not, and why. Then reflect upon your lessons frequently. Constantly challenge yourself to be a better manager and leader than you were the day before. Like those who have come before you, you too will be successful. Have faith in yourself and in those around you. Good luck on your journey!

Acknowledgments

I want to recognize and thank my wife, Susan, and children Kelly, Justin, Casey, and Brad. Their loving support has made my journey successful. Management careers can create difficulties and put strain on a manager's family, just as on the manager himself. Never forget your first priority—those who love and support you. It is because of them that the successes you earn will have true meaning. Always strive for a balance between your career and your family. Reaching a lofty goal with no one to share it with is truly a hollow victory.

Table of Contents

Foreword xiii
About the Author xvii
Preface xix
Introduction xxiii

1 The Transition into Management 1
   Objective 1
   Introduction 1
   Natural Instincts vs. Management Capabilities 3
   Leadership by Example 5
   Decisions, Conflict, and Controversy 7
   People vs. Process Issues 9
   Communication: A Strength or Weakness? 12
   Establishing and Communicating Expectations 15
   Bias in Management 17
   Hiring and Firing . . . the Good, the Bad, and the Ugly 18
   Dealing with Politicians 23
   Summary 25

2 Leadership in Perspective 27
   Objective 27
   Historical Overview 27
   Pressures of Leadership 31
   Pros and Cons of Leadership 32
   Change, Not Chaos . . . A Leadership Imperative 32
   Techniques of Good Leaders 33
   Communication 45
   Honesty in Management 51
   Reward and Recognition 52
   Developing Informal Leaders 53
   The New Manager 56
   Summary 66

3 Managing the Transition from Individual Contributor to Manager 69
   Objectives 69
   Preparing for the Transition 69

Walking the Talk: Pathways to Leadership

Table of Contents

New Roles and Responsibilities 70
Facilitating the Transition 73
First Success 81
Summary 81

4 Complying with Employment and Labor Laws 83
Objective 83
Federal Labor Laws 84
State Labor Laws 97
Summary 98

5 Management Skill-building Scenarios and Case Study Examples 99
Objectives 99
Scenario 1 99
Scenario 2 102
Scenario 3 104
Scenario 4 106
Scenario 5 107
Scenario 6 108
Scenario 7 109
Scenario 8 110
Scenario 9 115
Scenario 10 118
Scenario 11 119
Scenario 12 121
Scenario 13 123
Scenario 14 125
Scenario 15 128
Scenario 16 130
Scenario 17 131
Scenario 18 132
Scenario 19 135
Scenario 20 138
Scenario 21 138
Underlying Causes 141
Summary 141

6 Managing Disciplinary Problems 143
Objectives 143
Identifying Performance Issues 143
Disciplinary Action . . . A Step-by-Step Process 149
Summary 163

7 Employee Selection, Direction, Motivation, and Empowerment 165
Objective 165
Market Dynamics and Technological Change as Drivers 166
Maslow's Hierarchy of Needs 168
Employee Involvement and Empowerment 171
Closed-loop Management 182
Communication 208
Unorthodox Decisions 216
Tools for Success 219
Summary 223

8 Building Organizational Alignment 225
Objectives 225
Aligning Capabilitiy and Competency with Organizational Vision 225
Organizational Base-lining 227
Vision 229
Cultivate Essential Employee Skill Sets 231
Succession Planning 241
Leading Mature Organizations 241
Building Consensus vs. Consensus Management 250
Summary 256

9 Base-lining Organizational Capabilities 259
Objective 259
Practical Capacity Analysis 260
Situational Assessment 262
Summary 275

10 Effective Problem-solving and Decision-making 277
Objectives 277
Problem Analysis 277
Assessment Clues 284
Decision-making 293
Case Study 302
Summary 314

11 Turning Your Vision for Change into Action 317
Objectives 317
Why Transformations Fail 317
Successful Transformations—Organizational, Departmental,
  and Process 320
The Transformation Model 327
Summary 370

12 Organizational Politics 371
Objectives 371
Why Do Politics Exist? 372
Teamwork vs. Politics 372
A Time and a Place for Politics 373
Summary 377

Appendix: Competency and Capability Assessments 379
Manufacturing Process Capabilities and Capacities 379
Manufacturing Process Controls 380
Quality Systems 383
Quality Management 386
Raw Materials Compliance 389
Inventory Management and Control Systems 391
Technical and Product Support 391
Cost Controls 393
Management Commitment 395
Financial Stability 397
Industry Knowledge 398
Facilities Management and Maintenance 399
Distribution Process Control 400
Order-entry Process Control 402
Customer and Field Service 403
Regulatory Compliance 405
Labor Relations 406
Document Control 407
Product Reliability and Warranty 408

Index 411

Foreword

It is 3 a.m. and I am awake. My mind cannot sleep because of an employee issue from late yesterday that is gnawing at me. Twenty-three years of management experience told me not to respond to the issue yesterday. Twenty-three years of experience told me not to press the "send button" on my initial e-mail response. Twenty-three years of experience told me to sleep on it. Forty-five years of me being me told me not to trust my initial instinct and apply the leadership skills that I have been taught throughout my career.

At 3 a.m., it is the perfect time to take out Mike's book, reflect on its content, and share its importance with you. Mike would challenge me. Is this issue real or are you feeling a loss of control? Is this about you or is it a true employee performance issue? What is the issue? How does it impact the achievement of organizational goals? What are your proposed corrective actions? What are the implications of each of your proposed responses to the employee and, politically, to you?

Mike crystallizes what it took me 23 years to learn and unfortunately, many times the hard way! My journey has taken me from individual contributor to a vice president with Johnson & Johnson to a senior vice president at a $3 billion division of McKesson. Functionally, I have been in accounting, operations, engineering, quality, plant management, and sales and marketing. As you might be thinking, change management and managing transitions has been a theme in my career. Navigating into unknown waters is scary. Fortunately, Mike provides us with a map.

This book is content rich with the details well organized. Mike's hope is that you read this book *before* you decide to make the transition from individual contributor to manager. His first challenge to you—have you thought it through? Is this position a good fit? Are you ready to give up being the expert? Like all of Mike's books, this one has been developed from his seminars

Foreword

and teachings, so the concepts have been well tested. In fact, the impetus for the book is that all too often new managers are sent to Mike's course for development. Almost without exception, there is one person in each course who concludes that making the transition was a mistake. Mike tracks these people and, all too often, there is no road back without significant personal cost.

Once you have thoughtfully made your decision, Mike discusses the spoken and unspoken requirements of a successful leader. I cannot stress enough the value of the unspoken expectations put upon you in the areas of politics and leadership. Mike shares that "managers manage and leaders get promoted." I encourage you to highlight this statement and when you have finished reading the rest of the book, come back and you will know its meaning.

Why is Mike so effective? Simply put, he has dived into the uncharted waters and was thoughtful enough to document his journey for our benefit. Mike has gone from an individual contributor to a CEO of a major corporation. He is a Certified Executive Coach to Fortune 100 executives; in fact, it was at Johnson & Johnson that I was introduced to Mike. He has been a consultant to numerous Fortune 500 companies such as Johnson & Johnson, McKesson, Northrop Grumman, and Philip Morris. Each assignment was yet another opportunity to perfect his techniques and demonstrate their effectiveness across all industries. As a teacher and author, he has critically thought through the details and organized them.

Mike teaches us that leadership is about people, politics, regulation, and developing a continuously expanding personal toolbox. He discusses the importance of managing politics and encourages you to pick a project that will give you an early win. His "closed-loop" strategy provides everything you need to know to select, direct, and motivate a team, including how to deal with change-management issues, succession planning, and performance problems.

From a regulatory perspective, the bases are covered: Title VII, sexual harassment, age discrimination, affirmative action, federal labor laws, OSHA, and workers compensation, to name a few. Additionally, Mike makes a significant contribution to your toolbox by reviewing root cause analysis, voice of the customer, quality function deployment, and cost-benefit analysis, along with sharing how to make decisions by taking both a process and functional view.

In the tradition of all great masters, Mike brings it all together through the tradition of story telling and discussion, as true mastery is the ability to apply the individual details holistically. My recommendation is for you to read this book and keep it by your desk. Let it process in your unconscious mind; refer to it frequently so that your practice becomes instinctual.

Both my father and mother taught public school for almost 80 years combined and they frequently quoted the proverb, "When the student is ready, the teacher will come." Your transition from an individual contributor to a leader provides the incentive for you to be a "ready student" and you are fortunate that your teacher has arrived.

It is now 9 a.m. I have just received approval and kudos from my boss regarding how I plan to manage my employee situation. The answer is to provide a new assignment that allows this individual to practice the skill he lacks. The position is one of equal or greater responsibility. However, I am not putting the employee into a high-risk situation. Should he fail, it will not significantly affect him or me.

You may be wondering—after 23 years, has my frequent practice allowed for my response to become instinctual? Not exactly! Only you and I know that my first reaction was not appropriate. Practice made me smart enough not to act on my instinct and to consult Mike's book to critically think through my situation. As Robert Frost said, "I took the road less traveled by, and that has made all the difference."

James F. Jordan
Executive in Residence
Pittsburgh Lifesciences

About the Author

Michael J. Termini is President & CEO of The Consulting Alliance Group, Inc. With over 35 years of pragmatic industry experience, he has an expansive, exemplary record of achievement. He has held executive management positions in domestic and international venues for a variety of industry leaders including Billings Corporation, Dresser Industries, PACCAR Corporation, United Technologies, Hallmark Cards, Allis-Chalmers, and Gephardt, Inc.

Author of *The New Manufacturing Engineer—Coming of Age in an Agile Environment* (SME 1997) and *Strategic Project Management* (SME 1999), Termini has also authored over 100 articles and training programs in the fields of management and leadership, business process improvement, strategic planning, concurrent engineering, integrated product development, agile manufacturing, and organizational reengineering.

Michael Termini holds an MBA in Marketing from the University of Missouri-Kansas City and a BS in Aerospace Engineering from the University of Missouri-Rolla. He is a Registered Educational Provider for the Project Management Institute, as well as a frequent management trainer at numerous universities and professional organizations, including the Society of Manufacturing Engineers. Termini also has been featured as a host and guest speaker for numerous live television broadcasts for PBS, NTU, and FTN.

Preface

A publisher once said to me that technical professionals "don't buy books on management." Unfortunately, this misguided perception is shared by many in academia and business. The truth is, however, that most technical professionals have a keen interest in expanding their careers by moving into management positions. The problem is that neither the engineering and technical schools nor the business training programs offered by their organizations provide them with the basic skills, tools, and techniques necessary to successfully transition into management from a technical position. As a result, the transition is often difficult and disheartening. This is exactly why technical professionals *do* buy books on management and why I see several thousand of them in my executive development classes each year.

To prepare themselves, technical professionals must decide early in their careers if they want to work in management. Making that decision consciously is vital because, as many technical professionals have found, once they transition into management, it is difficult or impossible to go back into technical positions. The reason is that obsolescence sets in quickly, especially in today's rapidly changing technological fields.

The intent of this book is to provide valuable insight on management from the perspective of a business executive who has successfully progressed from engineer to CEO in his career. Based upon over 30 years of practical business and industry experience, the tools and techniques discussed herein will provide students, technical professionals, and experienced managers with the tools needed to successfully traverse the corporate minefields of today's fast-paced business environment. The old adage that *knowledge is power* is verified over and over again in the business world. Armed with the foreknowledge of what to expect and how to deal with it, you will learn how to avoid many of the traps that can sidetrack or ruin your career.

Preface

Accept the fact that there is no magic pill or business model that can be learned to ensure success. There simply is no substitute for hard work, dedication, and application of common sense. But there are management fundamentals that can be applied along with those requirements to greatly increase the probability of success as well as career enjoyment. Just as there are tangible rewards to be derived from a technical career, there are tangible rewards to be gained from management. But management is NOT for everyone. As this book will point out, the decision to move into management from a technical position must be weighed carefully against the intrinsic joys of a technical career. Dealing with people, motivating them, and at times disciplining them can be stressful and difficult. Some individuals thrive on the challenge of managing people, some absolutely hate it. Recognize your strengths and weaknesses, the things you do well and not so well, and how you want to spend your days on the job. Only if management is truly right for you, should you consider making the transition. It should not be a financial decision. Today, many organizations have created parallel career and financial tracks for technical professionals that allow them to grow professionally and financially without ever leaving the hallowed halls of the technical field. Make this career decision wisely.

In this book, a multitude of management tools and techniques will be discussed along with their practical application. Case studies from real-world companies will be utilized to illustrate how to apply those principles in a business setting. Differing viewpoints on management techniques will be explored. Nothing will be held back—nothing. Anything and everything that a manager will face, from sexual harassment to gender bias, will be discussed. The intent is to highlight as many of the issues facing today's managers as possible to better prepare them for what lies ahead.

One final point before moving forward—there is simply no substitute for common sense and common decency in management. Those two traits alone will enhance any manager's probability of success. Be *fair*, be *consistent*, and be *predictable* and you will earn the trust and respect of your employees.

SOME HUMOR TO GET YOU STARTED

A man walks into a café with a shotgun in one hand and pulling a large buffalo with the other. He says to the waiter, "Coffee please."

The waiter says, "Sure, coming right up." The waiter brings the man his coffee. The man quickly drinks his coffee, then turns and shoots the buffalo with his shotgun, making an incredible mess. He then calmly walks out.

The next morning, the man returns to the café. Again he carries his shotgun and is pulling a large buffalo. He walks up to the counter and calmly orders a cup of coffee. The waiter, somewhat shocked to see the man return says, "Hold on a minute. We are still cleaning up the mess you left in here yesterday. What the heck was that about anyway?"

The man smiles broadly and proudly says, "I am training for a management position. You know, come in, drink coffee, shoot the bull, leave a mess for everyone else to clean up, and disappear for the remainder of the day."

Introduction

Promotion into management for most technical professionals is only the first step in a long growth curve. Management is truly a growth experience for all who venture into it. Every day, successful closed-loop managers learn something new, make mistakes, and enjoy successes. As stated in Chapter 1, management is not for everyone. There are certainly challenges and risks associated with the move into management. Frustrations exist as well. But for those who brave those challenges, the rewards—both personally and financially—are excellent.

As discussed throughout this book, success is earned over time. It does not come as a perk; nor is it necessarily guaranteed by hard work and dedication. Situational drivers within the workplace and external drivers that influence the business environment often combine to create unique challenges for a manager. While there is no recipe for instant success in management, the closed-loop leadership principles illustrated throughout this book certainly provide a structure for success, as do the decision and communication tools discussed. Much will be learned over time and gained through the use of common sense and respect for others.

With experience comes the realization that each situation brings with it unique constraints and challenges for a manager. Past experiences provide insight on how to analyze a situation, not necessarily how to resolve it. In management, there are a few givens and no canned solutions. That is why every day is a learning process—another opportunity to expand upon existing skill sets and to create new ones. Yes, mistakes will be made along the way. But by working within the structure of closed-loop management, those mistakes will be contained so they are learning events versus career disasters.

A good starting place for a new manager is to create a journal to document those things done or observed that worked well, and those that did not. The journal is updated and reviewed frequently. It provides a basis of learning from the past to better prepare for the future. Too often, random events, daily pressures, even politics set the stage for success or failure of a management career. No manager should ever leave his or her destiny to fate. Career management is an essential aspect of success; it is one that is not to be taken lightly.

Success is earned through the leadership of employees. It is the success of the employees that guarantees the success of their leaders. No manager is deemed to be successful if the organization around him fails to meet the expected level of performance on a consistent basis. No manager can be successful without creating a dynamic work force capable of self-direction and self-discipline. And, no manager is successful unless he has developed a capable leader to take his place. In short, no manager can do it alone. That is why management exists—to provide leadership that ensures the success of the organization and its employees. When they succeed, so do their leaders. It is truly a closed-loop process.

ONE MORE THOUGHT

A man in a hot-air balloon realized he was lost, so he reduced altitude and spotted a woman on the ground below. He descended a bit and shouted to her, "Excuse me, can you help me? I promised a friend I would meet him an hour ago but I don't know where I am."

The woman replied, "You are in a hot-air balloon hovering approximately 30 feet above the ground. You are between 40 and 41 degrees north latitude and between 59 and 60 degrees west latitude."

"You must be an engineer," said the balloonist.

"I am," said the woman. "How did you know?"

"Well," answered the balloonist, "Everything you told me is technically correct, but I have no idea what to make of your information and, the fact is, I am still lost. Frankly, you have been no help to me so far."

The woman responded, "You must be in management."

"I am," he replied. "How did you know?"

The woman replied, "You don't know where you are or where you are going. You have risen to where you are due to a large quantity of hot air. You made a promise that you have no idea of how to keep, and you expect people beneath you to solve your problems. The fact is you are in exactly the same position you were in before we met, but now, somehow it's my fault."

Remember where you started from; then judge your success by how far you have come.

The Transition into Management

OBJECTIVE

In this chapter, several of the basic considerations relative to the transition of individual contributors into management roles will be explored in general terms with more detail to follow in subsequent chapters. In addition, the chapter will provide an overview of many of the tools and techniques available to facilitate the transition from being a technical professional to being an effective manager. The assumption that a good engineer or a good technical professional can be a good manager is not necessarily true. So this chapter will also address the myriad issues and problems the technical professional will often be forced to deal with early in this critical career transition.

> "The assumption that a good engineer or a good technical professional can be a good manager is not necessarily true."

INTRODUCTION

There exists a common belief among many technical professionals that, "If I want to make more money or advance beyond the ranks of my technical position, I can easily transition from being an engineer or technical professional into being a manager." However, the transition for most technical professionals is often times incredibly problematic. The reason is that most organizations fail to adequately prepare the technical professional in advance for that transition. Even in college, most technical professionals take only the minimum number of management courses required to get by. Unfortunately, those courses really do

The Transition into Management

not get into the real business issues that will be faced by today's functional, project, or departmental manager—employee problems, performance problems, organizational problems, process problems, strategic problems, tactical problems, financial and budgetary problems, customer problems, political problems, etc. These are the "make or break" issues of a management career. Thus knowing how to recognize and deal with them efficiently will make traversing the organizational mine fields much easier.

> "There is a significant difference between being an excellent individual contributor and being an effective business manager."

There is a significant difference between being an excellent individual contributor and being a solid manager. Organizations need managers who make good decisions, who lead effectively, who constantly mentor employees, and who work through their employees and peers to get the most difficult jobs completed successfully. Experienced managers are able to think organizationally, act tactically, and avoid the trap of "silo thinking."

While this book focuses on the real need for exceptional leaders and managers, there is also a great need for dedicated and skilled individual contributors within every organization . . . professional engineers, professional technicians, project management professionals, accountants, programmers, systems analysts, etc. Every organization requires these professionals to grow and prosper. Individual contributors are of tremendous value to an organization, because it is their daily contribution that ensures the organization's customers are served, operations are maintained, and objectives achieved.

In many enlightened organizations, alternate career paths are being developed for technical employees to grow both financially and professionally. For too long it was thought that for a technical professional to advance, it was a requirement to move into management. That simply is not the case. Many engineers, programmers, accountants, and other technical professionals are paid as much or more than managers within the

The Transition into Management

same organization. They have career paths that allow them to grow professionally, maximizing their personal and professional capabilities while staying within the confines of their preferred technical areas. In short, there is an option for every technical professional in every industry to stay within the discipline they love and enjoy; there are alternatives that provide growth with either career decision. So decide wisely.

The reason why alternate career paths are important is that management is not for everyone. The move into management is a conscious, well-thought-out decision, one that is made by the individual, not for him by a superior or other manager. It is made for the right reasons, both personally and professionally. Just as there are numerous tangible, personal rewards derived from a technical career, there are equally as many from a management career. But there are also numerous problems that a manager deals with daily that are not part of the responsibilities of the individual contributor. Therefore, the decision to move into management is always made with as much wisdom as possible. There is often no turning back once the decision is made. This chapter begins, therefore, with a brief discussion of several key considerations relative to the decision to move into management, as well as the requirements the decision will dictate.

> "The decision to move into management must be made with as much wisdom as possible."

NATURAL INSTINCTS VS. MANAGEMENT CAPABILITIES

Management, leadership, and decision-making skills are not something most successful managers are born with. Yes, many technical professionals have some of the inherent, natural talents that make a good leader. And, most are good problem solvers, good abstract thinkers, and rational in their assessment of process-related issues. As a result, they often do an excellent job in management if given the proper training and preparation. But in most cases, the management side—the people side of the business—is learned on the job through trial and error. To be successful in management, the technical professional goes beyond those basic instincts as well as the technical training received in school and on the job. Most of the strategic and tactical business, personnel, and operational issues that will be dealt with in any organization or work group are neither black nor white. In fact, managers now, more than any other time, are required to deal with shades of gray in which simple answers are elusive.

Most technical professionals use established theorems, calculations, and measurements in their jobs that are very clearly defined and have been proven over time. Management, as a discipline, is not blessed with those same quantitative tools that are universally applied time and time again. For managers, every situation is unique. And while as a technical professional it is possible to resolve a technical problem and replicate the solution a number of times for validation, this same approach simply is not workable in a business environment. Replicating a canned solution or business model used in another business situation will often yield less-than-desirable results, even if that approach was successful in the past. It is thus imperative for a manager to understand that each business situation is uniquely different, requiring careful and comprehensive review and analysis before a final decision is made or action taken. Each business issue, situation, or problem is assessed on its individual constraints and merits. Nothing is taken for granted or overlooked.

In every industry today the focus goes beyond that of simple management. Leadership and facilitation skills are in demand. There is a movement away from the difficult, if not impossible, task of trying to manage and control knowledge workers—professionals with highly advanced technical and business skills. These professionals refuse to be led around by the nose, to be micro-managed. Instead, these talented (often multi-talented) individuals want the freedom to utilize their creativity rather than follow strict direction or a methodology dictated by their superiors. Consequently, knowledge workers respond best to managers who support, guide, mentor, tutor, and coach them so they can constantly develop and enhance their personal and professional skills. Thus, the role of a manager in today's complex business environment is not to rule or dictate, but rather to lead and facilitate. This requirement necessitates that aspiring managers develop an entirely new set of skills to effectively lead these professionals. Even experienced managers are required to respond to this dynamic organizational paradigm, with its changing employee expectations and demands, and generational challenges to ensure personal and organizational success.

Dealing with People

The hardest task facing technical professionals who are making the transition to management is learning to deal with people. Many technical professionals simply are not good "people" persons. They prefer to do things on their own, groomed by years of working in their office or cubicle, doing their own work, alone and without interruption. Today, with the movement by organizations to encourage employees to telecommute, many technical professionals have found it possible to work at home, in the comfort of their own living room, office, or den. In the shelter of their own home, they are even more divorced from the requirement of dealing with other employees. The good part of this scenario is . . . "I can get a lot of work done if I don't have to answer all those phone calls; if I don't have to deal with all those irritating people; if somebody isn't always knocking on my door saying they need my help." The bad news is, as aspiring managers, they have lost the opportunity to learn first-hand how to deal with other peers and employees, address personnel and business issues, or to build self-directed work teams to handle tough functional or organizational issues. Without the opportunity to observe their leader in action, employees are not exposed to learning from his or her actions and mistakes, to seeing what techniques work effectively and which do not, and to learning the fundamental rules of management.

LEADERSHIP BY EXAMPLE

Successful managers have learned to lead by example. There's an adage that says, "An organization is a reflection of its leader." If an organization is not performing well, the first place a manager looks for answers is in the mirror. Specifically, is something he or she doing sending the wrong signal to the employees? For example, if it is a requirement for all employees to report to work at or before a specific time every day, at what time does the manager get in? Is the manager there right on the hour, a few minutes early, or consistently late? Is the manager actively working at the designated start time? Does the manager consistently drag in a few minutes late from lunch? Is the manager the first one out the door at quitting time? Does the manager's attitude seem positive and upbeat, or is he or she one of those people who drag in every day with a negative attitude? The bottom line is this: employees will mimic their leader and react as the leader does—for better or for worse. Employees look to their manager for leadership and direction. If the manager's words are in contradiction with his or her actions, employees will notice and respond accordingly.

Effective managers recognize that "walking the talk" is a vital part of leadership. Employees do as their leader does. Just as with raising children, follow-through, discipline, and structure are critical.

Example

The following is an example taken from an actual incidence at a Fortune 100 firm in the energy conversion industry.

A young, upwardly mobile technical manager built his stellar career around hard work, dedication, and results. As he moved up through the ranks of the organization, he quickly became recognized as a solid technical professional and an equally solid leader of his employees. His career path reflected the respect and admiration employees, peers, and senior management had for him. As manager of a large department, he also earned respect for his fiscal management, and the process and productivity improvements initiated under his direction. His career was definitely moving in the right direction.

At 38 years of age, he was named vice president of a midsized division of the corporation. Expectations of him were great. Part of the duties of his new position included developing close working relationships with the division's key customers and suppliers. He began entertaining customers by taking their senior managers and marketing representatives to dinner, and later, on golf outings. He purchased a golf membership at one of the local country clubs for the division and began using it regularly. In fact, so regularly that it became a daily ritual. His staff soon realized that anything requiring his approval would have to be submitted before 2:00 p.m. daily—before the boss left for his tee time. Things continued along well for a period of time. Then, gradually over time, his employees, recognizing that the boss would be gone every day by 2:00 p.m., began to take off early. As the practice became more widespread, productivity within the ranks of the organization began to suffer. As the productivity loss became more noticeable to upper management, calls began to come in from corporate headquarters. What was going on in the division soon became evident. When it did, a promising career came to an abrupt end.

DECISIONS, CONFLICT, AND CONTROVERSY

The decision to move into a management position begins with a fundamental question: "Am I comfortable making decisions?" Many people are comfortable in making decisions that affect the task at hand. And, many are comfortable taking on additional responsibility. However, most will avoid making decisions when faced with controversy, organizational politics, or conflict. And it is a fact that indecision is a detriment to any manager's ability to effectively lead.

There will be times when managers are forced to make unpopular decisions. It is a requirement that simply cannot be avoided, overlooked, or shirked. A manager's responsibility is to maintain momentum within his or her organization to keep the organization moving forward in spite of obstacles or difficulties. Decision-making is a vital and fundamental requirement of management. It is easy when everything is going as planned. But good managers clearly understand the requirement to make sound, timely decisions even when faced with an organizational

The Transition into Management

or business crisis. To be effective, managers expeditiously lead their organizations through numerous difficulties and change processes by making sound, logical, often out-of-the-box decisions.

Management and Decisions

Because of an inability to deal effectively with conflict, an aversion to politics, or a dislike for controversy, many managers have a tendency to back away from decision-making when faced with an uncomfortable situation. Rather than avoiding the discomfort, however, the manager's inaction actually creates additional problems that make the situation worse for both the manager and his or her employees. Effective managers make sound, supportable decisions, in a reasonable time frame, irrespective of controversy or conflict. Their decisions are well thought out and analytical, based upon the best possible facts surrounding each situation. Good managers never shoot from the hip just to make the problem go away for the short term. Short-term fixes usually allow problems to return later in far more dramatic ways.

Technical professionals do not jump to arbitrary decisions relative to design or development efforts. Each situation or problem is thoroughly assessed by looking at the numbers and taking measurements to gather quantifiable data before making a decision. Analysis is done expeditiously to allow the design or development efforts to move forward on schedule.

> "Whenever a good employee is coupled to a bad process, the process will win every time."

For successful managers, the process is the same. They deal with hard facts when making decisions. Equally as important, those decisions are made in a timely fashion to maintain momentum within the organization. And, once a decision is made, the manager stands firmly behind it.

Business decisions are critical to the organization's bottom line regardless of the level at which they are made within the organization. Since decisions have a rippling effect, managers recognize this and react to the requirement to make decisions quickly and accurately to constantly move the organization forward.

PEOPLE VS. PROCESS ISSUES

Successful managers recognize and accept the fact that employees do not come to work every day with the intent to make mistakes. If repetitive problems are plaguing an organization, in the majority of cases there are process and not personnel problems at the source. Experienced managers look first for processes that are uncontrolled and incapable of meeting desired performance levels, and secondly for those that are poorly defined. It is a fact that whenever a good employee is coupled to a bad process, the process will win every time. This is because no matter how hard an employee tries, the inefficiencies inherent within the process will overcome the employee's efforts, resulting in mistake or failure. So in cases where failures and mistakes are repetitive, good managers look first for process problems. Thereafter, they look for employee performance issues.

> "Decisions in business are not like making wine in Napa Valley where the manager can simply put a decision on the shelf for a few years and it will miraculously get better."

The likelihood of a process being at the root of a problem leads a manager to inquire about *how* the mistake can be avoided in the future rather than focusing on *who* made the mistake. When employees realize that their manager is more interested in fixing the problem than in fixing blame, they will be more likely to bring process problems to their manager's attention. And when all employees begin to take responsibility for identifying and resolving business process problems, the manager's organization has taken its first step toward self-direction.

Personnel Perspective

One of the primary objectives of any manager is to get maximum performance from his or her employees. This is often more difficult than it first appears. The majority of employees come to work with the intent of doing a good job, day-in and day-out. But many things come into play that influence the employee's ability to do his or her job effectively. There are organizational and process issues, political issues, and personal issues that arise each day on the job that the employee must deal with. There are limited resources, time constraints, budgetary issues, and numerous other problems that impact performance. Every manager's role is to provide the best combination of resources, timing, and capabilities possible to help every employee do the best job possible.

In essence, the organization's hierarchical triangle is now reversed. As a functional or departmental leader, the manager's role is to be an effective resource for his or her employees. It is the employees that get products out the door and customers serviced. Thus, it is the employees who actually generate revenue for the organization, controlling quality and productivity. A manager's job is simply to support the employees in their efforts to satisfy organizational and customer expectations. Consequently, managers are required to take the actions necessary every day to yield tangible results for employees and other functional managers or peers—the internal and external customers.

Organizational Perspective

Successful managers always think in terms of what is best for the organization in consideration of both its internal and external customers, rather than in parochial terms. They think organizationally versus in functional silos. As Figure 1-1 illustrates, there is a difference. Conversely, silo thinking considers first what is best for the department, discipline, or function. Horizontal thinking looks at the business as a process, with all of the disciplines and departments contributing to that process—the process of satisfying the customer.

There are times when functional issues, functional pressures, and functional priorities lead managers to become too focused on taking actions that benefit their own department or

The Transition into Management

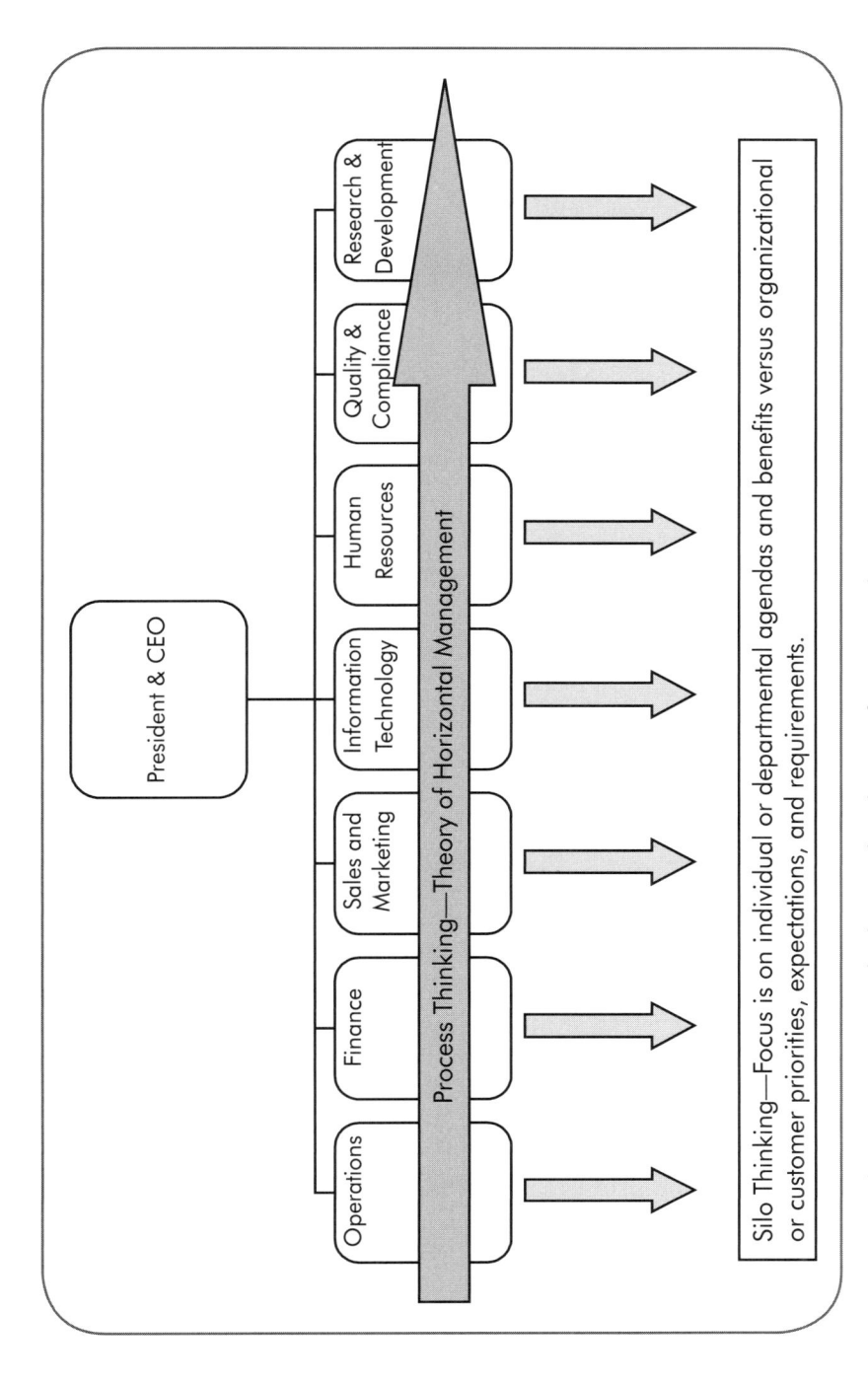

Figure 1-1. Silo versus process thinking—the Theory of Horizontal Management.

discipline at the expense of another department or discipline. Worse yet, to divert attention from their own departmental problems, ineffective managers often make decisions or take actions that seriously compromise other managers, departments, or the entire organization. Functionally focused actions are unacceptable. The decisions a manager makes and the subsequent actions taken must always address customer and organizational needs first.

COMMUNICATION: A STRENGTH OR WEAKNESS?

Do most technical professionals communicate well? Do they like delegating responsibility to others? In reality, the experience, training, and even the personality of many technical professionals work against them when moving into a management position. As a technical professional, there is a tendency to take the easy way out by telling someone, "Hey, just do it the way I told you to do it." Or, "Just get out of the way, I'll do it. We'll talk about how I did it later on. I don't have time to mess with it right now." But for a manager, this behavior is not appropriate. A manager's role is to accurately and comprehensively communicate what is needed and then assist the employee in getting the job done. When required, a manager trains and mentors his or her employee on those critical skills and techniques that will make the employee successful. Good managers share their valuable experience and are patient when employees make mistakes while learning. Employees learn from mistakes, trials, and successes, just as their managers did. Effective managers occasionally allow employees to experience mistakes, even to fail, because learning is a result. If employees never make mistakes, they are not trying anything new, and not experimenting to discover potential improvements. Without exploring the numerous alternatives to every work activity, process, or problem, progress is not made. Employees in that environment stagnate, as does the growth of the organization.

> "Deming said, 'Drive out the fear of failure in your employees.'"

A good manager constantly communicates to facilitate learning among his or her employees. In addition, a manager never assumes that an employee knows what is expected. Managers set out clear directions to ensure employees understand assignments along with how the results of their efforts will be measured. An employee who understands what is required does an effective job. There is no middle ground, no gray area. Successful managers make every assignment as clear and unambiguous as possible. They establish priorities, clearly communicate them, and then follow through. If there is a single word that summarizes effective managers from the employees' perspectives, it is *predictable*. When an employee knows what his or her manager expects every day, and the manager is consistent in priority, direction, and purpose, then that manager sets the stage for both employee and organizational success.

Conversely, communication lapses are often the reason why employees fail to perform as expected. A simple, but effective methodology used by many managers to avoid ambiguity in communicating assignments is to use simple 3 × 5 note cards. Before giving an assignment to an employee, the manager fills out an assignment card, such as the one shown in Figure 1-2, detailing the specifics of the assignment, which typically include:

- to whom the assignment is to be given;
- the scope of the assignment;
- the intended results to be derived from the assignment;
- the time frame for completion of the assignment;
- the recommended techniques or methodologies to be used for the assignment (if applicable);
- the budgetary or financial constraints associated with the assignment (if applicable);
- the specific metrics to be utilized to measure progress or results derived from the assignment; and
- any additional information or data sources that will be useful to the employee.

When communicating the assignment to the employee, the manager refers to the assignment card to ensure that nothing is left out. The card is then given to the employee for reference. This

The Transition into Management

Assigned to:	
Scope:	
Expected outcomes:	
When due:	
Approach:	
Constraints:	
Metrics:	
Data sources:	

Figure 1-2. Assignment card.

simple approach aids communication by forcing the manager to think through an assignment completely before discussing it with an employee. This, in turn, enhances employee understanding so the results from the assignment meet the manager's expectations.

One final comment is in order. Communication between genders remains a sensitive and somewhat delicate issue in the workplace. Studies conducted in the late 1990s have again confirmed that, in general, men and women communicate differently—not better, not worse, just differently. By understanding those differences, a manager can improve communication with all employees. For example, female employees are often transformational in their communication styles, meaning that they tend to think in participative, process-oriented terms. She will often bounce ideas off of her manager, using her manager as a sounding board. In doing so, her intent is to get feedback and not necessarily direction or problem resolution from her manager. She does not want the boss to give her the answer; rather she is seeking input so she can resolve the issue herself. For the manager to jump in with a dictated solution to the issue is thus a mistake. Male employees, on the other hand, are often more transactional in their communication, focusing on task orientation. He looks for specific, direct input from his manager relative to what is expected and how to accomplish it.

In all cases, managers are well served to be direct with employees of either gender. Successful managers communicate clearly, ask for understanding and agreement from their employees, and then close with a brief summarization of the assignment or comments. When employees know what is expected, they deliver.

ESTABLISHING AND COMMUNICATING EXPECTATIONS

When given a stretch goal or challenge, most employees will do whatever it takes to get the job done; but only if they believe that those goals are achievable. So the bottom line is, if a manager establishes an unrealistic set of goals and objectives for his or her employees, the employees may go through the motions, but they will not take ownership of the manager's vision or objectives. The manager will not be able to motivate his or her employees enough to achieve the expected results. A simple but important rule for managers is, therefore, to establish goals for employees, as well as for themselves, that are realistic and achievable. Those goals are not required to be easy to achieve, but they must be achievable.

> "Competitiveness and success are transitory. Unless an organization is constantly focused on improvement, at times radical improvement, failure is predestined."

Goals and objectives are dynamic. Each year, the goals and objectives of an organization are raised enough to stretch the organization and its employees to an enhanced level of performance. Within progressive organizations, employees are never permitted to rest on past successes, to become comfortable with current levels of performance or recognition.

The Transition into Management

One of the things most managers learn early in their career is that every organization will quickly develop one of two cultures.

The first culture is that of success. Success breeds additional success—it is infectious. Success results from consistent achievement of organizational or project objectives . . . making that first milestone on budget and on schedule, completing an assignment on time, getting a problem solved effectively. This is when success becomes a part of the psyche of every employee throughout the ranks. Successful organizations will continue to grow and prosper because of the momentum built by successful managers and supported by the enthusiasm of employees within the ranks. When a manager or employee works for a company that has a tradition of successful operations, products, or services, there is a belief that no other outcome is acceptable. People are committed to ensure that this level of performance is maintained. Failure is not a consideration: "We wouldn't consider a project failing to be completed on time or coming in over budget. We wouldn't consider a functional manager making a commitment and then failing to live up to that commitment." Success becomes the only way in which the organization, its managers, and its employees view themselves.

The second common organizational culture is that of failure. Failure comes as easily as success, often more so. It occurs when a manager or group of employees fails to live up to the performance level required by the company or its customers, and nothing is done by management to address the issues. Departments are constantly over budget and projects fail to meet expectations. Every manager tolerates an occasional failure. But consistent failure sets the tone for an organization to develop a culture for failure. The examples are numerous throughout the last several decades in a multitude of industries.

It is a manager's responsibility to create and maintain a culture in which employees believe they can be successful. The first step toward establishing a tradition of success is to set expectations that not only allow employees to stretch, but to actually reach the goals set before them. Employees who experience success grow with it.

BIAS IN MANAGEMENT

Occasionally, managers are forced to deal with tough personnel problems. There are situations where it is necessary to discipline an individual employee or a group of employees. Again, this is not something that comes easily to most technical professionals. When required to impart discipline, however, an effective manager does so quickly, fairly, and impartially.

Every manager, every individual, has biases or prejudices of one type or another. But good managers know to set aside all bias when the situation indicates the necessity for disciplining an employee. If the discipline is to be fair and effective, personal prejudices and biases must not be given weight. Similar to how a technical professional searches for the basis of fact in every problem, a manager must seek out the relevant facts within every business situation. In short, before a disciplinary action is initiated, a manager must clearly and completely understand the situation and the drivers behind it. There is more on this topic in a later chapter.

Many employee performance problems are the result of a manager's aversion to conflict and, thus, to facing personnel-related issues head-on with the employee. Confrontation on performance issues is unpleasant, but it will certainly be even more so if a manager continues to avoid the issue. As an employee's performance continues to move in an unacceptable direction over time, unchecked by honest and direct communication from his manager, a feeling of resentment begins to build in the manager. As the resentment turns from frustration to anger, bias begins to cloud the manager's judgment, making even the most insignificant infraction seem untenable. When the manager finally "blows," it is usually over something unrelated to the real performance issue, or over something so minor that, to the employee, his or her manager is blowing things completely out of proportion. The employee sees the manager's action as unfair and biased. This is when things get out of hand; the issue has been allowed to become personal.

Once a manager is aware of an employee's performance problem, immediate action is required to address the infraction with the employee, before it becomes "personal." By so doing, the issue is resolved quickly without personalities becoming involved. Again, there is no place for bias or prejudice in management. Effective managers judge their employees on the results that those employees generate, and on how effective and consistent they are in generating those results. An employee's gender, age, skin color, sexual orientation, or religion is of no bearing.

Example

To illustrate the point of how bias permeates many business environments, consider the following example from a rapidly growing, highly successful Silicon Valley company in the computer software/Internet industry.

During a conversation with a company visitor, a 24-year-old female department manager said, "We don't hire anyone over the age of 30 as a general rule. They just wouldn't fit into our corporate environment. Our staff is made up of young, aggressive professionals who have grown up with computers and the Internet. Older candidates just don't understand the new and emerging technologies." (She probably never gave any thought to the age of the technical professionals who invented computers, software languages, or the Internet.) Is this age bias? Of course it is; bias of this or any kind is unacceptable in the workplace, especially in the prevailing litigious climate. The issue of bias and discrimination will be discussed in detail in a subsequent chapter. For now, accept the fact that this is an arena where caution is strongly advised.

HIRING AND FIRING . . . THE GOOD, THE BAD, AND THE UGLY

One critically important aspect of a manager's job is hiring highly qualified employees for the organization. While this subject will be covered in significant detail in later chapters, for now suffice it to say that this aspect of the manager's job must be performed with great care and due diligence. To be surrounded with bright, dedicated, capable employees enhances any manager's potential to achieve organizational and career objectives.

Some managers, especially new ones, feel threatened by high-potential employees or candidates for employment. To minimize the risk that an employee might take his or her job, an insecure manager will often hire less-qualified employees, thus making the manager appear indispensable. This is obviously an erroneous and dangerous action on the manager's part. In fact, this often leads to the termination of the offending manager. Because the employees hired lack the essential skills to produce exceptional and consistent results, these subordinates are incapable of assisting the manager in getting quality work accomplished within the time and volume desired by upper management. As a result, the manager becomes bogged down and ineffective. Without the capacity to manage the organization's workload efficiently, that manager will eventually become a target for removal; exactly the situation he or she attempted to avoid in the first place.

> "Another given in management is that unless a manager has one or more employees ready, willing, and able to take his job, that manager will never be promoted."

Successful managers follow a cardinal rule: find the best qualified, enthusiastic, and motivated employees possible. The success of these high-potential employees always shines brightly on their manager, thus ensuring that the manager receives strong consideration when the next promotion becomes available. After all, it is not the manager's role to do the work within the department. Rather, it is the manager's responsibility to ensure that the work is accomplished efficiently and effectively by the employees within the department. Only in developing employees who are capable of making management-level decisions, thinking organizationally, acting expeditiously, and fulfilling personal job requirements and responsibilities to the organization as a whole, is a manager primed for a successful career path.

Hiring employees for the organization is enjoyable, as well as somewhat exciting once a manager develops a comprehensive succession plan (discussed in Chapter 8) and begins to execute it. But there also comes a time when a manager must take strong disciplinary actions against an employee or "free someone to pursue other endeavors." This is always difficult and potentially litigious, so it is imperative for a manager to handle this situation correctly. In situations like this, the manager's intent is to do what is best for both the employee and the organization. It is certainly not the most enjoyable aspect of the job, but it is a requirement. It is also a primary reason why managers fail to live up to the expectations of senior management. Managers often duck this highly emotionally charged situation. It is far easier to ignore an employee's poor performance than it is to take it head on. But addressing it directly, honestly, and firmly is exactly what is required. This subject is explored further in a later chapter.

It is essential for every manager to develop a comprehensive succession plan that defines a promotion/back-up candidate(s) for each critical employee or position within the organization, including that of the manager himself. Succession planning is vital at even the lowest levels within the organization. Contingency planning of this nature minimizes the risks associated with surprise losses of critical skill sets within the management and employee ranks. Risk management of this type ensures continuous operation within the department or function whenever a potentially disruptive change in personnel occurs.

Example

There was a gentleman who was attending a training session. At every break throughout the first day, the instructor noticed that he would run to the phone to call his office. He would ask the person on the phone a series of questions and then return with a troubled look on his face. At the end of the day, the instructor called him to the side and indicated that he seemed troubled. The instructor asked if there was a problem at the office. The gentleman responded that there were no problems, but that was why he was concerned. Things seemed to be running absolutely fine without him. The instructor suggested that he was doing an excellent job of managing his department and should be commended that his employees were so competent. The next day at the training session, the gentleman had a lot more fun.

Inherited Problems

In a new position, every manager inherits employees—some good, some not so good. A manager must quickly assess each employee for his or her strengths, commitment, capacity, capabilities, and chemistry within the organizational work group. There may be otherwise solid employees who are not synergistic with this work group, or with their new manager. Or, in some cases, employee skill sets are redundant or inconsistent with the new manager's vision of what the organization is to accomplish in the future. In such cases, a change is best for both parties.

Every manager finds it necessary to rebalance his or her organization from time to time to ensure that the skill sets and chemistry required to meet the organization's mission are in place. Over time, changes of this nature come through retirement, transfer, termination, resignation, or other means, creating openings within the employee ranks. Before personnel changes are initiated, however, successful managers develop a staffing plan to guide the selection and organizational development process.

Occasionally, personnel problems may exist that a predecessor failed to address. Those situations, too, will require immediate attention. It is common for a manager moving into a new position to be told, "There's a lot of dead wood in this organization. We need you to take care of it quickly." This always leaves an experienced manager perplexed. First of all, why wasn't the situation handled by the incumbent when the problem(s) first arose? Why didn't senior management address the problem once it was recognized? The answer lies in that most managers do not like conflict and will avoid it at almost any cost. It is easy to say to an employee, "You did a pretty good job this year. There are a few things that you need to work on, but in general you did quite well. We'll talk about the areas you need to work on later." It is far more difficult to have that tough face-to-face review with an employee that puts it all on the line. But that is exactly what is expected from a manager and what the employee deserves to improve his or her performance. Consider it from the employee's perspective. The employee knows that he is not performing up to the level of others within the department, and yet he still gets the same raises, the same performance evaluations. So why change? Then, several years later, a new manager comes along and wants to fire the employee for that same level of performance. Is it any wonder that the employee is confused, frustrated, and angry?

When working for a capable manager, no employee is ever surprised by a poor performance rating or disciplinary action. The reason is simple. Effective managers never fail to address or communicate these issues in a timely manner with their employees. They are keenly aware that it is always easier to address personnel performance problems in their infancy. When the problem is allowed to age, emotions will become an explosive factor—on both sides of the issue.

Unfortunately, new managers are frequently faced with the task of cleaning up carryover personnel issues before new initiatives can be implemented. This is where yet another problem arises. When the manager pulls the personnel files on this "dead wood" from Human Resources, what is found? Almost universally, these "dead wood" employees were rated very good or excellent by one or more former managers. Now their new superior is telling them their performance is not consistent with expectations and that disciplinary actions are being initiated. Or, worse yet, the employee is immediately terminated for poor performance by his new manager. Here there are some real legal issues involved. Consider that this is an employee who has a documented history of acceptable to excellent performance . . . "a very good performer" . . . "meets or exceeds job requirements." For the new manager to justify terminating the employee to an NLRB arbitrator, especially after being on the job for only a brief time, is a practical impossibility. The only alternative available to a new manager is to assess each employee based upon consistent, reasonable job expectations for a period of time. Then, only if the employee's performance is still not adequate after the manager has worked with the employee to improve his or her performance, can the manager initiate disciplinary action. Any attempt to shortcut the process will likely be met with disaster.

DEALING WITH POLITICIANS

Do politicians exist in today's organization? Well certainly if you live in Washington, D.C. they do. But seriously, do most managers have politicians within their own organization? The answer is a resounding, "Yes." Why are there politicians? In most cases, their managers have created them. Not only has management created the political environment, but in many cases they have nurtured those same politicians through the existing performance appraisal systems and performance metrics. Often managers inadvertently create "win-lose" scenarios. Departmental or organizational performance metrics are employed to measure individual success, which results in one employee winning at the expense of another. For years, the resulting political conflicts were side-stepped by managers. "The law of the jungle" or "The cream will rise to the top" or "The strong will survive" were commonly used justifications for inaction. But in truth, conflicting metrics create chaos, pitting one employee against another. The situation is especially critical today in the dynamic global markets where, to survive, every organization must have all employees pulling together toward a common goal.

Example

Consider the following example taken from a Fortune 200 U.S. electronics firm.

A new operations manager noticed severe infighting and politics within her organization shortly after being promoted into the job. In some cases, there existed open warfare between departments. All of her efforts to mediate the situation failed, and her overall organizational performance began to suffer.

The Transition into Management

In her search for an answer, the manager began looking at the performance metrics in place at both the department and individual levels within each department reporting to her. Her findings revealed a surprising series of facts.

The Purchasing department and its buyers were being measured against a commonly used procurement metric called PPV—purchase price variance. PPV is established when Purchasing and Accounting together establish a floor for price increases or decreases for the upcoming year. In other words, what Purchasing expects to pay for raw materials, goods, contract labor, etc. The prior year, the PPV had been set for a maximum 2% increase. The Materials and Inventory Management department also had been assigned a conventional metric against which every employee was measured—inventory turns (a measure of capital employed per period). The target had been set at 24 turns, or approximately two weeks of inventory on site at any given time.

The two metrics, in a steady-state business environment, did not appear to be in conflict. However, her organization was not in a static environment. Price pressures throughout the industry had become extreme. Purchasing was under constant pressure from suppliers who increased their prices while, at the same time, pressure came from management to lower prices. Materials and Inventory Management was also under pressure from senior management to meet or exceed their inventory turn targets to free up additional capital for other corporate projects. Purchasing employees found that the only way they could drive down prices was to purchase in larger lot sizes, which allowed them to get better quantity-price breaks. But that worked directly against Materials and Inventory Management's turn objectives, and vice versa. In short, open warfare had begun. As pressure mounted from management, employees within both departments began working against each other to achieve their own individual performance targets. Clearly, employees in both departments were working diligently to meet the performance targets established by management. But just as clearly, those targets had been poorly defined, requiring the two departments to effectively work against instead of with one another. When the new manager instituted a total cost metric in place of the other two metrics, and made both departments accountable for that same metric, the warfare ended and employees from both departments began working together.

Managers faced with similar situations look first at the metrics driving employee behavior and performance. If conflicts exist, common solutions that provide all employees with the opportunity to succeed are sought. Once deployed, these changes in performance metrics will quickly lead to a dramatic reduction in or elimination of politics within the department.

SUMMARY

In this chapter, a number of fundamental career transition and management guidelines were discussed relative to the technical professional who is considering a move into management. The more a manager knows about what lies ahead, the better job he or she will do in managing and controlling the business environment, thus making the transition occur quicker and less problematically. The bottom line is that an effective manager is always prepared for what lies ahead. Preparation, planning, and foresight are valuable assets for every manager in every situation. Subsequent chapters will address these and other critical issues in more detail with examples to illustrate how these principles are applied in real business and industrial settings.

2

Leadership in Perspective

OBJECTIVE

In this chapter, successful leaders from a broad range of radically differing industries will be studied. Their exemplary leadership qualities and techniques form the basis for learning how to be an effective leader. Historical management styles will also be discussed, along with the application of those styles in various business environments. The intent of this chapter is to provide readers with an overview of the individual qualities and basic requirements for successful leadership in the competitive business climate of today.

HISTORICAL OVERVIEW

Until the early 1970s, the predominant management style was known as *Theory X management*. This style was embraced by individuals whose approach to management was autocratic and demanding. These were the individuals who followed the credo, "It's my way or the highway." For many years, the Theory X approach was actually quite successful. In fact, within some environments and in certain business situations today, Theory X actually still works better than some of the more participative management styles. For example, in times of crisis when immediate action is called for, an effective manager takes control of the situation and leads decisively. The manager's role is to lead the organization to a solution or successful conclusion. In these situations, there simply is no time to train employees on how to resolve the crisis. The training is done after the crisis is resolved.

Leadership in Perspective

As industry moved into the late 1970s and the 1980s, employees had become better educated, more highly mobile, and far more independent. Managers found that employees wanted more of a role in making decisions that impacted their workplace and the security of their employment. In short, they wanted to participate. In response, *Theory Y management* came into being. This type of manager rewarded employees with pay increases, promotions, or more responsibility based upon the employee's ability to perform at specified levels set by the manager. Theory Y managers exercised power by bestowing rewards upon employees. This was the point in time when concepts like employee involvement, gain-sharing, and other incentive-based approaches to management came into fashion. The Theory Y management style worked well until economic conditions in the late 1980s, and again in the late 1990s, began to restrict an organization's ability to use salary and other perks as incentives for increased employee performance.

Today's successful business leaders use a carefully crafted blend of Theory X and Theory Y styles to maximize the motivation and discipline required to successfully guide increasingly complex organizations. Often referred to as *Theory Z management*, this is a style that combines the strength and drive of Theory X with the employee-focused, team concepts of Theory Y management. The secret to the success in the Theory Z approach lies in being predictable so that employees always know what to expect. That consistency in communicating the desired direction and priorities is paramount for success in dynamic, technology-driven industries where change is constant and often revolutionary in nature. It is not essential that a manager's employees always be in agreement with their manager's position. Nor is it essential that the employees actually "like" their manager. What is essential is that they respect their manager. That respect comes from the manager's consistency, predictability, and fairness in the way he treats all employees.

At one time or another in all of our careers, we have worked for or will work for a strong, almost headstrong manager. In the vast majority of those cases, those managers are respected by their employees because they know exactly what to expect from their manager. There is no second-guessing or difficulty in interpreting the manager. The manager is clear, fair, and specific in her expectations of every employee. Consequently, every employee knows what is required to be successful. Employees know that there will be predictable repercussions should they fail to live up to those expected levels of performance and conduct. This clarity in vision and action provides each employee with the structure needed to perform effectively in any business environment.

There are two additional leadership styles that merit discussion. Unlike the Theory X, Y, and Z styles, which can and should be adjusted as required to reflect the needs of the manager's organization, the following two styles are a matter of individual personality and as such, cannot be easily changed.

The first of the leadership styles is that of a *change agent*. This style reflects the leader who is a revolutionary thinker. He or she works best in dynamic environments requiring radical changes to organizational processes and structures. The change agent is rarely content with leaving even recently implemented projects stagnant for any period of time. He or she is always pushing the envelope to find better ways to operate. Easily bored, the change agent constantly seeks new challenges and new dimensions in organizational structure, operations, and performance.

The second style is that of a *sustaining manager*. As a leader, the sustaining manager is more of an evolutionary thinker. Slow, well-engineered, methodical actions reflect the approach. Continuous improvement versus radical change is the preferred methodology. The sustaining leader functions well in environments with solid processes and procedures requiring only minor enhancements to maintain expected levels of performance.

Both the change agent and sustaining leadership styles are necessary within an organization at varying times in its life cycle. However, they cannot be placed incorrectly or problems will occur. If, for example, a change-agent leader is placed in a management role within a static, well functioning, change-

Leadership in Perspective

resistant organization, he or she will likely fail. Constantly pushing the boundaries, he or she will alienate peers and employees who prefer to make only modest changes to existing processes and procedures. Conversely, a sustaining leader in a dynamic organization will run into similar problems as he or she tries to maintain a slower, more deliberate pace of change. Dragging down the momentum of the organization will create frustration among peers and employees, and thus ultimately generate problems for the leader.

As Figure 2-1 illustrates, change agent and sustaining leaders can utilize Theory X, Y, or Z styles to maximize performance within the business environment and culture of their particular organizations. However, because change agent or sustaining personality traits are not easily altered, successful managers recognize this limitation as they carefully select positions and roles that fit with their abilities to fulfill the requirements of a particular position and organization. An option for any manager who finds himself in a role that is contrary to his particular leadership style is to staff the organization with employees, managers, and informal leaders who reflect the opposite style, thereby bringing balance. This balancing through complementary skill sets and leadership styles aids in offsetting the potentially nega-

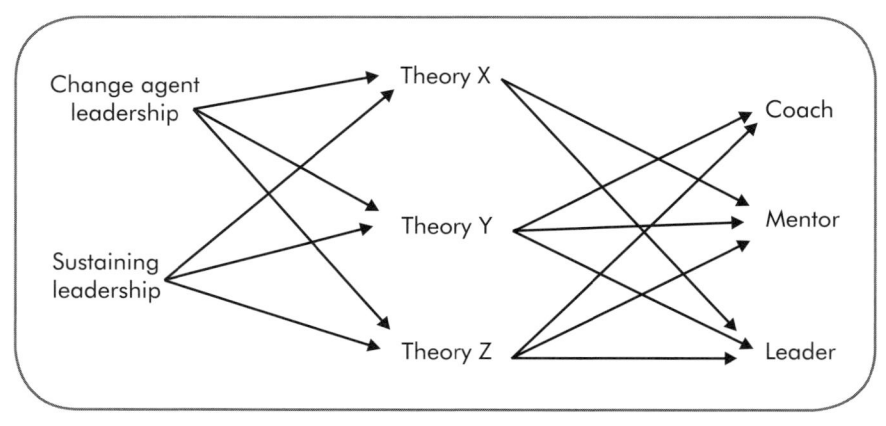

Figure 2-1. Situation-driven leadership style blending.

tive aspects of the manager's personal leadership style while bringing a fresh perspective to the situation.

Example

When Lee Iacocca took the reins of Chrysler Corporation, the company was in financial crisis. Customers were defecting in droves; the banks had forced the company into Chapter 11 bankruptcy; suppliers demanded cash-on-delivery for raw materials; and employees were in revolt. It certainly was not an ideal environment in which to start a new job. Which management style did Lee adopt when he came on board—soft and participative, or direct and autocratic? In the situation Lee was handed, there was only one management style he could have adopted. As Chrysler moved into equilibrium and ultimately into profitability, Lee shed his autocratic management style and adopted a softer, more participative team approach. Why did he change? Under the new business conditions, his former autocratic style would not have been accepted by the managers and employees of Chrysler.

PRESSURES OF LEADERSHIP

Leaders are now required to possess increasingly more diverse skill sets so they are capable of handling a larger number of responsibilities and managing a larger number of employees. Today's leaders must be team builders, employee developers, business and technology specialists, strategic thinkers, and tactical executioners. This expanded role brings with it a tremendous amount of pressure from every level within and outside of the organization. That pressure is driven from the boardroom, senior management, employees handling day-to-day activities, customers, bankers and financiers, and certainly the stockholders and external regulatory bodies. In short, there is a tremendous amount of pressure coming from numerous different directions. Success, therefore, is predicated upon the manager's ability to think clearly and make rational decisions in high-pressure, dynamic business environments.

Leadership in Perspective

PROS AND CONS OF LEADERSHIP

Here again is a point for those considering a move into management, as well as those already in management positions. Who is at risk if the manager or his/her employees do not perform? Who is at most risk if the organization does not perform? Is it the individual manager? Is it the employees? Is it senior management? Is it the board of directors? Certainly, each one of these groups has a distinct element of risk if the organization is not successful. But who is most at risk in a publicly traded corporation? It is the stockholder. If a publicly traded organization fails to meet its financial targets, it is stockholder dividends that get cut or stock pricing that gets downgraded, not the paychecks of managers and employees. It is the stockholder who sees real money go down the drain. The stockholder's investment in the organization is diluted or lost altogether because management did not perform. Examples of companies like Enron, Adelphia, WorldCom and numerous others illustrate this point clearly. It is a hard fact; stockholders today are no longer the silent majority. They are becoming very vocal—and litigious. They are putting tremendous pressure on the management of the companies they invest in for results—not just from time to time, but consistently and predictably. That means there must be quantifiable results throughout the organization at every level. Every manager is expected to play an active role in achieving those results. There will be rewards for so doing and tangible penalties for failure.

CHANGE, NOT CHAOS . . . A LEADERSHIP IMPERATIVE

Within every successful organization, change has become the norm. Driven by rapid technological advancements and expanded expectations in the marketplace, managers today assume the role of change-enabler. But change, even constant change, is vastly different from chaos. There are numerous books that promote the creation of chaos within an organization as a way to improve performance, for example, *Creating Chaos in Your Organization*, *Managing the Chaotic Organization*, or *Success Through Chaos*. Their message is universal: by creating chaos, change is guaranteed. That approach may sell books, but it will certainly not create permanent process improvements within an organization.

Every seasoned CEO knows that if he has an organization in chaos, by definition this means the organization is out of control. Management is not leading it, and subsequently there are no controls. The direction of organizations in chaos is set by destiny, not by a clearly developed and delineated strategic plan. This is not management. Yes, every good manager wants change to be the norm to guide the business culture. But there must be a plan to guide and control the change processes. *There must be direction.* For example, no sensible individual would set off in a car to drive from San Francisco to New York City without a map, without an idea of how far it is, how long it will take, how many clothes to pack, how much gas to buy, or how much money to take along. To blindly set off on an easterly course in hopes of finding New York would be illogical, even foolish. The astute traveler studies a road map, develops a route, plans for the trip, and packs the necessary provisions for the journey. That is exactly what a good manager does when planning a change process within an organization.

> *"Planned change is essential for every organization. Chaos should be avoided at all costs."*

TECHNIQUES OF GOOD LEADERS

Successful management careers are built upon the execution of management and leadership techniques that yield consistently excellent results. While every manager develops his or her own style and approach to management, there are fundamental tools and techniques that all successful managers weave into their individual management styles. These techniques are discussed in the following sections.

Getting Employees Involved

First and foremost, successful managers get all employees involved and keep them involved every day. No manager makes all the decisions, nor should she be expected to do so. Rather, effective managers encourage employees to make certain decisions that impact their day-to-day activities and responsibilities. These managers do not micro-manage. Instead, they let employees do their own work. This leaves the manager free to concentrate on the strategic issues that affect organizational performance and success.

It is very common for solid individual contributors who move into management positions to fall into the trap of taking on their employees' problems and workloads personally. Pretty soon, such a manager is working 12–14 hours a day, six days a week. The manager becomes totally overwhelmed and struggles desperately to keep up with his own responsibilities. The manager's effectiveness begins to erode, making him a target for termination. In the meantime, the manager's employees are going home at 4:30 every afternoon. From the employee's perspective, this is a great job. "If I have a problem, I simply give it to the boss and he'll take care of it. I don't have to worry about it. The boss works Saturdays anyway. I am free to enjoy my weekend at home."

A manager's job is to get every employee involved in carrying the organization's load, making decisions, and delivering what the customers want. If the manager could do the job alone, there would be no need for employees in the first place. The pace of change in technologies and business cycles, competitive conditions, and market dynamics prohibit any manager from taking on the entire load alone. No manager, no matter how good or how dedicated, can keep that many balls in the air. Successful managers work through their employees. The employees, in turn, appreciate the opportunity to be part of management decisions and planning, to address some of the challenges of the business, and to find ways to better satisfy the customer.

Establishing Dynamic Performance Goals

As discussed in Chapter One, departmental goals, personal goals, and the goals of employees are deliberately set high, but attainable. Good managers focus on creating an organizational culture of success through consistent attainment of each of these goals. Fundamentally, it is a manager's responsibility to ensure that all employees clearly understand each of these expectations. Goals and objectives are clearly and comprehensively stated and defined, along with the collective and individual employee performance metrics associated with each delineated expectation. Managers know to ask questions of employees to ensure that they understand expectations. Often, employees are reluctant to admit that they do not clearly understand what is expected of them or how their performance will be measured. It is a manager's responsibility to probe the employee's understanding by asking questions and seeking concurrence. Understanding is critical to the success of both the employee and the manager. If an employee knows clearly what her manager expects, then the employee's job becomes much easier and overall performance is enhanced.

Example

Thinking back in your career, have you ever worked for a manager who was very indecisive, who would say something one day, and then something else the next? Did you ever really know what to expect? Were the constant reversals in direction distracting? Was that individual an easy manager to work for? The answer to this last question is likely "No."

Effective managers set clear goals for their employees. And, if there should be a need to change those targets, they communicate the required changes to employees along with the reasons why they are necessary. By so doing, employees always know what to expect and what is expected of them.

Building and Maintaining Momentum

Anyone who has ever had to push their car any distance because it stalled knows how difficult it is to get the car moving initially. However, once the car starts to move (assuming it is not being pushed uphill), it becomes increasingly easier to maintain and even accelerate the car's momentum. However, if the car is allowed to come to a stop, the difficulty in getting

Leadership in Perspective

it going again is repeated. So it is with the momentum within an organization.

One of the key responsibilities of a manager is to build and maintain momentum within the organization. In other words, to keep every employee moving forward, resolving problems and issues, making decisions, and getting every element of the job done day in and day out. Every organization will stall or stumble from time to time. Employees will become complacent, comfortable with current levels of success within the operation, or overcome with difficulties. Maintaining status quo will become sufficient in their minds, especially in organizations with a history of success. In cases like this, a manager's job is to lead employees out of their comfort zones, thereby regaining forward progress and organizational momentum. Doing so may require the manager to scrap old business processes, policies, or procedures altogether, and to introduce new ways of doing things. "Burning bridges" to ensure that employees do not revert to the old methodologies also may be necessary.

> "Success is what every good manager works to accomplish. But in and of itself, success can be a death trap without the foresight to keep today's success in perspective for tomorrow."

Every organization must keep moving forward, take on new challenges, and look for ways to enhance performance or it will be doomed to ultimate failure. And to keep moving forward, an organization relies on its employees. Managers and employees alike can not be allowed to become comfortable resting on the successes of the past. To ensure that employees constantly focus on continuous improvement, a change in employee performance appraisal and reward standards is often necessary to keep employees from being recognized and rewarded for their compliance to old methodologies and procedures. If looking back is not possible, employees will always look forward.

There are countless organizations that are successful year after year because of good, often safe management decisions. Then all of a sudden, those same organizations get into serious trouble. They go flat, lose focus, and ultimately lose ground. Why does this happen? How can an organization with talented managers and employees, a history of successful operations, and a solid market base fail? The names of such companies come right off of the Fortune 500 listing . . . IBM, Motorola, Chrysler, Xerox, NEC, PanAm, Allis-Chalmers, K-Mart, etc. The list is an endless parade of corporations that experienced great success followed by significant reversals. Why didn't management see the problem coming? Why did they fail to take corrective action in time? The answer is that management failed to keep the organization moving forward. Success became a deterrent to the same type of continuous change processes that initially made the organization successful. Simply put, management failed to keep the organization's momentum and vision for change alive. When success became a way of life, managers and employees alike became complacent. Often before management could react, the organization was doomed to failure. (Organizational transformation is discussed in detail in Chapter 10, along with the techniques necessary to sustain change as part of an organization's culture.)

Example: Management and Employee Complacency

USA Today recently carried an article about a multinational electronics firm that found itself in a situation in which the organization had to be completely redirected and reengineered as a result of management's failure to recognize significant shifts in technology, customer expectations, and competitive trends in the marketplace. For years the organization was first in its industry. It had historically set the standard in product development, product quality, and product-line performance. But within a few years, its competition had all but driven the company out of its niche markets, thus forcing management to reconsider the direction of the company and ultimately move it into entirely new fields. Why did this happen? Managers and employees alike became too comfortable. Believing that they knew more than their customers, they began making decisions accordingly. Managers and employees assumed their organization was invincible.

Leadership in Perspective

When a senior manager finds his subordinate managers, supervisors, or employees becoming overly comfortable, it is time to make a change. It is time to challenge and encourage those employees to increase their momentum, productivity, and performance. Successful managers challenge every employee to find ways to improve individual job performance to a point that the job itself can be eliminated. Managers then reward those employees, find them a new assignment, and reissue that same challenge.

Example: Far-sighted Management

A large manufacturer of residential and industrial products in Mexico, number one in its industry, possesses over 90% market share. The company produces hundreds of thousand of units every year and its earnings before taxes are in excess of 40%. In short, it is an incredibly successful organization.

Though the company was not experiencing significant competition or customer dissatisfaction, the senior manager and his staff made a decision to reengineer the entire front-end of the business, eight departments in all. When asked why the successful company was making such a dramatic change, the senior manager's response was, "Because being successful today is no guarantee that we will be successful tomorrow. We must take the opportunity that our success affords us to make changes now that will ensure success well into the 21st century." This is the type of momentum successful leaders generate with their vision and sense of urgency. Instilling that same urgency in employees ensures that an organization will never rest upon past successes, but rather, will use them to build even greater successes in the future.

Example: Nearsighted Management

By contrast, consider the market-share trend illustrated in Figure 2-2. Have the leadership and management of GM lost sight of its goals, its customers, or its competition? Has GM's leadership failed to accurately gage and manage its core competencies? Has technology given the advantage to another

Leadership in Perspective

General Motors' Market Share*

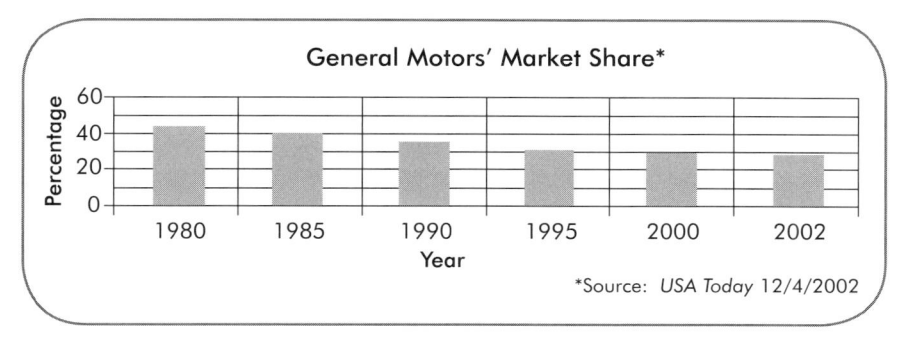

[Bar chart showing declining percentages from 1980 to 2002, with years 1980, 1985, 1990, 1995, 2000, 2002 on x-axis and percentage (0-60) on y-axis]

*Source: USA Today 12/4/2002

Figure 2-2. General Motors' declining market share.

competitor? Is there an understanding or recognition on the part of GM's leaders and managers that a potential disaster exists unless changes are enacted? As will be discussed in detail in an upcoming chapter, effective leaders are visionaries; they are always alert to changes in the business environment and the corresponding need for change within their own leadership styles and that of their management staff.

Driving Out the Fear of Failure

Employees will make mistakes. It is a given. If employees do not make an occasional mistake, they are simply not doing anything. Good managers recognize that fact and tolerate mistakes made by employees so long as they learn from their mistakes. Ed Deming said, "Drive out the fear of failure." That was an incredibly astute statement. Employees must not be afraid to make mistakes. But equally important, managers are required to control the downside of those mistakes so they do not become detrimental to employees or the organization. To do so requires the establishment and enforcement of rules and guidelines for all employees within the organization. So long as employees operate within those rules and guidelines, the mistakes they make will be controlled (see Figure 2-3). Their mistakes will not become devastating to their careers or the organization. However, if an employee is allowed to operate outside the organization's rules,

Leadership in Perspective

Policies

Rules

Within the structure of the operating constraints, mistakes are contained.

Guidelines

Procedures

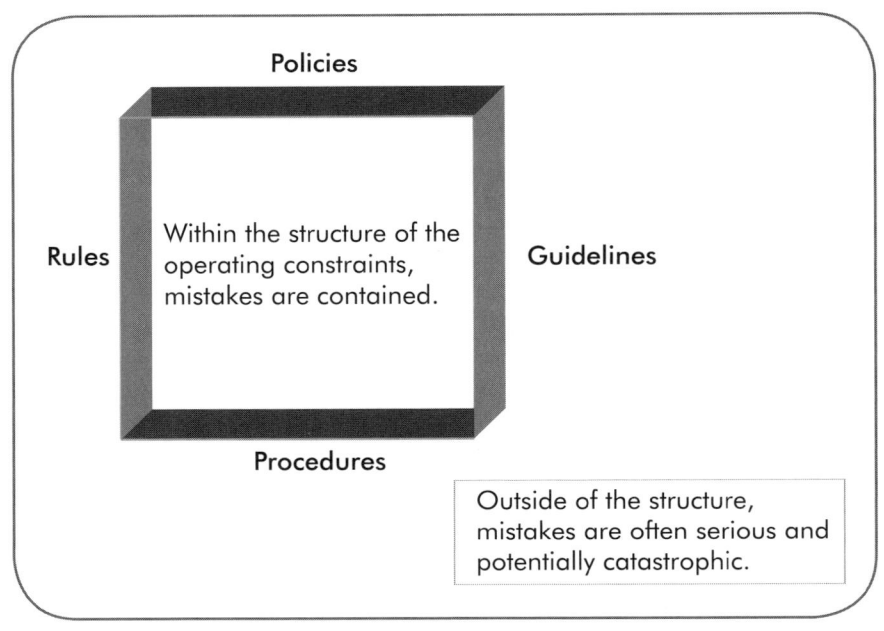

Outside of the structure, mistakes are often serious and potentially catastrophic.

Figure 2-3. Mistakes must be contained.

policies, and procedures, that same mistake has the potential to bring down the organization and the employee's career, along with that of his manager. So while managers carefully encourage employees to take controlled risks, and even allow employees to make mistakes, they also wisely control the downside. Those control factors are enforced to protect all parties.

Avoid Assigning Blame

When an employee has a problem and brings it to his manager's attention, effective managers are careful not to unintentionally shoot the messenger. The initial questions that a manager asks are, "How did the problem occur?" and "What can we do to prevent it in the future?" What a manager does not ask is, "Who did it?" By following this common-sense rule, employees are made comfortable in approaching their manager for help when they make a mistake. But seasoned managers understand that there is always a natural fear of those who have power over us. So it is with employees and their superiors. Effective managers work diligently to minimize that natural

> "Do unto others as you would have them do unto you."

fear by continuously reinforcing their support for the employees within the organization. It is a simple message, "Do unto others as you would have them do unto you."

Inspiring Employees to Take Risks

Engineers, technical professionals, business managers at all levels, even senior executives for the most part, are not risk-takers. They are, in fact, usually very conservative individuals. Rarely is a CEO found in Las Vegas pulling that crank on the old slot machine. They are simply adverse to unnecessary risk, especially with the organization's limited and critical resources. Managers acknowledge and accept the fact that they too are entrusted with the organization's money, capital assets, and human assets. They further understand that they are expected to make responsible fiscal decisions relative to the care and stewardship of those assets. In short, managers are expected to avoid unnecessary risks. However, they are also expected to take controlled risks when those actions will move the organization forward. So, there are times when risk is necessary. As markets change, business conditions change, or customer expectations change, managers are forced to challenge the status quo, to take a controlled risk to maintain organizational momentum. Forward momentum is always a requirement for consistently positive performance.

The situation is the same for employees. There are times when a risk on their part is beneficial to the organization. Experienced managers effectively control the downside of an employee's actions through training and mentoring. While employees are kept within the rules and guidelines of the organization, they are at the same time encouraged to step outside of their comfort zones to identify new opportunities for organizational and personal advancement. They are, however, advised to seek the

Leadership in Perspective

advice and approval of their manager as they proceed. Only then can employees effectively and safely take those risks, and subsequently be successful.

Good managers teach their employees fundamental risk management techniques. This allows employees to quantitatively assess the risks associated with their decisions, and then to initiate corrective actions where necessary to design those risks out or reduce them to an acceptable level. While risk-taking is encouraged, successful managers make sure every employee understands that there simply is no excuse for carelessness. Tools like preliminary failure analysis and risk criticality analysis are commonly utilized by managers. Such tools are used to identify potential problems or decision failure modes along with their possible impacts and probability of occurrence, and then to quantify the risk levels associated with each. As illustrated in Figures 2-4 and 2-5, these tools provide the basis for determining whether a decision or course of action is appropriate based upon the constraints of the situation (Termini 1999).

Making Time to Listen to Employees

Most employees have good ideas. Why then do many managers fail to listen to them? Most managers have good intentions when an employee comes to them with a suggestion or recommendation. The manager sincerely wants to act on the employee's comments or address the employee's problem. But pressures often overshadow the day, thus causing the manager to forget the conversation within a short time. The employee, however, does not forget that his manager made a commitment to act. When nothing happens after a few days, the employee feels as though his comments or concerns were of little or no importance to his manager. Trust is lost, communication stops, and the employee's performance declines . . . and the manager often has no idea why.

> "Good managers forget the open-door policy and begin wearing out shoes on a regular basis."

42 *Walking the Talk: Pathways to Leadership*

Leadership in Perspective

Preliminary Failure Assessment				
Project Description: Project Number:			Project Manager: Date Initiated:	
Failure Modes	Consequences	Risks (Before)	Corrective Actions	Risks (After)
List of All Potential Project Failure Modes	Budget / Schedule / Deliverable / Safety / Other	Failure Probability / Detection Probability / Magnitude / RPN	Corrective Action for Items with RPN > 1.0	Failure Probability / Detection Probability / Magnitude / RPN
1. 2. 3. 4. 5. 6. 7. 8. 9. 10.				
Acceptable RPN: Prepared By:			Go/No-Go: Date:	

Figure 2-4. Risk management tools—preliminary failure analysis.

Astute managers make the time to listen to their employees. When an employee comes forward with an idea or problem, the manager intently listens to the employee's concept and the intended approach for resolving the issue, and then takes decisive action. Even if the manager's approach to that same issue or problem is different than that recommended by the employee, as long as the employee's approach will work, the manager empowers the employee to address the issue in his own way. By so doing, the employee gains the opportunity to learn how to analyze a situation and, from the data, to make good decisions. By getting employees involved, listening to them, and supporting

> "Managers must make the time to listen to employees."

Leadership in Perspective

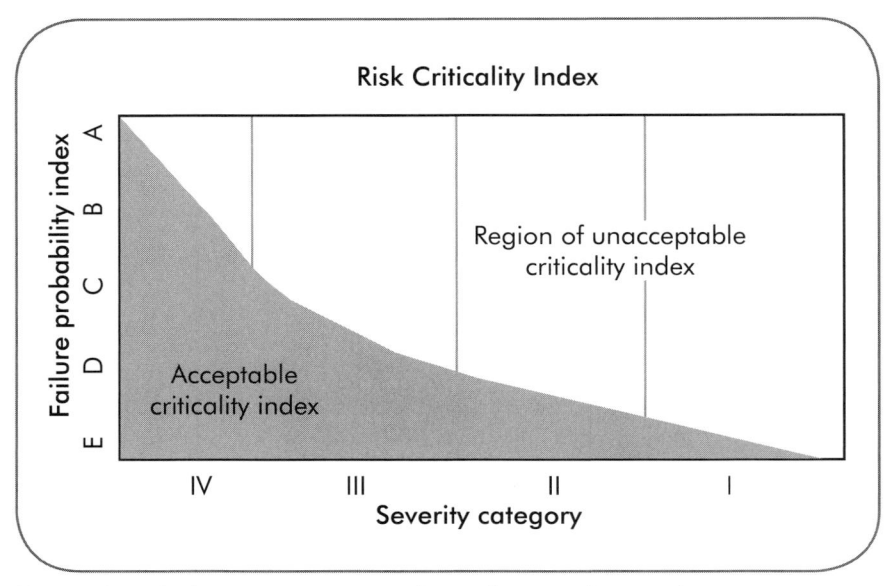

Figure 2-5. Risk management tools—risk criticality analysis.

their decisions, a manager plants the seeds of ownership for the resolution of the problem with the employee. Employees blossom as a result.

Unlike talking, listening requires effort. When a manager has many things vying for attention, phones ringing off of the hook, deadlines looming, etc., it is often difficult to stop everything to listen to what an employee has to say. But that is exactly what the manager must do. It is imperative to turn off the phone, put the current pressures in check, and give the employee full and undivided attention. If the timing is inconvenient, then the manager explains to the employee that she wants to give the employee her complete attention, but at that moment there are other things that must be addressed first. She asks for patience from the employee and then establishes a time to get back together (within one to two hours maximum). Now committed, she follows through. Her credibility as a manager is on the line.

It is a good practice to set aside a few hours every day just to walk around the organization to talk with employees at their workstations, see first hand the issues they face daily, and get a grasp on the magnitude of their problems. Employees will open up more to a manager who is frequently accessible and visible, more so than one who practices the "open door policy" (ODP). The ODP approach merely means to an employee that the manager's door is open, not necessarily that the employee is welcome inside. Good managers wear out shoes on a regular basis. They interface with employees on the employee's own turf to learn their perspectives, issues, and constraints. Managers who do are more highly trusted and respected—and far more effective. They are also more in touch with the pulse of their organizations, and thus are better positioned to act proactively before problems arise.

> "Good managers never make a commitment to an employee that they cannot or do not intend to keep."

So where do managers get the time to contribute one to two hours each day to talk with employees? A good place to start is by cutting out nonproductive meetings. After all, most meetings that a manager attends are of no measurable value to the organization or the manager. That time is better spent with employees—the people within the organization who really get things done for the customer and who need their manager's help to get problems resolved.

COMMUNICATION

Writing memos and sending e-mails is *not* communicating with employees. Communication of these types should be used only when it is impossible to talk with an employee face-to-face, or as a follow-up to a verbal conversation. Trust and respect are based on the strength of the relationship between superior and subordinate. A manager cannot know his employees, and vice versa, when the main form of communication is impersonal.

Leadership in Perspective

Good managers know the value of face-to-face communication. They make it a point to walk around and get to know what's going on within their organization from direct observation rather than filtered reports. Instead of writing policies to affect change, they get directly involved to ensure their vision for change becomes reality. In so doing, they become sensitive to the pulse of the organization, and thus better able to foresee problems before they become difficult to address.

Example

On the first day on the job, a new CEO was escorted to his new office by a board member. The office was huge, to say the least. It had three large potted trees, 12-ft-high ceilings, three walls of windows, a beautiful hand-carved, 8-ft-long oak desk, along with numerous chairs, couches, and assorted tables. In short, it was luxurious. As he looked at it for the first time, it became apparent to him that many of the company's employees would never come to such an office to seek help or information—the office itself was a barrier to communication because it was so imposing.

Later that day, the CEO called the production manager. He asked him to find a spare desk, chair, and telephone, and locate them within the production area where they would not interfere with the routine activities of the production floor. The CEO indicated that there would be a new employee working at that desk for the next several weeks. He didn't give him any more insight than that. The next day, the CEO went to his satellite office in the production area. An old, beat-up metal desk, worn chair, and a telephone became his temporary work area. As he began to work, employees began to notice a new face in the area. One person would ask, "Who is that?" Someone else would reply, "I don't know him." When the production manager told the employees who the new person was, the first comments that came out were, "Why is he down here?" "Is there something wrong?" "Do we have a problem?" The CEO was sure the supervisors and managers were thinking the same thing.

Throughout the next several days, the CEO would get up from his desk to wander around to talk with employees. He would start the conversations with an informal introduction, and begin by saying something like, "Do you have any problems with your work? Are there any issues you haven't been able resolve?" or "Tell me what you like or don't like about your job, and what you think should be done about it." After awhile, employees began to open up. They began talking about their problems and offering ideas on how to address them. Once they did so, the CEO would contact the appropriate manager or supervisor, advise them of the employee's comments and recommendations, and then ask the supervisor to look into the situation and get back to the employee (and to him) with their ideas on resolving the issue, the timing, and cost. In many cases, the CEO would simply ask the manager or supervisor to come to the employee's workstation to look at the issue first hand to determine what could be done to resolve it.

Soon not only were the employees on the floor actively identifying and resolving daily problems, but many of the supervisors and managers were on the floor, dealing with the employees where things were happening. That is when things began to get resolved. Management and employees began to communicate. The barriers to cross-functional communication and cooperation were broken. For the first time in years, people at all levels within the company began to work with one another in a collaborative effort.

Mentoring and Coaching

A common mistake made, especially by new managers, is failing to mentor and coach employees who have made a mistake. Instead of confronting the employee directly, the manager resorts to "papering the problem." The manager writes a new policy or procedure, prints it out, and then distributes it to all employees via interoffice mail or the company's intranet. Rather than focusing on the one employee who was at fault, the manager deems it less confrontational to address the issue in general terms through a new policy. But, of course, this only makes every employee angry, causes a general disruption in the workforce, negatively impacts productivity, and allows the offending employee to walk away without even a personal reprimand. Now that worked well, didn't it? The manager assumes the problem will never happen again because everyone now understands the new procedure. Is anything really resolved? No!

Good managers realize that writing policies and procedures solves nothing unless the source of the problem is resolved first. If a manager has a problem with an employee, he or she meets with that employee face-to-face to get it resolved immediately. If a new process, policy, or procedure is actually needed thereafter, it is then written and distributed only to the affected employees. No manager resolves operational, process, or employee performance problems simply by writing memos or new policies. Face-to-face communication always produces the best, quickest, and longest-lasting results.

Pros and Cons of Cybercommunication

Technology provides managers with the means to communicate with employees through numerous mechanisms much quicker, and in some cases, more effectively. In many cases, however, new technologies have actually hampered rather than improved communication. One example is e-mail. Often managers and employees use it as a means to avoid communicating face to face. Rather than confront a difficult, unpopular, or contentious situation directly, managers rationalize that the problem will go away by simply writing an e-mail and copying everyone in the entire organization. That way, every employee gets the word and the manager is not forced to confront anyone directly. To illustrate, when faced with political or polarizing issues, managers and employees who sit on opposite sides of a partition or in their respective offices send poison pen e-mails back and forth to one another. It would make sense for that manager or employee to walk around the partition and talk with the other employee. But why doesn't this happen? Because most people greatly dislike conflict and will avoid it at all costs.

While cybercommunication allows managers and employees to avoid face-to-face conflict, successful organizations discourage employees and managers from using it to resolve disagreements. When addressed face to face, problems are resolved quicker, managers and employees communicate more effectively, and misunderstandings are readily defused before they become personnel issues.

A Leader's Attitude and Its Impact

A manager's approach to resolving daily problems, attitude on the job, and even the way he carries himself influences the attitude and morale of his employees. Consequently, successful managers always set the example by maintaining a positive outlook. When a problem arises, it is treated routinely rather than as a crisis. Tempers rarely flare and voices are seldom raised (unless done for effect). In short, effective managers never "lose their cool." Exuding confidence, they are always in control of the situation. When under the influence of such a leader, employees emulate those same behavior patterns. And when they do, the productivity, capability, and capacity of the organization are greatly enhanced.

> "Good managers, when faced with a crisis, never ask 'who' created the problem or crisis. Rather, they ask 'how' the crisis arose and how it can be best resolved."

There are times when every manager is forced to think creatively to find ways to make the collective outlook and approach of his organization positive. Even though a result may be negative, there is always something positive to be learned from every business situation. A manager's job is to build upon those positive aspects, and not allow employees to dwell on the negative aspects of the situation. Sometimes just finding the root cause of a problem and getting it resolved is cause enough to celebrate. Whatever the case, a positive approach yields dividends for all parties concerned.

Leadership in Perspective

Example

The following is an example from a large manufacturing company in the capital goods industry.

The industrial engineering manager of the company had been with the organization for over 20 years. He was an incredibly articulate, bright, solid engineer. When given a problem or an assignment, no matter how large, within a matter of a few days he had it resolved. And, it was always done correctly. As a manager, he had surrounded himself with good, solid, technical professionals. As good as he and his employees were, however, no one in the rest of the organization would work with them. When there was a project that involved the industrial engineering department, it was always, "Man, I don't want to deal with this guy and his people." Why? Because they were always negative. The industrial engineering manager had this gruff, almost nasty outward appearance and approach. Most employees on the job had never seen the man smile. His employees and fellow managers were turned off by his attitude. As a result, they kept the industrial engineering manager and his staff at arm's length. Consequently, the organization was not as successful as it could have been. The chemistry and corresponding synergy did not exist.

In an effort to resolve the situation and avoid terminating the industrial engineering manager, his superior decided to try something a little unusual. He pulled together all of the employees who worked within the department, except for the industrial engineering manager and his staff. He asked the employees for their help with an experiment. He went on to explain that every day for the next two weeks he wanted every employee to go by the industrial engineering manager's office on their way to their office or workstation. Their assignment was to stick their heads into the industrial engineering manager's office and say, "Hey, good morning. How are you doing? It's good to see you. If there's anything I can do to help you, feel free to give me a call." They were then to proceed to their offices with nothing more said.

Every morning for the next several days, the employees followed the instructions. The industrial engineering manager's employees began watching the parade with great interest, wondering when their boss would explode. Within a few days, the constant outpouring of goodwill began to get to the industrial engineering manager. Everyone was so happy, so friendly; what was going on?

Finally it came to a head. The industrial engineering manager was walking in the main aisle toward the purchasing and production control department. His superior's office happened to be at the end of that main aisle, so he could see him coming and orchestrate the grand finale. At somewhat the same time, every one of the buyers came out of their offices. They addressed the industrial engineering manager, saying, "Hey, how are you doing buddy? It's good to see you. What can we do to help you?" He broke right there on the spot and began laughing. He was laughing so hard he couldn't stop. Soon, everyone was laughing with him. Now this was a guy who probably had never smiled in his entire life. As he returned to his office, he was still laughing out loud. His staff was totally taken aback. They had no idea what was going on. But their reaction was predictable—"You know what? This guy's human after all!" Then they, too, began to laugh. He, his staff, and employees elsewhere recognized that it was okay to lighten up and have some fun at work. It was okay to smile. It was okay to be positive. From that point on, the entire organization began to bond and grow. The chemistry grew exponentially because everyone adopted a new positive outlook.

HONESTY IN MANAGEMENT

Successful managers have learned the importance of honesty in every aspect of their day-to-day business dealings. Simply put, today's managers live in glass houses. Everything that a manager does is seen by his employees. The higher within the organizational structure a manager resides, the clearer those walls become.

Everything a manager does is visible, thereby intensifying the need to act appropriately and deal honestly in all situations. If a manager says one thing and does another, employees will see it. If that manager has a "discreet" affair with someone in the office, employees will see it. There is simply no such thing as a discreet affair in an office, especially when a manager is involved. It just doesn't happen. Political ploys are equally visible to employees. By saying, "We are all going to work as a team in this organization" and then doing the opposite, a manager sets himself up for a severe loss of credibility. Employees see right through it. Managers must be honest and straightforward in words and in action. Here again, a manager must "walk the talk."

Example

The national political scene bears out the fact that "honesty is the best policy." Even in the hallowed halls of the Oval Office, there is no such thing as secrecy when it comes to inappropriate behavior. There is one difference in a business environment, however. Business leaders and managers will *not* walk away from such behavior unscathed. Managers are generally terminated immediately for actions that compromise their integrity and thus their credibility. You may think that as a manager your personal life is your own and that it should have no bearing on your professional life. Think again! Senior managers, in particular, are conservative. They deal with impropriety quickly and severely. A manager's actions on the job, at business meetings, while entertaining customers, and even at home are factored into the credibility equation. Once that equation totals zero, a manager's time on the job is done.

REWARD AND RECOGNITION

When employees perform well, when projects are completed as scheduled, or when plaguing operational problems are finally resolved, it is time to celebrate. Good managers realize the importance of celebrating success within their organization. When their employees do a great job, they recognize them. They promote employees' successes throughout the organization. They have fun with it. Good managers understand the importance of "planned spontaneous recognition" of employee successes. They reward their employees with something personal. They bring in a pizza or a cake as recognition of a successful month, a successful week, or successful project. It becomes a powerful team-building experience. Simple acts of recognition like this go a long way in demonstrating that the manager cares and notices his employees' contributions. Because it is personal, it is powerful. So when in doubt, reach for the pizza!

> *"When it comes to reward and recognition, never underestimate the power of pizza."*

DEVELOPING INFORMAL LEADERS

By now, it is apparent that no manager can handle the requirements of the job alone. It is therefore necessary to develop informal leaders within the organization. These individuals have the ability and willingness to contribute to the organization's capabilities and capacities through their personal involvement with peers. Their skills complement the strengths and offset the weaknesses of their manager. By complementing their manager's skills, the synergy generated within the entire work group is greatly enhanced and the organization's capabilities greatly expanded.

Every employee has certain strengths and capabilities that, when properly identified and focused, can greatly enhance their manager's effectiveness in guiding the organization. Once those individual employee strengths are identified, the manager then assigns them specific roles and responsibilities. This allows the individual to grow professionally while, at the same time, contributing a complementary skill to the organization that increases its overall synergy and balance. These informal leaders are rarely vested with the formal power or position with which to force change through the organization. As a result, they have learned to work through their peers to get things done through the informal channels of cooperation and collaboration. It is that unique skill set that makes them so valuable.

Here are a few of the common roles that managers assign to informal leaders and how each role contributes to the organization's success.

Leadership in Perspective

- *Entrepreneurs*—these individuals are the non-traditionalists within the organization. They think outside-the-box when it comes to new concepts for product development, organizational change, or any new venture the manager is exploring. These employees are vital in situations where innovative thinking is required in a work group. The entrepreneur has the ability to create or adopt a new concept, and then sell it to other employees as a peer. This person is a change agent for the organization and plays a vital role in leading change movements for the manager.

- *Problem solvers*—these are the employees who thrive on resolving difficult organizational, process, or personnel problems. When a manager runs into a difficult problem or a barrier to the organization's progress on a particular operational issue, these employees are excellent at identifying root causes and soliciting the necessary support from other employees to get a solution implemented. Often incorrectly called "firefighters," these employees actually play a key role in ferreting out problems that hamper day-to-day performance. These types of problems are often difficult to address at the management level due to resistance or lack of trust at the employee level.

> "Nigel Bristow, President of Targeted Learning eloquently said, 'In today's dynamic and increasingly challenging work environments, organizations can no longer afford to have some people lead while others merely follow.'"

- *Mentors*—these individuals are the natural teachers, coaches, and facilitators within the organization. They thrive on sharing their skills and knowledge with other employees to enhance their capability and contribution to the organization. These are the employees that a manager relies upon to develop younger employees who may have an excellent arsenal of technical skills from a theoretical basis, but who lack the knowledge of how to practically apply those skills. Often recognized by their peers as a bountiful source of knowledge and support, these employees are a vital element in any team-based organization because of the credibility and trust they receive from their peers and superiors.

- *Team leaders*—these are the employees who have the ability to effectively build and lead a team of fellow employees. They build cohesiveness, maintain focus on the objective, and promote a positive outlook when difficulties arise. These are the employees who know how to select the right employees for a task, rally them to build a sense of urgency in reaching an objective (especially in cases of an emergency situation), and then lead them by personal example and commitment. Often termed "the go-to persons," these are the employees managers turn to when faced with difficult assignments or situations because they always get the job done.

- *Challengers*—these are the employees who look at situations from a number of perspectives to expand their understanding. They commonly challenge other employees to ensure everyone is working with facts versus opinion. These individuals will never accept answers like, "We have always done it this way." Challengers bring value to the organization because they constantly look for alternatives to maximize outcomes for the organization while minimizing the risk of poor decisions by groups. When managing a group of employees who have been together for a long time, smart managers often insert a challenger to shake things up. The challenger causes everyone to think differently by questioning or breaking down old paradigms.

- *Attack dogs*—these are the employees hired by managers to attack especially difficult challenges like organizational changes or transformations. These employees will consistently generate the desired results. A manager simply explains what is wanted and then turns them loose. Attack dogs will get the desired results, but they may well leave many dead bodies in their wake. These employees are not politically sensitive, thus they tend to create enemies along the way. While exceptionally useful in cases in which changes must be pushed through, they often find themselves the target of other managers and employees. Managers who have recruited and unleashed these go-getters must also accept the responsibility of protecting and supporting them. Too often, these same managers turn their back on these employees when things get political, allowing the attack dog to be thrown to the wolves. This is unethical and immoral—and will be obvious to other employees within the department. When this happens, the manager's credibility is lost.

THE NEW MANAGER
History and Its Impact

Chapter One discussed setting expectations for employees and concluded that expectations must be realistic and achievable to get employee buy-in. It is equally as important for managers to set realistic expectations for themselves.

When taking a management or supervisory position, every new manager inherits a history of performance problems, existing business or market opportunities, political issues, personnel problems, projects under way and planned; in short, an organizational history. For better or worse, the situation will require the new manager to initiate actions to resolve all of the open issues. That history and all of its associated problems, however, can not be resolved overnight. Every new manager must have time to assign priority to the issues. Selecting the "silver bullets" correctly will place the manager's attention on those issues of greatest importance and value to the organization and its customers, thus ensuring the appropriate application of corporate resources.

> "By jumping into action before knowing what the true problems really are, a manager causes more trouble for himself than is necessary."

Before setting priorities and initiating subsequent actions, a wise manager takes the time to assess each issue thoroughly, considering carefully the current business situation and environment so the correct priorities can be set. No manager ever assumes that the organization's problems can be resolved overnight. "Hit the ground running" does not mean running off in the wrong direction. Rather, it means quickly establishing the correct course of action based upon a realistic and accurate assessment of the situation so that the direction taken hits the target the first time. Yes, there is always an expectation that a new manager will begin to make corrective actions quickly to gain control of the organization. There is an equal expectation, however, that those actions selected by the new manager will be the correct ones ... and in support of the organization's strategic direction so that things will actually get better, not worse.

> "'Hit the ground running' does not mean running off in the wrong direction."

A technique used by successful managers in new business or organizational settings is to take the first few days to get as thorough an understanding as possible of his superior's expectations. Spending as much time with his superior as possible during the first few days on the job, a new manager utilizes this interaction to maximum advantage. The new manager learns his superior's concrete requirements, as well as his implicit expectations of the organization's performance. A seasoned manager knows to dig deeply during those conversations to uncover things that his new superior may neglect to mention that could prove important later—things like specific organizational performance criteria, budgetary concerns, or simply problems of the day. There are also implicit requirements that the superior may assume the new manager will know, and as such will not mention unless pressed. These are often things like personnel issues, strategy issues, or political issues—issues that can make or break a manager's career if they occur downstream as a surprise because the manager failed to ask about them early on.

Leadership in Perspective

Example

When calling to make a hotel reservation, a potential guest gives the reservations clerk a series of explicit requirements regarding his expectations for a hotel stay. If each of those expectations is met, the guest can expect to be reasonably comfortable at the hotel. What does the guest ask for? He asks to reserve a room for certain dates, within a certain price range, and with a particular size of bed: king, queen, or double. He may require a smoking or non-smoking room, a room with a particular view or easy access to workout facilities, or a room with wireless Internet access. Each of these things is an explicit requirement. But what about requirements for things like clean linens, clean towels, or enough hangers to hang a week's worth of clothes? Are these requirements any less important to the traveler? No? Then why isn't it necessary to ask for clean sheets, clean towels, etc.? The answer is that travelers implicitly expect them. Most travelers assume that every hotel provides those things. However, nothing should be considered a given. It is the same in the business world, but even more so. No manager can assume that because his superior did not mention something that it is not important.

Establishing Priorities

Based upon his superior's explicit and implicit requirements, the new manager sets near-term and longer-term priorities. Not every issue can be number one, so together they identify their order of priority. This allows the manager to concentrate his efforts, and those of his employees, on those things that are most important to the organization. If something is not clear, the manager asks for clarification. Once all of the priorities are established, the manager then reviews them again with his superior to ensure a common understanding and agreement in as much detail as possible. This final review is known as "mining for silver bullets." It is essential to weed out those issues most critical to the organization and set aside the nuisance issues that are frequent distractions with little organizational value.

Implementing Performance Metrics

Next, the manager and his superior establish a set of performance metrics based upon the expectations and priorities so that the manager's success in meeting those objectives can be quantitatively measured. Once agreed upon, the priorities, expectations, and metrics are documented for future use.

The metrics established are:

- few in number, preferably five to six maximum,
- consistent with the organization's overall direction and business strategy, and
- measurable in quantitative terms using readily available systems and subsystems supported by the organization.

Examples of performance metrics for a manufacturing concern are operational or process throughput, process or operational cycle time, operating expense, and inventory investment or turns. For an engineering or design operation, common metrics would include design cycle time, design reliability, design-to-cost compliance, number of engineering changes, and manufacturability measures. Every industry has its own set of key performance metrics. It is a manager's responsibility to identify, assess, understand, and comply with those appropriate to his organization.

The First Few Weeks on the Job

A smart manager uses the first few weeks to advantage, recognizing that as time goes on there will be less access to her superior than during the early days of her tenure on the job. Experienced managers set frequent review periods with their superior, typically weekly during the first six months on the job, monthly thereafter. These are set times in which the new manager and her superior review progress and take any corrective action necessary to ensure that the manager stays on course. Since progress is frequently reviewed, the manager and her superior are on the same page with respect to the course of action; there are never any surprises. A good manager recognizes the importance of making her superior her number one customer, as well as what is required to get and keep her superior's support. Successful managers have learned through experience that their superior, rightly or wrongly, has a significant impact on their career. That fact is never taken lightly.

Meeting with Internal Customers

The next step for a new manager is to meet with all internal customers: that is, the internal and external organizations, departments, or processes the manager's organization serves and supports. These are typically the departments to which the manager's organization provides information, materials, technology, or personnel in support of business process needs. Those organizations rely upon the inputs from the new manager's organization to generate the outputs required of them in support of their customers.

The new manager's role is to work with her counterparts to isolate their specific expectations and requirements, and then to ascertain if there is a gap between the internal customers' expectations and priorities and what the manager's organization is providing. If a gap exists, the manager and her counterparts work to find common ground. Their challenge is to identify ways to satisfy both groups while remaining consistent with the requirements of upper management. Once an agreement is reached on the expected levels of performance (and these can be dynamic expectations), the parties then establish a series of metrics that the two will use to measure the performance of the new manager's organization. The new manager then documents those metrics and integrates them with the metrics, priorities, and requirements of upper management.

Integrating External Metrics and Internal Performance Measures

The final step for the new manager is to develop a set of internal measurements that will guide her organization in meeting the expectations and requirements of all of its customers—a methodology that will allow the manager and her employees to measure their own performance.

The manager then clearly and completely communicates the new performance metrics and their origin to all employees to ensure that they understand the new expectations and priorities. As with all communication between a manager and her employees, nothing is assumed or neglected. Every employee must know precisely what is expected, how results will be measured, and how they relate or contribute to accomplishment of the organization's overall direction and mission.

Next, the new manager's task is to redirect all departmental and individual employee activities and projects within the organization to correspond to the newly formed performance targets. New performance metrics provide a road map of how the manager intends to accomplish her organization's vision through a series of projects and organizational process controls. The manager will decompose each of the organization's process performance targets into a series of functional metrics that will guide the day-to-day operations of the department. Ultimately, these will be used by department employees to measure their own success.

A Simple Tool

A simple technique that aids a manager in communicating organizational metrics to employees is the placement of a flip chart, bulletin board, or easel outside the manager's door. The chart displays a series of graphs depicting each of the organizational performance metrics along with the organization's current status against them. The manager then updates each graph weekly to illustrate the organization's progress. What will take place as a result is known as the "Hawthorne Effect." Having this visual reminder, employees are psychologically motivated to raise their level of performance to the expected level established by management. In most cases, performance will improve markedly (15%–20%) without any additional input from the manager. The secret to the Hawthorne Effect is the transfer of knowledge regarding the explicit expectations of the manager, along with the methodology to measure those expectations quantitatively by each employee affected. If employees know what their manager expects, know that the manager is measuring their performance, and know the methodology of that measurement, then they will refocus their attention to achieving that targeted level of performance. The Hawthorne Effect concept is simple and effective.

The Critical Linkage

When setting organizational priorities and performance metrics, an effective manager ensures that the linkage is evident between his organization's functional metrics and those set forth in senior management's mission statement. This ensures that employees at all levels clearly understand their role, as employees, in support of reaching key organizational objectives.

Most organizations have mission statements. But, even though that mission statement has been communicated in various ways, most employees and managers cannot repeat it from memory because it is neither applicable to nor understood by them personally. For the most part, these mission statements are nebulous, lacking the metrics to track the organization's progress in achieving senior management's desired outcome. There is a disconnect between what senior management wants the organization to accomplish and the day-to-day activities of most employees and managers. When that disconnect exists, employees simply do not know what to do to assist management because nothing is measurable. Employees are unaware of how the things they do daily will contribute to senior management's vision, so they simply do the best job they can even if it turns out to be counter to senior management's intended direction.

The same disconnect can exist with functional managers. Guiding the different functional processes within the organization effectively dictates that functional managers understand the link between senior management's strategic objectives and the process-level requirements necessary to meet them on a daily basis. Without that understanding, the functional manager may establish tactical, functional, and individual metrics that run counter to the objectives of the organization. The bottom line is that every manager must understand the linkage and communicate it clearly and frequently to every employee under his supervision. By following the process of identifying his superior's requirements, identifying the internal customers' requirements, and then integrating them into his functional requirements, that linkage is created and communicated.

Motorola Example

The operating initiatives established by Motorola's senior management in the 1980s serve as an excellent illustration of the critical linkage between the metrics set forth in a company's mission statement and the functional metrics used throughout the company.

In an effort to create a common focus and approach among its management and employees, Motorola's senior management created three key initiatives that ultimately became the basis of their vision for six-sigma operational excellence. The key initiatives were:

1. Achieve 100% customer satisfaction annually, as measured by customers. So whatever metrics, whatever methodology Motorola's customers used to measure performance, Motorola was required to comply completely.

2. Achieve a ten-fold improvement in the cycle time of every business process, every five years. Whether it was closing the books, designing a new product, or processing customer orders, over the course of the next five years that business process (and myriad others within the corporation) was required to be improved ten-fold.

3. Achieve a ten-fold improvement in product and process quality every two years, with an ultimate goal of six sigma quality levels throughout the corporation.

These are dynamic and measurable organizational metrics. They are understood by every employee within Motorola. Today known as "Process Excellence," these initiatives have become the basis of all employee and organizational performance measurements, performance appraisal criteria, and reward systems at Motorola.

Leadership in Perspective

Managers within Motorola use Process Excellence to easily correlate the organization's performance expectations to those of the individual employees within every department. By so doing, every employee, every manager, and every facet of the organization is pulling in the same direction. The linkage between what management sets as the organization's vision and each employee's contribution to that vision is crystal clear. There is no ambiguity or misunderstanding about what the organization or its employees are to accomplish.

Progress Reviews

Once departmental and employee performance targets are established and communicated, they are reviewed frequently. Weekly progress updates are the rule. These sessions do not require an hour-long department meeting. A quick 10–15-minute review with time for questions and the exchange of ideas relative to improvements is adequate. The direction the organization is taking should never be a surprise to anyone. Closed-loop communication combined with timely and effective corrective actions will ensure that every employee stays on target.

Corrective Actions

If a manager finds that his organization is failing to meet the expected level of performance, or is failing to meet the metrics and priorities established by senior management and internal customers, then rapid corrective action is required.

Too many managers, especially new ones, set the interval period between review of the organization's performance measurements and employee performance measurements too far apart. Monthly is common practice, primarily because the review of metrics can be made to coincide with the month-end closing of financials for the company. Project managers, for example, will look at their critical paths once a month, instead of once a day. Department managers look at the status of their budgets or their shipping quotas at the end of every month, versus daily. This delay in reviewing metrics means that 30 days of recovery time is lost. Enlightened managers monitor key performance metrics on a far more frequent (daily) basis. If there is a failure to achieve a particular metric, the response can thus be immediate and correction implemented without delay.

Example

Upon study of a manufacturing company's shipping schedule, it was apparent to the functional manager that the activity consistently followed a saw-toothed curve. Nothing happened the first two weeks of the month. In the third week, things picked up somewhat, and in the fourth week everything broke loose. Everyone had to work at a frenzied pace because they were out of time. When the next month began, everyone again relaxed because they knew they would not be measured again for another 30 days. The cycle kept repeating itself. As the manager began to analyze employee behavior and the organizational culture associated with this phenomenon, it became apparent that the interval between performance measurements was too broad. The time gap allowed employees to procrastinate without consequences until they were in a crisis. When employees missed the daily allotment of shipments, they simply rationalized that they would make up for it later in the month. Tomorrow became the fallback—that is until there was no tomorrow because the end of the month was looming. Only then would they get serious. But of course, by then it was too late.

To change the employees' behavior, and thus the culture of procrastination, required a simple change in metrics. Instead of setting monthly goals, the manager set daily goals (see Figure 2-6). By focusing on more finite measurement intervals, the employees were forced to alter their behavior to meet "today's" expectations. Things could no longer slip because the "end of the month" occurred daily. The net result was a dramatic improvement in shipping performance coupled with a dramatic reduction in budget variances. Was this rocket science? No, it was merely a pragmatic approach to the application of employee performance measurements. The Hawthorne Effect is an effective tool for managers if used properly. If things are not going as planned, it's up to the manager to make a change. No improvements ever

Leadership in Perspective

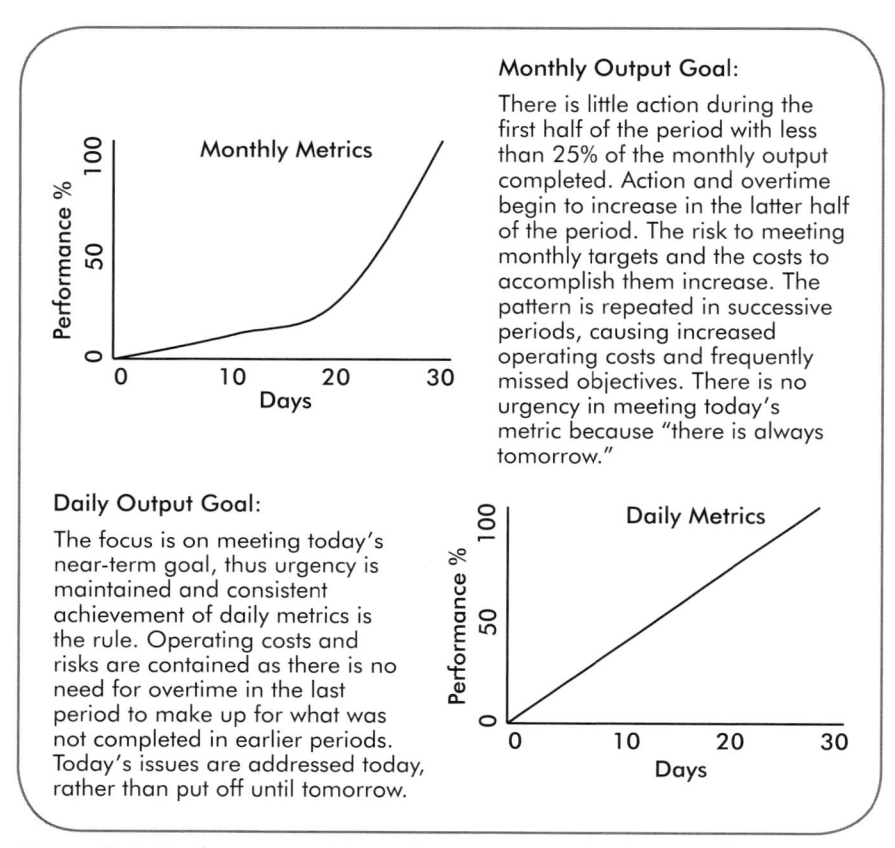

Monthly Metrics (graph: Performance % vs Days, 0-30)

Monthly Output Goal:
There is little action during the first half of the period with less than 25% of the monthly output completed. Action and overtime begin to increase in the latter half of the period. The risk to meeting monthly targets and the costs to accomplish them increase. The pattern is repeated in successive periods, causing increased operating costs and frequently missed objectives. There is no urgency in meeting today's metric because "there is always tomorrow."

Daily Output Goal:
The focus is on meeting today's near-term goal, thus urgency is maintained and consistent achievement of daily metrics is the rule. Operating costs and risks are contained as there is no need for overtime in the last period to make up for what was not completed in earlier periods. Today's issues are addressed today, rather than put off until tomorrow.

Daily Metrics (graph: Performance % vs Days, 0-30)

Figure 2-6. Daily vs. monthly performance monitoring results.

occur from inaction. There must be a sense of urgency instilled within every employee. That urgency can only occur if there are frequent measurements of performance.

SUMMARY

Throughout this chapter, various perspectives on leadership were discussed. In addition, those techniques and tools that solid managers integrate into their management styles and daily interactions with employees have been discussed in limited detail. In the following chapters, many of these same tools and techniques will be expanded through real-world examples and additional detail to illustrate their application in today's rapidly changing global organizations. In addition, many of the sensitive issues that managers will face in a business setting, from sexual harassment to age and gender bias, also will be explored.

REFERENCE

Termini, Michael J. 1999. *Strategic Project Management: Tools and Techniques for Planning, Decision Making, and Implementation*. Dearborn, MI: Society of Manufacturing Engineers.

3
Managing the Transition from Individual Contributor to Manager

OBJECTIVES

In this chapter, the issues associated with an individual's promotion to management from within a workgroup or department will be explored, along with some techniques to be employed to ease the transition. While moving into a management position as an "outsider" carries with it its own set of unique challenges, often being promoted from within the organization is even more difficult. The hurdle of transitioning from "one of us" to "one of them" can be difficult and problematic for the new manager.

PREPARING FOR THE TRANSITION

Too often, there is a tendency to wait until an employee is promoted into a management position before steps are taken to train him in the skills and techniques that will make him successful. The problem with this approach is obvious—the new manager is immediately placed in reactionary mode. He is forced to begin reacting to a series of operational and organizational issues, including those left over from his predecessor. He does not have the opportunity to grow into the job comfortably. The fallout that results is often tragic and unnecessary.

One of the key responsibilities of every manager is to prepare employees interested in an eventual move into management *before* they are placed in the position. While often easier said than done, this remains an essential ingredient to building depth and capability in an organization. A manager's goal is to get these management candidates ready, willing, and

Managing the Transition from Individual Contributor to Manager

able to take on a leadership role, even that manager's own role, as quickly as possible. That way when an opening occurs anywhere within the organization, aspiring managers are already trained and prepared to effectively handle the challenges that lie ahead of them.

Training, while vitally important, is only one element of the succession planning and transition process, however. To fully prepare a new manager for everything he will face in a management role is not always possible. It is a given; there will be things he will learn on the job and situations for which no amount of training or mentoring will prepare him. So ultimately, whose responsibility is it to prepare the new manager for what lies ahead? The answer is both the employee and his manager. If it is an employee's intent to eventually move into a management position, he too must take control of and responsibility for his own destiny. Every employee is required to actively manage his own career. If an employee makes a conscious decision to move into management, then it is wise for him to seek management training as soon as that decision is made. In such cases, managers encourage those employees to attend continuing education programs offered by leading universities and trade organizations. In contrast to many advanced degree programs, these continuing education classes are often taught by business professionals who have personally made the transition from technical into management positions, and who will provide insight and advice from their own experiences, successes, and failures.

> *"You will never be promoted unless there is someone ready, willing, and able to take your place."*

NEW ROLES AND RESPONSIBILITIES

Recently promoted managers who have spent time in the trenches with a group of fellow employees will find it particularly difficult to transition into management of that group. The transition involves more than a simple move from the role of an excellent individual contributor to that of a manager; it involves the management of friends and close business associates. It is almost as though when the individual takes on the manager's title, the expectations, perceptions, and relationships with those same employees change overnight. It is a difficult transition because it often strains or destroys long-standing personal relationships. The new manager is often isolated from the group because she is no longer considered one of them. There are many reasons why this phenomenon occurs.

Obviously, the responsibilities of a manager are different than those of an employee. A manager is forced to address strategic as well as tactical issues and to be organizationally focused versus detailed or functionally focused. The manager's responsibilities are now far greater than those of an individual contributor. A new manager finds herself not only responsible for her own work, but that of her employees. The job now includes heavy doses of coaching, tutoring, and mentoring employees—helping them learn, solving problems, addressing concerns and career and personal issues, etc. In short, the job is significantly larger and more complex.

There will be times when a new manager comes to realize it is a bit lonely at the top. Numerous late Friday nights, Saturday mornings, and Sunday afternoons will be spent in an empty, quiet office. After hours, employees are at home or doing things together, but the new manager finds herself in the office, working on problems she did not get a chance to resolve during normal working hours because she was busy helping others. In every manager's career, there comes the inevitable question, "Is this job really worth it?" Management requires a significant personal commitment on the part of every individual who ventures into it. It is a commitment that directly impacts not only the individual, but those around her as well. An employee considering a move into management is advised to be prepared for some tough going during the transition. She is equally advised to clearly understand what she is getting into prior to finalizing that decision.

With a change in title and more responsibility comes the requirement to look at things in a different way. There are

Managing the Transition from Individual Contributor to Manager

things that may have been blown off to another day before, but now the new manager must address them before leaving the office. A new manager is also placed in the position of being far more demanding of those same employees she socialized with previously. There will be times when the new manager is forced to require those friends and business associates to stay until the job gets done rather than to go out for drinks or golf after work. As a manager, friends, business associates, subordinates, and others are expected to respond to her requests. Old friends suddenly become subordinates, an entirely different and challenging situation.

Every individual wants to be liked and respected. We all want friends. But in a business setting, friends tend to have the expectation that they will be treated differently from other employees, that they will be given a little extra latitude or consideration. A successful manager does not allow this to happen. Every employee is treated the same; there is a level playing field for all. There can be no favors, no special treatment, no exceptions—every employee is treated equally and respectfully and given equal expectations for performance.

> "Every employee is treated the same; there is a level playing field for all."

Can a friendship be maintained between a manager and her employee? Certainly, but it is tough. It will take a special type of relationship and a special type of friend, one who understands the requirements the job places on a manager. Those that understand are true friends. But like children, even true friends will test a new manager from time to time. If a manager cuts a friend a little slack or shows favoritism in any way, she is immediately compromised as a manager.

In some cases, old friends will fail to understand why the changes discussed as peers are not being immediately implemented by the new manager. There will be an expectation, and pressure, to make policy or organizational changes immediately. Rightly or wrongly, every new manager is expected to uphold the party line, even if in the past she was openly opposed to it. Yes, changes can be made over time. However, until those changes are approved and implemented, every manager is required to conform to the organizational norms and hold employees to those same policies and procedures. Old friends do not always understand why it takes so long to implement change. They do not realize that organizational and cultural changes do not happen easily or quickly. But they must be encouraged to be patient. And since most of us are not born with an abundance of patience, this too will be a hard sell.

Living in a glass house, everything a manager does is seen by employees. Nothing is discreet or confidential. In addition to personnel and operational responsibilities, every manager has fiduciary responsibilities to the organization, its employees, and its stockholders. This deserves a manager's undivided attention and complete compliance. Legally, every manager is bound to take appropriate and correct actions to uphold the organization's policies and procedures. Managers act primarily for the benefit of the organization and its stakeholders in all matters concerning the business. Those who fail to do so face not only the possibility of organizational losses, but potential job loss and personal losses arising from litigation. Consequently, every manager will be forced to make some tough calls throughout their career to do what is legally correct versus what may be expeditious or politically correct at the time. A seasoned manager knows never to compromise her position or professional integrity by ignoring the responsibilities that come with the job. Management responsibilities exist 24 hours a day, seven days a week, 52 weeks a year.

In Chapter 4, other legal issues facing managers will be explored in significant detail. For now, it is sufficient to say that no manager should risk taking an action of questionable legality or fail to take action where the legal issues clearly dictate the need. Ignorance of the law is no protection in today's court system. When in doubt, a good manager seeks the advice of legal counsel.

FACILITATING THE TRANSITION

While it is evident by this time that a transition to management will require fortitude and due diligence on the part of an

Managing the Transition from Individual Contributor to Manager

individual, there are several proven tools and techniques that will make the transition easier.

- First, it is important that a new manager gains an understanding of the attitudes and morale of his new employees as quickly as possible, along with the drivers behind them. Organizational culture will frequently influence the behavior and performance of employees. Therefore, gaining an early understanding of the reasons why employees behave as they do allows a new manager to quickly develop and implement corrective action plans, where required, to alter the circumstances that reinforce negative behavior. For instance, it may be necessary to alter the reward and appraisal systems, current policies and procedures, or even operational processes to affect the needed changes. If a new manager fails to fully understand why employees behave as they do, he will be unable to institute permanent change. Because the manager has come from the employee ranks, he may believe he has a good understanding of the behavior drivers. The truth is, however, the manager's own bias and perceptions may be leading him astray. More tenured managers know to look for data that will clearly isolate the root cause of the current employee behavior, whether positive or negative. A good manager never lets personal bias cloud his judgment.

- Every new and experienced manager must recognize that his personal behavior will affect the behavior and performance of his employees. If a manager is negative and explosive, his employees will either adopt that same style or become excessively passive. If every time there is a problem, the manager throws up his hands in frustration, incapable of maintaining a semblance of rational thinking and reason, then his employees too will consistently falter whenever organizational or operational problems occur. If, however, a manager maintains a positive outlook, looks for solutions to problems rather than assigning blame, and constantly seeks opportunities even in difficult business situations, then his employees will maintain a similar proactive attitude. In short, every manager's employees are a direct reflection of that manager, for better or worse.

- A good manager constantly assesses the needs of his employees against the needs of the organization. There are times when a manager must break his employees out of the current business environments or constraints to allow them to think differently or just to give them a mental break. In today's high stress, heavy workload business environments, most employees are working well in excess of 40 hours a week, many in excess of the national average of 45 hours per week. They become mentally tired or locked into the organizational way of thinking, failing to see new and creative solutions to existing business problems. Effective managers stay in tune to their employees to spot the fatigue factors that inhibit performance. When those factors cannot be overcome through normal coaching or mentoring, it is incumbent upon a manager to find ways or venues that will provide the employees with a clearer or different perspective on the issues. Something as simple as bringing in pizza or holding a department meeting off site will yield measurable dividends, breaking the conventional mold and allowing employees to think and interface outside of the constraints and pressures of the organization.

> *"Stay in tune with employees to spot the fatigue factors that inhibit performance."*

- Communication barriers within a department are quickly addressed by savvy managers. Often, the physical layout or structure of a department inhibits communication between employees (partitions, offices, walls, etc.). An early look at the physical barriers to communication can provide a new manager with insight relative to why his employees do not work well together or communicate effectively. Simply put, if employees cannot see one another, communication declines. Good managers create ways to bring employees together physically. They redesign the department's layout to put employees in closer proximity to one another and remove the visual barriers between them. Communication areas are designed into the new layout. These are places where employees can talk together informally, exchange ideas, and work out problems. Providing such a venue also allows employees to build relationships with one another on a personal level. One of the things many Silicon Valley company employees complain about the most as their companies grow larger is the loss of the "Friday afternoon beer busts." No, it is not the beer and hot dogs that they miss. Rather it is the opportunity to interface with other employees and get to know them on a personal level, building an informal network that allows them to work together to resolve cross-functional problems. It is a fact that 95% of communication within an organization occurs informally. The physical structure of an organization will either reinforce that communication or destroy it.

- Successful managers communicate early and often, dedicating a significant amount of their day to talking with employees. Visible and accessible, they gather and utilize the input of employees to resolve day-to-day operational problems and make process improvements. Because employees are closest to the issues, they likely know them best. Employees appreciate their new manager's interest and his willingness to incorporate their ideas. New managers frequently use employees as a sounding board for new ideas and concepts. They encourage critique and accept it openly, building trust with employees along the way. They learn the triggers that motivate each employee, as well as those that create discomfort and concern. The circle of communication is expanded to other peers and managers. Nothing gets done within an organization unless employees and managers communicate openly and honestly with one another.

- Managers are the organization's cheerleaders. When success is realized, managers utilize the opportunity to praise employees on their accomplishments and contributions to the organization. Successful managers recognize the requirement to reward on an organizational level, while at the same time knowing that "there *is* an 'I' in 'team,'" no matter what the pundits say. Every employee has an internal desire and drive to achieve their own personal goals, to be recognized as a contributor, and to reach a level of performance that brings with it recognition. As Maslow clearly pointed out with his Hierarchy of Needs, individuals seek recognition and accomplishment. However, it is important that individual goals remain secondary to organizational goals to create the synergy necessary for a solid team. To that end, a manager rewards on a team or organizational basis consistent with what the organization or department has achieved as a whole, and then on the individual's contributions to those organizational successes. By so doing, the new manager acknowledges both outstanding organizational and individual performance.

  Successful managers recognize extraordinary efforts made by employees. When employees put in extra effort or work longer hours to meet a deadline or resolve a particularly difficult problem, recognition by their manager is appreciated. A simple acknowledgment of the act, along with a simple "thank you" will reinforce the employees' dedication while building relationships with their manager. However, effort alone is not enough. It is the results employees generate that bring value to the organization. Without results, the effort is wasted.

- Managers make timely, prudent decisions. While the topic of decision making is expanded on in more detail in a later chapter, for now it is sufficient to say that indecision is a catalyst for organizational failure. Effective managers make decisions and encourage employees to do the same. But there is danger when new managers too eagerly accept every problem that their employees throw at them.

Managing the Transition from Individual Contributor to Manager

In allowing employees to dump their problems and walk away, a new manager finds himself mired in situations without either adequate data with which to make an informed decision or the means to gather the needed data. The result is indecision. Successful managers encourage their employees to bring problems to them for resolution. But with the problem comes the requirement for the employee to:

– define the problem and provide the manager with the data used to validate it,

– define the assumptions made relative to the problem and the validation techniques used to ensure the assumptions are correct,

– define the alternatives available to the manager relative to the problem, how each was derived, its associated risks and implementation issues, and

– select which alternative the employee would choose if the decision were his to make, why he chose it, and the validated data used to arrive at his conclusion.

By teaching employees to follow this procedure, the new manager is ensured that he gets the information necessary to make informed decisions, while at the same time encouraging employees to make decisions independently.

- Effective managers ensure that assignments are understood. Busy managers, especially new ones, fall into the trap of barking out assignments in a rapid-fire way when numerous things are going on simultaneously. Buried in phone calls, operational problems, and looming deadlines, the new manager calls employees in, barks out assignments, turns them loose, and moves on to another task. An employee walks away from the encounter with a vague, incomplete idea of what his manager expects, but with a commitment to do his best to deliver what he perceives the boss wants. Upon completion of the assignment, the employee and the new manager are dismayed at the dif-

Managing the Transition from Individual Contributor to Manager

ference between what the employee did versus what the manager expected. Too often, new managers fail to think through assignments completely before giving them to employees. The result is always confusion, frustration on both parts, and decay in the trust between employee and manager. The solution is simple. Seasoned managers know to keep a stack of 3 × 5 cards handy. Before making an assignment, they fill it in with the details necessary for the employee to complete the assignment (see Chapter 1 for more information on the use of this tool).

- Managers reinforce the need for creativity and out-of-the-box thinking from their employees. There are times when the demands placed on the organization from senior management seem unrealistic. Employees and managers alike rapidly conclude that what senior management is seeking cannot be accomplished. Thereafter, nothing happens. When a new manager sees this condition setting in, she encourages her employees to look for unique, innovative solutions. She challenges employees to treat the assignment much as a child approaches a new video game. In the beginning, the child constantly fails. But because of the competitive nature that resides within us all, a child will not quit trying. The child learns something new from each failure. With every attempt, the child passes to a higher level until, suddenly, he breaks through to win the game. It is the same learning process with difficult business assignments. Employees are encouraged to look for new approaches, those breakthrough ideas. Plato said, "Necessity is the mother of invention." Employees are made to realize that nothing of significance comes without hard work and conscious effort. And good managers realize that innovation requires abandoning existing paradigms to reveal new approaches and solutions to business and process problems.

Another approach to encourage innovative thinking is to require employees to prepare a listing of 10 reasons why the assignment *can not* be done within the timeframe required given all the organizational constraints. Once this is completed, employees then brainstorm a listing of 10 reasons why it *can* be done. Going through this exercise breaks down the initial resistance on the part of employees, allowing them to vent their frustrations first and then refocus their thinking in a more open, creative way.

- New managers capitalize on innovative ideas. When an employee forwards a new, creative idea that has significant potential, successful managers seize the opportunity to reinforce the employee's thinking, encouraging him to further develop the approach or idea. However, a good manager never leaves it entirely up to the employee to work through on his own. Great ideas die a quick death without fertilization by management.

- New managers encourage employees to challenge one other. Innovative ideas are spawned from multiple points of view. Employees are encouraged to professionally critique the ideas of others and suggest alternative methodologies or approaches. Collaboration leads to an optimal solution for the entire organization. When employees begin to think alike, successful managers recognize the potential for a stalemate and seek diverse inputs and ideas from outside sources. They may invite other functional managers into department meetings to gain their perspectives. Further, they may benchmark concepts and methodologies developed by other departments within the company, other organizations within the industry, or best-in-class organizations from other industries.

  > "Innovative ideas are spawned from multiple points of view."

- Good managers encourage risk-taking by employees. When a new manager comes onto the scene, many employees become overly conservative in their approaches to problem resolution and day-to-day activities. This is especially true when the new manager has come from the ranks and has historically demonstrated consistency and doggedness in her approach to doing things. Under these circumstances, a new manager must quickly establish ground rules for the organization that promote risk-taking and innovative thinking. Every employee is encouraged to look for innovative solutions and take calculated risks that have been quantitatively measured and assessed. But while risk-taking is encouraged, the manager makes it abundantly clear that there is no excuse for outright carelessness; employees are required to engineer risks out.

FIRST SUCCESS

For the new manager, it is absolutely mandatory that the first thing he touches be successful. The reason for this is simple. If a new manager takes on a project or an organizational problem and is not successful, he becomes viewed as just an average manager, never capable of getting anything of significance accomplished. But if that first project or action is successful, generating measurable results, then he quickly develops a reputation as someone who gets things done. The stage for a successful career is set right up front. In the business world, perception is reality. When a manager is perceived as effective in resolving problems, implementing change, or leading organizational projects, his job will immediately become much easier. Conversely, if he is perceived as either "run of the mill" or a genuine failure, the job will be much tougher. That perception, for better or for worse, is difficult to reverse.

SUMMARY

Promotions from within an organization bring with them some unique problems for a new manager. Knowledge of and preparation for those challenges, however, will make the transition markedly easier. New managers will face challenges from former peers and comrades, legal challenges relative to the fiduciary responsibilities that accompany a move into management, and personal challenges to win the trust and respect of employees within the department.

Managing the Transition from Individual Contributor to Manager

Combined with a healthy dose of common sense and patience, the tools and techniques provided within this chapter will aid a new manager in launching a successful career, as well as avoiding early trouble. Above all, communication and consistency are requirements for success in a new management position. Knowing the expectations and seeing consistency in the direction, priorities, and approach of management are of significant importance to employees. They want to be led, not managed. Recognizing the difference separates the truly successful managers from those that just get by.

Chapter 4 will explore several of the legal aspects of management. Bias, discrimination, labor law, employment law, and other topics will be addressed in detail. New managers must be aware of the legalities associated with management. The simple fact is that gender, sexual orientation, religion, race, and nationality are of little importance when selecting, dealing with, and evaluating employees. What every manager is interested in are the results that employees generate. Allowing personal bias to enter into decision making opens a manager to personnel and legal problems.

4

Complying with Employment and Labor Laws

OBJECTIVE

This chapter will discuss several important aspects of employment and labor law. The intent is to provide a basic understanding of the legal requirements every manager is required to comply with when dealing with employees. In particular, this chapter will explore:

- sexual harassment and its implications in dealing with gender issues in the workplace,
- how various forms of race, sex, and national origin discrimination violate Title VII of the Equal Opportunity Employment Act,
- the accommodations managers make to avoid physical and religious discrimination,
- the requirements of the Americans with Disabilities Act and their impact on management decisions in the workplace,
- the scope and application of age discrimination laws,
- the remedies available to managers in cases where discrimination or harassment is alleged, and
- the issues faced by managers working within a union environment.

Today, more than at any time in the past, managers realize that their decisions and actions cannot be made arbitrarily. Managers are not free to act as they wish. They are required to comply with numerous federal, state, and local labor laws. To ignore the law is foolhardy and irresponsible.

Complying with Employment and Labor Laws

FEDERAL LABOR LAWS

Unionization in the workplace has been around since 1886 when the American Federation of Labor (AFL) was formed. Many government-sector employees are unionized, but only approximately 15% of private-sector hourly and salaried employees are members of an organized union or bargaining unit. While union membership has been on a steady decline for over two decades, the drive for expansion of unions into new business sectors continues. Thus for new managers to assume that federal labor laws will not impact their business decisions or influence their career because they currently work within a nonunion environment is a serious mistake. Federal labor laws directly impact both unionized and non-unionized workers, their employers, and their managers. Therefore, in this section several of the key elements of the federal labor laws will be discussed.

Equal Employment Opportunity Act

The courts have set forth specific requirements relative to a manager's role in dealing with employees in the workplace, which every new manager must be versed in. Of primary importance are the requirements and restrictions outlined in what has become known as "Title VII" or the Equal Employment Opportunity Act. In 1972, the Civil Rights Act of 1964 was amended to include the following provisions in Title VII.

"It shall be unlawful employment practice for an employer:

"1. To fail or refuse to hire or to discharge any individual, or otherwise to discriminate against any individual with respect to his compensation, terms, conditions, or privileges of employment, because of such individual's race, color, religion, sex, or national origin; or

"2. To limit, segregate, or classify employees or applicants for employment in any way that would deprive or tend to deprive any individual of employment opportunities or otherwise adversely affect his status as an employee, because of such individual's race, color, religion, sex, or national origin."

Title VII applies to employers with at least 15 employees who are employed for at least 20 weeks in a current or a preceding year, employment agencies, labor unions with at least 15 members, state and

> *"In essence, any form of discrimination by a manager is illegal and unethical."*

local governments and their agencies, and most federal government employees. The only current exemptions are Indian tribes and tax-exempt private clubs. In brief, Title VII prohibits any form of discrimination by a manager or business:

- in the selection and hiring of employees,
- in the decisions made by a manager relative to promotions and demotions of employees,
- in decisions made by managers involving offers of training or apprenticeship programs for employees,
- in referrals for employment made by managers,
- in decisions made by managers relative to the dismissal of employees, formulation of work rules, or any other "term, condition, or privilege" of employment.

In essence, any form of discrimination by a manager is illegal and unethical.

Civil Rights Act of 1991

In an interesting twist to U.S. labor laws, the court has ruled that Title VII extends beyond the territorial boundaries of the United States. It now applies to U.S. citizens (but not to foreign nationals) working in a foreign nation for a U.S.-owned or -controlled employer. The 1991 Act, however, contains an exception should the conduct required under Title VII cause the employer to violate the laws of the foreign nation. In that instance, the local laws shall prevail.

Sexual Discrimination

In general, most managers equate sexual discrimination to issues involving female employees and their male superiors. It must be noted, however, that discrimination on the basis of sex is strictly prohibited for either gender. This is a major issue facing managers of both genders today because the laws associated with sexual discrimination continue to change and proliferate almost on a yearly basis. For example, in 1978, Title VII was amended to include the Pregnancy Discrimination Act, which prohibits employee discrimination because of "pregnancy, childbirth, or related medical conditions." As a consequence, any manager who fails to hire a female employee, or terminates that employee because she is pregnant, is using discriminatory labor tactics.

Sexual Harassment

When it comes to dealing with someone from the opposite sex in a business setting, men and women are not yet completely comfortable. While major advances in dealing with gender issues in the workplace have been made, there remain certain biases and prejudices that still prevail. It is also a given that in today's gender diverse workplaces, it is common for coworkers to become sexually involved as consenting adults. It is equally as common, unfortunately, that unwelcome sexual advances occur among coworkers, as well as between managers and their employees. Indeed, sexual harassment has become a complex issue in the workplace.

Due to the preponderance of publicity that sexual harassment cases have generated, managers and employees remain genuinely confused about what sexual harassment is and is not. To aid managers in better understanding the nuances of sexual harassment, the Supreme Court has ruled that sexual harassment includes lewd remarks, touching, intimidation, posting pinups, and other verbal or physical conduct of a sexual nature that occurs on the job.

Refusing to hire or promote an employee because he or she refuses the sexual advances of a manager constitutes an obvious violation of Title VII. But not all situations are so clearly a violation. For example, the Supreme Court has ruled that Title VII *does not* require a victim of sexual harassment to prove that the conduct has seriously affected the employee's psychological well-being because the situation has created a hostile work environment. Rather the court has said that "a discriminatorily abusive work environment, even though it does not affect an employee's psychological well-being, can and often does detract from the employee's job performance, keep employees from advancing in their careers, or discourage employees from remaining on the job." In the court's opinion, Title VII encompasses any abusive conduct, sexual or otherwise, which could seriously affect a reasonable person's psychological well-being, whether or not the hostile workplace is actually psychologically injurious.

As a consequence of Title VII, managers continue to reel from myriad possibilities that could be considered sexual discrimination or sexual harassment. In their words, "How do I avoid it and what is my exposure as a manager?" There is also concern about the manager's own exposure should one of his subordinates sexually harass an employee. It is often questioned as to how liability for such an act can be extended to the manager even if he had no part in or knowledge of the act.

In 1997, the Supreme Court handed down several clarifying rulings regarding sexual harassment to provide managers with guidance relative to what they can and can not do, their legal obligations, and the actions they must take to protect themselves and their organizations.

In one of its rulings, the court stated that an employer is vicariously liable to a sexually harassed employee because of the hostile work environment created by the alleged harasser—a supervisor or manager with immediate or successively higher authority over that employee. The Supreme Court further ruled that companies can be held liable when a supervisor threatens an employee with repercussions resulting from the employee's failure or refusal to consent to the supervisor's sexual advances, even if the supervisor fails to follow through on the threat.

> "An employer is vicariously liable to a sexually harassed employee because of the hostile work environment created by the alleged harasser."

In addition, the court included a definition describing the requirements for an organization and its managers to use in preparing a defense against liability and damages from an alleged sexual harassment situation. The court stated that an employer must prove:

1. that it exercised reasonable care to prevent and promptly correct any sexually harassing behavior on the part of its managers and supervisors, and
2. that the employee claiming to have been sexually harassed failed to take advantage of any preventive or corrective opportunities or mechanisms provided by the employer, or to otherwise attempt to avoid harm.

What the courts will look for in such cases is:

- Did the employer have a policy specifically prohibiting sexual harassment?
- Did the employer have a process in place to quickly and confidentially handle sexual harassment complaints?
- Did the employer provide multiple channels outside of the employee's normal chain of command through which an employee could file a complaint?
- Did the employer publicize or otherwise inform all employees of its sexual harassment policies and of the processes in place to handle complaints?

In short, for the defense to be upheld, a manager must prove that he has taken an aggressive stand against sexual harassment and implemented a multi-pronged approach to deal with offenders—a zero-tolerance policy. A manager also must prove that this zero-tolerance policy has been communicated to all employees and that it is rigidly enforced at all times, and at all levels within the organization. A typical zero-tolerance policy includes statements of what the company considers sexually harassing conduct to include: physical assaults of a sexual

> "A zero-tolerance sexual harassment policy must be communicated to all employees and rigidly enforced at all times."

nature—rape, sexual battery, molestation; intentional physical conduct of a sexual nature like touching, pinching, patting, grabbing, poking, or brushing; unwanted sexual advances, propositions, sexual comments or gestures; sexually explicit jokes; comments regarding another person's sexuality; and sexually explicit or suggestive publications, posters, calendars, graffiti, or displays of any kind. Also typically included are statements covering the prohibition of preferential treatment or promises of preferential treatment in exchange for sexual favors or sexual conduct, as well as the prohibition of threats by managers and supervisors should sexual advances be rejected.

Title VII also expressly prohibits same-sex discrimination and sexual harassment of homosexuals.

Religious Discrimination

Title VII prohibits employers from intentionally discriminating on the basis of religious preference or practices. In essence, employers are required to "reasonably accommodate" an employee's religious practices, observances, and beliefs. The caveat that the court placed on this requirement reads, "if so doing does not cause an undue hardship on the employer." Many conflicts arise in the workplace when an employer's work rules come into conflict with an employee's religious observances and holidays. In most cases, a manager can make allowances for an employee's religious observances. In cases where so doing would cause significant difficulties for the organization, it is incumbent upon the employee to work with the employer to come to a compromise that is acceptable for both parties.

> "Employers are required to 'reasonably accommodate' an employee's religious practices, observances, and beliefs."

Equal Pay Act

The Equal Pay Act of 1963 protects male and female employees from discrimination in pay that is gender based. In essence, if two jobs are determined to be equal and similar in required skill sets, effort, responsibility, or working conditions, an employer can not pay disparate wages to members of the opposite sex. The court, however, has ruled that there are acceptable criteria that do justify a differential in wages between genders:

1. payment systems that are based upon seniority, merit, quality, or quantity of output such as piecework or incentive systems, or
2. factors other than gender such as shift differentials.

The Equal Pay Act covers all levels of private-sector employees, along with state and local government employees. Federal employees are not covered.

Age Discrimination in Employment Act

The Age Discrimination in Employment Act covers private-sector employees (employers with over 20 non-seasonal employees), employees of labor unions (with at least 25 members), employees of all employment agencies, state and local government employees (except those in policy-making positions), and certain federal-government-sector employees over the age of 40. It prohibits age discrimination in all employment hiring and termination decisions, decisions regarding promotions, compensation-related decisions, decisions relating to the payment of benefits, and decisions regarding terms and conditions of employment. An interesting quirk to the Age Discrimination in Employment Act is that it does not cover discrimination of employees under the age of 40.

Discrimination Against the Handicapped

Rehabilitation Act

The Rehabilitation Act of 1973 expressly prohibits employers from discriminating against handicapped persons in hiring when the person is qualified and can perform at the minimum level of acceptable performance or productivity expected from non-handicapped employees after reasonable accommodations are made for the handicap. The Act applies to all employers who receive federal contracts or federal assistance.

Americans with Disabilities Act

Enacted in 1990, the Americans with Disabilities Act (ADA) imposed obligations on all employers, providers of public transportation, telecommunications providers, and operators of public facilities to accommodate individuals with disabilities. ADA prohibits all forms of employment discrimination against qualified individuals with disabilities with regard to job application procedures, hiring and termination decisions, compensation plans and their application, training, and promotion decisions. The Act requires employers to make reasonable accommodations for disabled employees so long as those accommodations do not cause undue hardship on the employer. Expected accommodations include certain facility modifications, modified work schedules, modification of training materials, equipment, and examinations, and provision for qualified readers or interpreters where applicable. ADA applies to employers with at least 15 employees. Exemptions include United States government employees, employees of wholly owned United States corporations, and employees of certain tax-exempt private membership clubs.

"ADA requires employers to make reasonable accommodations for disabled employees."

ADA covers the following classes of disabled employees: recovering drug addicts and alcoholics; individuals who are mentally retarded; those who are speech, hearing, or visually impaired; and individuals with HIV, paraplegia, schizophrenia, muscular dystrophy, cerebral palsy, epilepsy, cancer, diabetes, and certain other afflictions. The Act expressly prohibits an employer from questioning job applicants about the existence, nature, or severity of a disability. The employer, however, may inquire about an applicant's ability to perform certain job-specific functions.

Affirmative Action

Recent Supreme Court rulings have changed the face of affirmative action as it applies to employers. In 1995, the court upheld lower court rulings in two separate cases involving reverse discrimination suits brought by white males against their employers under Title VII. In essence, the court demonstrated that the Equal Protection Clause of the U.S. Constitution and equal employment opportunity laws, in general, could be applied in cases involving white employees just as they had in cases involving minorities. The result of this action by the court will force many employers in both the government and private sectors to revisit and revise their affirmative-action programs or subject themselves to possible lawsuits from white employees who have been passed over for promotion in favor of less-qualified minority candidates.

As with all U.S. labor laws, affirmative action laws are continuously under scrutiny and change. At present there are three states that have abolished affirmative action laws (Michigan, California, and Washington). Several others will have ballot initiatives to either limit or restrict the scope of current affirmative action laws. As such, it is always wise for every manager to revisit labor law on a regular basis to ensure that any changes at the state or federal levels are clearly understood and complied with.

> "Revisit labor law on a regular basis to ensure that any changes are clearly understood and complied with."

Fair Labor Standards Act

Enacted by Congress, the Fair Labor Standards Act (FLSA) applies to private-sector employers and their employees engaged in the production of goods for interstate commerce. The FLSA strictly prohibits employers from utilizing oppressive child-labor practices and makes it illegal to ship goods produced by employers who violate the Act. Child-labor regulations restrict the employment of children in the workplace to the following:

- children under the age of 14 can not work in any employment with the exception of the delivery of newspapers,
- children between the ages of 14 and 15 may work limited hours in non-hazardous work environments, which are defined by the Department of Labor (restaurants, gasoline stations, grocery stores, etc.),
- children between the ages of 16 and 17 may work unlimited hours in non-hazardous jobs,
- individuals over the age of 18 are unrestricted.

The FLSA requires employers to pay non-exempt employees not classified as managerial, professional, or administrative, at least the prevailing minimum wage for regular work hours (up to 40 hours weekly) and overtime pay at a rate of 1.5 times regular pay thereafter. Each week is considered a separate event under the Act. The exceptions to this rule include students and apprentices, or cases in which the employer provides employees with food and lodging.

Family and Medical Leave Act

Passed by Congress, the Family and Medical Leave Act of 1993 provides workers with unpaid time off from their jobs for medical emergencies, such as:

- serious health conditions that prohibit the employee from performing his or her normal duties on the job,
- caring for a child, spouse, or parent with a serious illness or health problem,
- the birth and subsequent care of a child, or
- the placement of a child for adoption or foster care.

The legislation covers private-sector employers with at least 50 employees, and all federal, state, and local government employees who have been employed by their employer for at least one year and who have performed their job duties in excess of 1,250 hours during the previous 12-month period. Employers are required to provide employees with up to 12 weeks of unpaid leave during any 12-month period for a covered emergency. The employer is required to restore the employee

Complying with Employment and Labor Laws

upon return to either the same or an equivalent position with equivalent employment benefits and pay. Accrual of seniority for the employee during the unpaid absence, however, is not required. There is an exception to the restoration requirement when a returning employee's pay is among the highest 10% of all employees within the organization. In such a case, the employer may legally deny restoration to a salaried employee to prevent "substantial and grievous economic injury" to the employer.

National Labor Relations Act

The National Labor Relations Act (NLRA, also known as the Wagner Act) upholds employees' right to form, join, and assist labor organizations in bargaining collectively with an employer. In brief, the NLRA makes it incumbent upon an employer to bargain in good faith with union organizations that represent the employees as a fundamental right under the law. The Taft-Hartley Act later expanded the activities that labor unions could legally become involved in. It provided employers with rights to engage in free speech in opposition to unionization, and established the right of the President of the United States to seek injunctive relief for up to 80 days against any strike that would create a national emergency.

> "It is illegal for an employer to sponsor or attempt to control a union."

It is of particular importance for a manager to realize that, under the law, it is illegal for an employer to sponsor or attempt to control a union. It is also illegal for an employer to interfere with, attempt to coerce, or restrain employees from forming or joining a labor union. Statements or threats of business closure should employees unionize are, therefore, illegal because they are deemed an unfair labor practice.

Under the NLRA, collective bargaining must include discussions and negotiations regarding employee wages, work hours, conditions of employment, fringe benefits, health benefits, retirement plans and benefits, work assignments, and safety rules.

Other topics such as supervision, business locations, or business restructures are permissible, but not mandatory for collective bargaining. Negotiations regarding discrimination in any form are strictly prohibited under the NLRA.

Plant Closing Act

There are times when an employer makes a decision to discontinue doing business within a geographic area, or perhaps altogether. In many cases in the past, management has elected to keep their intentions a secret from employees for numerous reasons, some of which were ethical, some of which were not. These actions often brought severe reactions from employees that frequently led to property damage and occasionally personal injury, not to mention immediate and significant hardships on the employees affected. In 1988, Congress enacted the Worker Adjustment and Retraining Notification Act (commonly called the Plant Closing Act) to cover employers with 100 or more employees. The Act places a requirement upon employers to inform employees of impending business closures or related layoffs at least 60 days prior to initiating such actions, whether or not the employees are unionized. It governs temporary and permanent business closures that result in a loss of employment for at least 50 employees during any 30-day period, or mass layoffs involving over 33% of a site's employees within a 30-day period.

There is, however, an exception provided employers under the Act. If an employer, in good faith, reasonably believed it would be granted the needed capital to continue the business, it is exempted from the requirement. It is the responsibility of the employer, however, to prove that it was actively seeking such funding prior to the business closure. An employer is also exempted from the requirement to give notice if the need to discontinue business operations was not reasonably foreseeable in sufficient time to give notice to its employees.

Consolidation Omnibus Budget Reconciliation Act (COBRA)

COBRA was enacted in 1985 to provide employees of private-sector employers, and their beneficiaries, with the right to

Complying with Employment and Labor Laws

continue group health insurance benefits after the dismissal or death of the employee, or due to the loss of benefits resulting from certain qualifying events defined by law. It is the responsibility of the employer to notify the employee and his or her beneficiaries of their rights under the law. Under the provisions of COBRA, the employee is solely responsible to pay the required group health insurance premiums.

Immigration Reform and Control Act

With the increasing demand in the U.S. for professional, skilled, and semi-skilled employees, many employers have looked to foreign nations for workers. To restrict companies from recruiting illegal immigrants to fill those openings in the labor market, the Immigration Reform and Control Act was passed in 1986. In short, the Act makes it illegal for employers to hire illegal immigrants. It requires employers to provide evidence that all employees are either U.S. citizens or are otherwise qualified to work in the United States under a valid work visa.

Occupational Health and Safety Act

The Occupational Safety and Health Act was written into law by Congress in 1970. The intent of OSHA is to promote safe work environments for employees of private-sector companies. It should be noted that OSHA does not apply to federal, state, and local government employees, or to employees of companies regulated by other federal safety legislation. In addition to the requirement to maintain safe working conditions for employees, employers are required to maintain records of injuries to employees and promptly report them to the Occupational Safety and Health Administration. Employers are also required to post notices in the workplace to advise employees of their rights under the law.

The law permits OSHA personnel to inspect the premises of employers for health and safety hazards and other associated violations of the law. If violations are found, OSHA issues citations requiring the company to take immediate corrective action.

Failure to correct the violations in a timely manner subjects the company to civil and criminal penalties. Thus, managers must take OSHA violations seriously.

STATE LABOR LAWS
Right-to-Work Laws

It should be noted that nothing in the Taft-Hartley Act specifically requires employees to join unions or to pay union dues in states or U.S. territories in which it is prohibited by either state or territorial laws. So many states and U.S. territories have enacted "right-to-work laws" by either constitutional amendment or state statute. These outlaw the requirement for an employee to join a union, or to pay union dues to obtain or retain employment, even within companies where union representation exists. To date, 21 states have enacted right-to-work laws. They include: Alabama, Arizona, Arkansas, Florida, Georgia, Idaho, Iowa, Kansas, Louisiana, Mississippi, Nebraska, Nevada, North Carolina, North Dakota, South Carolina, South Dakota, Tennessee, Texas, Utah, Virginia, and Wyoming.

Workers' Compensation

Most states require employers represented within the state to provide either government-sponsored or private workers' compensation insurance for their employees. The cost of the insurance premiums is borne exclusively by the employer. The intent of the insurance is to provide compensation to employees who suffer work-related injuries. To be eligible for workers' compensation benefits, an employee must prove that he or she incurred the injury during the course of employment.

Workers' compensation is an "exclusive remedy" under the law. In other words, employees injured on the job and receiving workers' compensation benefits are generally not permitted to sue their employer for damages. A somewhat obvious exception to this law exists, however. If an employee is intentionally injured by his employer, even though that employee is receiving workers' compensation benefits, the employee is permitted to sue the employer for damages.

SUMMARY

This chapter focused on several of the legal aspects of management that every new manager must be familiar with. Ignorance of the law is neither a protection nor a defensible position in cases involving litigation. Management carries with it a significant degree of responsibility and accountability for compliance with organizational policies and procedures, as well as compliance with federal, state, and local laws. When conflicts exist between internal policies and established law, the law always prevails. No manager should ever place themselves or their employees in a position that is contrary to the law, whether directed to do so, or by intention. It is easier and more comfortable to be looking for new employment than it is to be looking at a new cellmate.

While there are certainly numerous other laws that managers must be familiar with, which are unique to their specific industries, the ones included in this chapter are those that apply to all industries and all employers. It is recommended that new managers spend some time with corporate counsel and employee relations professionals to learn more about specific issues that relate to their duties as managers. In addition, managers must realize that the laws are amended, changed, and expanded frequently. It is a good managerial practice to revisit them periodically.

In Chapter Five, several real business scenarios will be used as examples of the often difficult situations that a new manager finds himself faced with, along with suggested approaches to address each. In most cases, there are *few* "textbook" answers to business situations involving employees. Each situation must be evaluated on its own merits along with the business constraints and environment surrounding the situation. As stated previously, in all cases common sense and common decency are strong assets for any manager.

5
Management Skill-building Scenarios and Case Study Examples

OBJECTIVES

This chapter will explore several actual case studies taken from a broad spectrum of industry. The intent is to provide new and experienced managers with insight into the complexity of these situations and demonstrate the techniques used by seasoned managers to address them. As stated before, every employee situation must be evaluated on its own merits considering the business environment and constraints of the situation. The case studies included herein provide a framework for *possible* solutions. There is no "one size fits all" solution. Dynamic business environments, business constraints, and business processes will all dictate a comprehensive assessment of each specific situation with the corresponding managerial actions dictated by those findings.

"Assess, evaluate, plan, and then act."

The fundamental rule of management is to assess, evaluate, plan, and then act. Taking action before understanding the entire situation and the drivers behind it is ill advised and will often lead to trouble for even the most experienced manager.

SCENARIO 1

A technical professional with tremendous capability and talent is hired for a key position within a large electronics manufacturing company. Expectations are high that the new employee will make an immediate and significant contribution to

Management Skill-building Scenarios and Case Study Examples

the organization in his new role. Within a short time, however, it becomes apparent to his manager that the new employee is not conforming to even modest performance expectations. What is the problem? In a case like this, there are a number of possibilities for his manager to consider.

- *Problem*: The employee may not clearly understand what is expected of him.

  Response: To clarify the employee's performance expectations, the manager discusses the job requirements in detail with the employee, providing him with a comprehensive job description, which details expectations, metrics, data sources, process definitions, etc. Complex tasks and assignments are thoroughly explained to the employee by the manager and affirmation is sought to ensure understanding. The manager makes himself available to mentor the new employee during the first several days and weeks on the job. Seasoned managers realize that even the most talented professionals struggle for a period of time in a new position until a level of comfort is reached.

- *Problem*: It is possible that the employee has been placed in the wrong job.

  Response: Placing an employee in the wrong job is an all too common occurrence. Managers often make the mistake of placing an employee in a role or position that the manager thinks is best for the employee without consulting with the employee first. The employee tries to make the best of the situation, but quickly becomes disenchanted. When the situation is allowed to continue unresolved, the employee's performance declines as he becomes increasingly frustrated. In the end, the employee seeks other alternatives either within the firm or with another organization. This is especially true with Generation Y and young Generation X employees who get bored quickly when unchallenged and so are quick to jump ship.

Management Skill-building Scenarios and Case Study Examples

Here is a classic example of putting the wrong employee in the wrong role. When an employee is deemed by his manager to be an excellent contributor in his selected field of endeavor, for example, project management, his manager often assumes that he is equally as capable of leading a project in that field. Unfortunately, the skill sets required for a project management role are distinctly different than those of an individual technical contributor. The manager is later disappointed when the previously outstanding performer begins to struggle and fail, never realizing that he has inadvertently set the employee up for failure. The result is an unfortunate lose-lose situation for both.

- *Problem*: It is possible that the employee may not be challenged in the position. Managers often intentionally start new employees off slowly—letting them grow into the new job. But in today's fast-paced business environments, this is often a mistake. Many new, highly motivated employees want to get immediately into the fray to show off their talents to their manager in hopes of immediate recognition and possible promotion. When held back, they will often rebel or simply tune out while waiting for their chance to shine.

  Response: Good managers know to give these high-potential employees responsibility immediately. They provide them with guidance and clear direction, and then get out of their way!

Case Study Example

A large consulting firm found it was encountering an unusually high volume of defection among young engineers during their first year of employment. The company was paying competitive salaries and providing the young engineers with excellent upward mobility, an excellent working environment, and extensive training in systems engineering. The problem was that these were mechanical engineers, electrical engineers,

Management Skill-building Scenarios and Case Study Examples

and industrial engineers, not systems engineers. These young engineers had no interest in becoming programmers or system designers. Rather, they wanted to pursue the fields of engineering they had studied in school. After a period in which the company frequently committed to move them into their field of choice and subsequently failed to do so, these talented employees became bored and began to defect. These good employees with tremendous potential never seemed to work out. They were simply placed in the wrong job.

SCENARIO 2

An employee with an excellent track record of consistently outstanding performance suddenly starts going downhill. What is the problem?

- *Problem*: One of the first things managers look for is a dependency. Drug or alcohol addiction is a common cause of this type of rapid decline in performance. Perhaps the employee has gotten involved in something beyond her control.

    Response: If her performance is going downhill fast, quick action by her manager may be the only salvation available. Before taking action, however, seasoned managers know to consult with the Employee Support Program representative or corporate legal counsel to get advice on the legalities of management's involvement and the policies of the company on such matters. After framing a course of action with them, the manager calls the employee in for a candid conversation, which goes something like this, "Julie, I've always had the highest respect for your work. You've always been a great performer. I've always been able to count on you. Lately, however, you seem to be falling down on the job. Is there something I can help you with? I'm concerned that you may have a problem and I'd like to talk to you about it so we can come to a resolution for you and the company. Or, if you feel more comfortable, we have an Employee Support Program available to you that you can pursue anonymously. Either way, as your manager, I want to see that you get the help you need to work through this problem."

There is typically no immediate response from the employee in these situations. While waiting, the manager remains quiet, patient, and sincere. There is often an extended period of silence before the employee begins to open up. The silence is allowed to run its course until the employee breaks it. Her manager then listens intently, remaining conscious of the employee's discomfort in discussing the matter. The manager is prepared to provide the guidance and support the employee needs. Because Julie is an excellent employee who has shown consistent dedication to the company, she deserves all the help and support her manager can offer. It may take two or more conversations before the employee opens up fully. This is common. Experienced managers know to remain patient, but persistent. The situation must be resolved as quickly as possible for the benefit of the employee, her coworkers, and the company. It simply cannot be ignored.

- *Problem*: Still another possibility a manager considers in this instance is a personal problem that is plaguing the employee, such as a sick child or parent or an impending divorce.

  Response: Whatever the problem is, often just talking to the employee about it will help her get it out in the open. Once revealed, it can be addressed. It is the manager's responsibility to help his employee through these tough situations. Everyone faces difficulties at one point or another in their lives. By providing his employee with sympathetic but persistent guidance, a manager helps his employee through the coping and healing process. Ultimately, the employee must take charge of the situation to reverse the performance decline; but with his manager's assistance, that process is accelerated for the benefit of all parties.

Management Skill-building Scenarios and Case Study Examples

SCENARIO 3

The performance of a group of employees begins to decline rapidly. What is the problem?

- *Problem*: Assuming there is no across-the-board corporate action like a downsizing or sale impacting the entire workforce, the root of the problem in this scenario is often easy to identify but humbling to address. The fact that it is a group of employees typically indicates that the manager has done something to compromise her position or credibility. In some way, she has let her employees down. She may have made a commitment and then failed to follow through with the appropriate action. Or, her actions may have differed from her words, resulting in a loss of employee trust or confidence. Or, she may have failed to take action to address an issue that is plaguing her employees. Whatever the case, the manager is forced to face the fact that a corrective action on her part is warranted and necessary.

Response: In such a case, the recommended technique for resolving the issue and restoring employee confidence is to deal with the issue in a straightforward manner. The manager calls her employees together for a group discussion in a conference room. Prior to the meeting, she pulls the table out and arranges the chairs in a horseshoe configuration. One chair is placed in the middle of the horseshoe. Taking the chair in the center of the horseshoe, the manager asks her employees to join her for an "open forum" discussion on her management style. She begins by saying, "There is obviously something bothering you as a group. I believe it has something to do with my management style or something I have failed to do in support of you. Please tell me what is bothering you." The initial response is often total silence. Faced with the reluctance of her employees to directly confront their superior, she is forced to direct the question to one or more of the informal leaders within the group, "Tom, would you start it off?"

Management Skill-building Scenarios and Case Study Examples

In a situation like this one, emotions and tensions are highly charged. As a result, a definite protocol is required on the manager's part.

When employees begin opening up, the last thing a manager does is to become defensive and say something like, "Look Tom . . . listen, you don't understand. This is the reason why I had to do it that way." By defending or attempting to justify her actions at that time, the manager effectively shuts off all further communication. Smart managers listen instead of talking. When the employees see she is sincere in her efforts to address the issues, other employees will start to open up. The manager's role then is to quietly take notes, listen intently to what the employees have to say, and thank them for their candid input.

At the end of the session, the manager closes the meeting by describing the next step in the process, along with what the employees can expect from her in the near term. "Okay. I've taken extensive notes and I truly appreciate your candor. What I will do now is look at your comments and recommendations critically and make note of the things I need to address. From that, I will put together a corrective action plan and get back to you next week on what I intend to do to address the issues you have identified. Thank you very much." This type of candid, open discussion and follow-through will help the manager reopen communication channels with her employees and begin the process of rebuilding their trust and respect. It certainly is not an easy journey, but is an effective one.

- *Problem*: The organization has just announced a unilateral action, such as an across-the-board salary or overhead reduction.

Response: Actions like these are typically beyond a manager's control and outside the scope of his responsibilities. However, in such cases, it is best to be up front with employees. "Gang, we're all faced with the same situation. Just like you, I'm taking a 20% cut. I don't particularly like it either. But for the organization to survive, these are the hard decisions that management has had to make. Help me work through them so we can all get our 20% back."

Whatever the situation, savvy managers are as open as possible with employees given the confidentiality of the issue or situation. Not all problems can be immediately resolved, but the fact that a manager is willing to talk about them candidly with his employees will go a long way in bringing employees back into the fold.

SCENARIO 4

A series of repetitive errors begins to occur within the department. The errors are generated by either a single employee or several employees. What is the problem?

Problem: In general, situations like this are the result of process capability or control deficiencies and not human error. More likely than not, one or more of the organization's operational processes are out of control or are steadily moving in that direction. Over time it is not unusual for changes in business conditions, constraints, or products to stress old processes until they begin to break down. The breakdown occurs slowly at first, manifesting itself as employee errors or carelessness. As time progresses, the decline in process control and capability begins to accelerate. Often, a manager fails to recognize the issue as being process driven until significant damage is done and employee confidence is lost.

> "A good manager is not concerned with who produced the error, but rather why it occurred and how it can be prevented from recurring."

Response: A good manager is not concerned with who produced the error, but rather why the error occurred and what can be done about it to prevent its recurrence. The best approach is to discuss the error with the employees involved. The manager focuses the discussion on the problem as a "process" issue, opening the door to collaboration as he and his employees work to resolve it. The discussion is carefully crafted to reinforce the fact that the manager does not consider the problem to be a personnel issue. As a result, employees are more comfortable in bringing issues to their manager in the future because there is no fear of reprisal.

SCENARIO 5

One or more employees within the department or work group are becoming openly antagonistic, driving down morale among the other employees. What is the problem?

Problem: This behavior is a symptom of a deeply seated problem either within the workforce or with an individual.

Response: The manager takes immediate action to identify the root cause of the problem and initiate corrective action. Situations like this are addressed directly and quickly. No manager lets this situation linger in hopes that it will fade away.

To begin, the manager pulls the employees demonstrating the undesirable behavior aside to determine why they are so angry. The manager looks for the reasons behind that anger and works with the employees to curb it while a lasting solution is worked out. Prudent managers recognize that if the employees are allowed to demonstrate their antagonism openly and freely among other employees, problems will begin to grow exponentially. The manager makes it a point to let the offending employees know that they can come into his office, close the door, and blow off steam. He assures them that he will listen to their complaints, but that those complaints are to remain within his office and not spread throughout the workplace. It is also made clear to the offending employees that unless their antagonism is restrained, disciplinary actions up to and including termination for insubordination will occur in a quick and decisive manner. Situations like this require direct but fair leadership.

SCENARIO 6

Employees within the department or work group do not demonstrate any initiative. They respond to direct assignments from their manager, but nothing more. They simply do what is asked of them and demonstrate no willingness to think on their own, resolve operational or tactical problems, or implement changes of any type. What is the problem?

Problem: In this situation, the message being sent to the manager from her employees is that she has either intentionally or inadvertently "shot the messenger." An employee has come to the manager with a problem, an opportunity, or an issue of either a personal or business nature. Instead of addressing the issue or problem in a non-threatening manner, the manager has lowered her sights on the employee, sending the employee out of the office with his tail between his legs. The word quickly spread and employees closed the communication channels between themselves and the manager in fear of similar treatment.

Response: This is a particularly tough situation for a manager. It will be difficult to regain the trust of employees, especially the employee who has been burned. To rebuild trust will require a long-term commitment on the part of the manager. She will be required to "walk the talk" in word and in action, demonstrating daily that all employees are respected for their value as key assets of the company.

> "Trust is a valuable commodity; it takes a long time to earn, but only an instant to lose."

Trust is a valuable commodity; it takes a long time to earn, but only an instant to lose.

Management Skill-building Scenarios and Case Study Examples

SCENARIO 7

Just the opposite of Scenario 6, a manager is faced with an employee who is constantly taking on more responsibility or authority than is granted him under his present title and job description. The employee's enthusiasm and careless disregard for the formal chain of command has begun to ruffle the feathers of other employees within the department, as well as other managers from outside the department. How does a manager address this situation?

Problem: The issues surrounding this situation are multifaceted. In one respect, a manager certainly does not want to kill the enthusiasm being demonstrated by the employee. Employees such as this one have the potential to handle greater workloads and responsibilities; they are upwardly mobile and have the tenacity to get a multitude of things done for the organization. On the other hand, the employee's enthusiasm must be controlled and focused so it does not get the employee or his manager into trouble in other parts of the organization, cause a breach of trust between departments, or break down communication and cooperation between operating units.

Response: The manager talks with the employee about the situation candidly to explain the impact he is having on the organization, both good and bad. In the discussion, the manager emphasizes the requirement for the employee to stay within the bounds of his job assignment, department, or project. The manager clearly outlines the employee's level of empowerment and operational scope, offering advice and encouragement. The importance of mutual cooperation between operating units within the company is also reinforced. The employee is assured that his commitment and dedication to the organization are appreciated, as are his energy and enthusiasm. The manager, however, expresses his concern that unless properly controlled, those same attributes will be misinterpreted and, if so, will likely be detrimental to the employee's career.

Experienced managers recognize that these employees are rare and uniquely valuable to an organization. However, they can not be left unchecked. They must be made to understand that it is equally as important "how" a task is accomplished as it is to get good results. To properly focus the employee and reward his dedication and energy, the manager gives the employee additional assignments and/or responsibilities. The manager varies the employee's assignments to keep his interest and constantly expands the employee's operational breadth. Over time, the manager assigns the employee larger or more difficult projects, as well as tasks that will fulfill his personal need for growth. Other options include outside training, mentoring, or internal management development assignments for the employee. Experience tells a manager that the solution is to feed these employees with an endless stream of new opportunities that are consistent with the needs and culture of the organization. This approach keeps the employee and his manager out of trouble.

SCENARIO 8

A subtle pattern of absenteeism and tardiness becomes apparent with a long-term employee. He has not had these problems in the past and still does good work when on the job. What is the problem?

Problem: Absenteeism and tardiness are often telltale signs of a dependency problem, which must be addressed immediately (see Scenario 2). A second area for management to consider is the emergence of a serious personal problem. Employee morale also may be an issue in such a situation. Still another possibility is that the employee is simply averse to playing by the same rules as others within the department. This can happen for any number of reasons. Nevertheless, it can not be

> "Absenteeism and tardiness are often telltale signs of a dependency problem."

Management Skill-building Scenarios and Case Study Examples

allowed to go unchecked or it will affect other employees who see the rules being broken or bent without repercussion. If one employee is allowed to get away with the infraction, then others will feel free to join in. Once that begins, chaos follows.

Response: The first step is for the manager to talk directly with the employee in an attempt to get to the root cause of the problem. Thereafter, the manager works with the employee to improve his performance. The manager:

1. meets one-on-one with the employee,
2. outlines the policies and procedures of the organization, as well her own expectations for all employees within the department or work group,
3. listens to the reasons why the employee is not complying with policies,
4. reinforces the requirement for consistency in compliance with the organization's norms,
5. advises the employee of the disciplinary actions that will ensue should the employee fail to comply, and
6. follows through with the required actions to ensure compliance.

One of the things most managers learn through experience is that there are two kinds of employees. There are morning people and there are night people. For example, some employees will drag in on time and stumble around until 9:00 or 10:00 in the morning. They are on the job physically but not as sharp mentally as they will be later in the day. Once they awaken, they fly through the rest of the day full of energy. The later hours are their most productive hours; they often work well into the evening hours on a regular basis.

Conversely, there are those employees who hit the ground running at 5:00 a.m. and are in the office by 6:00 a.m., full

Management Skill-building Scenarios and Case Study Examples

of energy and vitality. Their most productive hours occur between 6:00 a.m. and 2:30 p.m. By late in the afternoon, however, these employees begin to burn out and rarely work much beyond quitting time.

So what does being a "morning" person, versus a "night" person, have to do with the issue of tardiness or absenteeism? Some employees find it difficult to get rolling by the appointed hour to start the workday on time. Others do not have that problem. Some employees will habitually work late hours while others do not. A manager must realize these human patterns and the reasons behind them before making a judgment about the dedication or productivity of his personnel. It is for this reason that companies began instituting "flex-time." It allows employees to vary their schedule to maximize their most productive time of the day, thus improving their personal productivity on the job. It is therefore of value, where permitted by company policy, to allow employees to vary their individual schedules around certain core times so their productivity can be maximized. There are circumstances within some companies, and even some departments, however, in which flex-time is not an acceptable solution. In those cases, managers are required to insist that all employees be on the job promptly at the starting time, without exception. Employees who fail to comply are addressed, disciplined, and in severe cases, terminated.

> *"Flex-time allows employees to vary their schedule to maximize their most productive time of day."*

Case Study Example

As a senior buyer within the purchasing department of a large pharmaceutical company, Pam was one of those dedicated, hard-working employees who could always be counted on to get the job done right. She was consistent, reliable, and predictable—everything a manager could ask for in an employee. One day her manager noticed that she came into work late. Dismissing it as an isolated event, no action was taken by the manager. Shortly thereafter, a pattern of tardiness began. Company policy dictated a starting time of 8:00 a.m. Pam had started rolling in consistently at around 8:15 a.m. to 8:30 a.m. At the time, flextime had not been adopted by the company.

Recognizing that Pam's tardiness was becoming a problem, her manager approached her on the issue. Pam apologized and indicated that she would make the effort to be on time. For the next two weeks, Pam's timeliness did improve. Her attitude was positive and her work was up to its usual level. Then, the pattern of tardiness began to reappear. The manager again approached Pam on the issue, this time with a higher sense of urgency in getting to the bottom of the matter. When the manager asked Pam about the underlying problem, she became very defensive. She said, "No, there's not a problem. And by the way, you don't seem to have much of a problem when I'm here at 5:30 p.m. or 6:00 p.m. do you? But you sure have a problem when I come in 15–30 minutes late in the morning. I don't understand your concern. You're getting your eight hours, plus some."

The manager indicated to Pam that while he appreciated the extra hours she consistently put in, and the quality of her work, neither was the issue at hand. Rather, the issue was that her starting time, like that of her coworkers, was 8:00 a.m. The manager further indicated that because she was a member of a service organization, it was important for her to be available during the same working hours her customers worked. She cooled down and talked candidly with her manager for several minutes.

Pam explained that she was a single mother and had a young son in daycare. She had found out that the daycare center she had been using for years planned to go out of business in the near future. She was faced with finding a new one. Pam had been trying a number of different daycare centers to ensure she was comfortable with her son's safety and care. After the first incident, she had asked her parents to fly in from out of town to spend two or three weeks with her to help her through the transition period. Once they returned home, the problem resurfaced. She had subsequently found a daycare center she was comfortable with, but it didn't open until 8:00 a.m. So, depending on traffic, Pam would get into the office between 8:15 a.m. and 8:30 a.m.

The manager empathized with Pam since he too had been a single parent with similar responsibilities. So the manager asked her, "Are you comfortable with this daycare center?"

"Yes, I am," she replied.

He then asked her if she felt it was a long-term solution that she and her son could live with. Pam indicated that she was happy with the daycare, but was faced with the fact that she could not make it to work daily by 8:00 a.m. After discussing other alternatives, the manager decided to alter Pam's working hours slightly to enable her to get to work on time. Instead of 8:00 a.m. to 4:30 p.m., Pam would work from 8:30 a.m. to 5:00 p.m.

The manager then called everyone in the department together to explain the situation and the solution agreed upon. He took the opportunity to ask if there were others who had similar problems that needed to be addressed. Though no one expressed the need to talk with him, he was surprised that the other employees rallied around the need to get Pam's problem resolved in a way that worked for her, as well as the company. Later, one of the other buyers offered to come into work at 7:30 a.m. to cover for Pam if she would stay over later in the day to cover for him. They adjusted the workload between them and the problem was resolved without compromising the needs of either the company or its employees.

What Made it Work?

The manager was effective in resolving Pam's dilemma because he:

- found the root cause of her problem through open, candid communication,
- worked out a mutually acceptable solution with Pam, and

- offered the same opportunity to the other employees within the department.

Many managers do not take the initiative to resolve straightforward personnel problems, such as altering working hours, because they feel they do not have flexibility as a manager. The reality is, however, that most managers do have this flexibility. In fact, one of the most frustrating things plaguing corporate senior management and Human Resource managers alike is that many middle- and lower-level managers do not take the initiative in addressing these issues within their own departments. Instead, they prefer to ignore them or move them up the chain of command for senior managers to handle. If in question, a manager can (and should) discuss the problem with Human Relations or the next level of management before moving forward. However, to be successful when doing so, he or she should recommend a solution too. There should not be the expectation that the higher manager solve the problem.

> "Managers sometimes do not take the initiative to resolve straightforward personnel problems because they feel they do not have the flexibility to do so. In reality, they usually do."

SCENARIO 9

Departmental employees have become individually (politically) motivated on the job instead of being focused on teamwork and organizational success. What is the problem?

> *Problem*: The underlying problem in this situation is typically the performance metrics the department manager has implemented for his employees. Unknowingly, managers often create a win/lose scenario within their organization by implementing individual or team performance metrics that are in direct conflict with those of other employees or teams within the same department. Wanting to be successful, employees work at odds against

one another, becoming almost cut-throat in their actions when someone stands between them and success.

Response: When politics begin to surface, experienced managers look behind the scenes for conflicts in individual performance measures. Those conflicts may not always be readily visible, but they are usually there. Once identified, it is incumbent upon the manager to make the necessary changes to find a common ground between the metrics so every employee can succeed. In successful departments, managers have focused the employee metrics on organizational success. That is, organizational and employee performance metrics are designed to force everyone to work cooperatively to accomplish the organization's goals and objectives. No employee can achieve success in meeting her individual performance goals unless her counterparts are equally successful. In other words, everyone wins or everyone loses. Every employee is thus focused on accomplishing a common set of goals and objectives, utilizing a common approach. When every employee is pulling in the same direction, there is no need or time for political action.

> "Organizational and employee performance metrics should be designed to force everyone to work cooperatively to accomplish goals."

Case Study Example

The materials manager of a large Midwestern capital equipment manufacturer is responsible for several departments serving the operations group. Two of those departments, Purchasing and Production/Inventory Control require significant performance and productivity improvements to meet the division's operating goals. To assist department personnel in meeting the goals, the materials manager establishes a set of industry-standard performance metrics for each department to govern the way the employees within each department operate. Purchasing, for example, is assigned the performance metric called purchase price variance (PPV). This metric governs how much the company is to spend for materials in support of ongoing operations, whether it be for conversion into products or for the company's own consumption—office supplies, production materials, maintenance materials, outside services, etc. Typically, Purchasing and Accounting get together at the end of each year to establish a cost baseline for the following year's material and services pricing based upon industry forecasts, commodity trends, corporate sales estimates, and a host of other factors. From that data, an annual pricing cap is established, which defines whether pricing will increase or decrease in the upcoming year. In this case, Purchasing and Accounting personnel determine that prices will increase a maximum of 6% in the following year; thus the purchase price variance is set at 6%. As long as material pricing remains under that threshold, Purchasing's performance metrics will remain favorable.

Next, the materials manager sets performance metrics for employees in the Production and Inventory Control department. The performance metric he selects is "inventory turns," which is a measure of capital employed. Success with this metric is the result of maintaining the lowest amount of inventory possible in order to meet the company's production and consumption needs on a daily basis. The intent is to keep the organization's capital free for other uses rather than tie it up in inventory where it remains inaccessible until the inventory is converted into finished products and sold. Following the just-in-time (JIT) theory, most companies target inventory turns to be in the neighborhood of 24–48 annually, or no more than one to two weeks of inventory on the shelves at any one time during the year.

On the surface, the materials manager institutes two common performance metrics that he assumes are compatible, allowing both departments to be successful. Unfortunately, that assumption is incorrect. Shortly after the beginning of the fiscal year, Purchasing begins receiving calls from several key commodity suppliers who say they underestimated the impact of labor and material costs for their products. Other commodity suppliers soon follow suit. Purchasing employees quickly recognize that their performance metrics are in jeopardy. Overall, their new calculations indicate that material pricing will likely increase in excess of 10%, not the 6% that was planned.

In an effort to meet their performance metric targets, Purchasing employees begin to negotiate with key suppliers for reductions in pricing. To hit the desired target pricing, they negotiate a different commodity price breakpoint. In other words, they agree to buy larger quantities of materials in a smaller number of lots. The end result is that material pricing declines to the desired level. However, inventory turns react adversely by dropping below the desired levels because of the receipt of more inventory than was planned for within a given period. Inventory carrying costs increase, capital availability is reduced, and product design flexibility is severely compromised. In short, the accomplishment of one performance metric causes a major failure in four other performance metrics, creating a win-lose situation. It is no wonder that employees from different departments are often at war with one another.

SCENARIO 10

In another firm, a programmer-analyst consistently comes to work each day with a well-developed plan to guide her in completing her work assignments on schedule. The employee is effective in her assigned tasks and in management of her time on the job. As a result, she completes her work assignments routinely in eight hours while producing high-quality work. The manager also has a second programmer-analyst working for him who typically requires overtime to complete the same quality and volume of work as the first employee. The second employee constantly complains to her manager that she is required to work significantly longer hours than her counterpart in the department and wants the work hours made equal so that she, too, can go home after eight hours on the job. How will the department manager resolve this issue?

Problem: The first action is to assess the assignments each employee has been given. Are the assignments actually comparable? Each assignment varies somewhat in complexity, difficulty, and scope. The department manager analyzes the workload of each employee to see if the second employee has been consistently given more challenging assignments than her counterpart.

Response: If there is an imbalance, the manager rebalances the workload of both employees, thereafter paying close attention to the overall load on each when handing out assignments. The manager alternates the difficult assignments so each employee receives an equal balance of difficult and easier assignments over time.

If, on the other hand, the assessment reveals that one employee is simply more productive than the other and/or a better time manager, other options are explored by the manager. For example, the employee who is less productive can attend outside training on time management, project management, organization control, etc. The intent is to provide the second employee with new or enhanced skill sets that will allow her to work at a more competitive, yet comfortable level. Another option is to ask the more productive employee to teach the second employee the tools and techniques she has learned that make her an effective time manager. Employee-to-employee mentoring builds personal relationships and trust among employees. It also improves communication and collaboration, opening the door to learning even more new skill sets from peers.

> "Employee-to-employee mentoring builds personal relationships and trust."

SCENARIO 11

Skill levels for technical professionals vary, as do their communication and project management skills. In many cases, a

Management Skill-building Scenarios and Case Study Examples

manager finds that she has a few employees within the department who consistently carry a heavier workload. These are the individuals capable of doing a wider variety of tasks—the people she can count on to get their assignments completed with little, if any, direction. Work assignments within the department are typically handed out by the manager based upon her comfort level with each of her employees, as well the risks she perceives in assigning specific tasks to certain individuals. It is thus common for one or more employees to be inadvertently overloaded while others are more lightly loaded. How and why does this happen?

> *Problem*: In many cases, there is an overload on the more competent employees because the manager knows from experience that they are simply more capable than others. They are the employees a manager trusts in times of crisis—the "go to" people. When a manager begins to unconsciously overload her "go to" people, workload discussions between employees begin. Discrepancies in workload are quickly identified and those same "go to" people begin pushing back. "Hey, wait a minute. Boss, how come I'm working so much longer? How come I'm carrying more of a load than anyone else? How can you justify doing this to me?" These are all fair questions.
>
> *Response*: When a manager has found that she has indeed overloaded her more competent employees, she addresses the issue openly. After honestly assessing the situation and validating her facts, the manager meets with the employee or employees in question. By saying to an employee, "You're right, Jeff, I must confess that I do place more of a burden upon you because, quite honestly, I can trust you to carry a heavier load. You have become one of my key 'go to' persons. I'm sorry if I've overburdened you, but now that you've brought it to my attention, I'll certainly rectify the situation." This type of candor has multiple benefits.

— It recognizes the employee for his accomplishments. There is a lot of pride that comes with this type of recognition from the boss.

— It reinforces communication between the manager and her employee. By admitting that she made a mistake, the manager seems more human and approachable to her employees.

— It builds trust.

But to rectify the situation, something must be done to either redistribute the workload, or reward the "go to" employees for the additional work they produce. Several options are available for a manager in this situation.

— Reward those individuals with higher raises.

— Promote them into lead or supervisory positions.

— Prepare them for a higher position with more responsibility so they can make more money.

— Ask them to become mentors for others within the department. Provide them with the opportunity to formally teach their skills and techniques to other employees. The increased competency and capability of a larger population of employees will allow the manager to distribute the workload more evenly in the future.

Experienced managers recognize that there will always be some employees in the organization who perform at a higher level than others. That is why some rise to higher positions within the organizational structure than others. They simply have more capacity, capability, and drive than their counterparts. It is a manager's responsibility to recognize these employees and find ways to reward their exceptional contribution to the organization.

SCENARIO 12

A 20-year technical professional progresses through the ranks and is promoted into a managerial position. Because she has come through the ranks, the new manager has a good understanding of her former peers, who now are her subordinates. As happens from time to time, favorites are quickly established, and the favoritism becomes evident to other employees. The employees who are not receiving the benefits of those favors begin to complain to their new manager's direct superior. What actions will the senior manager take to deal with this scenario?

Problem: Before initiating any action, the senior manager will confirm through his own due diligence and observation that what he is being told is accurate. There are times when perceptions are incorrect or deliberately slanted for personal reasons. The new manager deserves the benefit of a doubt until the facts are gathered.

Response: If the facts indicate that favoritism is being shown, then an immediate discussion with the new manager is definitely in order. The discussion is kept confidential. The senior manger indicates his awareness of what is happening and that it must stop immediately or further disciplinary action will be forthcoming. He then follows up to ensure the situation is resolved without repercussions to those employees who came forward.

If the facts indicate that no favoritism exists, it is still important that the perception be dealt with before further personnel problems arise. Too often, if left unchecked, perception becomes reality. The senior manager encourages his subordinate manager to have several candid conversations with her employees, rotate assignments among employees, and mentor those who feel left out of the loop. He encourages her to critically analyze her actions as a manager to see what it is that is giving the impression of favoritism and then to make the necessary changes to address it. The earlier it is addressed, the higher the probability that the subordinate manager's career will be successful.

> "Too often, if left unchecked, perception becomes reality."

SCENARIO 13

It is recognized that tenure and experience play a role in the amount of money technical employees are paid. Managers often find that their tenured employees have moved to the top of the pay ranges for their job classification over time. When this happens, increases become smaller; they are generally tied to cost-of-living adjustments versus performance. In some cases, these employees may be "red-lined." That is, they simply will not get another raise unless there are sizable adjustments made to the job classification structure. It may have taken some of these employees 20 years to get to that salary level.

To meet the demands of the organization's growth, managers must continually hire new technical professionals to staff newly created positions. These young professionals do not possess the years of experience that their tenured counterparts have, but they are often hired at or near the same salary level as those tenured professionals. Or, in other cases, they are moved more quickly through the salary ranges to keep them in line with the industry. It may take a younger technical professional 5 years to reach the same salary level it took the tenured professional to reach in 20. The tenured technical professionals, seeing this phenomenon, begin pushing back. They see the inequity and want a resolution that rewards them for the years of technical experience they bring to the job, which their younger counterparts can not possibly match. How will their manager address their concerns?

> *Problem*: There is no doubt that the tenured employees have a legitimate complaint. But in most cases, a manager has few options available to work with.
>
> First, there is the reality that technical professionals remain in significant demand worldwide and industry wide. With the deficit between the supply of graduating technical professionals and the demand for their services, there are simply not enough to go around. That supply and demand ratio drives up the salaries that companies are willing to pay. Sign-on bonuses, coupled with hefty

starting salaries, have become the norm just to get these young technical professionals in the door.

Second, there is the reality of business. Every job within a company is classified relative to its financial value to the organization. That value is predetermined by a system like the Hay System, where a company assigns job points (value) to each position within the organization based upon a series of factors such as industry segment, level of responsibility, profit-and-loss impact, area employment demographics, and numerous others. Unless that job is re-assessed for a higher set of job points, it will always maintain that particular level of value to the company. What that means is a manager is restricted to the pay scales defined in the job classification. He simply cannot give out more money to employees than what the company deems those jobs to be worth.

Third, every manager is faced with the fact that, to attract new employees, he must pay competitive salaries. Those salaries may well equate to the salaries the manager is paying his senior technical professionals. This may not be fair, but in reality, it happens.

Response: Senior employees do have some choices in this scenario. The manager's role is to help them evaluate the alternatives open to them.

— One alternative is to seek outside training to enhance their skill sets to qualify them for other, higher paying jobs.

— Another alternative is for the tenured professionals to go back to school to earn advanced degrees or companion degrees, which will broaden their skills sets and qualify them for another job.

If the tenured employee rejects these options, then the manager and the employee are left with no other viable alternatives. The employee has made a decision to accept the criteria and parameters of the job he is in. If the employee elects to resign and pursue other opportunities, the manager's hands are tied. And, if the tenured employee stays on the job but fails to perform within expectations, he is then treated like any other employee who is not performing. When all else fails, the manager can appeal to the employee's sense of pride and ask him to take on the role of mentor for the younger employees. The senior employees may find satisfaction in sharing their expertise with others and seeing their years of experience applied by others for the betterment of the organization.

SCENARIO 14

A manager has an otherwise good employee who frequently fails to show up for work without notice. Overall, the employee does a pretty good job of making up the lost time, and when she is on the job, she does good work. The employee is generally considered by her manager to be a valuable contributor. The problem is the employee simply fails to report for work on a regular, predictable basis. The manager has, on numerous occasions, talked to the employee about her unexcused absenteeism. In each case, the employee has committed to her boss that she will resolve the issue. For several days or even weeks, the employee reports to work on time faithfully. Then the pattern of absenteeism begins anew. Other employees in the office are aware of the situation and are openly complaining. They, too, want to see the problem resolved. How will the manager of this employee address this performance issue?

> *Problem*: By choosing not to perform, the employee has an unfavorable influence on the organization. Other employees are witness to it and are adversely impacted. If the manager does not take decisive action to resolve the issue, the message to all employees is either that their manager does not care or does not have the intestinal fortitude necessary to deal with it decisively. Neither will result in acceptable behavior on the part of the offending employee or her counterparts.

Management Skill-building Scenarios and Case Study Examples

Response: This is a difficult situation for a manager, especially with today's shortage of talented professionals. Terminating the employee will surely lead to workload problems for the other employees because the odds are that finding a suitable replacement will take a significant amount of time. The thought that "a warm body is better than nobody" begins to creep into the manager's logic. However, if the manager fails to adequately and quickly address the performance issue, there is a high likelihood that other employees will begin to exhibit similar behaviors.

The only course of action for the manager to take is to address the situation with immediate disciplinary action or termination. The manager places the employee on notice, documents the expectations, and follows through. If the employee fails to comply with the work rules established for all employees, then termination is the proper action. If the employee's performance comes up to expectations, then constant monitoring by the manager is required to ensure consistency over time.

Case Study Example

An engineering manager of a large manufacturing concern located in a small town in the Midwest is faced with a dilemma. His lead designer approaches him one afternoon declaring that he will no longer do the detailed documentation on new design projects. He says he will design but will not waste his valuable time completing the tedious bills-of-materials, detail drawings, and instruction notes. That, he contends, will have to be handled by someone else. He is a design engineer, not a detailer. And with that, he promptly leaves his manager's office. How will the manager deal with this situation?

The department manager is faced with a difficult choice: force the engineer to do the work as is expected of every designer in the department and risk his resignation, or allow the designer to do as he desires and risk a mutiny by the other design engineers. Compounding the manager's dilemma are these facts:

Management Skill-building Scenarios and Case Study Examples

— This design engineer is well known in the industry as an expert in his field. For him to find other employment in a short amount of time will be no challenge.

— In the past, the manager has had difficulty recruiting new engineers to the firm because of its small-town venue. To replace the petulant design engineer if he chooses to quit would be a daunting task.

None of the options is particularly appealing to the manager. After thinking about it, the manager concludes that he has only one option available to him. The next morning, he calls the design engineer into his office. His conversation is straight to the point, "Look, this is what I expect of you—just like I do anyone else. If you are not going to fulfill your obligations completely, then I will be forced to take other disciplinary actions."

The engineer replies, "If you're telling me to do documentation, I won't do it, I'll quit." This response leaves the manager with no other choice. He restates his requirements and asks for the engineer's compliance. The engineer tenders his resignation and storms out the door.

Three weeks later, the manager finds himself thinking, "You know what? It's kind of funny. Since he left, overall department performance has actually improved. I mean, I haven't even noticed he's been gone." Why had things transitioned so smoothly? Because every other employee in the department quietly picked up the slack left when the engineer left. It was their way of expressing their appreciation for the way in which their manager handled the situation. By setting the expectations for everyone within the department equally and sending the message through his actions that he was willing to make the hard decisions, employees learned they could count on their manager to do the right thing. He earned their respect and trust—a winning combination for any manager.

> "When a manager treats everyone within the department equally, it builds respect and trust."

Walking the Talk: Pathways to Leadership

Management Skill-building Scenarios and Case Study Examples

SCENARIO 15

The operations manager of a large IT department within a Fortune 100 firm is faced with a pretty tightly wound organization. That is, the department workload is heavy; employees are working at maximum capacity; unpaid overtime has been significant for an extended period; and she is saddled with budgetary constraints that prohibit her from hiring new employees to ease the burden. Compounding her situation is the fact that her boss continually brings in special assignments—additional work to be thrown in on top of everything else in process. This constant juggling of priorities creates confusion for her employees; they are on a project one day and then pulled off to start something new. A few days later, the first project becomes hot again, so they pull off of the project they are working on to go back to complete the first project, and so on. This start-stop process creates lost time and productivity, as well as frustration among the employees. Her employees are beginning to wear out; they are at maximum capacity and the overloaded situation has no outlook for relief. What are her options?

Problem: Working more overtime is not an option as she cannot pay her employees any more than what they already earn—40-hours pay for 80 hours of work. There is not a lot of incentive for them to willingly put forth extra overtime hours. It is simply not a viable option to ask them, or attempt to force them, to work longer hours.

Response: One viable option is to say, "No" when the boss comes in with new projects. There are times when a manager must simply say, "Boss, no. Enough is enough. We can't do it. The plate is full. I can't put any more on it." This approach is not as hazardous to a manager's career as it may at first seem. The secret is to maintain a quantitative organizational capability study that illustrates the department's or work group's practical capacity. Much like any other industrial engineering practical capacity study, this analysis compares the available labor hours factored in at a realistic productivity level against the current volume of work, again measured in labor hours. Something must give when the load exceeds the available capacity for an extended period of time. This type of quantitative analysis gives senior management a baseline to work against. They can see when the limits of the organization are being stretched unrealistically. Armed with this information, management can effectively rebalance the workload, delay or cancel less important projects, or readjust priorities to maintain focus on those projects and activities of prime importance to the organization.

Problem: There are situations in which the additional assignments must be scheduled irrespective of the workload, as budgetary constraints prohibit the hiring of additional permanent employees. These are situations in which a good manager becomes creative.

Response: There are alternatives available when adding more people is not an option, or when the department's workload continues to grow at accelerated rates over extended periods. Experienced managers recognize that most accounting systems treat permanent and temporary employees differently. That is, temporary employees and contract labor are treated as expense versus fixed overhead. As such, while the manager might not be able to hire a full-time employee, she may be able to hire a temporary employee, an intern, or an outside contractor. This approach is often acceptable to senior management so long as it is made clear that when the particular tasks or projects are completed, the temporary employees are dismissed.

Another approach is to seek the help of local universities and colleges. There are many graduate programs looking for projects or assignments that their graduate students can work on. Often, college and university professors, along with their graduate students, will work at a relatively low cost just to get experience on real-world projects. There is significant value for the money with this approach. First, there is an experienced professor to oversee the work of dedicated graduate students with the time and incentive to do solid work. In many cases, the cost associated with the use of university assistance is tax deductible as a contribution to a nonprofit institution. Secondly, it provides the manager with the opportunity to look at potential new employees and begin the recruitment process early.

Yet another option is to outsource some of the workload to outside firms. Yes, there are risks and costs associated with this option, just as there are with the others. But in some instances, this may be the only way to get the required work and projects completed without creating total chaos in the workplace.

SCENARIO 16

A new department manager in a fast-paced Tier One automotive engineering design firm finds he has inherited an employee in his department who can best be described as "Mr. Bad Attitude." What actions are appropriate in this circumstance?

Problem: The employee is openly demonstrating disdain for his manager, as well as upper management. His negative attitude is starting to impact some of the younger employees in the organization.

Response: The approach in situations like this is for the manager to be straightforward, candid, and expeditious in handling the issue with the employee. The sooner the issue is brought out, the quicker it can be resolved, even if the ultimate solution is to terminate the employee. The discussion will not be a particularly pleasant one, but nonetheless, it must be conducted.

The manager immediately meets with the employee to clearly and completely explain his expectations. The conversation begins, "Look, this is the only discussion we're going to have on this subject. Your behavior is insubordinate. It either stops right now, or you're out of here. If I need to have a second discussion with you, it's going to be an exit discussion. If you've got a problem, you discuss it with me. Or, if you prefer, talk with Human Relations. But you do not complain to your peers or disparage management. You will not be allowed to spread discontent within this organization. We simply can not and will not tolerate it. Do you understand?"

The manager then agreed to set aside 30 minutes each week for an extended period to meet with the employee. This allowed for open, candid discussions concerning the issues troubling the employee. Over time, the issues were resolved and the employee became a dedicated, loyal contributor.

SCENARIO 17

A new manager is assigned to the Accounting department of a mid-sized consulting firm. She finds she has inherited a supervisor in her organization who was promoted by her predecessor into a classification for which the employee is really not qualified. The manager inherited the supervisor, and along with him, the problems associated with his inability to do the job. The supervisor's employees recognize that he is in over his head, as do the supervisor's peers. Senior management is also aware of the performance deficiencies and is putting heat on the new manager to address them immediately. What can be done in this circumstance?

Problem: The first inclination for a manager is to immediately terminate the non-performing supervisor. After all, everyone, even senior management, recognizes that he is not performing. As a consequence, the backing for such a move is in place at all levels within the organization. However, terminating the employee is not so cut and dry. First, there is no documentation indicating anything other than acceptable performance from the supervisor. Thus, there are no supportable grounds upon which to terminate him. Secondly, the company, having placed him into this position, owes an obligation to the supervisor to help him grow into the job.

Response: An employee in this position can not simply be discarded. It was not the fault of the employee that he was placed in a job he was incapable of handling. Since management made the mistake, it is management's responsibility to help groom and develop the employee so he can become competent in the position. In other words, the supervisor must be given the opportunity to grow into the job. Whether or not the new manager personally put the supervisor in the job is irrelevant. The manager must support him as he learns the nuances of the job. To that end, the manager is required devote time from her schedule to work with the supervisor over a designated period of time, typically six months to a year, to help him improve. A written performance improvement program is required to:

— provide the employee with clearly defined expectations for his performance, including quantifiable performance metrics to guide his progress, and

— provide supporting evidence in the event that the supervisor is ultimately terminated or demoted into a position more suitable to his skill sets.

If after a reasonable period of time (6–12 months) the supervisor is still not capable of doing the job, then it is time to begin the transition to another position or begin termination procedures.

SCENARIO 18

The operations manager of a large aerospace company has a technical professional working within the department who frequently disappears from the office. The employee, whose name is Larry, leaves for lunch at noon and then shows up around 3:00 in the afternoon or sometimes not until the next day. When the manager questions Larry regarding where he has been, he always responds with a logical explanation like, "Oh, I was out on the job site running down problems." Or, "I was in the other part of the building." For awhile, the manager accepts Larry's responses, but is suspicious.

While out in the factory running down problems one afternoon, the manager takes the opportunity to check up on Larry. After searching for some time, the manager concludes that he is not in the building. The manager asks another employee if he has seen Larry around. Somewhat sheepishly, the employee directs the manager to the parking lot where Larry's car is parked. There, the manager finds Larry asleep in his car. How should the manager handle this situation?

Problem: The manager knows he has to deal with Larry's performance issue quickly and directly. It can not be ignored in hopes that it will go away or miraculously get better on its own. If he does not address it, the problem will likely get worse over time. The manager's initial thought is to terminate Larry on the spot. Grounds for termination are certainly apparent. The manager, however, recognizes the need to isolate the reasons why this problem has arisen prior to concluding what action to take. Experience has taught him the importance of seeking facts before reacting.

> "If a manager chooses not to address a personnel problem, the problem will likely get worse over time."

Response: The manager begins by looking for a drug or alcohol dependency. If a dependency does in fact exist, the manager recognizes his responsibility is to encourage Larry to get into a rehabilitation program. Most organizations have such programs, which are either handled by internal or external healthcare professionals. If Larry rejects involvement in the program, then it becomes a career choice on his part. The manager did what was ethically and legally appropriate.

Management Skill-building Scenarios and Case Study Examples

Before concluding anything, however, the manager decides to discuss the situation with Larry to isolate the specific issues surrounding the situation. Based upon the facts he uncovers, he will then develop an action plan that focuses on improvement. During his conversations with Larry, he learns that things are not as he assumed. Larry's situation, as it turns out, is not one of dependency. Because Larry's parents had reached an age where they were now incapable of taking care of themselves, he had moved them in to live with him and his wife. The move was creating serious financial burdens on Larry and his family as the medical expenses for his parents began to mount. To make ends meet, Larry had to make more money. He is moonlighting five days a week, plus working a third job on the weekends. At best, Larry is getting only four hours of sleep a day. Simply put, he is just worn out.

When confronted, Larry responds honestly, "You caught me, Mike. I'm sorry for letting you down, but I'm working three jobs to make ends meet. I'll try to do better."

After discussing the situation in depth, the manager gave Larry some personal advice. "Larry, you must come to a conclusion. How long can you maintain two jobs during the week and a third on the weekends, and do any of them effectively?" The next question the manager asked Larry was probably the most pointed. "Which job are you making the most money on?"

Larry responded, "Why?"

The manager replied, "If you're making more money here than on the others, then you had better not be sleeping on this job. I'm not paying you to sleep in your car. Go sleep on their time. That way when you're fired, it will have the least financial impact on you. Larry, you must make a decision. You simply can't do both."

While the manager utilized humor to defuse the emotions of the employee, he remained supportive, but firm. It was a choice that only Larry could make. Larry decided to give up his second job during the week. In turn, Larry's manager helped him secure a short-term loan through the company credit union to get him through his financial difficulties. Eventually, Larry paid back the loan and was able to quit his weekend job.

SCENARIO 19

Many companies began instituting no-smoking policies in the mid to late 1990s as a result of increasing pressures from employees and mounting legal liabilities. By 2000, the no-smoking policy had become almost universal throughout every industry. Its enforcement provides all employees with a work environment that is free of airborne pollutants and smoke—one that is healthier for employees and actually cleaner for business equipment, computers, and office machines. In short, it is a win-win scenario for everyone involved. But what about those employees who smoke? How does the policy affect them and is it discriminatory? This issue is a hornet's nest for managers to deal with because of its complexity. On the surface, it appears straightforward enough, but it is fraught with numerous potential problems and pitfalls.

Problem: A good manager enforces the no-smoking policy as strictly as he does all other company policies. Nonetheless, several times a day employees from other departments, his employees, and several company managers go outside the building for a smoke. One department manager has gone so far as to have "walking meetings" with her employees so she can smoke outside while discussing important issues.

Several nonsmoking employees in the manager's department question why those employees who smoke get an extra two to three breaks a day while the nonsmokers are in the office working. The complaints are becoming more frequent and increasingly sharp—"reverse discrimination" is often claimed. Upon looking into his

Management Skill-building Scenarios and Case Study Examples

employees' complaints, the manager finds that these frequent five-minute smoke sessions are in reality turning into several 15–30-minute breaks daily. When the manager questions his employees about their extended smoke breaks, he is told, "We are out there with other department managers talking business." The employees fully and honestly believe they are in compliance with company policy because they are talking about business issues while smoking.

Response: This is not a situation that can be handled individually by any manager. It is something that must be handled universally by all managers in the organization. When a corporate no-smoking policy is created and promoted, there must be specific rules and guidelines for all managers to use consistently relative to its enforcement. The company policy must define clearly who can take a smoke break, when, how frequently, for how long, and even where. Further, it must outline whether or not business is to be conducted during these breaks. Most importantly, enforcement of the policy by management must be equal for all employees. For example, all employees are given 15 minutes twice a day, or twice in the morning and twice in the afternoon to go have a cigarette, a cup of coffee, or use the restroom. By adhering strictly to the guidelines for enforcement, there can be no feeling of discrimination among any employee group.

In this instance, unthinkingly, management has created an environment that could well be considered discriminatory. In effect, if the manager acts alone, he risks giving the impression that he is favoring one employee group over another. Why is this so? Because he is enforcing the work rules differently from the way they are enforced by the rest of management. There must be consistency between and within all levels of management in enforcement of the policy. No manager is free to take the position that, "Nobody in my department will be allowed to smoke ex-

Management Skill-building Scenarios and Case Study Examples

cept at designated times and in designated areas. I don't care what other department managers allow, my policy stands!" Nor is a manager free to allow some employees more time during the day than he allows others. This applies to all company man-

> *"For better or worse, a manager who inconsistently enforces company policy without reprisal sets a new precedent for all employees."*

agers and supervisors. If a precedent is established by any member of management and that action consistently violates the company's no-smoking policy without reprisal, then those actions establish a precedent for all employees. Once this occurs, all managers are compromised and accusations of employee discrimination become defensible.

Case Study Example

Because management does not want customers or employees walking through a smoke-filled lobby or corridor, the no-smoking policy at a large international capital goods manufacturer dictates that employees go outside the building to smoke. By so doing, not only has management increased the time employees will be away from their workstations by adding additional distance, but the company has now exposed employees to the elements—cold weather, snow, and rain. Why is this an issue? Employees more frequently catch colds or the flu because management does not provide a sheltered location where they can smoke. The net result is increased lost time, medical leave, and lower productivity. When management disciplines employees for increased absenteeism, the employees have recourse because their health has been impacted as a result of their compliance with management's actions. Thus, management is at fault, not the employees.

The lesson learned is that policies and their effects must be thoroughly assessed before implementation. Once implemented, all managers must enforce the policies consistently. Exceptions create downstream employee problems.

Walking the Talk: Pathways to Leadership

Management Skill-building Scenarios and Case Study Examples

SCENARIO 20

A male manager has a female employee whose job requires her to occasionally work on construction sites where the workforce is mainly comprised of skilled tradesmen. In this environment, she frequently gets catcalls, whistles, and inappropriate remarks from the workers. Her male counterparts make every effort to shelter her from this environment. They often hover over her when she is on the construction site, or say to her, "No, you don't have to go out there. I'll take the work out. I'll get the information for you." They constantly try to keep her from being faced with what they perceive to be a hostile environment. Inadvertently, they are also blocking her from doing her job.

Problem: Frustrated, the female employee comes to her manager for assistance. Her comments are, "I feel harassed; not by the men out there on the construction site, but by my peers who are constantly sheltering me. I feel like I can't do my job effectively because everybody's hovering over me all the time. What are you going to do about it?"

Response: The response and corresponding actions in this scenario are clear. The employee has been assigned the job and must be allowed do it without interference from her coworkers, even if they are well intentioned. The manager's response is to call the offending employees together, instruct them to back off, and then monitor the situation to ensure that they do. Their fatherly instinct has no place in today's work environments.

SCENARIO 21

A new department manager is faced with a dramatically increasing workload within his department. Unlike the norm, in this scenario the manager has enough people to get the job done. However, the manager has only limited equipment and no budget to purchase additional equipment so that every employee has the tools needed to do the work. This is a common situation in software development environments, R&D

companies, or other technology-driven organizations. What is the manager's plan?

Problem: Utilizing the Theory of Constraints effectively, the manager concludes that lack of equipment is the obvious bottleneck. Because of this, the volume of work generated by his department is limited. In developing his strategy, he considers all the existing environmental constraints. The facts are as follows.

— There is no money in the capital budget to buy more equipment until at least the next budgetary period.

— There is a consistently growing demand for increased output from the department. The increased demand is not just a small blip that will level out in a short period.

— Common sense dictates that spreading the employees out over an additional shift will better utilize the available equipment. By so doing, the need for capital expenditures could be eliminated, the productivity increased at a minimal cost to the organization (primarily shift pay differentials), and the changes could be implemented immediately.

Response: Regardless of the need, whether it's short term, long term, or some combination thereof, the problem must be addressed for the work to get done. The decision to add a second shift will not be a popular one for all employees. It is one, however, that must be made.

The manager meets with his employees to explain the situation and his decision. His explanation goes something like this: "To satisfy the demands of the company and its customers, some of our department's employees will be deployed to a second shift so that we get better utilization of equipment and resources."

Employee response was predictable: "Oh well, yeah, that's understandable. Somebody else can go to second shift, but I can't work second shift. I don't work at night. I have certain family obligations." The excuses continued throughout the discussions. None of the employees volunteered to work the second shift. They, in fact, refused to consider the idea further. Given the circumstances, what options does the manager have?

— One option is to assign the second shift to all employees on a rotating schedule until the situation is addressed on a more permanent basis. The pros to this approach are that employees are all treated equally, the work gets done without unjustified capital expenditures, and there is no loss in productivity resulting from the learning curve for new hires. The cons include disruption in the work-home schedules of all employees and the subsequent disharmony that will likely result. If it is a short-term need, this approach will work. But if the need is longer term, the next option will provide better results.

— Determine the number of positions required for each shift and then open them for bid to all employees based upon seniority and ability. Those employees with the highest combination of seniority and job skills are awarded the first-shift positions. The second-shift positions are then opened for bid to the remaining employees on the same basis. If the remaining employees decline the second-shift positions, the manager begins the hiring process for new employees and terminates the remaining employees because of lack of work on the first shift. If the need is immediate, terminating these employees is the best option. However, if the manager has the flexibility to make the change over time, attrition is the preferred solution. As the organization continues to grow to meet the demands of the marketplace, or as attrition takes staff away, the manager hires new employees specifically for the second-shift positions. Thus, over time, the manager works himself out of the prob-

Management Skill-building Scenarios and Case Study Examples

lem. When hiring new employees, however, it is imperative that the manager makes it clear to all candidates that he is hiring exclusively for a second-shift position.

UNDERLYING CAUSES

Why do scenarios such as those presented in this chapter happen? Why do managers constantly run into these problems? In many cases, it is simply a misalignment of manager and employee expectations. In other words, there is a failure in communication. If a manager clearly defines employee expectations relative to the level of performance required, in most cases, employee performance will comply. If performance problems do begin to surface, the quicker the manager moves to resolve them, the better, as there is less chance of the problem becoming severe. When a problem is made visible to all involved, the difference between fact and fiction becomes readily visible. Thereafter, resolution can be achieved quickly and completely.

SUMMARY

In this chapter, several scenarios were discussed along with the pros and cons surrounding the various options available to managers in handling each circumstance. It is wise to remember that no single answer fits all circumstances. Successful managers analyze their environment and the drivers behind it. They look at the reasons why an employee or group of employees exhibit undesirable behavior, and assess the options available to correct it. Every business situation is unique and therefore must be handled based on its own merits and constraints. There is no "one size fits all" solution to employee performance problems that can be applied universally by every manager, every time. There is no handbook that describes the perfect course of action in every business situation. Successful managers think, analyze, assess, and then act. To do otherwise is a recipe for disaster.

In Chapter 6, the manager's role in handling various personnel problems will be discussed. Pitfalls and opportunities will be outlined. Disciplinary actions will be reviewed. And, dos and

Management Skill-building Scenarios and Case Study Examples

don'ts will be explored in detail, along with guidelines to keep managers out of trouble and out of court. It is wise to remember that for managers, prevention and early corrective actions will go a long way in preventing a broad range of employee problems. When a manager addresses and resolves employee performance problems quickly, potentially explosive situations are defused with the least impact on all parties.

6
Managing Disciplinary Problems

OBJECTIVES

While never a pleasant part of the job, occasionally every manager is faced with the requirement to discipline an employee. In this chapter, corrective actions relating to employee performance problems will be explored.

Many managers shun direct confrontation with employees. They find it far easier to ignore a performance problem in hopes it will miraculously improve than to face the employee with the negative aspects of his or her job performance. But unlike a fine wine that improves over time on its own, employee performance problems only worsen if left untouched by a manager.

Several tools and techniques for resolving employee performance issues will be explained in this chapter. As with all employee issues, if a manager is unsure of a particular situation, it is wise to seek advice from HR professionals or corporate counsel before initiating any form of corrective or disciplinary action. This is one aspect of management in which doing everything right the first time is essential. Mistakes can be painful to a manager. In some cases, they can be career limiting.

IDENTIFYING PERFORMANCE ISSUES

If a manager finds himself in a situation in which an employee is exhibiting either behavioral or performance problems, immediate managerial involvement is warranted. Again, the earlier the performance issue is addressed, the easier it is for both parties. However, before taking a radical

"Before taking action, stop, think, assess, and then react."

action and possibly getting into trouble, an experienced manager follows a simple rule . . . *stop*, *think*, *assess*, and *react* (STAR). The STAR rule forces a manager to critically assess the situation first to find the drivers behind the employee's action or inaction. Once those drivers are identified, plans can be developed for a corrective action that will yield the desired results for both the manager and the employee. The primary disciplinary objective is to help an employee improve his performance to an acceptable level. The only time termination is considered is after a manager has provided his employee with the opportunity, tools, and guidance with which to make the necessary improvements in performance and the employee has thereafter failed to improve.

The manager's first step is to examine the situation thoroughly. It is important to examine all aspects of the performance or behavioral problem to gain as much understanding as possible. Here are some key questions to ask in investigating the situation.

- Who has exhibited the behavior that is deemed unacceptable? Is it one person or is it a group of people within the department or work group?

- Is there a single issue or behavioral problem of concern, or is there more than one?

- Does the unacceptable behavior tie to a specific situation, condition, or environment, or is the behavior universal in nature?

- Where is the behavior being observed and how is it affecting other areas across the organization? For example, are all of the engineers happy but all of the Purchasing personnel unhappy? Are all of the Customer Service representatives up in arms while the Quality and Manufacturing personnel are contented? By isolating those areas where the problem behavior exists and where it does not, a manager makes the necessary comparisons that will lead to uncovering the specific drivers behind the performance problem.

- When did the unacceptable behavior first become apparent? Can it be tied to a specific event or situation in the workplace?
- How often has the unacceptable behavior occurred? Was it a one-time occurrence or is there a recognizable pattern of nonconforming performance or behavior? For example, a long-term employee comes into his manager's office screaming, yelling, ranting, and raving. He makes a complete idiot of himself over something minor. This is the first time he has ever done this—the only time in the 10 years the employee has worked for the company. It is unlikely he will ever do it again. Should his manager hold this instance against the employee? Is this one incident worthy of termination? Or, could it be a rare occurrence the manager should chalk off to, "Everyone is entitled to a bad day once in awhile." Repetitive behavior problems are those that are of concern to managers. One-time infractions are considered just that . . . isolated events.
- What is the extent of the performance problem? Is it an insignificant issue, minor irritant, or is it of real significance? For example, is the behavioral or performance issue negatively impacting the organization, its employees, and other organizational units?
- How widespread is this particular performance problem or behavior? Is it something that is within a specific work group or can it be pinpointed to a specific individual?
- Has the manager or his predecessor attempted to address this behavioral issue in the past? If so, what were the results of those efforts? If the results were positive at that point in time, why has the problem resurfaced? If the results were not positive, why was there no further action taken? In other words, why is the problem still occurring?
- From another perspective, why are other employees in the department not exhibiting that same behavior?

Managing Disciplinary Problems

- In addition to the employee's primary performance problem, are there others that could be present, but are not? Are there areas of stark contrast in the employee's job performance? Is his behavior radical in nature and how does it correlate to his performance? Are there certain parts of his behavior that are admirable while others are totally revolting? If this is so, why is there a difference and what is its root cause?

The purpose of this exercise is to isolate and clarify the issues so they can be dealt with in a logical, unbiased manner. A disciplinary action should never be the hasty result of a knee-jerk reaction by a manager; nor should it be the result of ill feelings harbored by a manager for an extended period of time. Poor or unacceptable performance should never be a surprise to an employee. It is a manager's responsibility to assess and communicate all performance issues with her employees openly and promptly.

Example 1

An employee does something her manager is not in agreement with on January 2nd. The behavior does not happen again and the manager never says anything about the incident. On December 20th of that year, the employee's performance evaluation interview is conducted by her manager. The manager rates the employee negatively for the year and places the employee on probation. When questioned by the employee, the manager reminds her of the January 2nd incident. The employee thinks to herself, and rightly so, "Why didn't we talk about it and resolve it back then? Why has my supervisor been harboring these bad feelings all this time without saying anything to me about the incident?"

Is it fair to the employee for her manager to maintain silence about performance issues, only to bring them up in her review months later? Does this action by the manager allow the employee to correct her performance deficiencies? The answer to both questions is a resounding "No." It is incumbent upon every manager to bring performance issues to light immediately with the employee so improvements can be made as quickly as possible.

Typically, there are several positive aspects of an employee's job performance along with a few that are less desirable. It is rare to find an employee whose overall performance is poor. When an employee's performance is less than desirable in some area, the question every experienced manager asks is, "Why?" Experienced managers seek insight so they can compare the good performance to the bad, which will often lead the manager to the root cause, and thus the solution.

Example 2

When a performance issue arises, the first thing a seasoned manager reviews is the accuracy and detail of the employee's job description. The manager looks for whether or not the job description that the employee has been asked to follow is correct, current, and comprehensive enough to yield the type of performance expected. In other words, is there a misalignment of the expectations of the manager and the expectations that can be reasonably derived from the job description?

> "When a performance issue arises, the first thing to look at is the accuracy and detail of the employee's job description."

It is not uncommon for department or employee job descriptions to be written by the department manager. In many cases, the department manager has performed many of those tasks as an employee within the department prior to his or her promotion into management. Those aspects of the employee's job that the manager is familiar with from personal experience are normally well written, comprehensive, and accurate. If, however, the employee has other assignments that the manager has no personal experience with, the description for those tasks is often less complete or totally incorrect. If the manager finds the employee is doing an excellent job with those aspects of his responsibilities that are well documented in the job description, but poorly on those that are not, is it the employee's problem

Managing Disciplinary Problems

or his manager's? Assessing the facts often will lead a manager to alter his viewpoint about an employee's performance. Before taking action, it is imperative for the manager to have good, solid facts. Investigating the facts helps managers dispel assumptions and identify real performance issues. In addition, the exercise provides documentation in the event that a disciplinary action is required at a later date.

Burden of Proof

A rule of thumb for a manager faced with a disciplinary situation is to practice *due diligence*. That is, the manager carefully compiles and documents supporting evidence of the problem. The burden of proof rests with management, just as does the burden of generating acceptable results. As a consequence, documentation is absolutely critical. Too often, the documentation developed by a manager in support of a termination or disciplinary action fails to adequately support the conclusions drawn by the manager. As a general rule, documentation must be comprehensive enough to lead an independent third party to reach the same conclusions as those of the manager. The linkage must be self-evident and supported by reasonable, quantitative performance measurements that are consistent with those of other employees performing the same or similar work activities. Qualitative measures that fail to provide evidence of the difference existing between what an employee is doing and what is required for the job will not be satisfactory to a National Labor Relations Board judge. It is also vital that the documentation contains the definitive corrective action plan that was presented to the employee to guide his performance improvement efforts. (Documentation will be discussed in more detail in the next section.)

Forced reversals of disciplinary actions initiated by a manager are generally the result of a manager's failure to:

> "A rule of thumb for a manager faced with a disciplinary situation is to practice due diligence in documenting supporting evidence."

148   *Walking the Talk: Pathways to Leadership*

- get the facts before initiating the disciplinary action,
- thoroughly document why the disciplinary action was initiated and how the conclusions were drawn, or
- follow through with the corrective action plans to monitor and aid the employee in improving his or her performance.

Acting without facts or cause is simply inexcusable and unacceptable behavior for any management professional. Neither is it defensible in a court of law. The first time a manager sits with an arbitrator in a National Labor Relations Board hearing or in a courtroom facing a discrimination suit, these lessons will be vividly engraved in that manager's mind. These are rarely pleasant situations. However, they are completely avoidable with a little care and due diligence on the part of the manager.

DISCIPLINARY ACTION . . . A STEP-BY-STEP PROCESS

If after a thorough analysis of the facts surrounding an employee's poor performance or unacceptable behavior a manager concludes that disciplinary action is warranted, then the following steps are required.

1. A meeting is called with the employee to discuss the specific performance issues, the quantitative measures of performance that support the manager's conclusions, and the expected levels of acceptable performance for the employee's job. Minimum performance expectations are documented for each task within the job description. All employees with that same job description are expected to perform at least to the minimum level, taking into consideration the facts and circumstances surrounding the work environment. The employee is not expected to perform as a superstar, but merely to adequately perform the fundamental aspects of her job on a day-to-day basis. An important point here is that the employee's performance is not to be measured against the performance of other employees doing the same or similar task. The employee's

performance is to be measured against the documented requirements of the job only.

2. The employee's input is sought. The manager may not be aware of justifiable reasons for a lack of performance on the employee's part.

3. The conversation is documented, including the employee's comments and reactions.

4. The employee is invited to take part in development of the corrective action plan for performance improvement. Even though the manager has prepared one in advance of the meeting, the employee's input is always of value. It is, after all, the employee's career, and he has a vested interest in building the criteria for his success.

5. A time frame is established, during which the employee is expected to bring his performance up to expectations. In most cases, a six-week to 120-day period is selected. This provides adequate time for the employee to improve and for management to assess whether or not the performance is sustainable.

6. Performance metrics are developed, which the employee and manager will use to quantitatively measure performance. By making the measures available to the employee, a manager gives more control to the employee over his own destiny. In addition, the Hawthorne Effect begins to set in to aid the employee's improvement efforts by providing him with the knowledge of what will be measured and how it will be evaluated.

7. A series of regular and frequent reviews are planned between the employee and his manager. Normally, once a week the manager and the employee review the metrics, discuss further improvement needs, and candidly assess the employee's progress toward the goal. The meetings open the communication channel so the employee gets the support needed from his manager to meet the targeted

levels of performance. The secret is to set the review periods frequently enough so the manager and the employee do not lose track of the employee's progress or lose the sense of urgency needed to make the effort successful.

Common Pitfalls

One common pitfall is that many managers fail to clarify the expectations for the employee by setting measurable performance objectives so that improvement can be measured. Another is forgetting to follow through with the employee on a regular basis to ensure he is provided with every possible opportunity to be successful.

> "Many managers fail to set measurable performance objectives so that improvement can be measured."

In essence, the performance improvement process forms a contract between the manager and the employee. As with any contract, both parties must comply with the terms and conditions set forth therein. Failure by either party constitutes a legal breach of that agreement. Therefore, the process must be taken seriously.

Example

Often managers succumb to daily pressures, get sidetracked, or simply forget to uphold their part of the performance improvement contract. The scenario commonly runs the following course. The manager and the employee agree on the terms and conditions of the corrective action plan, as well as to a review meeting every Friday afternoon at 4:00 p.m. The first Friday comes along and the two sit down to discuss the employee's progress, to address any issues, and to review the performance measurements. The manager solicits the employee's input and documents the employee's comments and his own. They discuss the various corrective actions required for the following week. So goes the process routinely for the next three to four weeks, during which time the employee is making steady progress.

Managing Disciplinary Problems

Then sometime into the fourth or fifth week, something comes up that causes the manager to cancel or reschedule the Friday afternoon review session with the employee. The manager calls the employee to advise him of the change in meeting time. "Listen, I'm going to be out of town on Friday. I'm not going to be able to make our normal meeting. Let's pick it up again Monday at 4:00. Is that okay?" The employee concurs. Monday brings with it another crisis, so the manager again calls the employee. "Listen let's just let the meeting go until next Friday. We'll pick it up then at our normal time." On Friday, the two get back together for the meeting. The following week, the manager again finds that other priorities will keep him from meeting with the employee at the scheduled time. So he calls again, "Listen, I'm going to be tied up again. The boss has got me working on a couple of extra projects. Let's skip this week and pick it up next week." Again, the employee concurs. During the subsequent week, the employee's performance slips a little. So the next Friday, the manager terminates the employee for failure to comply with the terms and conditions of the corrective action agreement.

The following scenario and corresponding dialogue occur next. The manager finds himself in a hearing with an arbitrator from the National Labor Relations Board, who begins asking the manager several direct questions.

Arbitrator: "Did you describe for the employee the expected level of performance?"

Manager: "Well, yes, I did."

Arbitrator: "And did you give the employee a corrective action plan and an opportunity to improve?"

Manager: "Yes, I did. We established guidelines and expectations, and then developed a set of quantifiable performance metrics."

Arbitrator: "Okay, that's very good. Now, did the employee improve?"

Manager: "Well, no, he didn't."

Arbitrator: "And so you terminated the employee?"

Manager: "Yes, I did."

Managing Disciplinary Problems

Arbitrator: "Did you set review meetings with the employee to discuss progress or the lack thereof?"
Manager: "Yes, I did."
Arbitrator: "Did you keep all of those review meetings?"
Manager: "Well, I kept most, but there were a couple of things that came up, preventing me from making two of them."
Arbitrator: "So, let me clarify. You established the review meeting schedule. Is that right?"
Manager: "Yes."
Arbitrator: "And you failed to keep all of those scheduled reviews with the employee?"
Manager: "Your Honor, you don't understand—we're a business. Things got busy. Things happened."
Arbitrator: "You failed to keep all of those meetings, right?"
Manager: "Well, yes, that's true."
Arbitrator: "Case closed. The employee is reinstated with back pay. Thank you very much."

The case is lost by the employer, as is the manager's credibility. All because the manager established a contract with the employee and then failed to comply with its terms. In the eyes of the law, this is considered a breach. The National Labor Relations Board's ruling concurs: the failure lies solely with the manager. The employee was there doing his best to comply with what his manager asked. It was the manager who failed.

Once performance improvement meetings are set, they must be kept. If the manager has a vacation scheduled, serious consideration must be given to canceling or rescheduling it until the disciplinary action is concluded. If a manager absolutely must miss a meeting (and this is truly the exception, not the rule), the manager must be represented in the regularly scheduled meeting with the employee to ensure continuity in the process. An HR professional is an excellent representative in these cases. But again

"The performance improvement contract must be honored by both parties to make it defensible."

Walking the Talk: Pathways to Leadership

Managing Disciplinary Problems

it is important to stress: *the performance improvement contract must be honored by both parties to make it defensible.* Failure to do so on the part of the manager is unacceptable and often embarrassing. It is management's responsibility and obligation to give employees the opportunity, tools, and support needed for them to improve.

Documentation

Upon completion of each review meeting, the manager thoroughly documents the results of the meeting, including the comments made along with his observations of the employee's behavior, attitude, and commitment. The documentation further includes any comments or conclusions that the employee specifically wants placed in the record. As this is the employee's improvement plan, she is encouraged to document her comments on progress. Content and context of the employee's comments are neither dictated nor edited by the manager, but entered into the record in the employee's own words. The employee's comments will often reflect her frustration, anger, and concern. This is to be expected. However, these comments are not used as justification to terminate the employee. The employee is provided every reasonable opportunity to improve. Over time, the employee's comments will become less emotional and more fact based. Comments such as, "My boss is an absolute idiot . . ." will give way to "I do not agree with my boss' conclusions for these reasons." Encouraging the employee to make comments emphasizes that this is her process. Once the employee takes ownership of it, she is focused on changing her performance, usually for the better.

The employee's performance is documented against the established targets and guidelines using actual measurements. If the employee is improving, the extent of that improvement is documented against the performance baseline for the job. There will be times when an employee is showing improvement, but because of the large gap between the employee's current level of performance and what is expected, the manager concludes that it is unrealistic to expect the employee to improve enough to meet the minimum job requirements. In those cases, the documentation will show a good faith effort from both parties and will justify the manager's ultimate decision to terminate the employee. The documentation will also allow the manager to give a positive recommendation to potential employers when the employee applies for positions that are more suitable for her capabilities.

THE DECISION TO TERMINATE AN EMPLOYEE

If within a reasonable time frame the employee is not improving, or is not improving quickly enough, or if the manager does not see the employee making an earnest effort, then the decision to terminate the employee is appropriate, even necessary.

There are other options, however, which managers can misguidedly select. The first is to pawn off the poorly performing employee's work to another employee. For example, rather than taking the performance problem on directly, managers often hire another employee to do the under-performing employee's work. Then they promote the under-performing employee into a higher position. Commonly known in the business world as the *Peter Principle*, this approach guarantees discontent among other employees because the manager is obviously dodging the issue.

Another common approach taken by managers is to spread the under-performing employee's workload among other employees, thus increasing their workload while allowing the under-performer to coast. This, too, guarantees discontent and often mutiny.

A third is to change the job description of the under-performing employee to correspond with his reduced performance levels without a corresponding change to the employee's grade or salary. The result is a highly overpaid, under-performer. Called *red-lining*, the net result is that the employee is never qualified for a promotion or raise again in the future. So there is certainly no motivation for the employee to improve, but it does allow management to dodge the tough personnel issue. It is not a motivation to the other employees either. For example, if an under-performing, high-level manager is asked step down to a new lower-level position without a decrease in grade and salary, it is unfair to the other higher-level managers. Each of those managers has a large number of employees reporting to them, profit-and-loss responsibilities, and extensive operational responsibilities to the organization. To maintain his grade and salary at a level commensurate with the other high-level managers in the company will create mass discontent, and rightly so.

In summary, there are three cardinal rules for a manager to follow when faced with the necessity to terminate an employee.

1. Do not reassign the employee to another department merely to avoid the distasteful termination process. Also, never promote a poor performer to get him out of the way (Peter Principle 101). The Peter Principle must not be allowed to infiltrate the organization. If faced with a problem employee, the manager deals with it professionally and responsibly.

2. Do not just continue to ignore the problem. This is the worst of all possible scenarios.

3. Do not lower the expectations for the employee and pawn off his work to someone else in the department or work group. There is no reason why another employee should be required to carry a heavier workload because his manager is not strong enough to deal with a tough personnel decision.

Successful managers never take the easy way out. They do what is right and appropriate for the organization and its employees. They do not go out of their way to find busy work for their under-performing employees. Poor performers are not given special assignments just to get them out of sight. Special assignments are transparent to both the employee and the organization. The employee is robbed of his dignity and the organization is robbed of the capital allocated for the job. When an employee is not capable, a good manager moves the employee into a job for which he is capable. If there is no such job, it is the manager's responsibility to terminate the employee so he is free to pursue other endeavors.

Employees watch everything their managers do with great interest. Action or inaction on tough personnel issues weighs heavily on

> *"Action or inaction on tough personnel issues weighs heavily on a manager's credibility and ultimate success."*

the credibility, as well as the long-term competency and success of a manager. She will either earn her employees' respect because she has made the tough decisions or lose it for ducking them.

An Exception to the Rules

While, in most cases, it is unacceptable to consider reassigning an employee with a performance problem, there is one exception that deserves mentioning. If an employee is diligently trying to improve her performance, working hard, putting forth a maximum effort, and yet is still failing, it may be a situation in which she was placed in the wrong job. In this case, the dedication and commitment are there; the capability is what is lacking. This happens far too frequently today. In situations like this, termination may not be the appropriate answer. A manager faced with this scenario is wise to work with Human Relations to find the employee another job within the organization. The employee has demonstrated a willingness to take on a difficult assignment. She is making the effort to be successful even though the job responsibilities are clearly beyond her capabilities. It is this type of personal commitment that every manager seeks in an employee. But that commitment must be matched with the capacity of the individual to perform the job. At times, there is simply a mismatch.

Example

An experienced senior manager has just accepted a new job with a large manufacturing organization as head of an operations group that is in disarray. The Purchasing and Logistics department, in particular, is performing at a level far below expectations. This is a large purchasing operation, responsible for several hundred million dollars in annual purchases domestically and internationally. With planned expansions to existing product lines, coupled with expansions planned in the European markets, it is immediately apparent to the new senior manager that this department is, and will continue to be, a bottleneck to the success of those organizational objectives. The new senior manager's due diligence quickly reveals that over the years the department has been staffed with employees who have been unable to perform acceptably in other departments or disciplines. So for this new senior manager, a complete and rapid turnaround of this critical department is his number one priority.

The senior manager's assessment begins at the top of the Purchasing and Logistics organization. It becomes readily apparent that the current department director is not capable of taking the organization to the level it needs to be to support the dynamic plans and objectives of the company. After an open and candid discussion with the department director, both agree that it is in the director's best interests to pursue other career opportunities. With that hurdle behind him, the senior manager immediately launches a search for a highly experienced purchasing director. The job criteria are stringent because of the broad range of responsibilities, the size and complexity of the procurement operation, and the urgency of completing the department turnaround. The requirements for the position include: an undergraduate technical degree, an advanced degree in business or operations, a minimum of 10 years experience in a multi-hundred-million-dollar purchasing operation staffed with over 20 purchasing professionals, broad international sourcing experience, and supply-base management expertise. It is an extremely critical set of requirements indeed, but they are deemed essential to fulfill the needs of the organization.

Working through an executive placement company, the senior manager is quickly able to identify several exceptional candidates for the position and he begins interviewing. During this process, the manager receives a call from the president of the division. The president asks the senior manager if he is con-

Managing Disciplinary Problems

sidering giving Tom an opportunity to interview for this job. Tom is an individual who works for the new senior manager in another capacity. Tom has been with the company several years and is generally considered to be a good, solid individual contributor. But Tom has only limited management experience and no purchasing experience. The senior manager responds, "Well, Pete, you do realize that Tom doesn't fit the criteria we've identified for this position. So no, I was not going to consider Tom."

The president responds, "I think we ought to give him a shot. He's been a good employee for a lot of years."

Now concerned that the conversation is moving in the wrong direction, the new senior manager explains his doubts once again, "Pete, I don't think there's a fit. I think it would be an injustice to Tom to put him in this position. I really don't see him being successful."

The president again responds, "I understand your concerns, but I still think we owe it to Tom to give him this opportunity."

Not always the politically correct person, the new senior manager puts it on the line, "Pete, let's cut it short. Are you telling me to put him in the job?"

The president's response is unambiguous, "Well, I guess you could say that I am. Yes."

The new senior manager discontinues his search and calls Tom into his office for a discussion about the job opening. The grade and financial aspects of the job, its requirements, and the senior manager's expectations are explained to Tom, along with the urgency associated with getting the department turned around within six to 12 months. Tom is excited, absolutely beside himself. The opportunity means a big promotion for him, from an organizational standpoint, a grade standpoint, and a financial standpoint. Tom accepts the position without hesitation.

Over the course of the next six to eight months, the new senior manager works with Tom, providing him direction, counsel, and advice on a daily basis. Tom regularly puts in 55–60-hour weeks. He works his heart out. Every week, Tom and the new senior manager review the department's performance metrics against the targets set by senior management, discuss

Walking the Talk: Pathways to Leadership

Managing Disciplinary Problems

the performance of the individuals within the department, reset and rebalance near-term goals and priorities, and talk about Tom's performance. The new senior manager shares his insight into ways Tom might improve employee weaknesses, expand cooperation with the division's supply base, and distribute the departmental workload more evenly among the buyers. Tom listens intently, then goes back to his office and works harder to try to meet expectations. Every time they discuss the department's continued decline in performance, Tom puts in even more time. After awhile, Tom begins working Saturdays and then almost every Sunday. Every time one of Tom's buyers has a problem, Tom takes it upon himself to solve it for the employee. Before long, Tom has a bigger workload than anyone else in the department. The new senior manager points out the need for Tom to delegate more to develop his employees so they are capable of working more efficiently. In a few cases, the senior manager encourages Tom to make personnel changes to bring more experienced professionals into the department. With each conversation, Tom becomes increasingly protective of his employees and defensive of their performance.

Even with all of Tom's hard work, things are not improving. Department performance continues to lag expectations, and often it even fails to meet the demands of day-to-day operations. The senior manager soon reaches the conclusion that Tom is not going to make it, but he still diligently works with him in an effort to guide him so he is successful. One afternoon, the new senior manager receives a call from the corner office. The president is on the phone. The new senior manager is asked for his candid opinion about Tom's performance and probability of success. The senior manager replies, "It's not working."

To the new senior manager's surprise, the president concurs, "You're right, it's not working. Why don't you terminate Tom and get on with finding a professional purchasing director."

Somewhat shocked by the president's cold response, the senior manager responds, "Wait a minute. You want me to terminate the guy?"

The president responds, "Yes, that's just what I mean. He's not cutting it." The new senior manager asks for a personal conference with the president to discuss the situation in more depth.

Later that day, the senior manager meets with the president and the VP of personnel. The senior manager takes the lead in the conversation, "Look, let me explain the situation from my perspective. Number one, we put the guy in the job. We're the ones who committed him to a position that he really wasn't qualified to do. He didn't ask for the job, we offered it to him. Now you're telling me, even after he's given it 100%, or more, to fire the guy? That just doesn't seem to be appropriate given the facts, so allow me to offer an alternative. I have another position that, quite frankly, is ideally suited for Tom. It's a critical position that we're going to have to fill anyway and I am confident that he'd do a great job in it. It is not a managerial position, but rather an individual contributor's position that will utilize Tom's strengths. It's a lower grade and a lower salary, but it's something that suits his strengths and capabilities perfectly. I propose that we offer the job to him." After much discussion, the senior manager is able to obtain the commitment of the division president for the job change. But that was only half the battle for the senior manager. There was still the requirement to deal with Tom.

The following week, the senior manager pulls Tom aside to broach the topic. Recognizing that this will be an emotional issue, the senior manager selects his words carefully. Although he is mindful of Tom's feelings, the senior manager leaves nothing open to interpretation. The senior manager systematically outlines the performance deficiencies within the Purchasing department, but always tempers the discussion with recognition of Tom's personal commitment and his efforts to address each one. The senior manager points out that despite Tom's efforts, the expected performance targets have simply not been met. Thus, he explains, there exists the requirement for a management change. While Tom is fully cognizant of the deficiencies, he expresses how heartbroken he is at being unable to affect the necessary organizational changes.

Managing Disciplinary Problems

As the discussion of the department deficiencies concludes, the senior manager broaches the issue of a new position with Tom. "Tom, I want you to consider a new job that I have created for you." But before the senior manager is able to finish describing the new position, Tom's emotions and frustrations begin to show. Tom becomes openly agitated and begins to argue his manager's decision to replace him. While Tom's reaction is expected, the senior manager knows that the situation must be kept under control. He immediately interrupts Tom, "Tom, before you stuff your foot any further down your throat, I want you to go home. Think about the new job; think about its scope; think about what it will do for you and what you can contribute to the organization. Then come back Monday morning so we can discuss it when your emotions are under control. But recognize one thing, Tom, Monday morning there will be a new purchasing director in that job. He has already been hired."

With that, Tom leaves. Early Monday morning, he comes back into the senior manager's office and they talk for several minutes. Tom is now relaxed. But he is still somewhat disappointed about being unable to meet expectations. He is appreciative, however, that his superior thought enough of him to consider him for another position. "Boss, I want to thank you for giving me the opportunity to take this new job. After I sat down to talk with my wife about it, she pointed out that I hadn't played golf in almost six months and you know I love to play golf. She also said that when I was home, I wasn't home mentally. I was always in a bad mood and the job had begun impacting my family life and my health. I just didn't see it. So I appreciate you saving my job. I appreciate you giving me another opportunity. I only ask one favor."

The senior manager responds, "What's that?"

Tom replies, "I'd like to introduce my replacement to the staff." The senior manager concurs.

Because of Tom's positive work ethics and attitude, the transition to the new department director goes smoothly. Tom works with his replacement throughout the transition. In his new position, Tom's contributions are again positive and measurable.

Why did the senior manager take the approach of offering Tom a different position versus simply terminating him? Because in this case, management placed the employee in the job fully recognizing that he lacked the experience and background necessary to be successful. Tom showed commitment and dedication to the organization, even though he was ultimately, and perhaps predictably unsuccessful. Thus, reassignment was a better decision than termination under these circumstances.

SUMMARY

In this chapter, the issues surrounding termination, reassignment, and reclassification of employees were discussed. Few people like conflict and confrontation. Unfortunately, it is part of a manager's job to make decisions even in the face of these undesirable conditions. Avoiding an uncomfortable confrontation by telling an employee that he is doing fine when, if fact, he is not performing up to expectations, is nothing short of poor management.

Every employee relies on his manager to help in career planning and the resolution of performance issues. Employees want to do the best job possible. At times they need help, and that help must come from their manager. Without a manager's guidance, encouragement, and discipline, employees will never grow to their potential. To make mistakes is human; to learn from those mistakes is wisdom. But wisdom requires nurturing.

Chapter 7 will explore the development of employee teams and work groups through selective recruitment, motivation, and discipline so they are capable of meeting and exceeding organizational performance expectations. It further discusses the techniques used by successful managers from diverse fields and industries in building effective teams. And it will look at the closed-loop approach utilized by one of the most successful managers in history.

7

Employee Selection, Direction, Motivation, and Empowerment

OBJECTIVE

This chapter will discuss many of the tools and techniques used by successful managers to build chemistry among their employees, an essential ingredient in creating the synergy that exists within today's most successful business organizations. Hiring the most talented, well-educated, most experienced employees is not always the key to long-term business success. Unless these high-potential employees work together for the common good of the entire organization, all of their talent and efforts, along with those of others, will be wasted.

Why is it that a group of seemingly less qualified, less talented employees succeeds against more talented, better-funded competition? How often has a small group of employees overcome overwhelming odds to achieve victory in the marketplace? What are their secrets? How do they achieve such success with so little apparent individual skill or talent? What is the source of the momentum within those organizations and how is it maintained over time? The secret to their success lies in the manager's ability to build an organization in which employees complement each other, offsetting the weaknesses of one employee with the strengths of another. Capable managers build balance within their organizations through the employees they hire.

> "Managers build balance within their organizations through the employees they hire."

A fundamental precept is that every action taken by a manager is tied to another. Nothing is done as a singular action. This concept is called *closed-loop management*. There is a master plan that ties everything together. From recruitment to motivation, from discipline to mentoring, every action has a reason behind it and ties directly to something else. In closed-loop management, nothing is left to chance.

MARKET DYNAMICS AND TECHNOLOGICAL CHANGE AS DRIVERS

Spurred by rapidly changing technology, the incredible period of change in the 1990s and early 2000s fueled competition and consolidation within every industry. Global markets and the demand for "better, faster, cheaper" performance in every industry segment placed incredible strain on organizations and their managers. Many organizations de-layered, downsized, or right-sized in an effort to reduce operating and overhead expenses, exacerbating the situation. Reengineering and lean techniques were employed to drive process and operational waste out, improve organizational throughput, and reduce operating expenses. New knowledge management systems brought managers and employees closer to the customer by processing and disseminating customer value data faster and more efficiently. Many corporations adopted the "virtual products and services" approach to minimize time-to-market and, thus, capture early market leads. E-commerce played a leading role in the change movement by creating new communication and distribution channels for businesses and consumers alike. In short, there existed a number of complex, challenging, and often contradictory dynamics that made every manager's job tougher.

By the time the new millennium was underway, global conflicts combined with economic disequilibrium had changed the dynamics of organizational constraints, cultures, and environments. Management requirements were again vastly altered as boom moved quickly to bust in many industry sectors. Competition within every market became more intense. Even the government sectors began to retrench to hold the line on costs. The game had changed for managers—once again. Effective managers immediately made the necessary adjustments and moved forward. Those who did not faced the potential for reduced effectiveness or outright failure. Making matters worse, over the course of the last two decades corporations have reduced the number of middle management jobs by over 2.5 million—making organizations flatter and increasing the span-of-control of the remaining managers. The driver behind this trend is capital. Corporations can no longer afford redundant and often unnecessary, highly paid managers.

The rule of thumb used by most Human Resource professionals for years was that a good manager had an effective span-of-control of seven to eight people. Beyond that, a manager began to lose effectiveness. In many of today's organizations, those same managers are required to oversee 200–300 employees. A manager's span-of-control is much greater and his job more demanding now than ever before even though many employees work in teams, which are sometimes self-directed. That situation exists by design, because global competition no longer allows corporations to maintain multiple levels of management as in the past.

With fewer management positions, organizations have recognized the benefits that come from moving decision-making through the organization to the lowest possible level. Shifting some of the fundamental management tasks and decisions to employees has become a reality in many industries, from high tech to no tech. Why? Other than the obvious answers of business need and management survival, employees are good at it. They are extremely customer-focused. In fact, when it comes to satisfying their customers, employees will always do what is right for the customer. Employees realize that their number one job is to meet their customers' expectations. They recognize, often more than management, that customer retention is vital if an organization is to survive. In addition, employees are non-political and openly question the motives of others within the company who may be politically motivated. They are also closer to the action. They know how business processes actually work versus what the procedures say happens. Employees know the real problems. And, they have a pretty good handle on the solutions to those problems. In reality, employees control absenteeism, productivity, and quality, and thus the organization's product and operational costs. Therefore, it makes sense to get them involved in the decision-making process.

In many cases, management has asked employees to do more, often with fewer resources and fewer opportunities for advancement, and sometimes for less money and a whole lot less job security. Even though employees may have received little notice and much less real action from management in the past, they are still more than willing to help so long as their managers recognize and support their fundamental needs.

MASLOW'S HIERARCHY OF NEEDS

Back in high school, most of us took basic psychology in which we learned about Maslow's Hierarchy of Needs (see Figure 7-1). At the time, most students probably felt like, "This is something I'll never use." The concept was memorized to pass the test and then likely blown off as trivia. However, the fundamental concepts behind Maslow's Hierarchy of Needs have proven to be critical tools for managers.

Maslow was right on target. The successive achievement of each one of the building blocks in his hierarchy is predicated upon the prior one being in place. What this equates to in a business environment is the recognition by a successful manager that before he can build teamwork into his organization, he must first satisfy the fundamental issues confronting his employees. Recognizing those needs within the organization provides a manager with insight to the correct methodology to implement to address personnel issues quickly and completely.

Fundamental Needs

Effective managers first recognize then satisfy their employees' fundamental needs. Once these needs are met, it is easier to get employees to take on larger roles in the organization, including decision-making, as well as gain their support of major

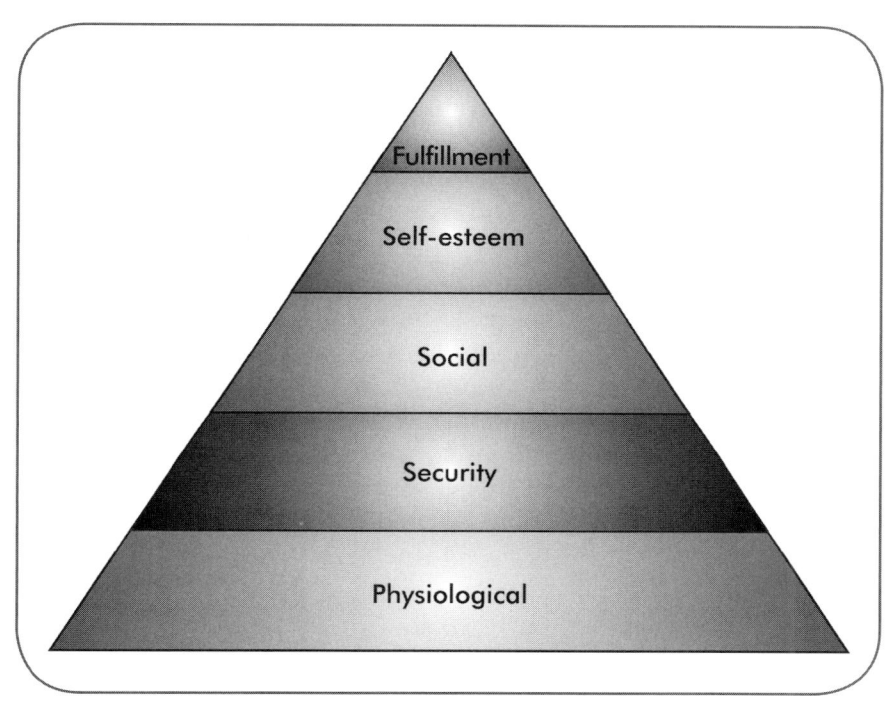

Employee Selection, Direction, Motivation, and Empowerment

Figure 7-1. Maslow's Hierarchy of Needs.

change processes. These needs exist at the personal level, social level, and even the financial level. Unless they are met, any initiative championed by management will not be successful. In fact, over 70% of all change processes championed by management fail miserably because managers do not accurately assess and address the needs of their employees before launching into the latest "flavor-of-the-month" program.

As organizations today move aggressively toward employee empowerment to offset the impact of fewer managers, leaders of organizational change processes often miss many of Maslow's basic building blocks. For example, the base-line building block in the Hierarchy of Needs is money. Every employee has a physiological need to earn enough money to pay bills, take care of a family, and meet the basic levels of subsistence. This in no way means that employees feel they must be rich before they are willing to move into the higher levels within the hierarchy. Rather, they must earn enough money to pay their primary bills. If an employee is deeply concerned about earning enough money to meet his bills at the end of the week, his manager can talk about the latest and greatest management program until he is blue in the face. All the employee is thinking about is, "I've got those bills coming due. Where am I going to get the money to pay them?" To the employee, nothing else matters until that problem is resolved. It becomes an all-consuming effort for the employee. Becoming active in a self-directed work team or launching a new product that will capture significant market share for the company will not be considered until the employee's financial problems are resolved. All of the selling, pushing, and talking a manager does is for naught in this situation.

> "Maslow's Hierarchy of Needs is a critical tool for managers."

Security Needs

The next level in the Hierarchy of Needs to be addressed by a manager is security—specifically, job security. For the employee, it is not only important to earn enough money to pay the bills today, but equally as important to have that paycheck come in consistently next week, next month, and next year. Only if these two key fundamental needs are met will the employee readily move to the next level.

Social Needs

At the social level, employees want to become members of recognized teams, taking part in team activities and projects. It is at this level that managers successfully launch initiatives that require the formation and support of employee teams. When social needs are being met, managers easily get employees involved in day-to-day decision-making and change processes. Thereafter, employees transition over time into the self-esteem and self-fulfillment levels. For example, they will move comfortably into self-directed work teams and eventually into higher roles within the organization as they ultimately seek self-fulfillment.

EMPLOYEE INVOLVEMENT AND EMPOWERMENT

Empowerment allows a manager to push decision-making down to the lowest level possible in the organization. Applied systematically, empowerment builds a balanced organization based upon the knowledge, skills, capabilities, and capacities of its employees. In essence, it builds upon existing employee capabilities by taking advantage of their proximity to the actual issues and opportunities surrounding day-to-day operations within the organization. It is that proximity and knowledge of how things actually work that allows employees to be effective in making decisions that will improve quality, cycle time, and operating performance.

Empowerment is a powerful management tool in that it focuses on giving employees all of the responsibility that they are both *willing* and *able* to assume. These are two very key points. Employees, for the most part, are uncomfortable with accepting responsibility for the decisions they make. There are a number of reasons for their reluctance. First and foremost is the acceptance of accountability for those decisions. Accepting accountability for something that is out of their control is a foreign and unwelcome concept. So, to be effective in making employees comfortable with empowerment, experienced managers thoroughly prepare employees through coaching, training, and application of the proper decision-making tools. It is only through experience that employees will to do an effective job at decision-making.

Managing Water Lines

In essence, empowerment is much like managing the water line of a ship (see Figure 7-2). A ship's captain constantly monitors the integrity of the ship's hull and the depth of draft the ship is drawing to ensure the vessel remains afloat. Substituting the organization for the ship, the role of the manager is like

Employee Selection, Direction, Motivation, and Empowerment

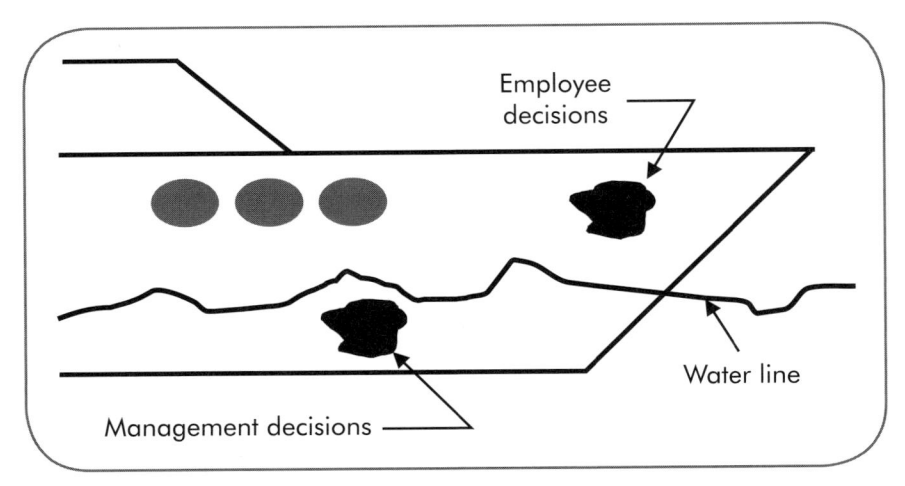

Figure 7-2. Managing the water line.

that of the captain—to monitor the level of empowerment (water line) within the organization as it changes over time. So long as the organization remains comfortably in equilibrium above the water line, everything is under control. But what happens to the captain if his ship unexpectedly hits an iceberg that punches a hole in the hull just above the water line? Is the ship in danger of sinking? The answer is obviously "no" if the seas remain calm and the hole remains above the water line. The first mate can easily handle the problem, make the appropriate decisions, and lead the ship's crew in making the necessary repairs. Certainly the captain will want input during the repair process, but his direct supervision is not required. If, however, the hole is beneath the water line, the ship's situation is much more serious. The captain will take charge of the repairs personally and make all of the required decisions until the ship is again safe and seaworthy.

Much like the captain, a manager's role is to make the beneath-the-water-line decisions for the organization. Those decisions (involving strategic, competitive, business, and financial issues, etc.) will always remain the domain of the manager. The above-the-water-line decisions, however, can be safely delegated

Employee Selection, Direction, Motivation, and Empowerment

to employees within the organization. They accept their roles as decision-makers regarding these important, but not critical, issues within their realm of expertise. They are capable and willing to handle these issues for their manager. This frees the manager to concentrate on those problems and decisions that can sink the organization if not handled correctly.

In today's business climate, no manager has the time to make all the daily decisions required for the organization to run smoothly. It is simply too much for any one individual to handle, no matter how capable and dedicated. Every experienced manager delegates some decision-making authority to his employees. That delegation, however, is done correctly to ensure the organization remains afloat. Successful managers monitor the water line of the organization carefully and often. As employees become more comfortable with decision-making over time and with experience, the water line is lowered by the manager without risk. With their manager's guidance, training, and patience, employees can and will take the reins of many above-the-water-line decisions. When this occurs, a manager's span of control is greatly increased, along with his effectiveness.

> *"Empowered employees are able to make the above-the-water-line decisions, freeing the manager to concentrate on higher-level strategic issues."*

Example

Are you comfortable with making decisions in the workplace? For most people, the answer is "Yes." Now, the questioning goes a step further. Are you comfortable with making decisions in the face of conflict or controversy? If your answer is "No," then management may not be suited to you because your personal water line remains relatively high. Successful managers understand the requirement to make decisions even in the face of conflict. Now answer the third question. Do you, or will you, feel comfortable making decisions that, if wrong, will cause your organization, department, or project to fail miserably? In

Employee Selection, Direction, Motivation, and Empowerment

other words, if your decision is correct, everything works out superbly. If your decision turns out to be incorrect, however, your organization will fail—your ship will sink. In many cases, non-senior managers are uncomfortable with making this level of decision due to lack of experience, training, or preparation. To ask them to do so is foolhardy and unreasonable. The answers to these questions define an individual's personal water line, which must be recognized and respected by management. To ask an employee to make decisions that fall beneath his personal water line is to ask him to do something he is neither willing nor able to do. The end result will always be failure.

Legal Issues Surrounding Empowered Teams

There are some legal issues that all managers must be aware of when planning to launch an empowerment initiative. For example, in December 1992, The National Labor Relations Board (the governing body over labor and employment law) ruled that several of the committees formed by the managers at Electromation actually violated the 1935 National Labor Relations Act. The court's reasoning behind the judgment was that those employee teams were actually employer- versus employee-dominated labor organizations under the letter of the law. Thus, the teams formed by management were illegal. The court issued a similar ruling the following year, adjudicating DuPont's employee teams to be similarly illegal under the guidelines of the 1935 National Labor Relations Act.

The court's decisions at the time, and to this day, are viewed as anti-employee. In essence, the rulings discouraged employees from taking part in decision-making. In light of these decisions, employee involvement and empowerment initiatives came to an abrupt stop while managers decided how to respond. The due diligence conducted by managers of many organizations with empowerment initiatives underway did, however, reveal an interesting fact. The court's rulings were specific to those two cases. When challenged, the court responded by saying that every other situation would be viewed on its own merits; the two decisions must not be viewed as an across-the-board rul-

Employee Selection, Direction, Motivation, and Empowerment

ing against the formation of employee teams. Any organization can, under other circumstances or conditions, form employee teams to assist management in making day-to-day operational decisions in support of the organization's business purposes. So, how do managers stay in sync with labor and employment laws? There are certain criteria that govern a manager's actions when initiating self-directed work teams.

Governing Law

Any employee team or individual employee can be involved in a number of decision-making processes within the workplace, subject to a few exceptions. They may *not* be involved in those decisions that impact:

- the rate of pay,
- the conditions of employment, or
- the hours of employment.

These decisions are off limits; they are the exclusive domain of management. By keeping employees and employee teams away from decisions in these three areas, managers will remain safely within the guidelines of the prevailing labor laws.

Union vs. Non-union Environments

Successful managers apply empowerment techniques in union as well as non-union environments with equal ease and success. In a union environment, however, a few common-sense steps always precede the actual launch of any change or transformation program. When working in a union environment, successful managers always negotiate the entire breath and scope of the empowerment process as they or their organizations have defined it with the union committee or its representatives in advance of launching the change initiative. The roles and responsibilities that managers and union representatives will assume in governing this process are clearly defined. A joint steering committee comprised of management and union representatives is organized. And a joint selection process is utilized by the steering committee to define the scope, timing, and membership in the initial teams. In short, total involvement is sought in all aspects of the empowerment process. Issues and concerns are handled up front in the process rather than battled out later. What these successful managers know is that communication, candor, and cooperation are essential elements of any empowerment process whether in a union or non-union environment.

Quality Circles

In the early 1970s, astute organizations and managers launched empowerment initiatives, dubbed *quality circles*, after a technique used successfully in Japan. In over 75% of the cases, however, quality circles failed to meet management expectations, resulting in their abandonment within a few months. In another 20% of the cases, only moderate tangible results were achieved. But in the remaining 5% of cases, organizations and managers alike found significant measurable benefits from this early attempt at employee empowerment. Why did a few organizations succeed at this early attempt at empowerment while most others failed? The answer lies in the structure and management of those quality circles.

In most cases, organizations formed quality circles as a competitive maneuver in reaction to the recognized successes being seen in the Far East, most notably Japan. Those successes had allowed Japan and China to begin to successfully penetrate many of the domestic and global markets long dominated by U.S. and Western European corporations. The basic intent of these early quality circles was to utilize this proven tool to regain market share that was lost to those foreign competitors.

Initially, U.S. quality circles consisted of groups of employees brought together for brief periods, several times a week. Circle members were given some basic business or process information, along with problems or issues to be considered for improvement. More often than not, the line supervisor or manager of those employee groups was designated as the circle leader. Chain of command prevailed over all circle decisions and recommendations. Recommended actions and solutions were submitted to the circle leader, who either agreed or sent the issue back to the circle for further analysis. If the suggestion was accepted by the circle leader, it was then passed up the organizational ladder for the next succeeding level of management to agree with it or kick it back as unworkable. The submit-reject-reassess process became endless and eventually failed to yield any tangible benefits for either the circle members or management.

Employees saw no difference between what they normally did on the job and the quality circle process. As could be expected, over time managers began to use the quality circles to promote their own agendas. The decision-making structure remained rigidly fixed in the old hierarchical structure governed and protected by management. Because of that rigidity, quality circles were unable to react quickly in a crisis or provide tangible support for management decisions. In frustration, management quickly abandoned quality circles, deeming them unsuitable for the U.S. corporate culture.

The Emergence of Empowerment

Empowerment in its present-day form came along some 20–25 years after quality circles. From a structural perspective, management had learned to delegate more decision-making authority to employees and teams, with less management intervention. The water line was well defined and employees were trained in the fundamentals of situational assessment and problem analysis. Salary scales and job security were well within acceptable levels for most employees, making them open to the concept of employee teams and involvement in the workplace. Most empowerment initiatives met with a modest degree of success initially. Soon afterward, however, employees and empowered teams began wielding their newly found authority as a weapon to achieve individual success and recognition, often at the expense of other employees and teams. Their actions quickly began eradicating the focus on teamwork, the fundamental precept of empowerment. Employees began to view the concept of empowerment more as self-empowerment, competing against one another, and losing sight of the fact that teamwork is vital

Employee Selection, Direction, Motivation, and Empowerment

for any organization to perform effectively. The focus became, "What's best for me?" Empowerment began to flounder.

What is the objective of empowerment? It is employees working with other employees to make decisions that affect their work. It is teams working with other teams, developing a network where all teams utilize one another as a resource and support base for their work. Rather than remaining autonomous, employee teams learn from one another, synergistically building upon the strengths and knowledge of other teams and team members to advance their own capabilities.

Why did so many empowered teams ultimately lose touch with the organization's goals and become internally focused? Why were they ultimately unsuccessful? The answer is simple. Most employees are not initially equipped with the basic skill sets, judgment, and decision-making capabilities required for broad-ranged empowerment. Many, in fact most, employees come from a history where training is job-specific, not inclusive of the broad-based organizational decision-making tools and techniques required to be effective. Most employees have no experience in managerial decision-making or in basic managerial skills. They have seen managers make decisions, but they have rarely been part of the analysis-decision process personally. Most employees have a history of following, basically responding to management's orders or lead. This is an easy, comfortable mode to be in for employees, but it does not serve them well when managers want to empower them to make decisions. In some cases, employees are afraid to make decisions. They tried it once, made a mistake, and were summarily burned for their initiative. Once burned, they now avoid the fire altogether.

Overcoming Fear

To overcome the fear of decision-making, effective managers quickly establish a clear set of rules and guidelines for their employees. Managers define specifically what empowerment is and what it is not, what it includes and what it does not, what decision-making authority is granted to the employees, and what is not. They then establish a comprehensive set of performance metrics and controls to provide the structure for their employees to work within while continuously monitoring progress. Managers also provide their employees with broad-based analysis and assessment training, which will provide insight into how a given team will resolve a business or process problem. All of this will take time. Successful managers always provide their employees with the time and support needed to become competent decision-makers. It will not happen over night; there will be mistakes made. A solid framework to work within combined with patience and consistency from management are important. The manager must be a coach, mentor, and tutor. This is not an easy transition for either a manager or her employees.

> *"Clearly communicated rules and guidelines help employees stay within the decision-making boundaries."*

A Change of Thinking

Empowering employees and employee teams to make decisions that influence the bottom line often requires a significant change in both thinking and action within the organizational hierarchy. It forces senior management to change from being internally focused to being more customer focused, and middle managers from being functionally focused to becoming process focused. In other words, all managers move away from being management centered to a position in which they are truly employee centered. The emphasis is on getting every employee at every level involved within the organization. Change like this, because it is typically completely opposite from how many companies operate today, will take time and consistency in action on the part of all managers to guarantee a successful transition.

Time Frame

Change of the nature required for employee empowerment often takes several months of consistent effort by managers at all levels. For example, the first phase of the empowerment process will typically take up to six months. Trust must be built up before employees will willingly follow their manager's or the facilitator's direction; that is, before they will begin to believe that management is serious about this process and will stay the course. It will often take another six to nine months for employees to begin providing feedback to their manager as they begin to test the concepts and processes behind empowerment. Another nine to 18 months will be required for employees to become truly involved. At this stage of the empowerment process, employees will begin participating on a regular basis in the planning, direction, and control of the critical operational processes within their department, while addressing the daily issues that impact performance. It will take another 18 to 24 months for employees to become truly self-directed, taking responsibility for their own actions. This is the apex of Maslow's hierarchy.

From management's perspective, a high level of control and hands-on supervision of employees will be required for the first six to nine months of the empowerment initiative. Thereafter, it will take six to nine months of active coaching, mentoring, facilitating, and tutoring. At this stage in the process, managers gradually begin to back out of the day-to-day decisions, handing responsibility to the employees for those above-the-water-line actions, but monitoring and coaching them to ensure that the downside of an employee mistake is contained. Once comfortable that employees are able to effectively make decisions, managers turn over responsibility for above-the-water-line actions to the teams. At this final phase of the transition, empowerment has become accepted and embraced by employees as a natural business process.

The empowerment process can, and often does, take two to five years of consistent effort by management. There are no shortcuts. In the past, employees have seen management get excited about new programs only to lose interest when things got tough. "Flavor-of-the-month" initiatives come along, management is excited for a time, and then pressures cause the program to be set aside for another day, which never comes. So it is easy to understand why employees treat new ideas with

Employee Selection, Direction, Motivation, and Empowerment

skepticism. Employees look to their manager to answer the obvious questions, "Why is this empowerment idea any different? You will talk about this for a few weeks or months and when the hype goes away, you will be off chasing something else. So why should I get behind another of your crazy schemes?" It will take time to gain employee acceptance and trust. Management must give it the time and consistency required.

Caution

Empowerment provides tremendous benefit to managers and employees alike. By delegating above-the-water-line decisions and actions to employee teams, managers effectively refocus their own attention on the strategic below-the-waterline issues. For employees, their involvement in the management of the business is a reward they have long sought. But empowerment, unlike many of the other initiatives launched by management in the past, is a two-edged sword. Once employees become actively involved and begin to embrace empowerment within the business culture, the process cannot be reversed without serious repercussions. The message is simple: do not launch into it unless the intent is to see it through. To do otherwise is asking for serious, long-term labor problems.

> "Once empowerment is embraced within the business culture, the process cannot be reversed without serious repercussions."

If management is unsure of the empowerment process or its scope within the organization, a safe way to start the process is to launch the change under the name of "involvement" versus "empowerment." By so doing, managers ease into the process with a focus on getting employees comfortable with the idea of working with their manager on concepts, suggestions, and ideas for process improvements. Once management and employees become comfortable with the process, additional efforts toward empowerment are initiated. If no further change in the scope of the effort is needed, then the process is maintained at that level.

Employee Selection, Direction, Motivation, and Empowerment

CLOSED-LOOP MANAGEMENT

Early in their careers, managers often develop a strategy or "technique" that drives their actions in dealing with employees, ultimately defining their style as a manager. In many cases, that strategy is a fractured, disconnected combination of methodologies and approaches to handling various situations in the workplace, often adopted more by default than by intent. Those techniques and strategies are then used as a template for all employee situations. But this "one-size-fits-all" approach limits a manager's ability to deal effectively with situations that simply do not fit into the template, thus compromising his effectiveness. The various individual aspects of a manager's responsibilities (hiring, motivating, and disciplining employees) remain disjointed with no apparent linkage. As such, the manager finds he is fully capable of dealing with certain elements of his role as a leader while being completely inadequate in dealing with others.

In contrast, more successful managers build their strategies around a closed-loop approach in which all aspects of their management style are interrelated; that is, they are tied by design to every other element in their management style. This linkage, while often invisible to employees and peers, provides consistency and predictability in the manager's style, which employees appreciate and respect.

Managers who apply a disciplined, closed-loop approach are rarely unprepared to deal with a business or personnel problem. They are rarely caught off guard by a surprise event because their approach to team building is predicated on balance, chemistry, and synergy. Every action these managers take is based upon a disciplined dedication to all aspects of their management style. Failure is foreign to them, while success becomes an integral part of the culture of their organizations.

Example

A relatively new manager, Michael was frequently encountering difficulty in motivating certain employees and in dealing with employee performance problems. Recognizing his

Employee Selection, Direction, Motivation, and Empowerment

shortcomings, he was constantly looking for ways to be a better manager. Specifically, he wanted to identify new ways to:

- get employees involved,
- guide and coach employees,
- develop employees,
- get employees to believe more in themselves so they would seek to improve their own skills, and
- get assignments done on time and correctly.

To learn more about proven management tools and techniques, Michael approached his manager and mentor, Roger Roy, for advice. He explained his concerns and failings with Roger, and asked for his input on how to improve. In particular, Michael asked for Roger's advice relative to specific tools and techniques he and other highly successful managers used to maximize performance within a dynamic organization where change is expected and must be dealt with on a constant basis.

Roger referred Michael to the local library to obtain information on Red Auerbach, pioneer of the closed-loop management style. Michael was puzzled as he did not recognize the name. He had expected to be referred to known gurus in the management field like Jack Welch of GE, Peter Drucker, or Chris Galvin of Motorola. Nevertheless, confident in Roger's capabilities as a manager, Michael went to the library that night after work to see what he could find on Red Auerbach. While at the library, he found a tape entitled "Dedication and Desire, the Red Auerbach Story." Michael checked it out, took it home, and stuck it in the VCR. The first frame revealed a little man with a big cigar talking about basketball. Michael was not a basketball aficionado and never even really watched the sport, so he was immediately turned off by the analogy. He was looking for business solutions and management techniques to implement them. So, dismissing the tapes applicability to his problems, Michael hit the stop button, rewound the tape, and took it back to the library without viewing it any further.

The next morning Michael saw Roger in the hall. Roger stopped to ask whether he had found anything on Red Auerbach. (Indeed, Roger was a closed-loop manager.) Michael indicated

Employee Selection, Direction, Motivation, and Empowerment

that he had found a tape on Auerbach, but did not listen to it because it was about a basketball coach and that really was not what he had in mind when he asked for input. Roger shook his head disappointedly. He proceeded to point out that, by prejudging the content, Michael had missed the key point. Yes, Auerbach was a basketball coach and a general manager. But more importantly than that, Auerbach had pioneered the closed-loop management style, which had been adopted by numerous business leaders throughout a multitude of industry segments. In short, Auerbach had developed a set of management tools and techniques that could be applied to any business setting successfully. Roger wanted Michael to learn about Auerbach's technique; his prowess as a basketball coach was unimportant.

That evening after work, Michael went back to the library, got the tape, and started listening to it. In fact, he listened to the tape at least a dozen times over the course of several days. Each time he listened, he got more out of it. Like Roger, and numerous other predecessors in leadership, Michael began to deploy Auerbach's techniques for selecting employees, motivating them and, when necessary, disciplining them. Throughout his career, he found that Auerbach's closed-loop methodologies worked consistently, regardless of the industry in which he worked. Those fundamental management techniques were equally applicable and equally successful in any environment.

Closed-loop Management Model

The closed-loop management approach consists of four key elements, all of which are essential in creating a management model that functions consistently (see Figure 7-3):

- employee selection,
- motivation,
- discipline, and
- tradition of success.

The true secret to closed-loop management is the interrelationships between each of these elements. No single element stands alone. They are all be linked to the others to maximize the synergy possible from this dynamic management tool.

Employee Selection, Direction, Motivation, and Empowerment

EMPLOYEE SELECTION
Self-disciplined and self-motivated
Role player, mentor, and student
Focused on team results and success
Complementary skill sets
Works well under pressure
Dogged and detailed
Manages risk effectively

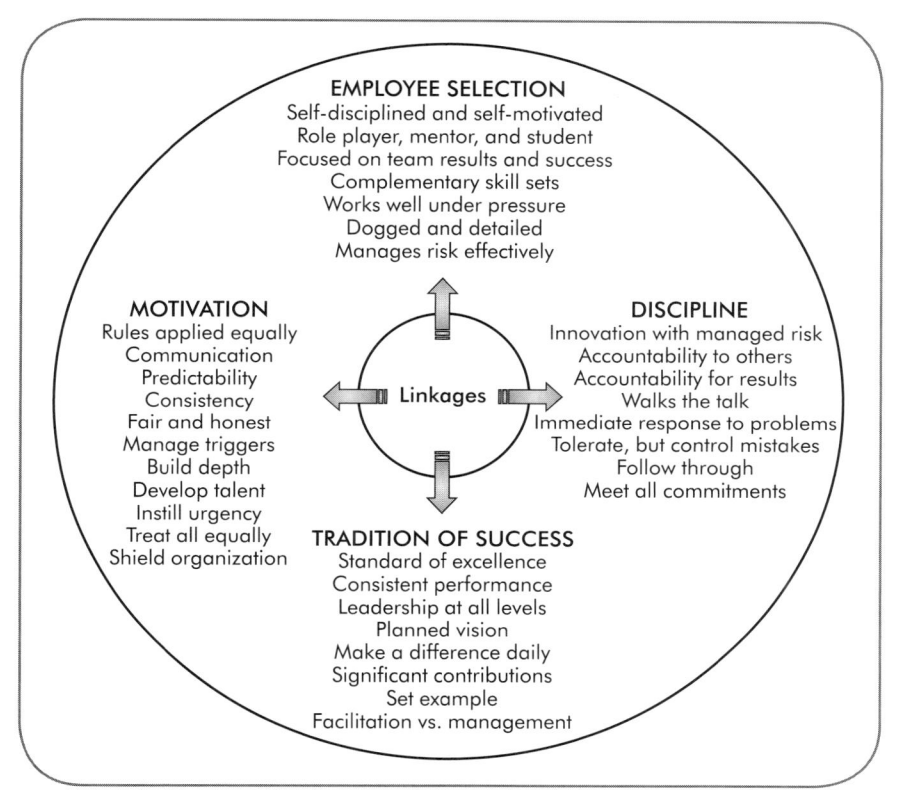

MOTIVATION
Rules applied equally
Communication
Predictability
Consistency
Fair and honest
Manage triggers
Build depth
Develop talent
Instill urgency
Treat all equally
Shield organization

Linkages

DISCIPLINE
Innovation with managed risk
Accountability to others
Accountability for results
Walks the talk
Immediate response to problems
Tolerate, but control mistakes
Follow through
Meet all commitments

TRADITION OF SUCCESS
Standard of excellence
Consistent performance
Leadership at all levels
Planned vision
Make a difference daily
Significant contributions
Set example
Facilitation vs. management

Figure 7-3. Closed-loop management model.

Employee Selection

Hiring the right personnel is paramount to building a cohesive, efficient organization. The selection of good employees, however, goes well beyond just their business, administrative, or technical skill sets. There are times when the most technically qualified candidates simply will not fit in. For an organization to reach its maximum potential, true chemistry must exist among its employees, both on a professional and a business level. It is that chemistry that ultimately creates the synergy evident in every high-performance organization. Thus, during the selection

Employee Selection, Direction, Motivation, and Empowerment

process, closed-loop managers routinely assess the technical and people skills the candidate possesses, as well as how effectively and comfortably that candidate will interrelate with the other members of the organization.

To illustrate, how often has a sports team comprised of "average" players succeeded in winning a championship? Possessing no exceptional talent or superstars, the team is forced to build upon the individual strengths and relationships that exist between its members. Team members are forced to rely heavily upon one another to be successful. Everyone is focused on one goal, one approach, and one outcome. They all pull together and back each other up to minimize the impact of a mistake. Team members support one another on and off the field. No one slacks off. Each member of the team has a personal obligation to put forth the maximum effort possible. This is why the team succeeds. Great organizations are not necessarily comprised of great individuals; they are comprised of great chemistry and teamwork.

The selection process assesses individuals based upon the following criteria.

- No room for superstars—each employee and/or candidate for employment is committed to the organization's success first and foremost. Every manager, every organization needs employees who are committed to achieving the performance and objectives the organization has been chartered to accomplish. The individual's goals in becoming part of the team are to support the other members of the team by contributing skill and talent for the betterment of the entire organization. In most organizations there is no room for superstars—individuals who only want to better themselves rather than (or sometimes at the expense of) the organization as a whole. In reality, superstars join an organization for solely personal reasons—to position themselves for promotion, higher salaries, or move on to another organization. They care little about the other members of the unit or the teamwork therein. Their interest is in letting their own star shine. If the organization

Employee Selection, Direction, Motivation, and Empowerment

fails, so be it. They, at least, still come out a winner. Most superstars have exceptional talent, capability, and technical skills. What they lack is the desire and dedication to work in a team environment. As they see it, there is no "I" in team. From a manager's perspective, a superstar lacking the ability to work within a team environment is of little value to the organization.

So how does a manager spot the superstar during an interview? The experienced closed-loop manager asks open-ended questions about the candidate's former position, company, or accomplishments. He listens closely for how many times the candidate uses "I" versus "we" in the conversation. He asks about the roles the candidate played in reaching the organization's objectives through accomplishment of various projects or assignments, along with his or her view of the strengths and weaknesses of other employees and managers in the former organization. No individual accomplishes anything of significance alone. If the candidate indicates that success was largely due to his or her efforts alone, then a superstar mentality exists and it is generally wise to look for other candidates.

- Select role players. Within every organization lies the requirement for employees who are capable of contributing different talents at different times. These individuals are comfortable performing a multitude of tasks and assignments outside of their normal roles. For example, when a manager takes a vacation or is otherwise out of the office, there is a need to delegate authority to a subordinate during the manager's absence. To do so, there must be employees capable of stepping into the management role for a period of time. Then once the manager returns, that employee is comfortable returning to his or her normal role within the organization. The same holds true in assigning project managers or project leads. In one project, a given employee may contribute as a project team member, yet in another as the project manager. Individuals willing

Employee Selection, Direction, Motivation, and Empowerment

to take on these differing roles give a manager more flexibility in addressing unforeseen business needs, as well as in accomplishing the organization's day-to-day activities. Because of their willingness to work with others in supportive and leadership roles, these individuals are also generally better received within the organization. They are often the informal leaders within the organization because they are trusted by everyone and feared by no one.

Michael Jordan is a good example of a role player. He was an exceptional basketball player, but was he a superstar? Of course, he was in the eyes of his fans. But was he an employee who focused on what was best for Michael Jordan? Or, was he an individual who focused on what was best for the Chicago Bulls? There is no question that he had superstar capabilities and talents. His greatness, however, came from his sincere focus on the success of his organization. For him, the "most valuable player" title was of little personal value. It was the team winning the championship that mattered most. Jordan was a true role player. At times a leader, teacher, coach, mentor, disciplinarian, and friend, he was whatever his organization required of him; he took on whatever role was needed for his organization to succeed. That is exactly what a manager needs from every employee. Contributors, in whatever fashion or form, are required for the organization to succeed.

- Select candidates with complementary skills. Hiring new employees with the same skill sets possessed by others within the department or organization is a common mistake made by inexperienced managers. Successful managers follow a policy of hiring individuals that bring complementary skills to the organization. Individually, every manager and every employee has strengths and weaknesses. A good manager analyzes those characteristics prior to the interviewing

> "Successful managers hire employees that bring complementary skills to the organization."

process to determine where the weaknesses lie within the organization. Then, when interviewing new candidates, they look for strengths that will offset those weaknesses. The reason for this practice is simple. To ensure organizational balance and alignment, it is mandatory to hire individuals possessing skills, capacities, and perspectives that will increase the overall balance, strength, and capability of the organization. Individuals bringing differing perspectives also enhance the creativity of the organization. When everyone thinks alike, the organization takes on a myopic perspective, and when that occurs, progress and creativity stop.

A Red Auerbach example illustrates the point. Early in his tenure, Auerbach drafted a young college player by the name of Bill Russell. To most industry experts, Bill Russell was deemed to be a mediocre basketball player coming out of college. Even though Russell's team had won the NCAA championship, Bill was considered to be a very one-dimensional player. He was, without question, a defensive standout. Offensively, however, he lacked the skills of many college players, such as Bob Cousey. Thus the industry experts concluded that Russell was not capable of performing successfully in the NBA.

But Auerbach saw Russell differently. He saw a skill set that was sorely lacking within his organization—defense. He also saw in Russell a dedicated, hard-working, focused individual who was unafraid to teach those critical skills to others. Russell was someone who had always demonstrated a strong desire to constantly learn new skills to enhance his value to his organization. The combination was exactly what Auerbach wanted in an employee. During their initial meetings, Auerbach advised Russell that his role, his complementary skill, was to bring balance to the organization through his defensive skills. He asked Russell to teach the other players his techniques so that they, too, would become better all-around contributors.

Bill was more than willing to share what he knew about defense. Equally as important to the organization, he was more than willing to learn offensive skills from the other players. Over time, Russell became one of the best all-around players in the history of the game. In his own mind, Russell was never a superstar. He simply brought another dimension to his organization. Humility and talent make a good combination.

- Look for individuals who will perform under pressure. A key trait to look for in an individual is tenacity—someone who will not buckle or become frustrated when the going gets tough. Things go wrong. Deadlines arise unexpectedly. New projects are assigned when the organization is least prepared to handle them. This is the real world. Managers need employees in whom they can be confident—those who are results-oriented and who will accomplish objectives. These employees adopt assignments as their own and are committed to seeing them through. If a problem arises, they inform their manager immediately. Then together, they find a solution. There are no surprises, just results. The "go-to" employees that managers rely upon in difficult circumstances, these employees always find solutions with little oversight from their manager because they possess an innate dedication and commitment to get the job done. During the interview process, closed-loop managers ask candidates about obstacles they encountered in their last assignments and how those obstacles were overcome. The manager then listens for the results achieved and makes note if they give excuses about why they failed.

- Hire a replacement. Smart managers look for individuals with the ability to both lead and follow. They look for individuals who are capable of stepping into the leadership role when their manager is unavailable. This is a key piece of advice: when interviewing new candidates for employment, savvy managers always look for an individual capable of replacing themselves.

Employee Selection, Direction, Motivation, and Empowerment

Some managers feel threatened by high-potential candidates or employees. So rather than take the risk that those individuals might challenge them for their job, they take the low road by hiring less competent candidates. There is a feeling of security in doing so; the manager is always recognized as being a step above his employees. The problem is, because there is no one within the department or work group capable of stepping up into that manager's position, the manager is always passed over for promotion. The promotion always goes to another manager who has developed a worthy replacement capable of doing that manager's job today. For senior management, it is simply the low-risk solution. Managers are promoted only when a suitable successor is immediately ready to step in.

> "Managers are promoted only if they have developed a replacement who is capable of doing that manager's job today."

During the interview process, experienced managers will always ask the candidate to respond to the question, "What do you want to be doing in three to five years?" The response they are looking for is, "I want to be in your job!" The next question they ask is, "So what plans have you developed to allow you to prepare yourself for my position?" These managers then listen for a logical career development plan that contains well-thought-out details and metrics. If, indeed, the candidate has a solid plan in place to accomplish the task, then this is someone who deserves a closer look. If there is no plan, or the response is weak on details, then the candidate has not yet developed a career plan that will allow him to accomplish that objective. Consequently, the person simply may not be a good candidate for the job.

- Hire creative thinkers. Today's business environments and technologies constantly demand new solutions and approaches. As a result, savvy managers are always on the look out for individuals with the ability to bring new perspectives to business challenges. These employees constantly challenge the status quo looking for alternative approaches and methodologies. They are never satisfied with the reasoning, "It's the way we have always done it, so do it the same way." In many organizations, these individuals are considered the rebels, the nonconformists. But without these off-the-wall thinkers, breakthrough ideas never happen and organizations become stagnant. Once that happens, good organizations fail simply because they continue to do the same things that always made them successful in the past. Change is a requirement for continued success, and closed-loop managers recognize that change typically comes from innovative employees.

A point of fact, creative thinkers are tougher employees to manage. They will keep even the most progressive manager on her toes. But the bottom line is they will also keep their manager, fellow employees, and organization sharp. Their job, their role, is simply to challenge the status quo—the establishment. That is the complementary skill they bring to the organization—the ability to keep everyone a little uncomfortable, to test the proven boundaries, to look for ways to improve even the best business processes and practices. Given the freedom to use their creativity, these employees will develop solutions that are unique approaches conventional employees and managers would never have considered. They can breathe life into stagnant organizations and make managers look brilliant. From a management perspective, however, their creativity must be properly channeled and controlled because they recognize no limits to the things that can be accomplished. Creative thinkers must be given a healthy dose of individual freedom, but that freedom must come with reasonable boundaries. They must be

> "Creative thinkers are tougher employees to manage, but they will keep the organization sharp."

led, because they cannot be managed. Managers of these highly motivated employees keep a bottle of aspirin in the top drawer of their desk. They will definitely need it. But the payback is worth it.

- Select teachers and students. While not to be taken literally, effective managers figuratively select candidates who are willing to share the things they have learned during their career with their fellow employees. These employees become the informal leaders within the organization because they openly share their skills and talents to help others perform better. Unlike many employees, they do not keep everything they know "close to the vest" to ensure their own job security or personal value to the organization. Rather, they openly embrace every opportunity to help another employee in whatever way they can. They are an open book to all.

> "Closed-loop managers look for both traits, teacher and student, in the people they hire."

But for the teacher to provide true value to the organization, the organization must also contain employees who are willing to learn new skills and techniques from their fellow employees. These individuals are not fearful of admitting that they do not have all the answers or that other approaches to a job, task, or problem might be superior to their own. They are open to new insights, perspectives, and approaches from whomever they can get them.

Closed-loop managers look for both traits, teacher and student, within the same person. They seek individuals who are willing to better themselves by bettering the organization and everyone in it. These are unselfish individuals who are willing to play multiple roles. Bill Russell was that type of employee—a teacher and a student. That is what made him so great, along with the organizations and managers for which he worked.

Savvy managers reinforce the teacher and student traits in their employees by sending them to outside training sessions on a regular basis. Not only will the employees learn new skills that will enhance their value to the organization, but they also can teach those new skills to others. An employee who receives outside training is asked to share what he learned with others in the department or work group by giving a one to two hour overview of the material. This technique broadens internal mentoring among employees which, in turn, strengthens interpersonal relationships. Employees are recognized for their skills, making them even more comfortable in assuming other roles within the organization.

Motivation

Selecting quality, capable employees is important, but it is equally important to effectively motivate these high-potential employees to get the maximum performance possible from them. Recognizing that these are talented, highly skilled individuals, closed-loop managers focus much of their effort building upon those strengths by incorporating motivational techniques.

Closed-loop management practices provide a balance between motivation and discipline, with the distinction between the two often being narrow. But effective motivation always begins with an understanding of the drivers behind employee behavior. In other words, determining the personal, managerial, and organizational factors that drive an employee or group of employees to react or respond to a manager's direction differently than either expected or desired. Results from two recent studies of employee behavior have yielded a consistent perspective on why employees do or do not respond to various motivational techniques utilized by management. To begin with, the myth that American workers are less motivated or less efficient than their international counterparts has been proven false. As Figure 7-4 illustrates, American employees are typically more productive and more committed to their employer's success than their peers in Europe. This fact is reinforced by the results of

Employee Selection, Direction, Motivation, and Empowerment

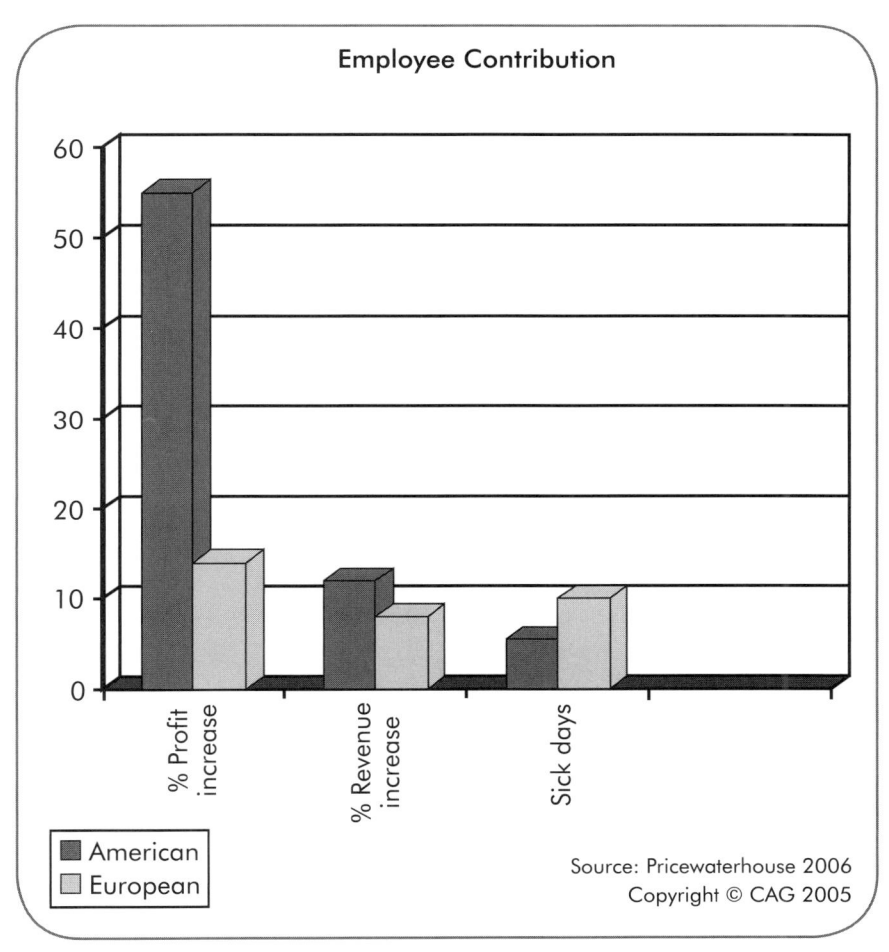

Figure 7-4. Comparison of U.S. vs. European employees.

a recent report sponsored by 12 Fortune 100 corporations (see Table 7-1). The data provides insight for managers into the two overriding factors driving employee behavior:

1. Employees are increasingly concerned about job security.
2. Employees recognize that their personal success and that of their employers are directly linked.

Employee Selection, Direction, Motivation, and Empowerment

Table 7-1. Report of Families and Work Institute of New York.

- The average work week exceeds 45 hours
- 65% of employees indicate they are required to work very fast
- 80% of employees indicate they are required to work very hard
- 58% of employees indicate they do not have excessive amounts of work
- 59% of employees indicate they are stressed on the job
- 60% of employees indicate their jobs can be frustrating at times
- 42% of employees indicate they have experienced a layoff or downsizing personally
- 64% of employees indicate they are extremely loyal to their employer
- 90% of employees indicate they are willing to work harder to ensure their employer's continuing survival and success
- 98% of employees indicate they try to do the best job possible no matter what obstacles they experience on the job
- 52% of employees indicate they receive personal satisfaction from knowing that they have done a good job versus 30% who indicate respect and recognition from their superior was most important

Successful managers incorporate these two critical factors into their motivational techniques on a day-to-day basis. They focus on communicating operational and financial results, providing employee performance metrics that are quantifiable and focused on organizational success factors, and honestly recognizing employee performance against those criteria, both good and bad. Closed-loop managers also know to apply different motivational techniques to their employees, recognizing that every employee is different.

Effective motivation techniques work in tandem with an overall management strategy that includes the following.

- Add depth to the organization. Successful managers realize the critical importance of personal growth for employees and for the organization, so they constantly work to build depth throughout the work force. Many managers openly point to the importance of building depth within their organization through succession planning, cross-training, and a multitude of other skill-set-broadening approaches. Yet those same managers will fall back on the excuse that they simply do not have the time to develop that depth. That logic is pure foolishness.

Building depth within an organization is a dual-phased process that begins with the hiring and promotion of individuals who are willing to learn and take on expanded responsibilities—those who are capable of performing numerous roles within the organization. Once hired, however, these individuals require guidance and leadership to expand their skills to prepare them for additional responsibilities. Closed-loop management principles promote the use of internal mentors to develop these employees. Each senior member of the organization is required to select and train one or more replacements. New employees are assigned to senior employees for development and mentoring. This use of the teacher/student philosophy has multiple benefits to employees and managers alike.

> "Closed-loop managers assign senior employees to mentor new hires."

1. The senior employees are motivated to take on the role of mentor for younger employees, thus allowing them to share their knowledge among those eager and willing to learn from their experiences. By mentoring, the senior employees develop a qualified backup who is capable of sharing the project and/or operational load. In so doing, the senior employee is made available for upcoming promotional opportunities.

2. The new employee is motivated to make her mentor look good. New employees will work hard to prove they

Employee Selection, Direction, Motivation, and Empowerment

are worthy of the gift of knowledge given them by their senior. The relationship, over time, becomes personal. When that happens, a true bond develops between the employees, making the chemistry between them stronger.

3. A network of communication and cooperation forms among the manager's employees, which promotes a team environment. This culture encourages employees to take risks without the fear that a failure will bring down their organization or their careers. With capable backups at every level, mistakes can be controlled through backstopping. This control mechanism encourages all employees to push the limits, challenge the status quo, and alter organizational paradigms with minimal risk. As trust and chemistry grow over time, the employees increase their individual and mutual capacities and capabilities; thus overall organizational efficiency is improved.

- Expel the politicians. Politicians exist within many organizations for various reasons; some are the result of poor management or conflicting performance metrics, others because of individual superstar personalities. Once recognized, closed-loop managers move expeditiously to address the problem by altering the metrics so that all employees are focused in the same direction. If that is unsuccessful, the next action is to rid the organization of the politically motivated through termination or reassignment. If left unchecked, politicians will introduce negative outside influences that will keep an organization in turmoil and destroy the chemistry within the group. To avoid confrontation, ineffective managers use the excuse that these are talented individuals who are needed because of the unique skills they possess. Others reason that

> *"If left unchecked, the negative influence of the politician will destroy the chemistry of the work group."*

a warm body is better than no body. Neither is correct. Politicians, while individually productive, always lower organizational productivity to a much greater extent.

- Rotate assignments. Closed-loop management promotes the rotation of assignments among employees to aid in their personal growth and development. This often entails moving employees into assignments that they are not formally trained in but will need experience in to prepare them for the next promotion. While this facet of closed-loop management seems unusual to many, it is actually of dual benefit. First, it broadens the perspective of the employee by exposing them to the constraints and problems in other areas. That knowledge provides the employee with a better understanding of how other disciplines impact or hinder the operations of other departments. Secondly, those within the new department benefit from the differing perspective of outsiders who view their department as either a customer or supplier of information, materials, or resources. The value in rotating assignments exists for both the employee and the organization. The more employees know about the day-to-day operations, problems, and constraints faced by other departments within the company, the better decisions they will make as they go about their own routines.

> "Closed-loop managers promote assignment rotation to aid the personal growth and development of employees."

For example, it is a good practice to move an engineer into departments like Purchasing, Manufacturing, or Marketing where he is exposed to supply base, production, or customer issues. Once returned to the Engineering department, the engineer brings a broadened perspective of the importance of design and drawing accuracy, manufacturability issues, and sourcing limitations. That knowledge will make him a better engineer. In the same respect, the engineer will leave behind a better understanding of the engineering requirements associated with designing new products and processes, how sourcing issues impact design reliability and cost, how process capability and repeatability affects design reliability, and how the initial accuracy of customer specifications influences the timing and cost of the product development cycle.

The same holds true for employees in other areas. Marketing professionals will bring Engineering and Manufacturing departments a better understanding of customer needs and perceptions. Accounting professionals will reinforce the need for fiscal responsibility in product design, manufacturing operations, and supplier development. Technical services professionals will bring a dose of reality into sales functions that have a tendency to sell products the company does not commonly manufacture.

A similar technique is to bring functional managers from other organizations into department meetings on a monthly basis to discuss how the departments impact or influence one another. The benefit of this two-way sharing of needs, expectations, and problems is often invaluable to increasing understanding and cooperation between the departments. Again, knowing more about the big picture and how each department or function fits into it brings perspective and clarity for employees and managers alike.

- Identify the triggers. Closed-loop managers understand their employees very well. It is this understanding that makes them excellent facilitators. A closed-loop manager quickly learns the individual triggers of each employee, those that motivate and de-motivate. Every employee in the organization has a different set of triggers. If a manager uses the wrong trigger in an effort to motivate an employee, the end result will be that the action will actually de-motivate the employee, exactly the opposite of what was expected and desired.

Employee Selection, Direction, Motivation, and Empowerment

For example, some employees are motivated by money, while others are motivated by a pat on the back, recognition, or acknowledgment as a leader within their peer group. These are the individual triggers that stir employees into action; they create a positive level of anxiety. That's right, "positive anxiety," also commonly known as the "sense of urgency." Managers recognize that from time to time, it is necessary to raise the level of performance within the work group beyond that of normal steady-state operations. Under normal circumstances, the routine performance level is totally acceptable. But in times of crisis when there is a deadline to be made or a project milestone to be met, every employee is required to step up his or her contribution to the organization. To create that sense of urgency in meeting the targeted objective, managers utilize the triggers, which are specific to each employee, to bring out that extra effort.

> "The application of motivational triggers allows a manager to ramp up productivity in times of crisis."

Isolating an employee's triggers requires a conscious effort on a manager's part to study the individual through interactive discussions and observations. Anything that elicits a behavioral reaction in an employee is a trigger, either positive or negative. Keys to an individual's triggers include:

- actions, assignments, or events that seem to energize the employee;

- individual hobbies or extracurricular activities of particular interest to the employee;

- situations that create anger or frustration in the employee;

- actions or events that cause the employee to pause and reassess;

- actions or events that create indifference in the employee; or
- things, actions, or situations that make the employee laugh openly.

Closed-loop managers recognize that an employee's triggers are often impacted or influenced by the individual's place within the hierarchy of needs. For example, if an employee who is normally motivated by more responsibility or lead roles within projects suddenly finds herself in a financial bind, her trigger will shift to overtime opportunities where she can earn additional wages to alleviate her present situation. To ensure maximum organizational effectiveness, closed-loop managers constantly evaluate and weigh the needs of their organization against the needs of their employees. Adjustments are then made to ensure that expectations and capabilities remain in sync.

- Shield the organization. Another of the closed-loop management fundamentals, and one of the things that Auerbach was absolutely brilliant at, is shielding employees from negative outside influences. Closed-loop managers control negative influences that can impact organizational performance or chemistry so employees can go about their daily routines without the frustration of politics, constantly changing priorities, the addition of unsupportable projects, unreasonable expectations, etc.

Productivity and efficiency are the direct result of employees who are afforded the opportunity to work day-in and day-out without unreasonable interruptions. The opposite is also true. When employees are consistently hassled by issues and problems outside of their control, disrupting the normal work patterns of employees, frustration quickly sets in. Once that occurs, employees become engrossed in daily fire-fighting, ignoring or overlooking obvious opportunities for improvement. Organizational productivity quickly wanes as employees are constantly whipsawed from one assignment to another, never completing any.

In many respects, management is like a one-way valve. When things are going well, compliments are flowing, and operations are running at peak efficiency, the credit passes through the manager directly to the employees. But when things are in turmoil, criticism surrounds the organization, and performance is well off expected levels, the buck stops with the manager. Why? Because the responsibility for failure lies with the manager; he failed to provide his employees with the opportunity to succeed by not shielding them from the outside influences that disrupt organizational chemistry and synergy.

Discipline

High-performance organizations are highly disciplined organizations. It is the structure, and the acceptance of that structure, which allows each employee to maintain focus on the common goals, performance, and ultimate success of the organization. With discipline comes pride, integrity, and trust. But there can be no structure without rules and guidelines that establish boundaries of permissible behavior and expected performance, just as there can be no discipline unless those same rules and guidelines are enforced equally upon all employees.

> *"Strict enforcement of organizational rules and guidelines promotes self-direction and makes micro-management unnecessary."*

Few organizations are self-disciplined at first. It is the responsibility of the closed-loop manager to solidify the organization's infrastructure by instituting rules and guidelines that will govern all employees. Thereafter, rather than micro-managing every facet of the organization's day-to-day operations, the manager simply monitors the perimeter to ensure all employees remain within the established guidelines (see Figure 7-5). Over time, the organization

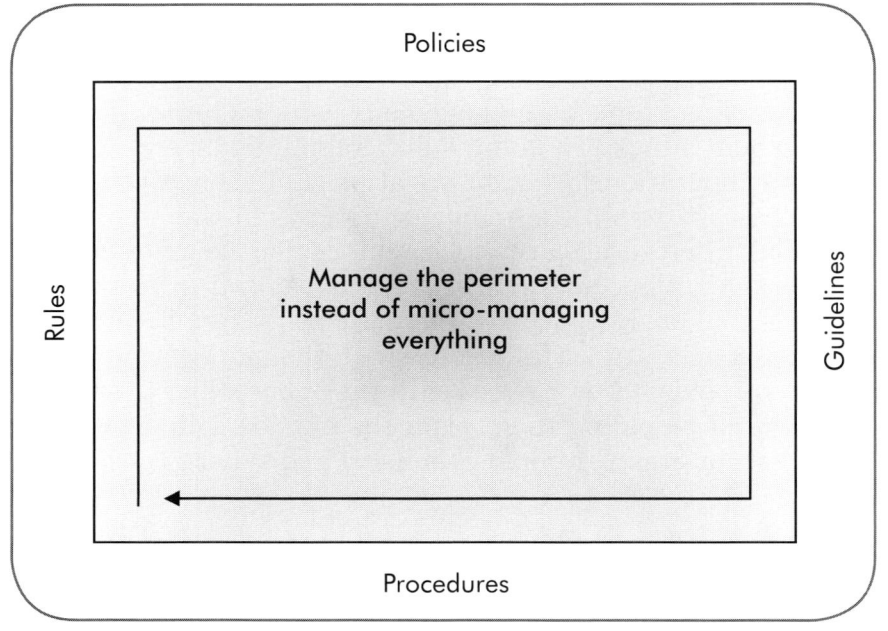

Employee Selection, Direction, Motivation, and Empowerment

```
                    Policies

    ┌─────────────────────────────────┐
    │                                 │
    │                                 │
Rules│    Manage the perimeter         │Guidelines
    │    instead of micro-managing    │
    │    everything                   │
    │                                 │
    │ ←                               │
    └─────────────────────────────────┘

                   Procedures
```

Figure 7-5. Managing the perimeter of the organization.

becomes self-disciplined; mistakes are contained and controlled within the group through strict enforcement of the rules by all employees.

Within any organization, discipline involves:

- handling the requirements of the job—in other words, doing what is expected each and every day,
- working within the rules of the organization,
- making personal sacrifices for the betterment and benefit of the organization, and
- exercising self-control.

Discipline also entails encouraging employees to make a difference, not just to be content with being part of a good organization or to just look busy. Rather, every employee is required to make himself an invaluable part of the organization through his contribution, work ethic, and commitment in good times and bad.

Employee Selection, Direction, Motivation, and Empowerment

A technique used by many closed-loop managers to reinforce self-discipline is to ask each employee to write his or her own epitaph. In other words, employees document how they want to be remembered by fellow employees after they leave the organization. Once an employee has completed the assignment, the closed-loop manager incorporates it into the employee's performance evaluations. In addition, the employee is challenged to review the writing at least once weekly and critically evaluate how effective he was in living up to his own goal. It is surprising how well employees perform when they are required to live up to their own standards.

Experienced closed-loop managers recognize that problems occasionally occur whenever people work closely together on a daily basis. Therefore, an effective manager is constantly watchful of the group's dynamics, paying particular attention to what's going on within the organization and its employees. In particular, a manager looks for personality issues that will negatively impact the chemistry within the group. When isolated, these issues are quickly and firmly addressed. This is a critical aspect of discipline because for individuals to work closely together in a high-performance organization, they must trust one another. Simply put, employees do not trust those they do not like or respect.

Auerbach was a master disciplinarian. Red established rules and guidelines that governed his organization. Once those rules and guidelines were established, he did not micromanage. Red simply stepped back, allowing and encouraging his employees to become self-directed. Employees developed their own plans, executed them, and took responsibility for the results, over time becoming totally empowered. However, if any employee broke the rules or stepped outside of the established guidelines, Red reacted quickly and predictably. It did not matter who committed the infraction. He treated everyone equally—everyone was expected to uphold the rules. There were no exceptions; no one received any special treatment. It made no difference to Red if the employee had been with the organization for an extended time or had just joined the organization, if he was the most valuable individual in the organization or the least. Everyone was treated the same.

Treating every employee the same and holding all accountable to the same standards is absolutely vital to building chemistry. Employees quickly recognize that management looks at each individual as a contributor in a different role, with each being as valuable as the other in reaching and maintaining the targeted level of performance. That recognition brings into focus the fact that it takes every employee, pulling his or her own weight, to make the organization succeed. This is the beauty of closed-loop management. It creates an environment in which each employee knows the expectations and rules, and why it is essential to perform to expected levels. Peer pressure becomes a key driving force behind the organization's success. Once the employees recognize that their manager will, in fact, consistently enforce the rules of the organization, they will conform and become self-policing. When that happens, a manager rarely is forced to discipline an employee for any reason.

Tradition of Success

The fourth element of closed-loop management is derived from the manager himself. It is the tradition that the closed-loop manager creates through his own history of successes. When employees are associated with a manager who has developed a reputation of consistently sound and effective leadership and of consistent and positive achievements, employees recognize the requirement to sustain that legacy. By association, the employee, as part of an organization led by a recognized successful leader, becomes himself recognized as a winner. With that recognition comes the responsibility to ensure that the tradition is upheld through the employee's own contribution. This is a strong motivational factor that drives each employee within the organization to achieve excellent results consistently, while at the same time supporting all other members within the organization to ensure their success as well. It requires self-discipline to make the right and not just the easy decisions, to do what is

Employee Selection, Direction, Motivation, and Empowerment

right for the organization versus taking the easy way out, and to face organizational challenges directly and overcome them as a unit.

Auerbach had a history of success. His organizations were always well-managed, effective, consistent winners. Becoming part of his organization was recognized as the apex of achievement. Every professional wanted to become part of Red's organization, as did every back-office, staff, or support professional. His employees created their own credo, called "Celtic Pride." To employees within the organization, failure was not an option. Success was the only acceptable result; every employee was expected to contribute to that success each and every day—no exceptions.

Leadership traditions are based upon the manager's philosophy and his consistent execution of those beliefs. In other words, closed-loop managers "walk the talk." They set high standards of excellence for themselves and their employees. They build and reinforce strong leadership skills at all levels within their organizations. Their vision for the organization is well planned, well executed, and clearly understood by all. They set the example through their actions and words. They encourage every employee at every level to make a difference to the organization each day and to have a positive impact on those around them. They recognize that success is built upon every decision and every action. As a result, nothing is random or reactive. The plan for success is comprehensive, realistic, and achievable. Every employee within the organization wins, or no one wins.

> "Closed-loop managers 'walk the talk.'"

Closed-loop management, especially when dealing with technical professionals, dictates that managers take on differing roles at various stages in the organization's evolution. When an organization is struggling or in its youth, and generally during the first five to six months after a new manager comes on board, the manager is required to play the role of a strong, almost Theory X type of manager. Thereafter when

Employee Selection, Direction, Motivation, and Empowerment

the organization stabilizes and employees become more self-directed (the next 9–18 months), the manager transitions into a facilitation role. At this stage, employees are capable of accepting higher degrees of empowerment without the manager's intervention. It is at this time that facilitation is the proper management style.

On a good day, technical professionals are tough to manage. They do not want to be micro-managed. They want to be guided; they want to be led. Self-motivated, they want to work for a manager who will set the priorities, guidelines, and ground rules, then let them do the work themselves. This puts the manager in the role of a facilitator—an individual who assists his employees in making decisions rather than making decisions for them. Facilitating is not directing or managing, but rather guiding, coaching, tutoring, and mentoring employees through consistent positive stimulation and reinforcement. Key to facilitation is identifying things that help employees to be successful, and then building upon those successes to create a culture and tradition of success within the department, which becomes self-perpetuating.

COMMUNICATION

Organizations that fail to communicate, fail. The same holds true for managers. Closed-loop management is based upon an infrastructure of effective communication because communication is the key element in teamwork. Effective managers create a vision for their organization; they then communicate that vision through word and action. The mission statement acts as a roadmap, providing precise instructions and directions regarding how the manager's vision for the organization is to be realized. Performance measurements track progress toward achievement of the organizational goals. Simply put, employees must know what is planned and how they will be measured if they are expected to execute those plans. In all cases, communication precedes action.

"Organizations that fail to communicate, fail."

Employee Selection, Direction, Motivation, and Empowerment

Though certainly important, it is not enough for employees to know what their manager expects or what other employees within the department are doing under routine circumstances. Employees also must know what their manager and fellow employees will do under abnormal circumstances. In other words, there must be predictability among the members of the unit so its members work in harmony and unison under all circumstances.

It is an unfortunate fact, but many managers fail to set aside time to communicate with employees. Instead they write memos or e-mails that send a blanket message to all employees. They lose touch with the "individuals" within the department because they never communicate with them personally. Communication is a two-way activity that involves both speaking and listening. Many managers do a poor job of speaking . . . and an absolutely horrendous job of listening. Closed-loop managers allocate a minimum of two hours each day to walking around and talking with employees in their workstations, listening to their ideas and problems, and working through the details of a solution. Managers that are highly visible and accessible are better respected and less feared. Yes, feared . . . there is a natural inclination for employees to fear someone who has authority and control over them. Accessibility and responsiveness to addressing the employee's problems or just listening to his ideas helps to break down that innate fear and convert it into respect. Just where do managers get the extra two hours out of a day to talk personally with employees? They stop attending useless meetings that accomplish absolutely nothing. The time is always better spent with employees working out problems and formulating plans for the future.

Closed-loop managers adhere to a cardinal rule. If they do not have time to stop to hear what an employee has to say, then they do not stop. They recognize that simply going through the motions is worse than not listening at all. If an employee comes into his manager's office with a problem or recommendation when she is in the middle of something, with papers all over her desk, the phone ringing, and a million other things going on, there is a high probability that communication will be one way. In that situation, a good manager does one of two things.

1. She shuts the phone off, pushes everything away, gets up from her desk, and walks around to sit down next to the employee to talk face to face. Or,

2. She simply says to him, "Bill, I want to hear what you've got to say. It's incredibly important to me that I give you my complete attention. But right now, I'm right in the middle of something that I must address first. If you will, let me get this wrapped up, then we can sit down to discuss your ideas. Give me 30 minutes to get this finished. Tell me where you will be then and I will find you." Then she follows through with her commitment.

What's the message? Bill's manager cares enough about his ideas or concerns to take the time to listen intently. It is this genuine interest in the employee that builds a high level of trust and respect between a manager and her employees.

Generational Challenges

With communication being a vital element in the creation of organizational chemistry and employee-management cooperation, it is important to recognize the fact that each generation of employees communicates differently in the workplace. Thus they will respond differently to management based upon their own unique perspectives. This is especially true today with three distinctly different generations in the work force—Baby Boomers (born in the late 1940s through the mid-1960s, representing 48% of the work force), Gen X'ers (born between the mid-1960s and late 1970s, representing 36% of the work force), and Gen Ys or Echo Boomers (born after the late 1970s, representing 16% of the work force). Each of these generations is driven by

> "It is important to recognize that each generation of employees communicates differently."

radically different personality types, needs, and expectations. Thus, to effectively manage and communicate with these employee groupings, closed-loop managers have developed an understanding of their unique differences and adopted different management styles to address the unique motivational triggers of each.

Today's closed-loop managers recognize that there is no "one size fits all" when it comes to effectively leading such a diverse work force. The differences between each work group dictate that they be managed differently, but with the same expectations for job performance and results. What makes this situation differ from the past is that managers today are faced with three versus the historical two employee generations. This vast spread in age and demographics, coupled with the technological competency differences between the generations, has created a unique challenge for managers of all ages. For example, how effective is a Gen Y manager in attempting to communicate and motivate a senior Baby Boomer, when the two have such different perspectives on life and work? The same holds true for a senior Baby Boomer manager when trying to understand what makes a Gen Y'er tick. In short, the challenges are real and daunting for experienced and novice managers alike.

Table 7-2 compares and contrasts the unique characteristics and expectations of each generation. Resources such as this table help managers to better understand the generational gaps. Where do the conflicts generally arise between managers and their employees, as well as between employee groups? The answers lie in the numbers:

- 60% of employees of all ages indicate there is tension in the workplace between generations, often driven by nuances in communication styles and a lack of respect for the abilities of other generations. Even simple differences in music appear to be a contributing factor to the communication gap.
- 70% of Baby Boomers are dismissive of the abilities of their Gen X and Gen Y counterparts.

Employee Selection, Direction, Motivation, and Empowerment

Table 7-2. Generations in the workplace.

Characteristic	Baby Boomers	Generation X	Generation Y
Age	More senior, ranging into their late 50s and early 60s	Young to middle aged, typically in their 30s	Young, typically in their early to mid-20s
Work force	Approximately 77 million	Approximately 37 million	Approximately 26 million
Education	Moderate, over 10 million with little or no high school	Educated, most college degreed	Educated and intelligent, most college degreed or higher
Skills	Minimum to moderate technological skills	Sound computer skills	Technologically competent
	Single-task oriented	Mult-tasking within limits	Strong at multi-tasking
Priorities	Live to work, early retirement may not be an option	Family first priority, career second	Work to live
Job/career	Job security and longevity is important	Will change jobs to facilitate family over career needs	Comfortable changing jobs frequently
	Career tenure is high priority	Career tenure within an industry segment is valued	Career tenure has low to no priority
	Comfortable working rigid schedule, overtime, weekends	Prefer flex-time and value family time	Want flexibility in work hours—job sharing, telecommuting, etc.
Recognition	Low maintenance	Require frequent input and recognition	Typically high maintenance requiring constant recognition
Change acceptance	Change is not readily received or valued	Change is accepted and valued if explained	Change optimized, focused change is key to retention

Table 7-2. Generations in the workplace *(continued)*.

Characteristic	Baby Boomers	Generation X	Generation Y
Personality traits	Depression and recessions molded them	Children of "flower power" generation, got what parents did not	Highly pampered and nurtured
	Openly challenging authority is not common	Independent, outside-the-box thinkers	Challenge, push back, and question frequently
	Quiet, thoughtful, conflict avoiders	Typically good, conflict adaptable	Rude, brash, quick, and bold
	Easily intimidated when job security is involved	Can be manipulated but rarely intimidated	Typically not easily manipulated or intimidated
	Conformance-driven from years of experience	Typically nonconformers, challenge status quo	Value independence in thought and action
	Patient and easy-going—go with the flow	Like a balance between challenges and routine tasks	Quickly bore with mundane work assignments
	Comfortable with status quo, adequate performers	Strong performers driven by change tempered by risk	Creative high performers
	Respond well to most management styles	Prefer Theory Y participative management styles	Do not respond well to Theory X management
Values	Value is a measurement of results generated	High expectations for themselves and employees	Place high value on self-worth
	Financial security	Recognition and challenge	Self-fulfillment
Fiscal responsibility	Retirement funding is primary financial concern	Still receiving financial guidance from parents	Financially capable, savvy and knowledgeable

- 50% of Gen X and Gen Y employees are dismissive of the value, capabilities, and experience of their Baby Boomer counterparts.

Other typical areas of conflict between Baby Boomer and/or Gen X managers and their Gen Y employees include:

- business attire,
- use of technology versus face-to-face communication,
- frequency of expected input on employee performance and job status,
- disparity in perceived technological skill sets,
- requirement for instant gratification and recognition,
- results versus effort-based recognition and rewards,
- organizational constraints and politics,
- lack of respect for tenure and experience, and
- lack of socialization skills and cultural sensitivity within the workplace.

So, to be effective, managers of all ages are required to:

- become better communicators with all generations within the work force,
- identify and apply the motivational triggers that are unique to individuals within each generational work group, and
- promote cooperation between the generational work groups by building bridges of understanding that reinforce the value each generation brings to the workplace.

Once employees begin to communicate openly and freely with one another, cooperation and group dynamics dramatically improve. Leading by example, effective managers make it a priority to work with all employees individually and collectively to build open channels of two-way communication that break down the generational barriers. Ignoring the critical differences will lead to continued conflict and organizational performance problems.

"Open channels of two-way communication break down generational barriers."

Employee Selection, Direction, Motivation, and Empowerment

Disagreements

In today's business environments, it is often frowned upon for employees to argue. The focus of many managers is harmony and consensus on all issues. Arguments, however, are a productive form of communication, so long as employees remain professional rather than personal in their comments. Many managers actually encourage employees to disagree, indeed argue, challenging one another to air differences. This candid honesty will often breed an understanding and acceptance of the other employee's opinions and positions. When employees openly disagree without personalities becoming an issue, breakthrough ideas and solutions are often the result. But when honest disagreement becomes open conflict, it is time to take a break from the issues in question, let emotions stabilize, and revisit the issues later. When employees become aggressive or withdraw from aggression, communication comes to an immediate halt, often for good.

Employees who are allowed to become too committed to their own opinions and concepts can, and often will, disrupt communication within the department. Effective managers are constantly on the lookout for these situations. When it becomes apparent that an employee has become too self-ingrained, the manager gently but firmly encourages that employee to consider other opinions and approaches and how they can be applied, rather than accepting the employee's reasons as to why they will not work.

Clearinghouse

It is often desirable for a manager to be the clearinghouse for communication within the organization. This does not mean, by any stretch of the imagination, that all communication is to be directed solely through the manager. Rather, it means that the manager assimilates, validates, and distributes information to all employees on a regular basis. The reason this is such a key function for a manager is that employees often get only bits and pieces of information, and rarely is that information validated to ensure its accuracy. As a result, misinformation leads to misdirection, confusion, and communication problems. By constantly pasteurizing and disseminating good information, problems are short-circuited before they become barriers to communication.

UNORTHODOX DECISIONS

There are times when managers are forced to make radically different decisions, decisions that may appear from an outsider's perspective to be a bit unusual. Intuitive managers know when to call those shots to revitalize employees or bring them back into their steady-state routines.

> "Radically different decisions are sometimes necessary to revitalize employees."

Example

This example is of a new product launch at a large company in the Pacific Northwest in early 2004. A consultant was hired by its Executive Committee to review the status of a new product introduction that was critical to the longevity of the corporation. The consultant was to assess the risks associated with a possible failure and create contingency plans so senior management would be prepared to address the critical risks found. When the consultant came on board, there were less than two weeks left before the committed delivery date to the customer. The timeline was extremely short and reaction time was at a premium.

Sitting through the design review meeting the first morning was enlightening for the consultant. The new product development team had apparently done an excellent job in bringing the product through the concept, design, and prototyping stages. In short, they appeared to be close to achieving their objectives. However, there were a few nagging issues that had not yet been addressed adequately, introducing an unacceptable degree of risk to the project. Discussions centered on action items for those issues. Individuals assigned the follow-up tasks headed out immediately afterward to get started. During the next two days it became apparent that there had been little progress in coming to grips with these issues, although the effort was nothing short of exceptional.

The consultant's assessment of the individuals versus the project drew a quick conclusion. The members of the project team were burned out. They had been working 70-plus-hour weeks for at least six months. Fatigue was causing them to make mental mistakes that, under other circumstances, would never have been made. An analysis of the failure magnitude and probability further revealed that if the product was not delivered on time, the customer would pull all future orders. Given that the customer represented over 80% of the company's gross revenues, the failure would be catastrophic.

Asking the team members to work longer hours was not the answer, nor was assigning additional resources to the team. A parallel development path was also out of the question given the remaining time. There had to be another solution that minimized the risk. It was time for one of those unusual decisions.

The consultant met with the Executive Committee to outline the situation and present the recommended actions. After gaining their approval, he then met with the project team . . . to give them another assignment! The assignment was for every member of the project team to take Thursday off. There was predictable resistance. The team members knew the risks associated with missing their objectives and thus they were reluctant to give up those precious hours on the consultant's folly. Nevertheless, they agreed to take the day off. Giving away a significant portion of the remaining time left in the project without a recovery plan must have appeared to outsiders to be foolish. But in reality, the risks were minimal. Directions for the day off were detailed:

- Every team member was required to take it off—no exceptions.
- Even though they were not to be in the office, the team was required to spend the entire day together doing something fun.
- Finally, the team was not allowed to talk about the project for the entire day.

Employee Selection, Direction, Motivation, and Empowerment

On the day off, the team played golf, saw a movie, and went to a late dinner and drinks. They spent the entire day together having fun. What did they talk about all day? Why, they talked about the project, of course. By breaking them out of their normal work environment, the pressures and frustrations that had clouded their judgment were eliminated. Problems were identified and addressed. The team returned to work on Friday morning fresh, clear headed, and ready to hit the ground running. By the end of the day, the team had completed its assignment. The product was ready to introduce into production as scheduled on Monday morning. By the following Wednesday, the first shipments were on the way to the customer.

What made the decision to take a day off successful was identification of the individual needs of the team members and recognition of how organizational constraints exacerbated the risk of not meeting the team's objectives. By altering the environment and applying the appropriate triggers for each individual, team performance was dramatically increased without a corresponding increase in individual effort. Will that equation work in all situations? Certainly not—there are no canned solutions in management. Every situation is assessed and addressed on its own merits. This is the challenge that managers face. It is what keeps them sharp.

How does a manager recognize the needs and constraints of individuals? He listens, observes, and analyzes. When pressure is great, managers will often do a poor job of listening to their employees. Under those circumstances managers talk a lot, but they are not really hearing what the employees are saying. Closed-loop managers, however, listen carefully so they clearly understand what their employees are saying, how it is being said, why it is being said, and the conditions under which it is being said. They do not immediately start talking, rather they stop and listen.

> "Listen, observe, and analyze to uncover the needs and constraints of employees."

218 *Walking the Talk: Pathways to Leadership*

TOOLS FOR SUCCESS

Closed-loop managers build the confidence of employees by providing them with the tools they need to do their jobs efficiently. If employees require outside training to enhance their efficiency or expand their skill sets, it is the manager's responsibility to get them the necessary training. If employees require other tools to get their jobs done, successful managers find ways to ensure those tools are provided as quickly as possible within the constraints of the business.

> "Build employee confidence by providing the tools needed to get the job done."

Performance Metrics

Performance metrics are tools that allow employees to measure their own performance and progress. Experienced managers ensure that these metrics are not in conflict, but rather that they are based on common goals and objectives for all employees within the department or work unit. Thus, performance measures guarantee that every employee can be successful without negatively impacting others within the organization.

The true value of performance measurements lies in that they allow employees to track their own performance, thus encouraging them to be proactive in their own behavior to achieve good results. Good managers ensure employees understand how these metrics integrate with the strategic vision and mission of the organization. They train their employees on how to apply them within their areas of responsibility. And they require employees to report their progress on a weekly basis, along with any required corrective action plans. To meet requirements, employees quickly begin to take ownership of their own performance.

Is there No "I" in Team?

Performance metrics are utilized not only to facilitate individual improvements in performance, but also to aid in organizational improvements. The purpose of organizational teamwork, thus, is to maximize the efforts of individuals working together for the benefit of the organization first, and the individual secondly. This fact is emphasized by the commonly utilized phrase, "There is no 'I' in team." Yet, managers spend an inordinate amount of time working with employees to enhance their individual performance. So, where is the disconnect? Is there truly no "I" in team? Certainly there is an individual component. Employees work to grow professionally, earn promotions, and make more money. To take away that individual component is to create a work force of drones with little self-motivation and discipline. By removing the ability to earn individual rewards, a manager effectively removes the employees' motivation to succeed. Yet, if the individual is so focused on personal achievement that he loses sight of the needs of the organization, then the organization suffers due to a lack of synergy and chemistry within the work force.

Recognizing the dichotomy, closed-loop managers reward first on a team or departmental basis, then upon the individual employee's contribution to the team or organization's success. By so doing, each employee realizes that only if her organization is successful can she be successful. If the organization fails to deliver upon its requirements, then every employee therein is deemed to have been unsuccessful. When the organization is successful, employees are recognized for their individual contributions to its success. Thus, the "I" is effectively put in team, but managed to achieve maximum benefit.

Planned Spontaneous Recognition

Closed-loop managers find reasons to recognize and reward employee successes not just with money, but also with items such as T-shirts, hats, pizza, dinner tickets, and tickets to sporting events, concerts, or social events. In short, the list includes anything and everything that has value to the employees and that adds a degree of fun and competitiveness to the day-to-day business environment. The technique is called "planned spontaneous recognition" because while the manager's actions seem spontaneous, in reality, they are well planned and executed. For example, when an individual has been putting in countless hours of unpaid overtime, the astute manager recognizes and rewards the effort. Something as simple as saying, "Thank you, I really appreciate your dedication and your efforts," means so much to an employee. Closed-loop managers never underestimate the fact that a little recognition goes a long way in making employees feel appreciated.

Closed-loop managers recognize, too, that recognition means even more to employees when it comes directly from their manager on a personal basis. Employees know that their direct supervisor is far more knowledgeable of the effort required to accomplish their assignments than a member of senior management. Therefore, when their direct supervisor recognizes their results, the acknowledgement has credibility, and thus more value than if it had come from higher up in the management chain.

> "Recognition means more to employees when it comes directly from their manager."

Closed-loop managers look for one thing each day that employees do correctly. While many managers concentrate on those things that employees do wrong, closed-loop managers concentrate on the positive aspects of employee performance. Then, these managers plan how to respond, but make it appear that the response is spontaneous. The response may be as simple as a handshake and a thank you, to something even more personal like bringing in cookies, soda, or pizza—something that says to the employees that their manager truly appreciates their efforts. It takes effort on a manager's part to see the positive every day. But in the end, that effort yields tremendous dividends.

Avoid Problem Transference

Decision-making, as has been discussed previously, is a major part of a manager's role. Managers accept the fact that decision-making is a requirement to maintaining direction and momentum within an organization. If an employee indicates the

Employee Selection, Direction, Motivation, and Empowerment

> *"To avoid problem transference, take the time to instruct employees on the decision-making process."*

need for a decision that is beyond his or her level of empowerment, managers will often take it upon themselves to make those decisions. Herein, however, exists a trap if additional steps are not taken. It is a manager's role to teach employees *how* to make decisions, not to just allow them to transfer their problems to their superior. Closed-loop managers take the time to instruct employees on the decision-making process, explaining what is needed to make a sound decision and why. Employees seeking a decision from their manager are required to provide the following information or data with their request for help:

- a complete definition of what the problem is and why it is critical that a decision be made immediately;
- how the employee defined the problem and the correlating data;
- how the employee validated the data along with all assumptions made in so doing;
- a listing of all alternatives available to the organization to resolve the problem, and of those alternatives, which ones introduce the least risk;
- how the risks were assessed and validated, and the data and methodologies used;
- the alternative the employee would select, given the data and analysis, and why.

With this, a manager has everything required to make a supportable business decision on the spot; and the employee learns what is required to make a sound decision. Not only teaching employees the proper methodology for making good decisions, it also provides them with a safety net. The employee knows that if help is needed, his manager is there to assist. This approach provides encouragement, motivation, and discipline—the structure required for closed-loop management. If, on the other hand, a manager allows his employees to simply dump their problems in his lap and walk away, then he effectively owns the problem and all of the headaches that come with it.

Example

George was the quality control manager of the engineered products division of a Fortune 100 manufacturer. He was well educated, technically competent, and detail oriented. George, as a manager, had just one flaw. Every Friday afternoon at 4:00, he had the habit of running to his manager's office with a major crisis. George then proceeded to dump that crisis in his manager's lap and head home for the weekend. Saturday morning, there was the boss at the office working on George's problems. It took George's manager just a couple of Saturdays to figure out what was going on and what to do about it. He figured that he had only two options. One, he would simply refuse to see George after noon on Fridays. Or alternatively, he could throw the problem back to George to address. He selected the second option (after giving option one due consideration). Every time George would bring in a problem, his manager would send George back to resolve it along with specific instructions on how to assess and resolve it. George quickly learned to handle his own issues and ultimately became a better manager in his own right.

SUMMARY

In this chapter, the application of closed-loop management techniques was discussed along with examples of its merits in a business setting. The key to closed-loop management is a disciplined, structured style of leadership that begins with building a synergistic organization from a core set of employee profiles that complement one another. Once those skill sets are resident within the organization, closed-loop management builds capability and control through the application of sound motivational techniques that focus on the triggers inherent within each employee. Rules and guidelines that apply to all employees equally are then administered, coupled with the

Employee Selection, Direction, Motivation, and Empowerment

freedom to learn and make mistakes within the boundaries of those rules. Next is the application of discipline to provide the structure that all employees and organizations alike require to sustain momentum and focus. Over time, a tradition of success permeates the organization, forming the basis for sustained levels of high performance and accomplishment.

Closed-loop management requires a manager's commitment to stay the course, even in the face of business constraints, organizational politics, or employee problems. It requires doggedness and flexibility on the part of a manager, with a focus on adherence to the organization's mission and metrics. Closed-loop management is a long-term proposition. It is not easy, but it is highly effective in generating exceptional long-term results for a manager, his employees, and his organization.

Chapter 8 explores the techniques used by successful closed-loop managers to maximize the capability and performance of an organization. It will discuss the importance of aligning management's vision with an employee base capable of meeting ongoing organizational needs. Team building, cross-functionality, and maturity factors will be addressed, along with the management techniques required to capitalize on the benefits possible from them while minimizing risk to the organization.

8

Building Organizational Alignment

OBJECTIVES

In this chapter, several of the techniques used by closed-loop managers as they begin to build an organization, and the teamwork within it, will be discussed. The concepts of closed-loop management will be combined with that of "visioning" to bring alignment between what managers intend to accomplish and the personnel required to make those visions reality. In addition, the techniques and tools required to create organizational alignment will be discussed.

ALIGNING CAPABILITY AND COMPETENCY WITH ORGANIZATIONAL VISION

As Figure 8-1 illustrates, before an organization can achieve consistent operational excellence, there must be alignment between the objectives and vision of its manager and the capabilities inherent within the organization's employees. The combined skills and competencies of the employees must be sufficient to generate expected results day-in and day-out. Without that balance, no amount of management or leadership will generate the level of sustained performance necessary to transform the organization into that envisioned by its manager.

As Figure 8-2 illustrates, when the requirements of an organization exceed the combined capabilities of its employees, a "performance" or "quality gap" is created. In situations like this, no matter how hard employees and management work, no matter how many hours they put into the job, no matter how dedicated they are, the organization will fail. The reason for this phenomenon is that the organization lacks balance. Employee

Building Organizational Alignment

Organizational Alignment

Y-axis: Customer or organizational requirements
X-axis: Departmental competencies and capabilities

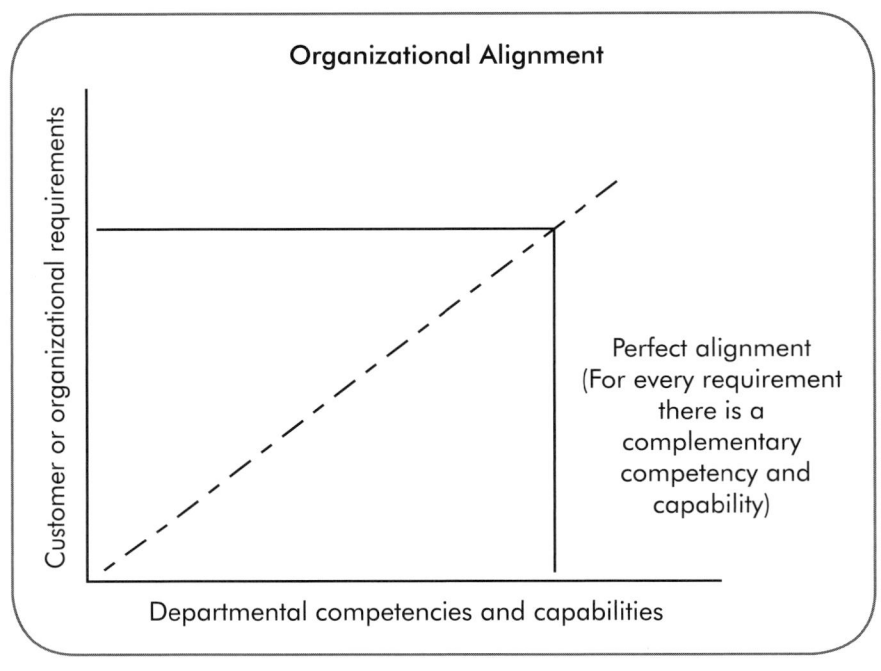

Perfect alignment
(For every requirement there is a complementary competency and capability)

Figure 8-1. Alignment between organizational needs and employee competencies.

skill sets fall short of what is required to generate consistent results and performance. The problem is not a matter of commitment or dedication. Nor is it a matter of poor leadership. In many cases, the employees give 100% every day . . . until frustration and fatigue set in. Managers, too, are giving 100%. It is simply that, together, they lack the skill sets necessary to accomplish the tasks placed before them. A change is needed to establish the required alignment.

Conversely, as Figure 8-3 illustrates, when the combined skills and competencies of the organization's employees and management exceed that required to meet organizational requirements, an "opportunity gap" is created. This is the best of all worlds; it is the direct result of the application of closed-loop management techniques discussed in Chapter 7. In this environ-

Building Organizational Alignment

Organizational Misalignment

Y-axis: Customer or organizational requirements
X-axis: Departmental competencies and capabilities

Ongoing quality and compliance problems—misalignment (Requirements exceed competencies and capabilities)

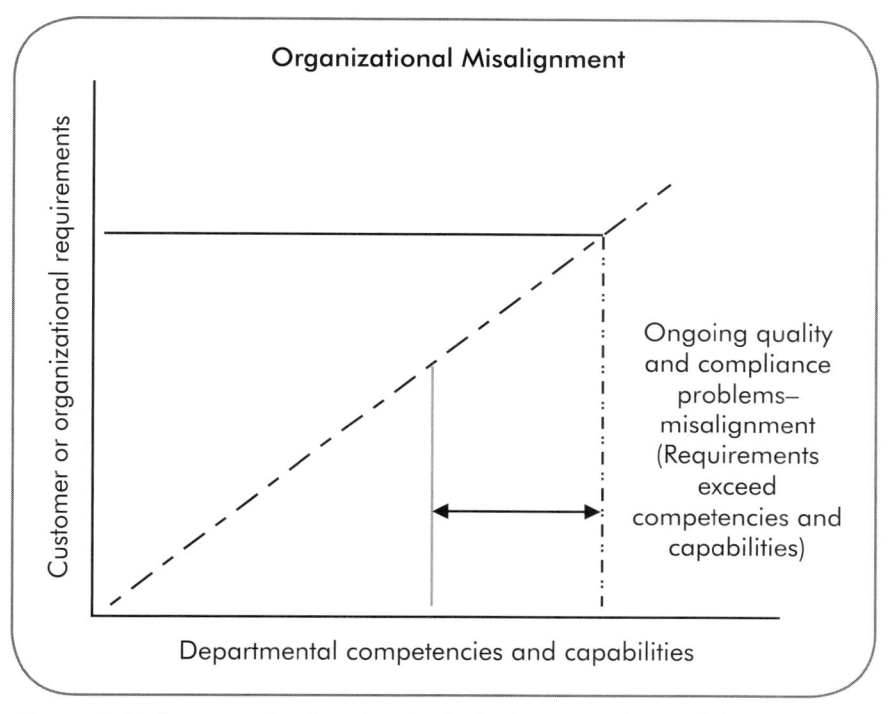

Figure 8-2. An organization that lacks balance and capability.

ment, an organization's acceleration to higher levels of sustained performance far exceeds that of the balanced organization. The reason is simple; excess capability exists within its personnel and management. Performance is pulled quickly from its present level to that which is consistent with the competencies of the employees. This acceleration often requires little extra effort because employees are working at their normal, sustainable levels. Employees are comfortable and confident in their ability to meet what management has envisioned. Because the goals are achievable to the employees, success is assured.

ORGANIZATIONAL BASE-LINING

Before a closed-loop manager begins evaluating and adjusting personnel within the organization to create alignment,

Building Organizational Alignment

Optimized Alignment

Y-axis: Customer or organizational requirements
X-axis: Departmental competencies and capabilities

Ongoing compliance to expected performance

An ideal scenario for any manager, the core organizational competencies and capabilities exceed current requirements. Thus, the organization is poised to advance at a faster rate, providing a competitive advantage.

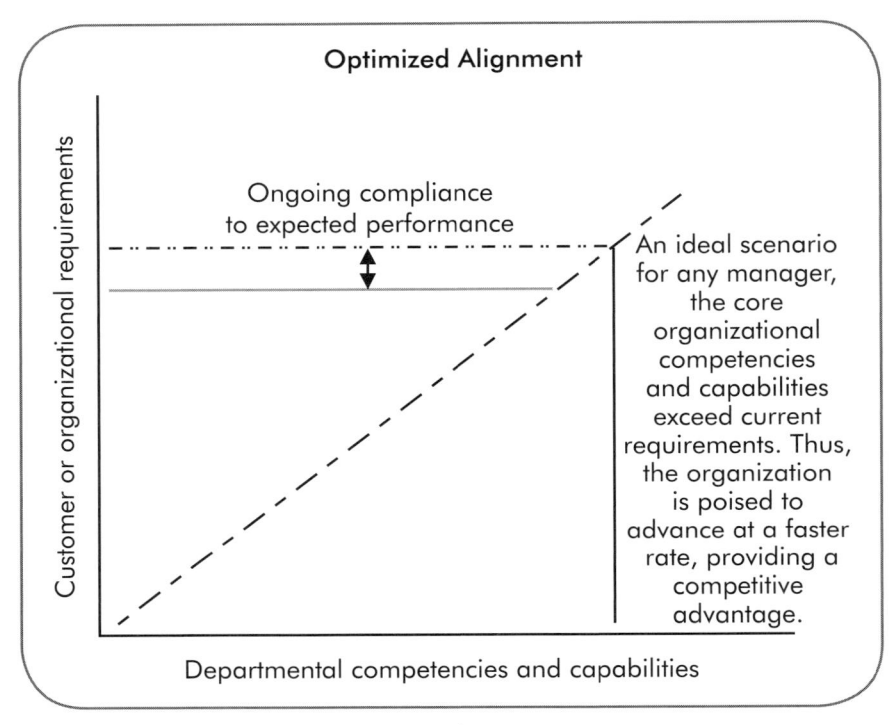

Figure 8-3. The "opportunity gap" phenomenon.

she first assesses the core competencies and capabilities currently resident within the organization. She then contrasts those competencies against those that will be needed to ensure organizational alignment with her vision. Misalignment is then addressed through her strategic and succession planning activities.

Core competency analysis is discussed in detail in Chapter 11, but for now, it is sufficient to say that its intent is to quantitatively measure and assess the capabilities and capacities within each department or function against an established base-line of expected performance. This analysis will clearly illustrate those areas in which quality gaps exist, and thus, where priorities must be established to bring personnel skills in line with current and future needs. It is here where a manager begins making critical decisions regarding what she intends to accomplish and the ability of her staff to make that transition successfully. The decisions and priorities are predicated upon the discussions held between the manager and her superior relative to senior management's strategic direction, vision, and mission for the organization as a whole. Those priorities are then balanced against those of the manager's internal and external customers, ultimately creating an overall organizational priority listing. The corresponding organizational metrics that guide the manager are then incorporated into the competency analysis to ensure that all aspects of the transition are considered.

VISION

The next step in the process is for the manager to create her vision of the organization throughout the next year, three years, and five years. Both near-term and long-term visions are absolutely necessary to support her succession planning activities.

For years American management was widely criticized for its near-sightedness. Management's focus was on short-term results, primarily those that were to be accomplished within the upcoming fiscal year. On the other hand, Japanese management was generally thought to be far more effective because their vision horizon typically ranged between five and 10 years. It was believed that it was this longer-term vision that gave them such excellent preparation for the competitive challenges of the future. This viewpoint was supported, so it was believed, by the fact that many Japanese firms dominated the global markets while Western firms constantly chased versus led their Far Eastern counterparts. In the late 1990s, this fallacy became apparent with the decline of the Japanese economy. The truth is, if a manager is so focused on the future that she ignores the problems of today, then today's problems will often overcome the organization, thus effectively eliminating the future altogether. Conversely, if a manager is so near-term focused that she fails to plan for the future, future events will occur at random rather than as strategically planned. As a consequence, managers today do not have the luxury of choosing either long- or short-term visioning—both must exist to ensure corporate longevity and success.

Visioning requires managers to plan for the future by building a set of strategic goals and objectives for the organization matched with a tactical plan that clearly defines how those objectives are to be met in the long term. Performance against those goals and objectives is then monitored and controlled through the use of quantifiable performance metrics and scorecard techniques. But this is only half of the requirement for effective closed-loop management. The second element of the equation is a short-term vision that monitors daily operations and performance to ensure short-term requirements and obligations are met consistently. In summary, managers today must be both long and short-term visionaries. One without the other places an organization at significant risk.

> *"Strategic goals and objectives must be matched to a tactical plan that defines how they will be met."*

Example: Malcolm Baldrige National Quality Award Winners

This example illustrates the fallacy of selecting a singular-term vision. Throughout the 1980s and 1990s, many American organizations actively sought the prestige associated with winning the coveted Baldrige National Quality Award. Winning the award, it was thought, ensured future success because customers would naturally seek out the provider of the best product or service. Competition throughout the early years of the award was intense. Early competitors for the award focused every employee and every manager on the goal of winning. Decisions were made and priorities set based upon their impact on winning the award in the upcoming year. As competition intensified, even more exhaustive effort was put forth to win the award.

With their concentration solely on the goal of winning the award, many managers lost sight of the fact that their customers were going unsupported, or at best, poorly serviced. Ultimately, it was the customer who suffered. Yes, a few of these firms did win the award. But in the process, some of the winners found they had lost many of their old customers forever. What was the net result? Many of those early winners faced financial insolvency. They lost focus of the near-term requirements of running their businesses, letting their longer-term vision take priority. There must be balance; without it, the future is always compromised.

CULTIVATE ESSENTIAL EMPLOYEE SKILL SETS

Many managers initiate the next phase of the process by critically assessing performance at three levels: the organizational level, the process level, and the individual level. Because each plays a vital role in the overall success of the organization, managers look for links between performance deficiencies within all three. To gain or maintain balance within the organization, employee skill sets must match or exceed the competencies required to meet near-term operational performance requirements, as well as longer-term strategic requirements.

The question that must be answered is, "Do the skill sets of each employee individually and those of the combined work force meet those near-term and longer-term needs?" If not, then employee skill sets must be enhanced either through training or through changes in staff. Decisions regarding staffing changes are difficult to make. To conclude that an employee who has given the organization years of dedicated service will not fit into the future plans and needs of that same organization is often heartbreaking. But to force that employee into a role he is incapable of handling is wrong for the employee and the organization. There are times when a change is best for all concerned.

A series of infrastructure questions, such as those in Table 8-1, is used to begin the analysis. These examples are by no means universal or complete. In all cases, closed-loop managers utilize situation-specific assessment questions designed to provide insight into the organization's unique circumstances,

Building Organizational Alignment

Table 8-1. Introspective questions regarding infrastructure for organizational base-lining of performance issues.

- At what organizational level do performance problems typically arise?
- Are the organization's performance problems strategic, tactical, or operational?
- Do the organization's performance problems impact other critical business processes, functions, or operations?
- Is there a justifiable urgency to addressing the performance problems?
- Have attempts been made in the past to address these same performance issues? If so, why were those efforts not successful?
- Is there a universal commitment at all levels to resolve the performance problems?
- Are the resources needed to resolve the performance problems available for immediate deployment? If not, when will the resources be available?
- Are the performance expectations realistic given all business, organizational, and operational constraints?
- Are the performance problems cross-functional in nature?
- If multiple departments or disciplines are affected by or contribute to a performance problem, is there common ground that will allow every affected department or department manager to be successful?
- Are all affected functional managers currently informed and involved?
- Other than the processes and disciplines identified, are there any outside factors that will inhibit a successful resolution to the performance problem?
- What strategic actions will be required to resolve the performance issues?
- What tactical actions will be required to resolve the performance issues?

environment, constraints, and processes. Answers to these and similar questions aid the manager in deciding the level within the organization on which to focus his initial priorities. Before making any decision or taking any action, however, the

Building Organizational Alignment

closed-loop manager evaluates performance issues at all levels to ensure that the actual drivers behind the current situation are thoroughly identified and understood. To do otherwise is simply an exercise in futility. In particular, each performance issue is evaluated based upon its overall impact on critical business functions, such as product, service, or operational cost structures; cash flow; profitability; market share; or competitive positioning. Those performance issues that impact one or more of the critical business issues always receive a manager's attention before any secondary issues are addressed. It is the establishment of these initial "silver bullet" priorities that influences the employee skill set analysis and any subsequent personnel decisions made thereafter.

Another consideration in the initial decision process is the urgency required in dealing with each issue. A manager quickly comes to the realization that everything can not be done at once; priorities must be established before anything can be accomplished. There should only be one number one priority followed by a singular number two, three, four, and so on. To assign top priority to many issues is to guarantee that none will be effectively addressed. It is also important to determine quickly whether or not the selected priorities have been addressed before. If so, why were permanent solutions not enacted, and what can be done to ensure the same failures are not repeated? It is an enormous waste of resources and time to battle the same issues time and time again. Savvy managers hit each organizational performance issue hard, effectively killing it so it will not arise later. By so doing, they can more efficiently plan future actions without concern that unexpected surprises will arise from a half-baked corrective action that only temporarily satisfied a performance deficiency. Doing it right the first time saves a great deal of pain and time downstream; and time is something, quite frankly, that is not in abundance for most managers.

Whether or not senior management is committed to address the particular issues at this time is another consideration. There is little sense in trying to fight an uphill battle to gain senior management's support when their priorities are focused in areas they perceive to be more critical. Senior management's support of a manager's staffing, operational, and budgetary needs will be an initial requirement. Without it, a manager's strategic and tactical plans will go nowhere. Again, experienced managers know to address the issues early with their superiors before launching into action. To do so saves time and embarrassment. It takes only a minute for a manager to solicit and receive concurrence from his superior relative to his priorities. It is time well spent, especially early in a manager's career.

> *"The time a manager takes to solicit and receive concurrence from his superior is time well spent."*

The support a manager will receive from peers is another consideration when establishing early priorities. For example, are other managers deeply involved in addressing similar or related performance issues? If so, then a united front may serve both managers well. To fight organizational and personnel performance issues without the support of other peers is doubly tough for any manager. No manager, department, or work group is an island unto itself. Success comes from cooperation and collaboration within the department as well as from those external forces that directly influence a manager's ability to get things done. Businesses today are less silo-driven and more horizontally or process-driven. No manager can survive for long within an organizational silo without help. Every manager learns quickly the necessity to reach outside his organization for help. It is not an indication of weakness or lack of competency. Rather, it is the mark of a wise manager who knows that things get done within an organization through cross-functional cooperation.

Matching Skill Sets to Organizational Needs

Once the organizational competencies are identified and priorities set to address needed corrective actions, closed-loop managers are then able to match the skill sets of department personnel against those needed to accomplish near-term and longer-term objectives. In doing so, it is wise for a manager to consider cross-functional skill sets that are not currently part of his typical organizational makeup.

Example 1

It is common for the manager of an engineering department to enhance his organization's competencies and capabilities through the addition of an "outsider" from operations, accounting, or marketing. These employees bring a different, often broader perspective into the department that gives every employee a better understanding of the entire organizational process. By breaking the silo thinking associated with a singular skill set, managers bring diversity in thinking, assessment, and action to the department. It is that diversity in thinking and perspective that often generates innovative, breakthrough ideas, greatly enhancing overall organizational performance.

Example 2

As a result of a recent merger with another institution, a banking manager is faced with the requirement to reengineer her department as part of an overall organizational transformation. In a case like this, is it a wise move for her to recruit a process analyst or industrial engineer to help? Absolutely! The skill sets that will be required include those that are functionally specific and relating to the various banking operations, as well as those needed for process assessment, which will be used to identify and eliminate the non-value added elements within each banking process. Those are the skill sets of a process analyst or industrial engineer. It is the combination of those skill sets that will yield the best results for the manager as she embarks upon the reengineering project.

Near-term and Longer-term Needs

In selecting the appropriate skill sets, closed-loop managers consider the near-term as well as longer-term needs of the organization. To illustrate the importance of this element of the decision process, consider the previous example. Often in

Building Organizational Alignment

an organizational transition brought on by reengineering activities, the post-reengineering operations are uniquely different from those of the current state. As such, the banking manager is required to consider the following factors when evaluating her staffing needs:

- the skill sets needed to maintain operations during the transition,
- the skill sets needed to plan and execute the reengineering activities, and
- the skill sets needed to operate the reengineered organization once the project is completed.

Each of these skill sets is uniquely different, yet vitally important to ensure the ongoing success of the organization. Technology changes, competitive conditions, strategic direction changes resulting from new visions of senior management . . . all of these, and more, can alter the skill set requirements of an organization. Managers must remain mindful of the requirement to maintain a multi-pronged perspective of the needs of their organizations.

Time-phasing Skill Set Requirements

Different skill sets are needed at different times. Because some skill sets demand a high financial commitment from the organization, many closed-loop managers opt to utilize a timing chart, such as the one in Table 8-2, to carefully plan the addition or temporary retention of certain skilled employees. The intent of the table is to segregate those skill sets that will be needed for only a brief time (for example, during a transition period) from those that will be needed continuously to support ongoing operations. The use of temporary employees or contract consultants is always carefully planned to minimize the financial impact on the organization and maximize the contribution of those talents during times of critical need.

When employing time-phased personnel planning, experienced managers consider not only those skill sets required within the department but also those required from support

Building Organizational Alignment

Table 8-2. Skill set timing.

Required Employee Skill Sets	07Q4	08Q1	08Q2	08Q3	08Q4	09Q1	09Q2	09Q3
Design engineering	X	X	X	X	X	X	X	X
Reliability engineering	X	X	X	X				
Product and process validation engineering		X	X	X	X			
Quality engineering	X	X	X	X	X	X	X	X
Supply base management	X	X	X	X	X	X	X	X
Drafting and detailing	X	X	X	X	X	X	X	X
Project management	X	X	X	X	X	X		
Embedded systems-RF					X	X	X	X
Compatibility engineering		X	X					

Building Organizational Alignment

departments or groups. Working with other managers, a comprehensive personnel plan is developed to ensure the appropriate skill sets are available when and where needed. Cross-functional personnel planning eliminates skill set redundancy, along with the fixed overhead associated with it. It also helps to avoid costly reactions when required skill sets are overlooked until the need is imminent.

Example

Many organizations today are moving aggressively to outsource functions deemed non-critical, those exceptionally high in overhead rates, or those in which management has determined the organization lacks the core competencies necessary to ensure a consistent level of acceptable performance. Organizations are outsourcing everything from accounts payable to payroll, from purchasing to human resources. Outsourcing has become the norm rather than the exception.

For purposes of example, assume a company has recently hired a new engineering manager. Further, as part of an overall organizational transformation project, senior management at the same time has made a decision to outsource all of the engineering design functions over the course of the next 18–24 months. Document control and the sustaining engineering groups, however, will remain. Knowing that the need for those design skill sets is limited to two years at the outside, the new manager would be foolish to hire permanent employees only to terminate them in the foreseeable future. The better decision is to either hire temporary or contract designers, or to outsource the function now.

Training

Another aspect of staff planning is to determine if available skill sets can be enhanced through training versus replacement. This is especially critical when demand exceeds supply in a tight job market like that experienced in the late 1990s and early 2000s in most domestic and many international venues. It is key for managers to isolate those training needs that will be required over the foreseeable planning horizon to transition existing or planned employees from where they are today to where they will be required to be to meet organizational objectives of the future.

Today, global markets and supporting business technologies are incredibly dynamic. Computers are everywhere. Innovations in systems, software, and communications occur almost daily. Any manager running an organization that is competing with firms that possess more advanced technologies is well advised to secure advanced technology training for his employees. Whether that training is on basic software or computers, advanced wireless network data management, or whatever else the business environment requires, it is necessary to keep his employees competitive. It is also wise for the manager in this situation to look beyond "catching up" with the competition. Rather, savvy managers seek advantage by projecting where technologies or competition is headed, then securing training for employees that will allow them to leap beyond the competition to reach the targeted competencies before others achieve that same level.

> "Secure the appropriate training for employees to develop the skill sets needed for the organization to remain competitive."

Example

For years, the Japanese utilized a theory espoused by Miyamoto Musashi in his *The Book of Five Rings* that encouraged managers in competitive environments to seek advantage by disguising their intentions, thus creating a false impression of where their strategic direction was leading (Musashi 1994). Then, as Musashi instructed, managers launched an offensive that totally surprised the competition because it came from a direction or a position of strength that the competition had never considered. This "element of surprise" approach served many Japanese managers and organizations well as they captured numerous markets in the last three decades of the 20th

Building Organizational Alignment

century. It was not until Western managers became enlightened about rapid product deployment that global competition became more equally balanced.

A Simple Tool

A simple training plan, such as the one shown in Table 8-3, is often used by managers to plan and monitor critical skill set training needs over a one to three-year period. There is obviously nothing complicated in this tool, yet it provides a quick and easy means to ensure that the required training is accomplished.

A related technique used by closed-loop managers is to require every employee who attends an internal or external training session to provide an overview to fellow employees. The overview includes the salient points or techniques learned during the training, as well as how those techniques can be applied to achieve improved performance. This internal mentoring en-

Table 8-3. Employee training plan.

Training Need	\multicolumn{8}{c}{Employee}
	ST	KT	MB	JC	DK	LS	AH	JK	TK
Wireless data management	X	X					X		X
Knowledge management			X		X		X		X
Intelligent agents			X		X			X	
Digital communications	X		X				X		
Programmable logic systems design			X		X	X		X	
Embedded systems design			X			X		X	
Strategic project management	X			X		X			X

courages collaboration, builds trust among employees, and equally as important, fosters depth throughout the organization.

SUCCESSION PLANNING

The assessment, selection, and preparation process is critical to succession planning. Building depth is always a paramount consideration during the early organizational planning periods. For every position, there must be at least one capable backup. For critical positions, there must be at least two.

As part of the assessment, selection, and preparation process, closed-loop managers identify one or two key candidates for each position, as is illustrated in Figure 8-4. Typically candidates for each position are classified as either:

- ready now,
- ready in one year, or
- ready in three years.

The required skill sets for each position are identified and then compared against the particular skill sets of each succession candidate to identify existing deficiencies. Closed-loop managers critically assess the strengths and weaknesses of each candidate. Weaknesses are addressed through training before the employee is allowed to transition into a supervisory, management, or executive position. All too often, an employee is promoted into a position for which she is ill equipped or poorly trained. That is a failure on management's part, not on the part of the employee. It is a manager's responsibility to ensure that an employee is ready, willing, and able to fulfill the requirements of a position before being placed into it.

LEADING MATURE ORGANIZATIONS

While the previous discussion has focused on building a synergistic organization when one does not exist, it is equally important to explore the managerial pros and cons of inheriting a mature, well-functioning organization. Many of the same issues and requirements apply, but this situation carries with it several unique nuances for a manager to consider.

Building Organizational Alignment

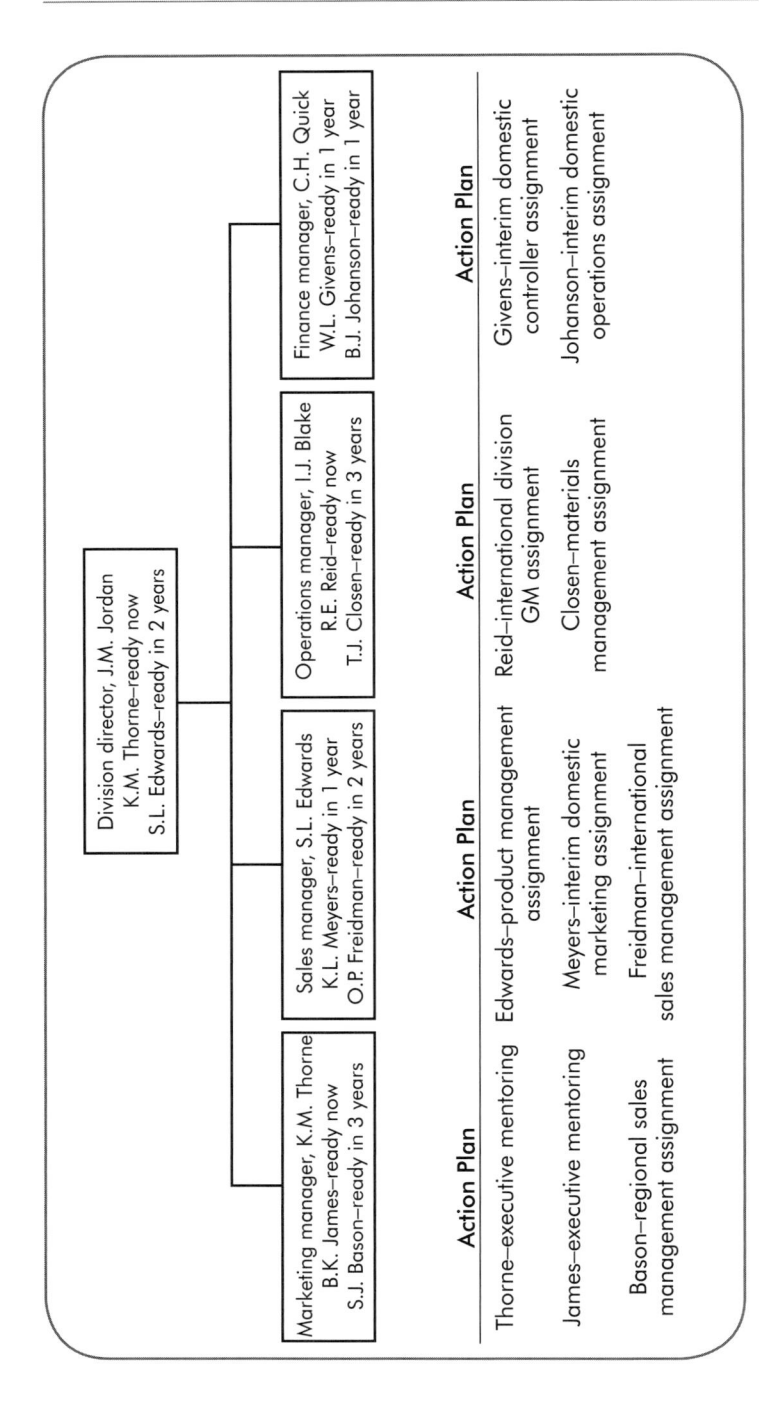

```
                    Division director, J.M. Jordan
                    K.M. Thorne—ready now
                    S.L. Edwards—ready in 2 years
```

Marketing manager, K.M. Thorne	Sales manager, S.L. Edwards	Operations manager, I.J. Blake	Finance manager, C.H. Quick
B.K. James—ready now	K.L. Meyers—ready in 1 year	R.E. Reid—ready now	W.L. Givens—ready in 1 year
S.J. Bason—ready in 3 years	O.P. Freidman—ready in 2 years	T.J. Closen—ready in 3 years	B.J. Johanson—ready in 1 year

Action Plan	Action Plan	Action Plan	Action Plan
Thorne—executive mentoring	Edwards—product management assignment	Reid—international division GM assignment	Givens—interim domestic controller assignment
James—executive mentoring	Meyers—interim domestic marketing assignment	Closen—materials management assignment	Johanson—interim domestic operations assignment
Bason—regional sales management assignment	Freidman—international sales management assignment		

Figure 8-4. Succession planning model.

As an organization matures, employees, work groups, or organizational teams become self-managed. The employees understand the organization, its challenges, and its capabilities. Because of that knowledge and experience, the employees are willing and able to handle the majority of issues that arise during the course of a normal business day with little, if any, involvement from their manager. The required skill sets for the present and future are resident within the group. As the manager, it is a great environment to work in because:

- Employees know what to do and they do it well and consistently.
- Job functions and responsibilities are based on detailed guidelines that have been established by previous management and adopted by employees.
- Responsibility and accountability are comfortably shared by all employees.
- Employees take an active role in setting direction, managing their individual job functions, and resolving day-to-day problems.

Dealing with mature organizations is, under most circumstances, fun for a manager. First, the manager is dealing with a group of employees who have very distinctly solidified roles and responsibilities. They know what to do. Everyone has a role to play; they accept and perform their roles well. Secondly, the employees set their own goals and objectives, and they get them done. When assignments are made by the group's manager, micro-management is not required to ensure that those assignments are completed as desired. Third, personality issues and politics are rare because there is a history of good chemistry among the employees. Everyone cooperates. Work is considered fun and employees enjoy coming to work. Communication and feedback systems function seamlessly between management and employees, as well as between employees within the group. Strong interpersonal relationships exist, building trust between employees. Thus, employees support one another and back each other up in times of difficulty.

Enforcement of Rules and Guidelines

While it sounds like a perfect world for any manager, a mature organization comes with its own unique set of challenges. Employees and employee groups, if not properly managed, tend to become independent, looking at themselves as entities of their own, separate from the rest of the organization. They will often perceive their constraints and level of empowerment to be different, less binding, than their counterparts within other departments. They are likely to set their own direction, rules, and expectations of acceptable performance. If these differ from those of their manager, rebellion often results. It is thus essential that managers in a mature organization continually reinforce the fact that the autonomy and self-direction enjoyed by the group cannot be construed, under any circumstances, as complete independence from the remainder of the organization. The group's activities are always to be restricted to the rules and guidelines that have been established by corporate management. They are required to adhere to corporate policies and procedures; they are not free to break them. The boundaries of the group's empowerment are reinforced regularly, as are senior management's performance expectations for the group.

If the manager and group reach agreement that certain rules, policies, or procedures require change, then they work together to recommend, gain approval for, and implement the needed changes. Employees are never permitted to arbitrarily change corporate or department policies on their own. Actions involving these issues are the realm of senior management, and senior management alone.

Performance Metrics

Attuned to the pulse of their mature organizations, closed-loop managers initiate proactive measures to avoid the onset of problems by making organizational performance metrics dynamic. Each year, the bar is raised. At times, adversity is introduced intentionally to recharge and refocus employees. Managers recognize that the tougher the challenge, the tougher the

Building Organizational Alignment

situation, the quicker employees will pull together, reinforcing their interpersonal relationships. When things become comfortable, employees have a tendency to relax those relationships. To keep them strong, managers promote outside activities for the group. Experiential training centers, department social outings, even an occasional sharing of a pizza over lunch work well to reinforce trust between employees.

Performance metrics are constantly monitored to ensure the group remains in compliance with management's expectations, not their own. Discussions between the manager and the group are frequent and results oriented. Things that can make the group function better are a frequent topic of those discussions.

Recognition

In mature, as well as growing organizations, it is imperative that every employee understands how he or she, as an individual, is contributing to the organization's success. In much of today's contemporary literature and teachings, managers are encouraged to focus solely on organizational or team success. The commonly heard phrase is, "There is no 'I' in team." While this is absolutely true and certainly vital to organizational cohesiveness and success, there remains in every employee an individual need to be recognized as well. As Maslow delineated in his Hierarchy of Needs, once employees move beyond the second tier of the triangle by satisfying their financial and security requirements, the next tier is one of self-actualization and self-fulfillment. In short, there exists a real need for employees to be recognized for their individual contributions to the organization and their work group in particular. To ignore that need is to invite mediocrity at best, or at worst, outright employee revolt. The secret here is to recognize the organization's success first and foremost, then to recognize the individual employee's contribution to that success. By so doing,

> "Recognize the success of the organization first, then recognize each individual's contribution to that success."

Building Organizational Alignment

employees recognize that only through the organization's successes can their own personal recognition be assured.

Challenges

One drawback of a mature organization is that it is often less open to challenge. This problem goes beyond merely functional organizations. Examples abound in which large, successful corporations have consistently demonstrated a tendency to be less open to market challenges, resting comfortably on prior successes. Ultimately, many have seen that resistance to change has led to dire results.

Another concern facing the manager of a mature organization is that over time many of the employees begin to view their own day-to-day activities as mundane. The excitement that created the high-performance organization has subsided, leaving behind a bland sameness day-in and day-out. The enthusiasm, emotion, and energy that made the organization successful is lost, and with it the sense of urgency and satisfaction that drove employees to achieve continuously excellent performance. If left unchecked, boredom will set in. When that occurs, intra-organizational communication and cooperation will become strained. At that point, the once successful, dynamic organization will begin to pull apart.

One approach used by managers to reinvigorate stagnant employees or work groups is to provide them with information on how other departments are performing, addressing operational or process issues, or managing projects. Managers then compare and contrast departmental successes or opportunities for improvement against those examples to benchmark best practices within the organization. A good action in this regard is to periodically invite other functional managers to address the employees to share ideas and observations. At times, joint department meetings with other functions also serve to enlighten the stagnant em-

> *"Closed-loop managers use benchmarking to stimulate creativitiy and innovative thinking."*

ployees on new approaches and methodologies that can be applied to their job responsibilities.

External benchmarking is yet another tool used by closed-loop managers to instill creativity and innovative thinking in mature work groups. The intent is to introduce new and often wildly differing perspectives on how to address internal process or performance issues. This external vision provides insight into the way other successful organizations address similar problems and opportunities. Introducing a new perspective can effectively start the creative juices flowing again.

In mature organizations or work groups, it is wise for a manager to consciously and continuously expand the organization's horizon, scope, and objectives. The intent is to introduce increased responsibility, and with it expanded competencies into the organization. These new challenges keep the employees sharp by constantly moving their collective and individual standards of acceptable performance to higher levels, thus stretching their capabilities and commitment. To complement these additional challenges, managers will often:

- increase the group's sphere of influence,
- expand the group's level of responsibility,
- change the group's scope of work, or
- encourage or assign the group to work with other functional managers on projects of mutual benefit or concern.

Example 1

When the Japanese came into the American automotive markets, the Big Four (yes, there actually was a Big Four at the time) ignored their Japanese competitors. The belief was, "People aren't going to buy that Japanese stuff. They're always going to buy our stuff. We don't feel challenged, because we understand our markets better than our customers or our competitors do." Even as market share began to erode to the benefit of the Japanese manufacturers, some of the Big Four responded and some did not. Prior successes, size, and branding blinded them to the danger. Even those who survived have

Building Organizational Alignment

remained close-minded on the subject throughout much of the management ranks. As a result, their global market share has continued to decline year after year.

Because they are less open to challenge, mature organizations and their employees are often less creative and innovative. The employees feel comfortable doing things the same old way. After all, in the minds of American automotive manufacturers, their approach brought them recognition and success over the last 80 years, so why change it? The phrase, "If it ain't broke, don't fix it," though never openly stated, was often thought of by American automotive company employees.

To break out of complacency, there are times when a manager is required to change even successful processes or methodologies to guarantee consistently excellent performance. In fact, several blue-chip organizations have adopted what has become known as the "Theory of Deliberate Change" in which every employee is challenged to improve his or her job to the point that the job can be eliminated altogether. Doing so, however, does not mean the employee will be out of work. Just the opposite is true. The successful employee is rewarded with a new job, a bonus, and a challenge to do it again. The fact is, when challenged appropriately, even the most "comfortable" employees will demonstrate the creativity and innovation required to perform at higher levels. The net result is a win-win scenario for everyone. The message is clear—successful managers constantly challenge employees to be creative and innovative. Often, these same managers create deliberate change within the organization to ensure that stagnation and complacency never set in.

> "Successful managers constantly challenge employees to be creative and innovative."

Example 2

A successful Milwaukee firm follows the practice of reinforcing employee relationships by holding social events that take place in an outdoor setting. One of the more unusual outings promoted by management is called the "Arctic Open." The second Saturday of every February, every employee in the department, male and female, is encouraged to participate in a company-sponsored golf tournament. Make no mistake, in Milwaukee the second week of February is very cold—snow is the norm accompanied by single-digit temperatures (or less). Nonetheless, participation is always excellent. Employees from numerous departments and functions brave the elements to enjoy the camaraderie of bundling up to play golf with tennis balls on top of the snow, eat hot dogs, and drink a few beers—all the while sharing stories of former Arctic Opens. Some might say it is plain foolishness—maybe, maybe not. It is an activity that pulls everybody together simply because it makes no sense. Activities like the Arctic Open reinforce employee relationships and organizational communication. Events like this become social activities that employees look forward to. They introduce a little fun to the organization. Sometimes, getting a little crazy keeps employees from becoming stagnant.

> "Sponsoring fun activities builds employee relationships and communication."

Example 3

To encourage continuous improvement in both its supply base and internal operations, Honda has implemented a supply management program. It is directed by the purchasing organization, which assigns a group of supplier quality engineers to work hand-in-hand with suppliers. This active supply-site interaction has allowed Honda's purchasing organization to expand its sphere of influence. Not only are the purchasing professionals at Honda working more efficiently as a procurement organization, but the employees are reenergized by the expanded challenges, operational problems, and varied perspectives this new assignment requires. By sending these tenured employees out to work with suppliers who have specific operational needs, problems, and issues, Honda's managers have effectively elevated their employees to Maslow's level of self-actualization.

BUILDING CONSENSUS VS. CONSENSUS MANAGEMENT

Consensus is an interesting term that is not always given sufficient attention or priority within an organization. Many managers feel that reaching consensus among employees is time-consuming and thus impractical. The diversity of opinions within the organization is sited as a barrier to consensus, versus being a major contributing element to the consensus process. Is consensus mandatory? No, but it is preferable.

Consensus is a tool managers utilize to build a common focus or approach for all employees. It is a means to get everyone pulling in the same direction toward the achievement of mutual goals. Consensus does not mean that each individual subscribes to the idea that the selected approach or methodology is the best one. However, all employees will accept and support consensus as a reasonable compromise to address the issue at hand. Some managers find it expedient to simply take a vote among employees regarding a methodology or approach, opting to follow a democratic process. The belief is that the majority rule will ensure success and following among all employees. Quite the opposite is often the case. Simple votes produce a dramatic polarization of the employees, resulting in some pulling in the opposite direction to the one adopted by management and the "majority." This polarization leads to either active or passive resistance among the dissidents, which in turn, will lead to personnel or performance problems for the group downstream.

Again, consensus is simply an agreement on an approach. While it may not be the exact approach proposed by an individual employee, it is an approach—given all the circumstances, conditions, and constraints—that all employees can and will support. All of the pros and cons of the various recommended approaches have been discussed and assessed, and every employee has had an opportunity to present his or her position. Agreement is then reached on an approach or conclusion deemed by

> "There is a higher probability of success when consensus is reached because employees are supportive of the agreed upon action."

Building Organizational Alignment

the group to represent the best compromise for all involved. Total support is then expected, and realized, giving management and employees a higher probability of success in implementation of the selected approach.

The process for reaching consensus is as follows:

1. The issue at hand is thoroughly described including all relevant details, data, and influencing factors. Managers describe the issue in frank terms laying the groundwork for complete understanding by all.

2. The manager then sets a time limit for reaching consensus. The use of time in the decision-making process is instrumental in keeping all employees focused on the issue at hand. Selection of "odd" time constraints is especially useful. For example, most meetings are scheduled for an hour (no one really knows why, probably because that is the way business calendars are printed). But an hour is often too long, giving plenty of opportunity for the employees to lose focus through discussions of irrelevant issues. Seasoned managers utilize time limits that are unusual. For instance, they may choose to have a time constraint of 19 minutes, 23 minutes, or 27 minutes—rarely in excess of 30 minutes. The reason for this unusual selection is that because it is out of the ordinary, employees pay more attention to it. Focus is maintained and resolution of the issue through consensus is more readily attained.

3. As agreement is achieved on particular issues or items, managers remove them from further discussions, moving forward on only those issues still open. This approach maintains focus.

Employees are free to disagree at any time. Disagreement, however, must be accompanied with an explanation of why the employee feels the proposed approach is inadequate along with a new recommendation. The intent here is to force the employee to come to grips with the reason behind their resistance, and whether or not it is personal or justifiable. In addition, this approach forces all employees to repackage their ideas to make them more easily understood by all. Often, great ideas are lost because they are presented (packaged) incorrectly. By forcing every employee to present their ideas in a different manner, managers encourage them to market their ideas or approach in a way that ensures that their customers "get it" and "buy it."

One of today's frequently practiced management techniques is known as *consensus management*. The premise behind this management approach is to guarantee agreement among all participants through continuing discussions until everyone involved buys in to the recommended approach. Weak managers find this approach especially useful because it relieves them from the responsibility of making the difficult, often unpopular decisions required of managers. If total agreement is not reached among employees, the manager simply tables the issue until the next meeting, effectively avoiding conflict.

While good managers recognize the importance of consensus building, they also recognize the fallacy of the consensus management approach. While the objective of consensus is to pull employees together, there are times when it is impossible or impractical to do so. Managers cannot sit back and let their organization grind to a stop because of organizational gridlock. This is particularly true in situations where the manager is dealing with below-the-water-line issues requiring immediate attention. When a stalemate develops in the consensus process, closed-loop managers step in to make the decision to ensure organizational momentum is maintained. In such a case:

1. The manager gathers hard, fact-based, validated information regarding the issue.

2. The manager discusses with each employee their perspectives, ideas, and recommendations regarding how to address the issue.

3. The manager employs fundamental decision-making processes (discussed in Chapter 9) and problem analyses to reach a decision.
4. Once a decision is reached, closed-loop managers describe their selected approach to the employees and request their support for its implementation.

This approach is effective and motivating. Employees are given the opportunity to take part in the decision-making process. If they falter, the manager will step in to move the organization forward, thereby providing the employees with the security of a safety net. By so doing, this approach drives out the fear of failure among employees, thus ensuring a learning process.

Importance of Quantitative Analysis

Often when given a new assignment, employees within mature organizations will exhibit the tendency to take shortcuts or employ incomplete analyses of the situation. Rather than conduct the required situational and root-cause analyses (discussed in detail in Chapter 9), employees rely upon their individual and collective experience in similar situations to carry them through. Analysis is deemed unnecessary because their experience has taught them what to do. The same remedies are applied, often with less than acceptable results. This is a particularly difficult pattern to break for a manager. To do so, closed-loop managers become actively involved in leading the employees through a detailed set of analyses, providing them with new approaches and perspectives to consider as the exercise progresses.

Every act of resistance, active or passive, is met with persistence in the pursuit of quantitative analyses and the results that they yield. Closed-loop managers know that every business situation is unique, and while some may be similar to past experiences, they are also in some ways different. As such, each requires a thorough review before any actions are initiated. This dogged pursuit of verifiable evidence and facts keeps employees focused on the new challenge, thus rekindling their entrepreneurial instincts and internal competitiveness.

Building Organizational Alignment

The Dangers of Like Thinking

An unavoidable consequence of a mature organization is that employees often think and act alike. Much like a man and woman who have been married for 30+ years, they think alike, they act alike, they look alike, and after awhile, they even smell alike. Over time, employees who have been together for extended periods become myopically focused on a single perspective of how to conduct their individual and collective activities. While a homogenous viewpoint certainly facilitates consensus, it equally invites a loss in innovation and creativity among the employees. The willingness to challenge another employee's position, ideas, or opinions is offset by a feeling that such an act is unprofessional or simply inappropriate between friends. Because employees no longer challenge one another, outside perspectives and the benefits they bring to an organization are lost. Culture drives the organization—at least until a crisis occurs. By then, the ability to challenge the status quo and think outside the box are lost, leaving the organization vulnerable to the inflexibility that results.

In cases like this, the manager's role is to shake things up by introducing new challenges, performance targets, and responsibilities. New initiatives and projects are launched to reinvigorate mature employees. Mentoring assignments are given to seasoned employees to prepare newer or younger employees for the next step in their careers or simply to build depth within the organization. Employees are kept aware of their importance to the organization and their respective and collective roles in ensuring its success and longevity. They are encouraged to build upon past successes to take the organization to new levels of performance and customer service. In short, it is management's responsibility to recharge employees to capitalize on their many talents and maximize their contribution to the organization's future success.

> "It is the manager's responsibility to recharge employees to capitalize on their talents and maximize their contributions."

Challenging Others

Managers of mature work groups know to encourage employees to professionally challenge one another; at times even taking on the role of devil's advocate to get the ball rolling. Every comment or suggestion made by an employee is evaluated against the datum of facts. In the absence of fact, the employee is challenged to provide evidence in support of his or her position. Everything is considered an assumption until it has been validated. Soon the employees begin to re-adopt the proven methodologies they once employed to identify the realities of the business. Once refocused, they again begin challenging the ideas and comments of their peers, as well as their own perceptions and misconceptions. It is at this point that innovative thought patterns re-emerge.

> "Employees are encouraged to professionally challenge one another to validate assumptions."

Challenging a peer is not always comfortable for an employee, especially when that peer is recognized as an expert in his field and is highly vocal about his views on a particular topic. Organizational position is also a deterrent, as is tenure. It is imperative that these barriers be breached so every employee within the department participates and is heard.

Closed-loop managers openly encourage employees to state their position or opinion, and the facts in support of them. Direct questions to reluctant employees often yield a definitive response. When they do not, the manager talks privately to the reluctant employee. The employee is reminded of the importance of his input and his obligation to be an active participant in all organizational discussions and decisions.

One-on-one discussions are also undertaken when the so-called experts attempt to dominate discussions or decisions. In this instance, closed-loop managers advise the employee to tone down the rhetoric and to speak only after all other employees have expressed their positions. These dominating employees are advised to openly and honestly consider the opinions of other employees, and to show their peers the courtesy and professionalism they deserve. Often, one such discussion will suffice. If it does not, then more direct corrective action is necessary.

On the opposite end of the spectrum in the mature organization is the individual who rarely speaks up. Perhaps it is due to shyness or simply a feeling of inadequacy. Whatever the reason, it is the manager's responsibility to engage these employees in all department discussions and decisions. In most cases, these employees exhibit tremendous insight because their time is spent listening and analyzing rather than talking. They view all issues from a multitude of perspectives, thus giving them the ability to identify potential and real problems that other, more vociferous employees often overlook. Closed-loop managers extract this hidden knowledge base through direct questioning, reinforcement, mentoring, and coaching. Closed-loop managers recognize the value these quiet employees bring to the organization and work diligently to draw out their opinions.

SUMMARY

This chapter discussed visioning and the importance of organizational alignment to ensure that management's vision can be accomplished. It also discussed the critical importance of accurately and honestly base-lining the organization's current competencies and capacities, and then comparing those capabilities against the needs of the future. Employee skill sets are then analyzed in the near term and longer term to ensure compliance with the vision. If shortfalls are found to exist, employee training and development becomes a requirement for management. Where those skill set shortfalls cannot be addressed through training and development alone, succession planning becomes critical to meeting management's future plans.

Also discussed in this chapter were the difficulties of managing, developing, and motivating mature organizations along with the tools and techniques to effectively address the associated management challenges. And finally, the chapter addressed the pros and cons of consensus management and how managers can use it to their advantage.

Chapter 9 discusses several of the quantitative decision-making tools used by managers to minimize the risk and the possible impact of bad decisions on the organization.

REFERENCE

Musashi, Miyamoto. 1994. Translated by Thomas Cleary. *The Book of Five Rings*. Boston: Shambhala; New York: Distributed in the United States by Random House.

9
Base-lining Organizational Capabilities

OBJECTIVE

Every manager makes a mistake in judgment at one time or another, especially early in his career. Work is piled on employees at an unreasonable pace, unrealistic deadlines are set without apparent consideration of the current backlog of work, or extra projects are undertaken when the organization is already in excess of its practical capacity. Why do managers allow this to happen? Are they not aware of the problems facing the organization? Do they not realize how much work is already on the plate of every employee? Why are managers reluctant to say "No" to superiors who constantly push for more? These are the issues that will be explored in this chapter.

No, managers are not blind to the plight of employees. In most cases, they simply have too few quantitative tools with which to measure organizational capacity and capability. Simple tools like practical capacity studies provide reasonable solutions to many problems. But those practical capacity studies only provide so much insight. Often, a manager is required to dig deeper to find the drivers behind the problems facing his organization. Rather than settle for a short-term fix to a problem, successful managers address the problem's root cause to eliminate it at its source. If the business process is redesigned or reengineered to make it capable and controllable, then organizational capacity, performance, and capability will improve dramatically.

In this chapter, the fundamental tools of situational assessment are described along with their application in a business environment.

PRACTICAL CAPACITY ANALYSIS

Closed-loop managers use a simple management tool to measure organizational load factors: *practical capacity analysis*. It is used to measure the "practical" level of workload that an organization is reasonably capable of handling on an ongoing basis. The calculation of practical capacity is straightforward:

$$P_C = E_n \times P_f \times L_n \qquad \text{(Eq. 9-1)}$$

where:

P_C = practical capacity (maximum sustainable workload)
E_n = number of employees per period
P_f = productivity factor (usually no more than 55–60%)
L_n = number of available labor hours in a given period per employee

When practical capacity is compared against the ongoing departmental or organizational load factors (daily requirements, special projects, and other labor-consuming activities), the closed-loop manager quickly determines if the organization is in an overload situation and, if so, for what length of time that overload situation will exist. The same equation is used to determine projected capacity versus projected load over time so trends can be identified and adjustments made to personnel or load factors. Periodic overload situations are handled with overtime. Extended or frequent overload conditions, however, require more proactive solutions like outsourcing, in-sourcing, staff increases, work reprioritization, etc.

> "Practical capacity analysis helps managers match staffing requirements to workload."

Why is determining practical capacity so important? Simply put, it provides a mechanism for managers to determine if there is capacity to accept additional work within the department. Managers are able to plan for additional help; or, conversely, when excess labor exists, the department is capable of taking on more work. Armed with this information, managers are able to make good decisions regarding the various elements impacting their organizational capability and performance.

There is one caveat, however. Productivity, a major piece of the practical capacity equation, is often an elusive factor. Intuition and estimations for most organizations are rarely good enough to base organizational decisions on. It is here where risk begins to escalate for many managers. Thus, it is imperative for managers to apply quantitative measures versus qualitative estimations. Situational assessment, a quantitative measure, is often used to minimize risk to the manager and his organization.

Example

Here is a simple example of how productivity is commonly impacted within an organization. Consider an employee's job description. In many cases, employees work every day without one; or, if they do have a job description, it is frequently inaccurate. Does that make much of a difference? Consider this. Productivity is defined as doing exactly what is expected each day; in other words, what the job description defines. So 100% productivity is doing exactly what the job description calls for, nothing less, nothing more. This means no fire-fighting, no rescheduling, no waiting on information, no reworking, no redoing anything. Employees simply come to work every day, sit down at their desks or workstations, and perform the work as it is described in the job description. If that is considered to be 100% productivity, few employees give the company 100% productivity each day. In fact, when measured, most range between 55% and 65% productivity, simply because of all of the inefficiencies that exist within their work processes. So what are employees doing the remainder of the day? They are fire-fighting, chasing unimportant issues, reworking information or reports, rescheduling work activities or projects, redoing everything. They are doing things they would not need to do if the process and organizational problems impacting them were effectively resolved. These types of problems are the priorities that managers put ahead of all the others because they inhibit performance improvement within the organization.

SITUATIONAL ASSESSMENT

The tool used by closed-loop managers to correct business process problems and minimize risk is *situational assessment*. Situational assessment forces a manager to recognize each of the actual and potential issues that must be dealt with in the near term. These include carryover issues from the past, issues occurring now, and issues that will be forthcoming in the near future. All will impact organizational performance and capability.

> *"What do I know? What do I not know? What do I need to know?"*

A situational assessment focuses on isolating the drivers behind a current condition or problem. By understanding exactly what is happening and why it is happening, the closed-loop manager is better able to prepare for the risks that may lie ahead. As a result, proper contingencies are developed to offset the likelihood of risks occurring or to minimize their impact on the organization. Risk management is an essential and critical part of every manager's responsibilities.

In many cases, the current conditions are a result of an unrecognized or unmanaged problem, issue, opportunity, or change in:

- organizational, functional, process, or individual performance;
- market, industry, or business dynamics;
- personnel attitudes or morale;
- customer service;
- the quality of the organization's products or services;
- profits, cash flow, or other financial metrics; and/or
- operational or process cycle times, design, or controls.

Similar or unique issues, problems, and opportunities may occur in any or all of the critical business processes. The same problems may have occurred in the past. Or, there may be indications of an impending problem or opportunity in the near or foreseeable future. In any case, the closed-loop manager recognizes and addresses the ramifications of these problems, issues, or opportunities on the organization before a corrective action plan is developed and executed. They begin their assessments with a series of probing questions designed to highlight:

- the changes that occurred, creating these problems or opportunities,
- when those changes occurred,
- the breadth of those changes, and
- where those changes occurred.

Armed with this information, the closed-loop manager begins to isolate the root cause of the problem so that an effective plan of corrective action can be developed and implemented. Closed-loop managers recognize that every situation is uniquely different. As such, their assessment focuses on those conditions surrounding the unique characteristics and constraints of a particular situation. Utilizing approaches that generated past successes on other similar assignments or projects will not guarantee the same successful outcome.

Unresolved issues or problems of the past often have a significant impact on the conditions identified in the present day. Past actions taken to resolve those issues or problems are explored as well as the reason(s) why those attempts failed. Obviously, the last thing any manager wants to do is to repeat the failures of his or her predecessor. Thus in addressing such problems or issues, closed-loop managers turn first to the present to isolate any actions currently underway so as not to duplicate efforts or inadvertently hamper the progress of other functional or departmental managers by launching actions of their own.

Once the current conditions have been thoroughly defined and assessed, all related issues or opportunities are broken down into manageable components. There is an old adage,

Base-lining Organizational Capabilities

"You eat an elephant one bite at a time!" The same applies to business process problems and opportunities. They are quickly broken into their smallest elements so that a more thorough understanding of each element can be developed and the common links between those elements identified. One of the first questions closed-loop managers ask is, "Is there more than one issue or problem impacting the organization's performance in several areas, or is there a single issue or problem manifesting itself in different areas at different times, in different ways?"

Because resources are typically tight, it is necessary for every manager, new or experienced, to prioritize which issues or problems to pursue first based upon:

- the potential impact each problem, issue, or opportunity has on the organization's operational and budgetary performance;
- the potential for performance improvements, which can be documented by operational metrics;
- the level of risk in the near and long term for the organization;
- the impact on resource consumption or utilization; and
- the impact on customer satisfaction or customer expectations, internally and externally.

The next step is to apply fundamental problem-solving techniques (discussed in Chapter 10) to identify the root cause of the issue or problem creating or impacting the current situation. Then fundamental decision-making techniques are used to identify the best alternative to resolve the problem.

When assessing the situation, closed-loop managers will be working with a significant amount of both relevant and irrelevant data. Before an action plan is devised, all of that data is assessed and validated, then converted into usable information. By so doing, closed-loop managers maintain objectivity and minimize the likelihood that bias will lead

> "All data must be assessed and validated before it becomes usable information."

to incorrect conclusions and corresponding inappropriate actions.

Example

This example illustrates how situations can be different from what they appear to be and, thus, why a situational assessment is so vital.

A consultant is hired by an organization to conduct an analysis of its internal operations and recommend improvement opportunities. Early in the assignment, the consultant is told by the vice president and general manger that the new purchasing director, who has been on the job about a year and a half, is simply not performing at an acceptable level. The VP explains that the prices being paid by purchasing for raw materials and component parts has increased over 8% during the director's time in office, despite frequent oversight by top management. After significant deliberation by the VP and his staff, a decision is made to terminate this employee because his organization simply is not performing. The consultant is asked to assess the situation and to validate management's conclusions.

As the consultant begins to assess the situation within the purchasing organization, and the individual manager's performance in particular, he looks closely at the day-to-day operations within the department. The consultant assesses the director's cost control measures and his supplier development initiatives, as well as the way he deals with internal customers. On the surface, the director's actions appeared to be correctly focused and effective. Things just did not add up the way they had been explained. So the consultant digs further into the hard data. The records of actual purchases for the prior three years are researched. The consultant compares and contrasts actual pricing for the same commodities over that three-year period. The data from the situational assessment clearly reveals that prices have not gone up 8% as senior management thought. Rather, prices have actually gone down approximately 3% during his tenure. The purchasing director has, in fact, reversed an

Base-lining Organizational Capabilities

upward trend that started under his predecessor. He has actually brought prices back under control by negotiating several excellent long-term contracts.

In this case, senior management is convinced that their conclusions are correct. They are preparing to terminate the purchasing director for failure to perform to an expected level. However, they know they need validation before action is taken. The consultant's findings clearly indicate something to the contrary. Why is senior management apparently not in sync with reality?

Before approaching senior management with his findings, the consultant assesses the financial records used to calculate price variances. The controller lends his assistance. To support senior management's conclusion that prices have risen, the consultant requests a breakdown of every element of cost included in material pricing. From this analysis, the consultant finds that overhead is overly burdened as a result of the vastly increased sales force. And for some reason, this excess is being incorrectly applied against material pricing. So, on the surface, it appears to senior management that the director is not doing an effective job of controlling costs. Thus management's conclusion to terminate him seems justified. However, after a thorough assessment of the situation, the only conclusion that can be reached is that the director is doing a great job. The real problem lies in the way the controller is applying SG&A overhead rates to the material accounts.

When the consultant presents the contrary conclusion, the vice president and general manager is predictably shocked. A poor management decision was about to be made based upon a lack of solid information and a host of invalid assumptions. In many business situations, this is exactly what happens. Managers assume certain things to be true. They look at cursory data and fail to accurately assess the situation, resulting in a bad decision.

Assumptions and Their Risks

Every closed-loop manager's initial assessment of a particular situation will be based upon certain assumptions. The closed-loop manager, however, validates those assumptions before moving forward to ensure that he is on sound footing and personal or organizational biases have not clouded his judgment. The validity of the manager's initial assumptions will impact the ultimate success, costs, and timing of any actions or projects he launches—as well as his career.

One way closed-loop managers confirm their assumptions is through a simple analysis, such as the one shown in Table 9-1. To begin, the assumptions made in assessing the situation and corresponding business processes and environment are listed and then rank-ordered according to their degree of risk to the organization. The level of risk is defined as:

- High—If incorrect, these assumptions will result in probable failure of any corrective action or project. There is little chance that a successful recovery will be possible at any cost. These are the most critical assumptions; thus they carry the highest priority for analysis.

- Medium—If incorrect, these assumptions will adversely impact the organization's performance, budget, timing, and/or primary responsibilities. Recovery is possible, but only with a significant impact on the organization and its resources. These are the number two priorities for the manager to assess and address.

- Low—If incorrect, these assumptions can be contained with normal management control methodologies and techniques. Their impact is typically modest, thus rendering them to the lowest priority for assessment.

Once the assumptions have been ranked, the next step for the closed-loop manager is to assign the responsibility for validating each assumption to an employee within the department who possesses the requisite skills required to accurately complete the task. Validation is a fact-finding activity. It is not intended to support the assumptions made by the manager, but rather to confirm their accuracy or inaccuracy. These analyses are done carefully. The data sources utilized to substantiate or show the error of an assumption are included on the risk analysis worksheet. There is no guessing in this analysis.

Base-lining Organizational Capabilities

Table 9-1. Example assumptions matrix.

Assumption	Risk Level	Data Source(s)	Confirmation Assigned to	Validation	Action Plan
1. Systems hardware is adequate to support implementation.	High	IT manager and system specifications	S. Edwards	Yes	
2. Systems support from MIS and vendor will be adequate to ensure user readiness.	High	MIS skills set analysis	S. Shanks	Yes	
3. New applications software can be implemented and tested within 6 months.	High	Vendor user group analysis	B. Johanson	No	Reschedule for 10 months
4. Users will accept new software.	High	MIS survey	C. Schmidt	Yes	
5. Database conversion can be completed within 3–4 months with 99%+ accuracy.	Medium	CAS data user group analysis	M. Termini	Yes	
6. Issues have been resolved by vendor and in-house MIS personnel.	Medium	IT manager and software specifications	J. Armstrong	Yes	
7. User training can be completed by in-house MIS personnel.	Medium	MIS skills set analysis	J. Kimbrough	Yes	
8. Vendor will deliver software on or before contracted date.	Low	Contract terms and penalties	C. Calcara	Yes	

New Managers

Rarely in a new position is a manager given a grace period to grow gradually into the job. The first day, there is pressure from all fronts to fix nagging problems and address performance deficiencies; in short, he must hit the ground running. With the dynamics of global markets and rapidly changing technologies, there is even more of an expectation that managers know immediately what to do and how to do it. They are expected to quickly act to implement solutions, regardless of their limited tenure in the position.

New managers are faced with a host of looming problems immediately upon starting a new job. These are often serious problems, sometimes strategic in nature, which must be resolved immediately. There is also a backlog of older problems that his predecessor left behind—personnel problems left unresolved, budget overruns to address, pending project deadlines—the list is endless. In addition, there are actions, projects, and activities in progress, which will require the new manager's attention so momentum is not lost. Real and potential problems will surface; all will require attention from the new manager. There is simply no opportunity for the new manager to gracefully ease into the job. Obviously, this situation puts pressure on the manager. Compelled to take some sort of action, many give into temptation, making bad decisions with dire consequences. Before a closed-loop manager launches an action, he clearly and completely understands exactly what is happening and why. There are three questions the closed-loop manager endeavors to accurately answer:

1. What do I know?
2. What do I not know?
3. What do I need to know?

Good management decisions are based upon a thorough assessment of all the issues, their root causes, an evaluation of the various courses of action available, and the consequences of each alternative. Seasoned managers have learned the secret to success: *assess, analyze, decide,* and then *act*. Before

Base-lining Organizational Capabilities

making decisions, they uncover the root causes of problems. Only then can opportunities to resolve them be understood. To do otherwise is to shoot in the dark and hope for the best.

With so much to do, new managers must effectively prioritize and allocate the available time and resources to those issues that are most significant to the organization. These are the issues and opportunities that will yield tangible positive results for the organization. To prioritize the issues, closed-loop managers often begin by asking a series of questions to help assess the infrastructure or base-line the organization. These questions are intended to assess each of the issues impacting the manager's organization, as well as those impacting other departments. What the manager seeks is supportable information that will allow those within the organization to stop fire-fighting and fix the problems.

> *"Assess, analyze, decide, and then act."*

All managers base their priorities on the facts before them. However, the initial information they receive is typically comprised of relevant data, irrelevant data, important data, unimportant data, facts, and just plain fiction. As a consequence, all data will require a degree of assessment and validation before it can be utilized in the decision-making process. Experienced managers know the importance of moving quickly through the data collection and assessment phases of situational assessment by first determining what they do not know, then acquiring only the amount of data that will be required to answer the relevant questions.

New managers often complain that they have insufficient data with which to make a decision. As a point of fact, no manager has the luxury of spending an inordinate amount of time or resources to acquire every possible fact. To maintain momentum, managers are required to make decisions based upon data that is readily available. This by no means, however, is an excuse to shoot from the hip. Rather, it is intended to bring reality into the equation. Situational assessment requires that managers assess the available data, identify the additional information required for a supportable decision, gather the required additional data, and make a decision. There simply is no time to study it to death.

Typical Questions

Each situational assessment focuses on identifying what a manager knows, what she does not know, and what she needs to know to satisfy organizational objectives. In this case, "know" refers to validated facts rather than assumptions. A series of introspective questions is developed to uncover the answers to those issues where hard facts do not exist or are not known. The following questions are typical of those asked during a situational assessment to uncover missing facts or to validate a manager's assumptions.

- In what specific areas is the organization failing to achieve the desired levels of performance? In what areas is the organization's performance acceptable? Is the gap between expected levels of performance significant or minimal? What factors exist to explain the performance differential?

- Are personnel issues contributing to the organization's failure to meet the expected levels of organizational performance? What personnel issues are contributing to the acceptable levels of performance in other areas? What factors exist to explain the differences?

- Which business processes are delivering consistently acceptable results? Which are not? Are the inputs for those inadequately performing business processes in full compliance with what is required to effectively support them? If not, what is the gap between what is required and what is delivered? Are the non-performing business processes adequately managed and controlled? Are the non-performing business processes capable of delivering the expected results under normal circumstances and operating constraints?

Base-lining Organizational Capabilities

- What projects or actions have been launched in the past, or are now underway, to address these specific performance issues? If those actions were successful, why has performance again declined? Is there a direct correlation that can be found? If, on the other hand, the former actions or projects were not successful, what are the factors that led to the failure? Are those factors still in existence?

- Are organizational, process, and employee performance appraisal criteria in alignment with management's expectations and requirements? Do they align with the expectations and requirements of all internal customers? Are they consistently applied, measured, and understood by all employees? Are they consistent with industry standards, competition, or evolving trends in customer service?

- Is management of the organization (at all levels) effective in leading and motivating employees to achieve organizational goals and requirements? If so, why is the organization not responding? If not, what changes are required?

- What external factors are impacting organizational, process, or employee performance? Can those external factors be eliminated, reduced adequately, or controlled consistently? If so, what actions are required to do so? If not, what actions are required to address those factors?

These surface questions will often lead to the requirement for a more detailed analysis of one or more areas within the organization. In effect, they will begin to define for the manager her limits of knowledge. To ascertain why performance deficiencies exist, fact-finding and data analysis is required. Ultimately, an action plan(s) is developed, followed by the launching of a project, or projects, to address the areas where corrective actions are needed.

> "A situational assessment breaks down complex processes into smaller components to enable better understanding."

In essence, situational assessment is used by closed-loop managers to break down complex business processes and situations into smaller components so that a better understanding of each can be achieved. Once the manager understands exactly what is happening, she is in a better position to fix existing problems or capitalize on opportunities for performance improvement.

For managers, the secret to successful assessments is to find the data necessary to expand understanding of the situation, then to look for links between the various factors observed to determine if a common cause exists for all performance problems within the organization. A single problem may be manifesting itself in a number of different ways, making it appear that numerous problems exist in many areas within the organization. Or, multiple problems may be impacting organizational performance. Knowing the answers provides a manager with an idea of the scope, timing, and resource load required to bring performance back to acceptable levels. Effective managers always deal with causes, not with symptoms.

> *"Effective managers deal with causes, not symptoms."*

Setting Priorities

Not every issue is critical. Priorities are set based upon which problems introduce maximum risk to the organization or impact organizational performance most severely. High-risk, high-severity issues always receive first priority. Once those are addressed and resolved, the closed-loop manager moves down to the next level to start the process again.

Setting priorities is never easy. It is even harder to keep them. Tremendous pressure exists to constantly alter priorities to suit political or personal agendas. Often managers will gravitate toward those things they like doing, or are more comfortable doing, to avoid politically charged issues. No manager has that right. Without exception, priorities must be set solely upon the results of a situational assessment and executed accordingly. To do otherwise is to compromise the organization's ability to compete effectively.

Base-lining Organizational Capabilities

Example

There was an incredibly brilliant inventor who was the chairman, president, and CEO of a publicly traded company, which he founded. In that position, he was responsible for setting the strategic direction for the organization, managing the organization's overall performance in the marketplace, and making the tough decisions relative to ensuring compliance with customer and stockholder expectations. Above everything else, however, he loved to invent new products. Thus, he frequently gravitated back into the R&D lab to invent whenever there was a critical or urgent business problem that required his involvement. He was not comfortable making tough business decisions, so instead he chose to avoid them. In the end, his inability to deal with difficult issues led to his downfall and dismissal by the company's board of directors. Managers, no matter at what level within the organization, are never free to work only on those things that come easy or are enjoyable to them.

Similar to the brilliant inventor, many technical professionals have the tendency to gravitate back into their individual comfort zones in times of crisis, preferring to stay close to those things that they know best, that are less risky, or less challenging. But once they become a manager, that avenue is closed forever. A manager is required to assess the situation, develop a thorough understanding of all salient factors, and then make the appropriate (and sometimes tough) decision relative to how to resolve the issue.

Nuisance Issues

No matter how much anyone complains, threatens, or nags, nuisance issues are never included in a manager's top priorities. The "squeaky wheel syndrome" often leads new and experienced managers to assign critical or limited resources to non-critical issues just to quiet another manager or employee. This is always a poor use of resources and a poor management decision.

Here is a common scenario. A new manager takes the reins of his organization. Within the first two to three days on the job, another functional manager or some other employee

Base-lining Organizational Capabilities

corners him. "Hey, glad you're on board. Listen, I've had this nagging problem for the last three years. Your predecessor would never take care of it for me, but I know you'll get right on it." After numerous follow-up visits from the functional manager, the new manager relents and assigns a key employee to solve the other manager's problem even though it is minor in the scheme of things. In the meantime, critical issues are ignored, leading to a continuance of performance deficiencies and organizational problems. As the spiral continues, the new manager loses credibility, then support. The end result is inevitable.

If the other manager's issue is an important priority, that is one thing. If it is not, it is best left for later. In the case of a nuisance issue, the new manager's response is, "Listen, I know that it is important to you and I will address your problem in due time. But quite honestly, there are other things that are more urgent and requiring immediate attention. I will get to your issue as quickly as I can. But I can't do it now."

Constant juggling of priorities to meet even senior management's wishes will result in confusion, frustration, and a lack of direction, all of which cripple organizational efficiency. There are times when every manager must just say, "No." Senior management will understand. They, too, fix priorities based upon their relative impact on organizational performance objectives, operational cycle time, operational costs, overhead, resource utilization, financial impact, and customer service. It is the same at every management level.

SUMMARY

A fundamental rule of management is never to attempt to resolve an issue until it is completely understood, including the drivers that have created it. This is why situational assessments are utilized. They uncover the facts surrounding the situation and the assumptions that exist regarding it.

One final example is used here to illustrate the importance of situational assessment. The CEO of a major electronics firm contacted a consultant because he needed help with a problem.

Base-lining Organizational Capabilities

The conversation went as follows: "Mike we're losing market share. In fact, we have lost over 13 percentage points in market share over the last several months. We need your help in developing a solution to the problem." The consultant's response may have shocked the CEO—"Believe it or not, loss of market share is not your problem. It is merely a symptom of it. Before we can effectively implement a plan to regain your lost market share, we must first find out the reason why you lost it in the first place, then fix that problem."

Fire-fighting is a common ailment for managers. To be effective, a manager must stop, assess the situation carefully, identify its drivers, set priorities, create an action plan, and then implement the plan. This is what situational assessment is all about; separating those issues that must be addressed from those that merely consume valuable resources with little, if any, return for the investment. Situational assessment is a critical tool that has saved many a manager significant downstream grief.

In the next chapter, the decision-making process will be outlined using quantitative versus qualitative techniques to ensure an unbiased, supportable action plan that minimizes the overall risk to the organization as well as to its manager. As before, the tools and techniques will be applied in real-world scenarios from industry to illustrate their application by experienced managers.

10
Effective Problem-solving and Decision-making

OBJECTIVES

In this chapter, the principles of problem-solving and decision-making will be reviewed. Every effective manager utilizes quantitative methodologies to identify the drivers behind current operations, business processes, and performance deficiencies. Shooting from the hip is never an option. Actions are based upon the results of a comprehensive situational assessment and accompanying decision analyses. By so doing, poorly conceived actions are greatly minimized.

Closed-loop managers are keenly aware that the results of a poor decision are always visible to employees and senior management. And while sound decision-making practices do not ensure career safety, they do greatly improve the possibility of career advancement.

PROBLEM ANALYSIS

The basis for accurate evaluation of a given issue, opportunity, or problem is cause-and-effect reasoning—isolating exactly what has gone wrong and what has caused the identified situation to occur. A *problem* is the visible effect of a cause that occurred at some time in the past. The key for every manager is to relate that exact cause to the exact effect being observed, because only then can the problem be effectively resolved and kept from recurring.

Problem-solving begins with a comprehensive, accurate definition of the problem.

Effective Problem-solving and Decision-making

- Exactly what problem or issue is to be resolved?
- Where was the problem or issue first observed?
- When did the problem or issue first appear?
- What is the significance or magnitude of the problem?

The answers to these questions will yield important information with which to isolate the scope of the problem or issue, and thus the breadth of the corrective actions necessary to resolve it. For instance, if the gap between the expected level of organizational performance and the actual performance is narrow, the corrective actions will likely entail a straightforward process improvement effort. If, on the other hand, the gap is wide, then the corrective actions will likely involve more extensive reengineering or redesign efforts requiring more resources, time, and money.

> "Throwing employees and money at problems will not yield optimum results for the organization, its customers, or its stockholders."

In defining the problem, it is essential for the closed-loop manager to isolate both what is and *what is not* happening. This approach provides the basis for comparing what actually is happening versus what should be happening, as well as defining the gap between the two, along with the factors that have impacted or magnified the deviations.

Closed-loop managers look for changes that have occurred in each of the "should be" conditions or performance. Once identified, the manager explores the what, where, when, and magnitude of each. The true root cause of the problem will result from a thorough assessment of the four questions above. Only the true root cause can create the effect being observed. No other cause can. So, once the potential root cause has been identified, it is confirmed through a replication of the problem or situation. Only then can the manager be assured he has found the true basis of the problem. With technical problems, simulation techniques are employed to determine if the true root cause has been identified. With business process or performance issues, however, simulation techniques are often not available. In such

Effective Problem-solving and Decision-making

cases, common sense is utilized to ascertain if the cause identified realistically creates the same effects as have been observed. Deviations are taken back in time as far as necessary to isolate when the problem was first observed. This leads to the changes that occurred and ultimately to the root cause.

The goal is to isolate the singular root cause from the field of multiple, probable, possible root causes. As illustrated in the root cause model in Figure 10-1, the objective is to come down the model as far as possible, ultimately minimizing the number of possible root causes associated with the issue or problem under analysis.

Ultimately, the manager's responsibility is to minimize the cost, minimize the risk, and maximize the return on investment for the organization. A thorough root-cause analysis of each problem/issue is vital to meeting those objectives.

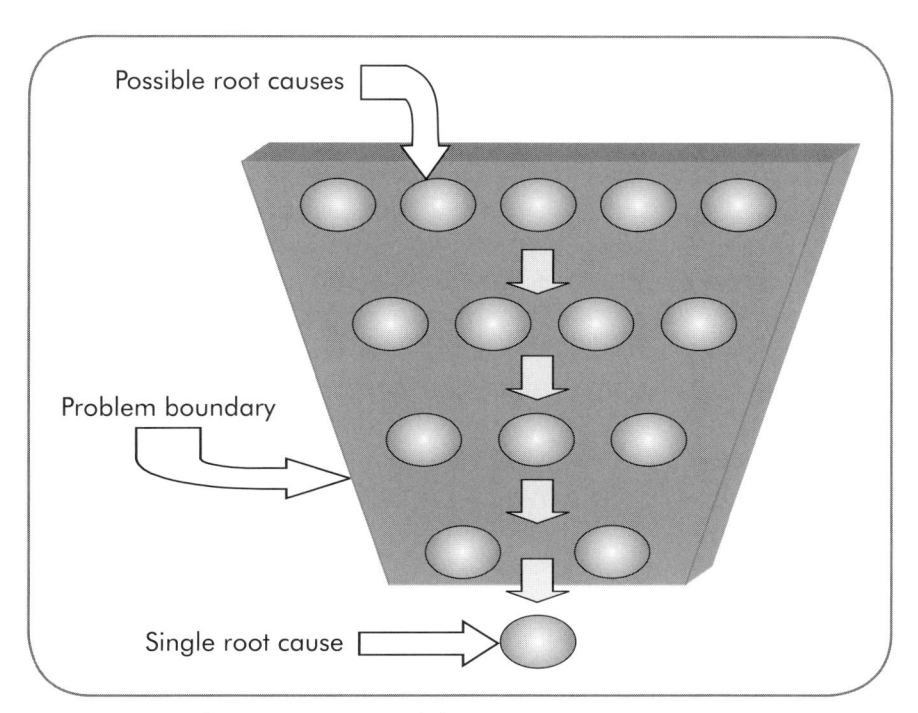

Figure 10-1. The root cause model.

Effective Problem-solving and Decision-making

No Shortcuts

It is important to note that pressure and stress often lead managers to make poor decisions or take unwise shortcuts in the problem analysis process. In fact, the more pressure a manager feels, the more risk he is willing to take to relieve it. To illustrate, consider the numerous product and/or business decisions launched in the past that were poorly conceived and executed. Why did those managers fail to see and address the risks? Why did they not see the flaws in their own decision processes? Were these simply careless or incapable managers? No, they were not. Either they did not assess the situation accurately or they succumbed to the external or internal pressures that increased their willingness to take unjustifiable risks.

Constraints in Assessing the Root Cause

In working through the root cause model, there are three possible constraints that occasionally prohibit a manager from reaching the singular root cause. The constraints are real and must be addressed by every manager as part of the situational and root-cause analysis phases to ensure that an accurate decision is made regarding the correct course of action.

The first constraint is *time*. There are instances in which a manager is forced to stop at a level above the singular root cause because time constraints are forcing more immediate action. For example, a manager may find it takes only one month to work through the model to a level where there are three remaining possible root causes, but an additional 10 months to work his way through to the singular root cause. In such cases, the manager is forced to stop further analysis to move the improvement efforts along quicker. If such a decision is made, the manager includes solutions to all three possible root causes in his planning. Arbitrarily selecting just one of the three is risky and ill advised.

The second constraint is *financial*. With many business problems, the financial costs associated with arriving at the singular root cause may outweigh the benefits of the effort. In short, the return-on-investment for additional analysis is not justifiable. In situations like this, it is the wisest choice for a manager to stop at a level above the singular root cause, and then include all remaining possible root causes in the ultimate solution. The implementation may be more complex, but the total return-on-investment will generally be much greater.

The third constraint is *technology*. For example when TWA's flight 800 was lost, several government agencies became involved in analyzing the flight data to determine what had occurred. From the multitude of possible root causes, the agencies quickly reduced the possibilities to three: missile, bomb, or mechanical failure. Due to the nature of the catastrophe and its potential impact given the number of 747s in service, it was also quickly concluded that stopping at that level of the root cause model was unacceptable.

To find and retrieve all possible pieces of the plane, an extensive search of the sea floor was begun. Once found, each piece was carefully examined and the plane reconstructed. Evidence revealed that a missile was not the cause of the crash. They moved down the model one more level: bomb and mechanical failure were the remaining possibilities. Wave front, flame propagation, and chemical residue studies were conducted along with a series of other tests. The results confirmed that the crash was not the result of a bomb, but rather a mechanical malfunction in the center fuel tank. Immediate actions were then taken to implement the required repairs on all remaining 747s and all other Boeing planes with similar fuel tank configurations.

> "Time, finance, and technology are constraints that can hinder a manager from reaching a single root cause."

If the investigators had merely guessed at the root cause of the disaster, many more such incidents would have likely occurred. However, had the NTSB been unable to recover sufficient evidence in their investigation, they would have been forced to consider all three possibilities equally. The ultimate conclusions and actions would then have had to incorporate actions to address and prevent all three possible causes of the crash, as technology would not have allowed further definitive analysis.

Problem-solving Tools

Most managers from technical disciplines have a background in utilizing basic problem-solving techniques. For some reason, however, they forget that those same techniques can be used to resolve project and business management issues. Application of basic problem-solving techniques is essential in isolating the problems and/or issues (and their associated drivers) that must be addressed during the tactical planning and execution phases of every corrective action.

Commonly used problem-solving tools include:

- evaluation and planning tools, including brainstorming, process maps, gap analyses, and cause-and-effect diagrams;
- data collection tools, including quality function deployment techniques, voice-of-the-customer analyses, surveys, focus groups, questionnaires, interviews, measurements, and observations; and
- data display tools, including run charts, histograms, check sheets, Pareto charts, and trend analyses.

The use and application of these tools is widely understood and generally practiced by most technical professionals and managers in their daily work. However, the tools are typically applied too narrowly to be useful for management-level decisions. In general, a combination of these techniques is better suited to aid a manager in working his way down the root cause model. Figure 10-2 illustrates how different combinations are employed to yield tangible results.

The analysis begins with a brainstorming session to identify all of the possible, probable root causes of the problem or issue. The closed-loop manager then begins to combine and categorize those possible root causes through a cause-and-effect analysis

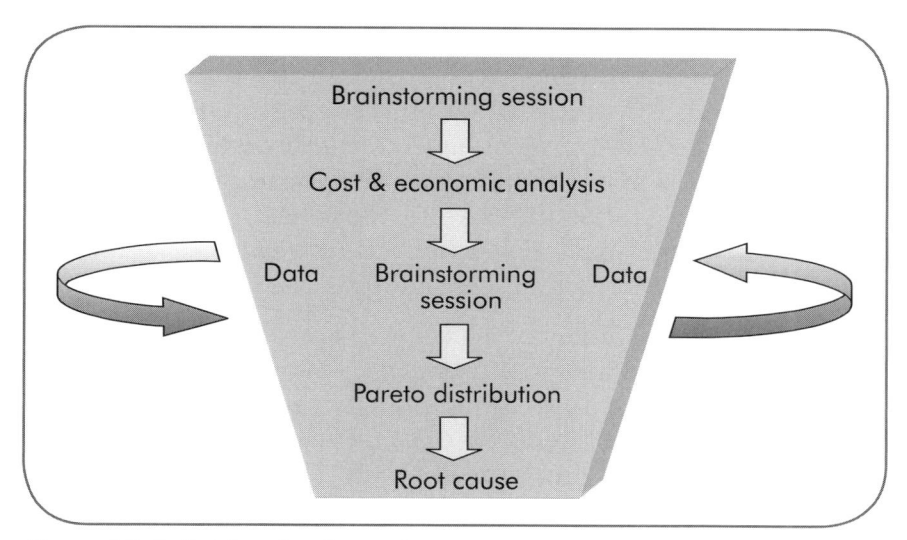

Effective Problem-solving and Decision-making

Figure 10-2. Solving for the root cause.

(fishbone diagram), gap analysis, or process analysis. Subsequent iterations involve the collection of data to support the manager's analyses and assumptions. After several iterations, the results will take the form of a standard Pareto distribution, yielding the one or two most probable root causes. The manager then determines if time and money will allow additional analyses to get to a singular root cause. For the closed-loop manager, this final business decision is based upon the unique conditions and constraints surrounding the particular situation he is facing.

Collecting Data

Often the data used during problem-solving sessions is found to contain a significant amount of error. As a result, there are several rules to follow in collecting data to ensure that additional variables are not introduced into the evaluation process.

1. Identify exactly what is required to know or learn, and then determine the type and amount of data necessary to satisfy those requirements. Ask: "What do I know?,"

Effective Problem-solving and Decision-making

"What do I not know?," and "What do I need to know?" It is important to remember that data costs money and its collection consumes valuable resources and time. While data is an essential element in the problem analysis phase, the collection of redundant or irrelevant data is a waste. Therefore, restricting the effort to collecting only the data necessary to make a sound decision regarding the cause of the problem is an essential first step.

2. Sanitize the data by correcting obvious errors and filling in the gaps. Caution is in order here. Closed-loop managers know *not* to assume the data is accurate as collected, even if it is computer generated. Inaccurate data will mislead a manager, causing him to reach the wrong conclusions and initiate invalid corrective actions.

3. Organize the data by type, category, time, frequency, etc. Thereafter, the data is condensed by computing descriptive statistics such as averages, mean, or range. Finally, the data is converted into useful information using the data display tools identified previously.

4. While collecting and analyzing the data, the closed-loop manager continues to monitor the situation to ensure that nothing has changed that could render the initial analysis invalid. This is part of ongoing risk management and is an essential step that cannot be overlooked.

ASSESSMENT CLUES

There exist a number of both soft and hard clues to performance problems. Closed-loop managers use them in assessing each particular issue. In general, the soft clues are those that provide insight from a general perspective. They act as a signal for managers to explore the hard data clues more intensely in an effort to isolate the drivers behind the business environment in question. Every discipline contains its own clues to performance problems.

> "Soft and hard clues help to isolate the drivers behind the situation in question."

The following discussion will provide a sampling from several functional areas to illustrate where and how these clues can be found.

Rejection and Rework

Soft Clues

In a manufacturing company, a typical soft clue is large volumes of materials constantly requiring rework or review by the quality inspectors. In an information technology company, the presence of a significant number of source-coding errors requiring debugging is a common soft clue. In a financial institution, a useful soft clue is an unacceptably high number of customer account errors. Errors like these are an indication of either process-related errors or process control deficiencies.

Still another soft clue to bottlenecks, rework, and errors is an untidy work area. Overflowing inboxes, for example, often represent information bottlenecks. The same holds true in a manufacturing plant or construction site. When materials are left in disarray, or machinery is left poorly maintained, delays and mistakes result.

Hard Clues

The first hard data sources for managers to explore are reject reports: not only the number, but the aging of those reports and the repetitiveness of the same or similar errors. In reviewing them, there is frequently a common link or root cause that a little due diligence will uncover.

A second hard clue is a high volume of change notices. When change notices are frequent, it is usually an indication that something upstream has gone awry or is out of control.

A third hard clue to the cause of rework and rejections is the complexity of information and/or material flow. Common sense dictates that the more complex a process flow is, the more likely the occurrence of errors. A simple flow map provides the information necessary to identify redundancies, bottlenecks, and backflows in an information or material process flow. Multiple

Effective Problem-solving and Decision-making

handling or keying is also a visible culprit leading to frequent rework, rejection, or errors. A simple rule of thumb is: *The longer a process takes, the more complex and convoluted its routing; and the more people involved in a process, the higher the probability that an error or mistake will result.* Or, in more simple terms:

$$Time + Complexity + People = Errors \qquad \text{(Eq. 10-1)}$$

A final hard data source is a backlog report. It will reveal how long information or materials are typically delayed. Backlog reports identify the queue time within each process step, or in other words, the time within the process that adds little, if any, value to the organization.

Example

Many engineering managers accept numerous and frequent engineering changes as a way of life. So too, have purchasing managers accepted purchase order changes as routine. In fact, both are indications of defective processes or control deficiencies within the business processes.

From a managerial perspective, change orders cost money—often thousands of dollars each. If a proposed change order does not generate an acceptable return-on-investment, the change is denied by the closed-loop manager. This action ensures that the root cause of the problem is surfaced and that corporate resources are not wasted on non-value-added actions. Few managers have taken the time to isolate the actual cost to the organization of engineering or purchase order changes. By taking the time to work with accounting to correctly isolate the cost of those changes, managers are better prepared to make an informed business decision relative to the actual value of a proposed change.

Performance Variations

Soft Clues

When performance variations occur between individuals or between shifts, the reason behind those variations is often at-

Effective Problem-solving and Decision-making

tributed to experience, seniority, or lack of support. The reality, however, is that none of these commonly held beliefs are valid. Performance variations are often due simply to the absence or inaccuracy of process or functional documentation. Closed-loop managers commonly find that newer employees and off-shift employees lack the information necessary with which to do their tasks consistently. The information to do so exists, but it is often created by more senior employees and is rarely shared. This uncooperative behavior ensures that the more experienced employees always achieve higher performance levels, and thus higher pay and recognition.

Hard Clues

When performance variations occur, experienced managers know to look first at the documentation and compare it to the actual "best practices" within the work group. When differences are identified, the optimum approach or methodology is documented. Training on the identified best practices is then conducted (often by the employee who developed the approach) to ensure compliance among all employees and across all shifts. After proper training, performance variations either stop completely or diminish significantly.

Another hard clue is an employee's job description. In many organizations, employee job descriptions are poorly written, inaccurate, or overly general. In some cases, they are nonexistent. When employees are left to "figure it out for themselves," it is no wonder that performance variations exist. Without guidance and structure, employees will gravitate to approaches to their jobs that are most comfortable.

Effective job descriptions include specific requirements, specific performance metrics, and the specific actions required, along with the expected results of those activities. Closed-loop managers frequently incorporate a detailed process map of the employee's job-related processes into the job description, which includes

> "All business processes under control of the closed-loop manager are mapped."

Effective Problem-solving and Decision-making

internal supply and support functions as well as internal customer requirements. All business processes under the control of the closed-loop manager are mapped. No action of value occurs without a plan. The job description and process definition provide the basis for that plan.

Documentation errors provide hard clues to performance variations and are the root cause of numerous performance variations along with their related budget overruns.

Example

A simple bill-of-material document drives all major subsystems within an integrated business system—item master files, vendor master files, cost master files, and manufacturing master router files. A minor error in this single document of 3% will often lead to a compounded error of up to 20% within the master subsystems over time. The resulting inefficiencies within all major organizational functions are rarely linked to this root cause. Therefore, functional managers are left to scramble within the confines of their organizations to patch business processes as best they can. Performance and budget variances will continue until the true root cause of the problem is identified and corrected.

Customer Service Deficiencies

Soft Clues

There is an old sales and marketing axiom: "Unsatisfied customers just fade quietly away without a single vocalized complaint." But on their way, they tell 10 of their friends, family, or business associates. As a result of this quiet customer defection paradigm, market share erosion remains a constant worry to many business managers. But there is a financial factor in this equation as well. It will often cost an organization 10 times more to replace a lost customer than it will to retain that

> "It often costs an organization 10 times more to recruit a new customer than it does to retain one."

same customer. Consequently, common sense dictates that customer retention is the number one priority; growth in market share is a distant second.

If a manager identifies significant customer "churn," there is a customer service problem within one or more processes or departments within the organization. A soft clue to this problem is found by observing the customer service representatives (CSRs) in action. Their pace, morale, and even the sheer number of CSRs, are indicators. High stress levels, rapid pace, long hours, frustration—all indicate that significant customer service issues exist.

Hard Clues

The obvious hard clue to a customer service problem is the number of customer complaints. Closed-loop managers spend at least one day every month either observing or actively involved with customer service personnel to understand their problems and how the manager's department, work group, or processes contribute to those issues. The most commonly adopted cross-functional performance metric for customer service is the reduction in customer complaints and defections. Performance metrics such as this are the drivers behind every organization's and every employee's performance evaluation criteria. By tying every manager and every employee to common metrics, daily decisions are made by every employee and manager to benefit the customer versus any internal agenda, priority, or need. Organizations that adopt this focus not only stay in business, but they thrive in business.

Other hard clues include the employee turnover rate within the customer service operation and escalating warranty costs. These too are harbingers of customer service deficiencies that demand immediate management attention at all levels within the organization.

The ratio of customer order processing time to product/service delivery time is another hard clue to customer service problems. Closed-loop managers know to compare the amount of time it takes to process a customer order against the amount

Effective Problem-solving and Decision-making

of time it takes the organization to satisfy that order. If the order processing time exceeds the production or delivery time, serious system or process problems exist. It is not uncommon, for example, for a manager to find that it takes up to four times longer to process a customer's order than it takes to satisfy it.

Example

Car buyers have long recognized that if time is an issue in their decision to purchase, they must select from the available cars on a dealer's lot. To order a car from the factory with specific options, and only those options, most customers must be willing to wait up to 12 weeks or longer for the manufacturer to produce and deliver the car. Yet, it takes the manufacturer only 18–22 hours to actually produce the car. So what is the difference between the one- to two-day production cycle and the 12–16-week delivery time? The answer is queue time, order-entry time, order-processing time, and a host of other non-value-added activities that drive the customer to another provider.

Toyota and Nissan recognized this issue early and capitalized on it as a market differentiator to garner increased competitiveness and market share. Through a series of decisive management actions, both companies offer to customize any customer order and deliver that vehicle within three days. Consequently, the competition has been forced to introduce other incentives to entice customers to wait or select from available inventories. These incentives come at a cost to the dealer, often resulting in a significant reduction in the dealer's margin.

Personnel Problems

Soft Clues

Unhappy employees are apt to perform poorly, make frequent mistakes, and present a poor image to customers. Seasoned managers have long recognized that if employees are not happy, if their morale is down, immediate action is required to identify and fix the root cause of the discontent. Doing nothing leads quickly to measurable losses in employee productivity and retention. This is especially true if a company has a history of labor unrest.

Hard Clues

Hard clue indicators of personnel problems include high absenteeism, high turnover, or noticeable "attitudes" among employees, especially key employees, which drive productivity down. Caution, however, is a requirement in isolating and understanding the drivers behind performance issues. In some industries during the last decade, especially the high-tech or "dot-com" industries, turnover rates remained consistently above historical levels as organizations raided talent from competitors or other regional firms to sustain growth. Managers in these industries quickly recognized that a high turnover rate was the norm and not necessarily an indicator of a business or management problem. In other industries, however, turnover rates in excess of 2–3% annually sounded the alarm. The secret to success for a manager is to compare the trends within his specific industry or geographic area against the norm for that industry or region to determine if the turnover or absenteeism rate is within the norm. When a manager finds that his rates exceed the norms, immediate assessment and corrective actions are in order.

Another caution involves cultural norms. Managers who have been given international assignments (these, by the way, are absolutely great career accelerators) often attempt to apply the cultures and norms from their country or culture of origin to the employees in the new location. This is a recipe for disaster. Managers with experience in international venues recognize that the cultures and norms inherited with the new international assignment drive employee behavior and cannot be arbitrarily altered by a manager, especially if those cultural changes are in conflict. As Japanese and German managers learned when their companies opened operations in the United States during the 1980s and 1990s, cultural norms are resilient when it comes to resisting change. As those managers learned, a change in management style is often the secret to success.

Effective Problem-solving and Decision-making

Blending cultures and norms allows managers and employees to meet halfway, making it a win-win for all parties concerned.

Supply Chain Problems

Supply chain problems plague many, if not most organizations. Because of the importance of the supply chain to an organization's success and the complexities involved in effectively monitoring and controlling it, closed-loop managers remain actively involved in supplier development and in resolving compliance problems. To illustrate, during a recent discussion with over 300 senior executives from a broad array of industries, the single biggest concern expressed was the willingness and ability of the supply chain to support their organizations' growth well into the 21st century. As an organization's greatest ally and at times its most determined enemy, the supply base impacts every process and every discipline within an organization. It is therefore a strategic element of every manager's operational and control planning.

Each of the following soft and hard clues is indicative of process and/or performance problems requiring a manager's immediate attention. Only by isolating the root cause or drivers behind each unique situation can a manager resolve the issue correctly and efficiently.

Soft Clues

Soft indicators of supply base performance problems include a variety of cross-functional issues such as operational or process interruptions or delays; quality compliance issues; product, project, or service cost/price-point difficulties; and project scheduling and control problems.

Hard Clues

The drivers behind supply base problems include: the absence of an effective supplier certification or qualification methodology; inadequate internal controls in the inventory forecasting, planning, and control processes; insufficient IT systems capability or database accuracy; poor sales and operations planning integration; internal or external documentation errors; and/or poor procurement/logistics process design, management, or control. Hard clues include: trend analyses of quality, pricing, or delivery performance; premium freight variances; surplus and obsolete inventory levels that drive inventory performance below established targets; statistical measures of supplier process capability and control; and the frequency of shortages of critical materials or services.

DECISION-MAKING

Once the root cause of a problem has been identified, a decision is made regarding the best alternative to resolve it. The alternative selected provides a manager with an opportunity to succeed or fail. The objective is to resolve the problem or issue in the most cost-effective, time-sensitive, risk-adverse means possible. When a risk is unavoidable, it is thoroughly analyzed, quantified, and considered. The rule of thumb for a manager is to "engineer risk out" of each decision through thorough analysis and quantification. In most cases, this "by the numbers" approach to decision-making provides a manager with a course of action that differs from what the manager originally considered as optimum. This is because when first looking at a problem, in most cases, managers display the tendency to concentrate on the symptoms or to comply with the loosely defined desires of their superiors. However, the way those issues are ultimately addressed is rarely of concern to those higher in the management ranks. Higher managers are simply looking for results. The successful manager realizes the difference and works to accurately define the problem as well as the various alternatives to resolving it before initiating action.

Many managers consciously or subconsciously avoid making decisions because of the controversy or direct confrontations

> *"With every decision managers set the stage for career success or failure. Careers are made one decision at a time."*

Effective Problem-solving and Decision-making

commonly associated with the decision-making process. Often, a manager's decision results in a contest between differing points of view. Politics play a role, whereby the person with the most political clout prevails and the loser suffers the embarrassment of defeat in front of her employees, peers, and superiors.

While few individuals enjoy confrontation, every successful manager eventually comes to grips with the fact that one of his most important roles and responsibilities is to make decisions—sometimes critical or unpopular ones. Indecision is deadly—for a manager and the organization—and for a manager's long-term credibility.

Any good decision is based upon a comprehensive understanding of the strategic and tactical requirements of the manager's organization. This is coupled with the results of thorough situational assessments and problem-solving efforts, which have isolated the root cause of the problems or issues impacting organizational performance. Next there is a complete assessment of the possible alternative courses of action available to resolve each issue or problem. Then there is an analysis of the results possible from each of the alternative solutions—good and bad.

> "Decision-making is the responsibility of every manager—even in the face of conflict, politics, or controversy."

Early in their careers, most managers recognize that there is not an expectation that they make the perfect decision. Managers and employees alike understand that there simply is no perfect or ideal solution to most business problems. Compromise is generally an accepted part of the process. Thus, the best decision is often the solution that comes closest to fulfilling all of the organizational requirements and management expectations in the most cost- and time-effective manner possible, with the least amount of risk. There are times, as well, when current conditions are an alternative that must be given due consideration. Simply put, there are times when doing nothing is the best course of action.

Effective Problem-solving and Decision-making

Example

In late 1997, the CEO of a large company called a consultant to discuss an intended course of action that his company was considering. The MIS project team had recommended that the company scrap its existing business systems and purchase a fully integrated package from one of the leading manufacturing software providers. It was the team's belief that the old systems were simply incapable of supporting the company into the 21st century.

After listening to the CEO's description of the intended software, it was immediately apparent to the consultant that the project team's selection was an excellent one given the type of business and industry involved. The consultant suggested, however, that the company not proceed at that time. When the CEO asked why, the consultant advised of the Y2K issues facing most businesses and the fact that the fix for the problem had not yet been implemented in the software they had selected. The CEO agreed that there was a real risk in moving forward. He thanked the consultant for his input, and said he would discuss the matter with the project team.

A few days later, the CEO called the consultant to advise him that they had decided to move ahead with the purchase based upon the IT manager's assurances that the Y2K issue was under control. The consultant recommended that if they did proceed, they not modify the software in any way so the fixes that ultimately would be developed by the software provider could be implemented without delay or problem.

In early 1999, the CEO again called the consultant complaining that he had just been informed by the IT manager that the new business systems would not operate in 2000 as a result of the Y2K problems. The CEO asked if he had any suggestions regarding available alternatives. The consultant gave him the only two feasible solutions:

1. Buy another fully integrated business system with the Y2K fixes in place and scrap the one purchased in 1997. (The company had extensively modified the system since

Effective Problem-solving and Decision-making

its purchase, and thus the provider was no longer supporting the system).

2. Hire as many mainframe programmers as possible and begin reprogramming the existing software in an effort to fix the coding problems.

This is a perfect example of the risk that management decisions introduce to an organization. The correct decision initially was to wait until the Y2K fixes were in place. Now, the alternatives available to the company were not only more costly, but more embarrassing. Ultimately, the company bit the bullet and started fresh with new software.

The Decision Process

While no manager can avoid the responsibility of making a decision, neither can he avoid the downside accountability for that decision if it is flawed. Thus, a structured methodology is required to minimize the risks introduced from biased decisions or those made with less than complete information. The decision process begins with an accurate description of what the decision is intended to address or resolve (objectives, issues, opportunities, and problems) and includes the known alternatives available to the manager to accomplish those business or operational objectives.

> "The actions a manager takes must reflect the lowest cost, lowest risk, and lowest organizational impact possible."

The tool utilized by many successful closed-loop managers is a decision matrix (see Table 10-1). The objectives established for the decision process are listed by the manager with input from her employees, peers, and superiors, and then divided into two categories:

1. The objectives that "must" be achieved to guarantee the success of the initiative, and

2. The additional or "desired" objectives the manager would like to include, but that are not necessarily mandatory to

Table 10-1. Blank decision-making matrix.

Objectives		Alternative "A"		Alternative "B"	
"Must"		Data	Yes/No	Data	Yes/No
A					
B					
C					
"Desired"	Weight	Data	Score	Data	Score
D					
E					
F					
Total					

the successful completion of the initiative. The desired objectives are used for comparison of one alternative against another. They become the differentiators in the decision process and are weighted relative to their importance to the manager's or the organization's strategic and tactical objectives. The weighting scale used is a one-to-ten scale, with a one representing those objectives with the least importance and ten representing those of significant importance.

All objectives, "must" and "desired," are quantifiable and measurable. The "must" objectives function as a go/no-go filter against which all alternatives are initially assessed. Unless an alternative fulfills each and every "must" objective, it does not meet all of the base-line criteria essential for a successful decision. Thus, it is immediately removed from consideration.

Once the "must" and "desired" objectives (and the corresponding weighting factors for the desired objectives) have been selected, the next task is brainstorming alternatives. It is a good idea to brainstorm using a clean sheet of paper *without* the objectives in view. With the objectives in sight, managers

Effective Problem-solving and Decision-making

tend to unconsciously force-fit alternatives, and thus, overlook many creative solutions. Just to clarify, the objectives are *what* the manager is attempting to accomplish, while the alternatives are *how* the manager intends to accomplish them. In other words, the alternatives are the courses of action the manager considers to accomplish the objectives. The brainstorming session will yield numerous possible alternative courses of action. Each alternative is entered into the matrix.

Example

Table 10-2 shows a completed decision matrix. Note the alternatives and how each objective has been quantified to ensure that all alternatives are compared against the same base-line. In this way objectivity is ensured in the decision-making process.

Every decision has consequences, both positive and negative. All must be considered and assessed for their potential impact on the organization and the risks they introduce. Further, they must be considered *before* a final decision is reached. This is the only opportunity a manager will have to address any negative consequences at little or no cost to the organization or her own career. Prevention is always less costly than failure. Negative consequences resulting from a flawed management decision will always introduce additional problems to the organization. There is a famous literary quote that applies here, "The evil that men do lives after them; the good is oft interred with their bones." The same can be said for a poor decision at the management level. It will outlive all of the good work done by even an exceptional manager. The business journals are filled with examples every day. Overlooking negative consequences that make the decision unworkable or organizational objectives unreachable is a fundamental and potentially career-limiting mistake that no manager wants to make.

> "Before a decision is made, it must be weighed to determine its potential impact on the organization."

Once all of the alternatives and objectives have been identified and entered into the matrix, the alternatives are then

Table 10-2. Completed decision-making matrix.

Objectives	Reengineering Process		Out-source Function	
"Must"	Data	Yes/No	Data	Yes/No
Reduce cycle time to 5 days	Cycle time data	Yes	Cycle time data	No
Ensure a 15% margin	Value engineering study	Yes		
Reduce overhead by 50%	Value analysis study	Yes		
"Desired"	Weight	Data	Score	Data	Score
Reduce cycle time to 3 days	10	Cycle time data	10.0		
Implement in 180 days	8	Project management study	7.2		
Ensure 55% return on investment	8	Value analysis study	7.2		
Return market study in 180 days	7	Market study	3.5		
Address "mine"	5	Industrial engineering study	5.0		
Total			32.9		

compared against the "must" objectives. The decision about each alternative is either black or white—either it meets the "must" objective or it does not. A "no" means the alternative is no longer under consideration; the manager proceeds to the next alternative, and so on. The data field of the matrix is used to

Effective Problem-solving and Decision-making

note where the information was obtained to support the answer. In essence, it contains the source of the decision regarding the alternative's conformance or nonconformance to the "must" objective. It is there as a reminder of how the decision regarding that alternative was made.

Only those alternatives remaining, which satisfy *all* of the "must" objectives, are compared by the manager against the "desired" objectives. Scores for each alternative are then calculated. This is done by multiplying the probability that the alternative will satisfy the "desired" objective by the weighting factor for each "desired" objective. All of the scores for that alternative are then totaled.

> *"The greatest challenge facing a manager may not be making the right decision, but rather implementing it."*

The alternative that best conforms to the manager's objectives, based upon the highest score, is the recommended course of action.

Typical Questions a Closed-loop Manager Asks

Once an action is determined from the analysis, closed-loop managers know to apply a reality check to their proposed alternative. While it may look good on paper, there are times when the selected alternative really is not workable within the operating or financial constraints of the business environment. The following list of questions aid in this reality check. The list is provided as a springboard to illustrate the approach.

- Can the selected alternative be implemented in a reasonable time frame without introducing unreasonable risks to the organization?

- Is the selected alternative economically feasible? Will it provide the expected level of performance or financial return required for the organization and/or its customers?

- Have all functional, organizational, and political barriers been breached?

- Have all necessary management approvals been received?
- Will the selected alternative meet all strategic and tactical objectives at the organizational level?
- Will the selected alternative be acceptable to the customer and/or senior management?
- Can the selected alternative be maintained by operating personnel without undue burden, overhead, or life-cycle costs?
- Is the selected alternative robust enough to withstand current and future business and market environments and constraints?
- Will the alternative selected allow the organization to expand business within current markets or enter into new markets?
- Will the alternative selected provide demonstrable market differentiation?
- Will the alternative selected project the image desired by senior management?
- Will the selected alternative require an investment in personnel, facilities, technology, or equipment beyond what is realistic and/or acceptable to the organization?
- Do the employees possess the essential skill sets required to implement and maintain the selected alternative?
- Is the selected alternative compatible with current core competencies, operations, and distribution methodologies?
- Will the alternative selected expose customers or the organization to any undue business, financial, or competitive risks?

If the answers to these questions confirm the manager's initial assessment and conclusions, the manager moves forward to implement the decision. If not, further review and additional assessment are necessary.

Effective Problem-solving and Decision-making

The actual questions closed-loop managers utilize for each decision process are dependent upon the unique conditions, environment, and constraints surrounding each business scenario. Every situation is unique and must be analyzed on its own merits.

Pro/Con Analysis

A pro/con analysis is a simple, but effective practice that provides a degree of protection in evaluating the alternatives under consideration. Savvy managers prepare a listing of each of the pros associated with every alternative course of action under consideration. Next, the manager lists all of the corresponding cons possible from each alternative. This simple pen and paper exercise forces a manager to think through all of the potential upsides and downsides (benefits and risks) of the alternatives under consideration. The closed-loop manager considers each course of action, first based solely upon the benefits to be generated from it. Thereafter, the potential risks of each are weighed to see if a different decision would generate a potentially better outcome.

There are certainly numerous examples of decisions in every industry that were less than stellar. Equally numerous are the after-the-fact critiques of those decisions by senior management, as well as other internal and external sources. Table 10-3 illustrates an example pro/con analysis. This particular analysis is in no way a reflection upon the manager who was responsible or his organization, but it does illustrate the importance of considering the benefits and the potential risks associated with the options selected for implementation.

CASE STUDY

The following case study on situational assessment (see Chapter 9) and decision-making is typical of the scenarios facing all managers. While the situation, discipline, and departments will vary, the example illustrates the complexity that exists within most business settings and highlights the areas in which managers typically stumble. As with all case studies in this text, this is an actual business scenario.

Effective Problem-solving and Decision-making

Table 10-3. New Coke® example.

Pro	Con
Market tests indicate that many customers and potential customers prefer the taste of New Coke over Coke.	Brand loyalty for both Coke® and Pepsi® is strong.
Many of the customers who indicated they liked the taste of new Coke are Pepsi drinkers. Thus, a potential for market share growth from Pepsi customers is real and potentially significant.	Replacing Coke with new Coke as the singular offering would be placing all eggs in one basket. If customers do not respond as predicted, market share losses may be significant and immediate.
Cost of entry is low as New Coke is simply a formulation change over Coke.	
New Coke costs less to make as a result of the use of synthetic sugar vs. real sugar.	
Packaging changes will be insignificant and of low cost.	
Existing bottling and distribution channels will require no change as a result of the introduction of New Coke.	

In reading this, it is important to consider the situation from the manager's perspective and reflect upon how the situational assessment can be best completed. The object is for the manager to generate a complete understanding of what is happening, the drivers behind this situation, and the priorities he will set for the decision-making phase of his activities. It is important to recall the three fundamental questions of situational assessment (see Chapter 9).

- What do I know?
- What do I not know?
- What do I need to know to make an informed decision?

Effective Problem-solving and Decision-making

> *"There is no one-size-fits-all solution. Every situation is unique and must be analyzed on its own merits."*

For a manager to understand how all aspects of a situation interconnect and interrelate, it is preferable to first view the situation from a macro perspective; then as the picture becomes clearer, explore the details. Getting into the details too quickly often leads a manager to overlook the obvious, resulting in a poor decision. Taking any action before understanding exactly what is happening and why will always be disastrous for a manager and his organization.

In addressing specific issues, managers are expected to implement changes and corrective actions that are the most cost effective and that pose the lowest risk to their organizations. Throwing people and money at a problem is never a wise decision.

Alliance Consumer Electronics Group (ACEG)

After a successful project management role involving the reengineering of ACEG's return goods process last year, Ted Knight and his team received several accolades and awards from ACEG's senior management. Based upon Ted's demonstrated leadership during that assignment, he has been promoted to the purchasing department as director of domestic and international procurement.

Ted's initial assignment is to address an issue that has been plaguing the purchasing process and its internal customers; including senior management. Like other manufacturing concerns, ACEG's production operations are heavily dependent upon purchased materials to support the production lines. In addition, ACEG's maintenance staff is dependent upon the purchasing operation for repair parts and maintenance supplies, sometimes requiring procurement with little advance notice. Further, ACEG's administrative and support staff relies upon the purchasing operation to provide office supplies, printed materials, engineering materials, and subcontracted services on a regular basis.

Ted has discussed his initial priorities with his superiors and he is expected to resolve the identified problem quickly. The symptoms of the problem have been identified by senior management and were described to Ted as follows.

- It takes 45 days from the date of request for the purchasing processes to deliver needed materials, whether production, maintenance, or office supplies. Shortages are frequent in all areas (averaging 12-15 stock-outs weekly), yet inventory turns are only at 2.34 (senior management dictates that turns be maintained at a minimum of 12, but would like them in the range of 24).

- The investment in inventory has created a serious cash-flow problem for ACEG's management. Inventory accounts for 85% of sales revenues year to date, versus a budget of 63% of sales revenues for the same period.

- Suppliers are complaining that they receive incomplete or inaccurate purchase orders (POs) from ACEG on a regular basis. Approximately 26% of all POs have at least one error or omission and 37% are past due when issued, all but ensuring that the supplier will be late in delivering the needed materials. Further complicating the situation, ACEG pays its suppliers regularly in 90–120 days, even though the agreed upon terms are net 30 days.

ACEG's Purchasing Process

The existing purchasing process begins with the receipt of a manual purchase requisition from the internal requestor by the purchasing clerk. The process then continues as follows.

1. The purchasing clerk dates the requisition and manually enters it into the purchasing system (15 minutes).

2. The clerk pulls the vendor history cards to determine the last purchase price and from whom the materials were purchased (5–6 minutes).

Effective Problem-solving and Decision-making

3. The clerk manually updates the history card with the latest requisition information and sets the card aside (6–8 minutes).

4. The system prints a purchase requisition for review (4–6 minutes).

5. The purchasing clerk, upon receipt of the printed purchase requisition, compares it against the vendor history card to ensure agreement, then refiles the history card (10–15 minutes).

6. Four times a day the purchasing clerk sorts the purchase requisitions by commodity (15–18 minutes) and distributes them to the appropriate buyers for action (5 minutes).

7. The buyer, upon receipt of the commodity purchase requisitions, contacts the designated (or an alternate) supplier to confirm the current pricing and lead times (10 minutes).

8. The buyer adds supplier data (date, price, part number, terms, unit of measure, shipping instructions, etc.) to the purchase requisition (15–20 minutes).

9. The buyer pulls and updates the vendor history card with that information and refiles the card (6–8 minutes).

10. Each purchase requisition is required to have a unique number assigned to it for internal control purposes. So, the buyer pulls the purchase order (PO) log, assigns a number to the requisition, and updates the log accordingly (8–10 minutes).

11. The buyer manually enters the updated purchase requisition information into the system (10–12 minutes).

12. All purchase requisition information is batch processed nightly by the systems department and delivered the following morning to the purchasing clerk (12–24 hours). In addition, the systems department prints an exception report in buyer sequence nightly, which denotes any dif-

ferences between what the buyer entered into the system and the last actual purchase of that material (for example: price differences, different vendors, different terms, etc.). These reports, too, are batch processed overnight and delivered each morning to the purchasing clerk for distribution to the respective buyers (12–24 hours).

13. Upon receipt of the purchase orders and exception reports, the purchasing clerk separates each into the appropriate buyer code and then distributes them to the appropriate buyers for review and subsequent action (45–60 minutes).

14. Upon receipt of the purchase orders from the purchasing clerk, the buyer reviews each one and signs it, then returns the purchase orders to the purchasing clerk (25–30 minutes).

15. Upon receipt of the signed purchase orders from all of the buyers, the purchasing clerk places them in the in-box of the purchasing manager for review and approval (120–180 minutes including wait time for all buyers to respond).

16. The purchasing director reviews and signs each purchase order and returns them to the purchasing clerk for processing (8–24 hours).

17. Upon receipt of the signed purchase orders from the purchasing director, the purchasing clerk separates the purchase order copies: copies 1 and 2 are sent to the vendor; copy 3 is retained for the purchasing file; copy 4 is sent to the requestor; copy 5 is sent to receiving; and copy 6 is forwarded to quality control (90–120 minutes).

18. The purchasing clerk matches the purchase requisition from the file with copy 3 of the purchase order, and places the matched paperwork in the respective buyer's open order file (30–45 minutes).

19. Upon receipt of the material, the receiving clerk pulls purchase order copy 5 from the file and matches it against

Effective Problem-solving and Decision-making

the vendor's packing slip to ensure agreement (8–10 minutes).

a. If agreement exists, the receiving clerk prepares a receiving report, matches it with the vendor's packing slip and copy 5 of the purchase order, and sends the documentation to the purchasing clerk (15–20 minutes). A copy of all documents is maintained in the receiving department in the event of a question or lost shipment.

b. If a disagreement exists, the receiving clerk contacts the buyer for instructions. Upon receipt of the documentation from receiving, the purchasing clerk pulls the open purchase order file and matches the documentation with copy 3 of the purchase order and the purchase requisition, and files it in the closed order file (5–7 minutes).

   i. The purchasing clerk then updates the open order file on the system (3–5 minutes), which processes all receipts daily by batch (8–24 hours), updating the accounts payable system to release payment to the vendor.

   ii. When all parts and line items on the purchase order have been filled, the purchasing clerk notifies the buyer (2–3 minutes).

   iii. The buyer closes the purchase order on the system and updates the vendor history card, then refiles it (5–10 minutes). Overnight, the system generates a closed order file (8–24 hours), which is then sent to the purchasing clerk the following morning.

   iv. From the closed order report, the purchasing clerk updates the PO log (3–5 minutes).

Your Solution

The process is completed. Given the preceding data, what course of action would you recommend for Ted considering all of the

Effective Problem-solving and Decision-making

facts and constraints? Compare your intended actions against his solution, which follows. Who do you think made the better decision?

Ted's Solution

Ted began his analysis from the situational assessment that mapped the actual purchasing process from receipt of purchase request to the delivery of goods. He then began to assess the possible factors that could lead to the symptoms the department was experiencing. His assessment considered all factors. For example, he was concerned that the company's suppliers were not being paid in a timely manner. This could create a significant degree of ill will and subsequent lack of support for any of the corrective actions he might consider. His initial thought was that the cash-flow problems resulting from the excessive inventory levels were the reason why supplier invoices were not being paid on time. To validate his assumption, he spoke with the Accounts Payable (AP) department personnel who were responsible for supplier payments. What he found was contrary to his initial assumption. While cash flow was an issue facing the company, it was not the reason why invoices were not being paid. The reason was that the AP staff was unable to complete a three-way match (invoice, receipt verification, and matching purchase order) as required under Generally Accepted Accounting Principles (GAAP) because the required documents were not available in a timely manner. Armed with this data, Ted was able to eliminate one possible source of the problem. In addition, he now had another piece of the puzzle that pointed to a process problem impacting the timely generation or processing of critical procurement documentation.

Ted next looked at the integrated business systems that supported the procurement, forecasting, and planning processes. Recognizing that those critical integrated systems were driven from the same data sources as his purchasing system, Ted worked with his IT Systems Support Team to evaluate the database's accuracy. His assumption was that if the database was corrupted, that may well be the reason why all of his direct and

Walking the Talk: Pathways to Leadership

Effective Problem-solving and Decision-making

support systems were failing to perform as required. The soft clues to his analysis (late purchase order generation, purchase order errors, late invoice payments, etc.) certainly supported his theory. Indeed, the analysis confirmed that the database had been severely corrupted. But before it could be corrected, Ted knew he must first understand why the corruption had occurred. That led him back to the use of the system by his personnel, as well as the processes in place within the Purchasing department. That investigation uncovered the root cause of the problem.

The integrated business system used by the company, like any other business system, is based upon the ability to forecast and predict the ordering of materials. As Ted's initial decision matrix (Table 10-4) illustrates, production and office supplies are repetitive commodities, meaning that they are regularly used, and thus could be forecasted. The system was capable of forecasting their usage and planning order launches appropriately. However, maintenance supplies were discrete and could not be accurately forecasted. Because of that, the Purchasing department staff had developed "workarounds" that bypassed the system to allow them to order maintenance items manually. Unfortunately, these manual processes, over time, began

Table 10-4. AGI/ACEG case study decision matrix.

Internal Customer	Criticality (Business Impact)	$ Volume Purchased (Financial Impact)	Unit Volume Purchased (Effort)	Repetitive or Discrete Orders	Actions to Resolve
Production					
Maintenance					
Office supplies					

Note: Lowest criticality commodities represent the lowest total dollar volume of procurements along with the highest overall volume and corresponding highest labor impact. Low-value, high-cost activities are to be eliminated from internal operations through out-sourcing of the activity.

Effective Problem-solving and Decision-making

to degrade the database, as well as slow down the procurement process, the accounts payable process, and ultimately service to the department's internal customers (production, maintenance, and office support staff).

Ted now had the data he needed to launch a corrective action. As he considered his options, he recognized that several factors would influence his ultimate decision. To assist him in his decision analysis, Ted developed the matrix shown in Table 10-4. A key "must" objective was that any solution he selected must place an emphasis on utilizing the existing business systems to eliminate the need for additional capital expenditures. In addition, he must consider the requirement to reduce the excessive overhead costs of the department by out-sourcing the high labor, low-value activities. Prior to Ted's promotion into the department, departmental staffing was increased to 28 employees by his predecessor to handle the increased workload. Ted knew that for the implementation, departmental staffing must be reduced to a minimum of 14 employees, a level consistent with prior operations. In addition, all the targeted performance improvement objectives of the purchasing department relative to customer service, inventory management, logistical costs, and supplier development would have to be achieved. And obviously, the issue of system forecasting would be of prime concern in any corrective action he implemented. Finally, Ted realized from his prior experiences that the solution he selected must represent the lowest-cost, lowest-risk solution possible considering all the pros and cons of the alternatives under review.

Utilizing Table 10-4 to isolate the key decision criteria and influencing factors, Ted first considered the level of criticality that each internal customer had on the organization to establish his initial priorities. Production and maintenance were assigned high criticality because their operations have a direct impact on customer service, operational performance, and financial objectives. While not as important, office supplies had significantly less criticality to overall business performance, thus it was assigned a low criticality rating.

Effective Problem-solving and Decision-making

Next, Ted considered the financial impact that each internal customer had on the operation based upon dollar volume purchased. Production was rated first, maintenance second, and office supplies last. Next, he considered the personnel impact in supporting each of the internal customers, recognizing that overhead reduction was a key "must" requirement in his decision analysis. What he found was that because of the number of items purchased in each category, office supplies actually required more effort than the other two categories, followed by production items, then finally maintenance items. As before, the ability to forecast was considered for each internal customer category to evaluate the impact on the use of the integrated business system. Now Ted had the data he needed to begin his decision process.

Beginning with Production as the most critical customer, Ted concluded (as shown in Table 10-5) that the integrated business system was fully capable of providing the required level of performance and internal control needed to support daily operations. As such, he launched a project in conjunction with the IT Support Team to clean up the database and put controls in place to monitor system use to eliminate the possibility of degradation in the future. This approach met the requirements of senior management to avoid another major capital expenditure, while at the same time providing a mechanism to eliminate many of the redundant and non-value-added activities within the existing purchasing process.

Next, Ted addressed the maintenance customers. As Table 10-5 illustrates, he was faced with the constraint that the integrated business system was unable to forecast demand for these items as they are discrete, meaning they occur without warning. He recognized, too, that the time and effort required to develop the necessary database criteria once a maintenance crisis occurred would not only delay the purchase and receipt of the needed materials, but it would be a waste of resources to prepare the required data for the system for an item that may never be needed again. Thus, the use of the system for these commodities was *not* the best solution.

Effective Problem-solving and Decision-making

Table 10-5. AGI/ACEG case study solution.

Internal Customer	Criticality (Business Impact)	$ Volume Purchased (Financial Impact)	Unit Volume Purchased (Effort)	Repetitive or Discrete Orders	Actions to Resolve
Production	High	1	2	Repetitive	System
Maintenance	High	2	3	Discrete	Credit card
Office supplies	Low	3	1	Repetitive	Out-source

Note: Lowest criticality commodities represent the lowest total dollar volume of procurements along with the highest overall volume and corresponding highest labor impact. Low-value, high-cost activities are to be eliminated from internal operations through out-sourcing of the activity.

In considering the low-cost, low-risk options, Ted concluded that a hybrid approach would address the requirements for immediate response time, internal control, and GAAP compliance. So, he contracted with two maintenance suppliers, one for electrical components and the other for mechanical components. Each supplier was required to carry a sufficient inventory of maintenance items to enable response to a request within a maximum of two hours for normal preventive maintenance items, and a maximum of 24 hours for breakdown items. The maintenance manager was given a credit card account that could only be used for these two suppliers with a cap tied to his annual budget. Once a need arose, he simply had to place a single call to the appropriate supplier. The needed materials were delivered including a receipt of materials. At the end of each month, a statement was received from the supplier providing the needed documentation for the three-way match to comply with GAAP.

In addressing the procurement of office supplies, Ted again considered all "must" and "desired" objectives, as well as the

Effective Problem-solving and Decision-making

business constraints impacting the performance of his department and that of the supporting integrated business systems. As Table 10-5 illustrates, Ted once again sought a low-cost, low-risk solution. His analysis had revealed that even with utilizing the integrated business system combined with an enhanced purchasing process, the cost to generate a purchase order exceeded $200. Considering that many of those purchase orders were for office supplies that totaled less than the cost of generating the purchase order, use of the business system for these items was not cost effective. Secondly, Ted's analysis concluded that over half of his staff was assigned to purchasing these items due to the overall volume of purchases required to meet daily demand. Thus, much of the overhead was allocated to procure items of insignificant financial or business importance to the organization. This, too, indicated the need for another approach.

Ted's solution was to contract with a single supplier of office supplies. The supplier was required to set up a small inventory of office supplies on site, provide on-site inventory management and issuance support, and provide monthly invoices for the items procured by the company's personnel. In short, if an employee from any department required office supplies, he or she would simply go to the supplier's warehouse store on site, write the department account code on a purchase request sheet, and acquire the items from the supplier's personnel. By implementing this approach, Ted was able to reduce his staff to the required level by eliminating the planning, forecasting, order launch, and receipt of high-volume, low-value goods. All of these activities were now the responsibility of the supplier.

SUMMARY

Every good decision is based upon a careful and comprehensive assessment of the drivers behind each unique business situation, as well as the benefits and risks associated with each possible course of action to address that situation. Decision-making is not a "shoot from the hip" or emotionally driven process. It is a structured process that quantifies each possible action to minimize the bias and subjectivity that infects a poor

Effective Problem-solving and Decision-making

decision. Managers get few second chances. It is too late when a poor decision negatively impacts the organization or reflects poorly on the senior management staff. Management careers are made or broken with each decision a manager makes. While recovery is possible in some cases, those cases are few. Thus, it is imperative that each decision be supportable, objective, and fact-based.

Closed-loop managers have learned to apply structured tools to their decision-making process each and every time a decision is needed. They take the time necessary to assess the situation, understand the drivers behind it, and analyze the alternatives available to resolve the situation in the most time-, cost-, and risk-sensitive manner possible. To introduce additional risk or problems to the organization is simply unacceptable in the business world.

In the next chapter, organizational change management is discussed along with the unique requirements necessary to ensure that change is successfully implemented and sustained.

11
Turning Your Vision for Change into Action

OBJECTIVES

The purpose of this chapter is to provide new and seasoned managers with the framework for a typical organizational change process, whether in a service, industrial, or government setting. In this chapter, the tools and techniques utilized in an effective organizational transformation process are explored:

- techniques for developing a vision for change and defining its associated mission;
- methods for communicating the mission to employees, peers, and management;
- tools to isolate and address barriers to the proposed change processes;
- techniques for forming and leading an effective transformation team; and
- methods for sustaining change once achieved.

Change processes, especially within organizations, are never quick or easy. Managers and employees alike talk about the necessity of change, but few embrace it. Change management represents one of any manager's greatest challenges. As such, it is always effectively planned, executed, and controlled from beginning to completion.

WHY TRANSFORMATIONS FAIL

The 1990s and early 2000s represented a period of dynamic organizational change driven by business process reengineering, six sigma and lean techniques, the move to reinvent government, and growing global competition and stability challenges. The

Turning Your Vision for Change into Action

emphasis was on enhancing productivity, profitability, and market position by introducing new business concepts that would radically alter an organization's culture by changing the behavior and actions of its employees. In every industry from banking to the high-tech sectors, managers at every level attempted to introduce new tools, techniques, and concepts to facilitate change. In many cases, however, those efforts proved unsuccessful. Many managers attributed their failure to the resistance of their employees to change, or more often, poor leadership and support from senior management.

> "Change is a powerful competitive tool for an organization; but change has its enemies —and they can be ruthless in their pursuit of the status quo."

Senior managers, for their part, placed the blame squarely on ineffective management at the lower levels. Finger pointing was the only thing that all parties commonly shared. Careful analysis, however, has shown that most transformation failures were the result of one or more root causes, most of which were not only foreseeable but also avoidable.

- Many change managers failed to take an active leadership role in the change processes they promoted. Their lack of direct, hands-on leadership left their direct reports free to interpret and guide the change process as they deemed appropriate. Hidden and often conflicting functional or political agendas took precedence over the goals and objectives of the transformation process. Employees saw inconsistencies between what senior management stated as the goals for the transformation efforts and the day-to-day actions taken by lower-level managers. The resulting conflicts and constantly changing priorities immediately created confusion and frustration among employees who were unsure of who to follow or what approach was going to eventually win out. The result: employees took no action and made no changes. They simply waited. After a period of time, the leaders of the transformation process focused their attentions on other projects or business activities. Eventually, things settled back into the normal business culture.

- Many change managers failed to develop a comprehensive vision of what their intended change process was and was *not* to include. By failing to thoroughly define the scope of the transformation efforts, they left those responsible for implementing the change processes with little direction and few rules within which to work. Lower-level managers, supervisors, and lead people were left with no direction and little, if any, structure to lead their employees through difficult organizational and process changes. They floundered early and often until ultimately the transformation efforts were abandoned.

- Many transformation managers lacked the patience necessary for the proposed organizational, functional, or process changes to take hold. There was simply a lack of understanding or acceptance of the fact that changes to business cultures require time and dogged persistence. When managers became frustrated at the pace of change, they began to apply downward pressure within the organization. As time went on, the pressure became greater until employees and lower-level managers ultimately rebelled. When that occurred, the transformation processes came to a stop.

- Conversely, in some instances, the change manager failed to introduce a sense of urgency into the transformation process. Thus there was no momentum to drive active participation in the transformation initiative. As a result, lower-level managers and employees placed lower priority on the change efforts than on their daily activities. That lowering of priority for the transformation efforts meant they would never again surface as something that needed immediate attention. Seen as just another "flavor-of-the-month" program, the initiative faded away and was soon forgotten.

Turning Your Vision for Change into Action

- In other cases, the targets for improvement set by the change managers for the transformation process were unrealistic given current business, budgetary, or personnel constraints. In many cases, no specific, measurable goals were developed. Employees, for the most part, are dedicated to the longevity and profitability of their organizations. They will work diligently to assist management in achieving transformation objectives, but only if those objectives are understandable and attainable. If they are not, employees will fail to respond positively and actively to the transformation efforts.

SUCCESSFUL TRANSFORMATIONS—ORGANIZATIONAL, DEPARTMENTAL, AND PROCESS

For a transformation to be successful, the change manager or change leader prepares by creating a concrete set of measurable and achievable expectations. These are derived from a clearly delineated vision of the transformed organization, process, or function. Coupled with these clear deliverables, the transformation process is driven by a comprehensive project plan that considers the strategic and tactical issues to be addressed before, during, and after implementation of the desired changes. As part of that project plan, integrated controls and performance measurements are incorporated to ensure ongoing compliance with the transformation targets. Equally as important is the capability of the organization and its employees to achieve the desired objectives given the real constraints that exist. Finally, the transformation process is led by a change agent or the senior manager of the organization, communicated to all of the organization's personnel, and sold as a change that will personally benefit each employee.

> "If you think it will be either easy or quick, better think again."

On the manager's part, there is consistency and tenacity to overcome the inevitable organizational resistance and politics, a willingness to make tough, sometimes unpopular decisions, and the patience to see the transformation process through to completion. Finally, there is sufficient political power behind the transformation efforts to ensure that the vision for change becomes the accepted culture for the transformed organization.

Examples

There are numerous success stories about managers who have pulled off organizational transformation initiatives, just as there are numerous stories of failed transformation efforts. Some of the better-known success stories include Galvin at Motorola, Welch at GE, and Iacocca at Chrysler. These were, for the most part, examples of forced change where market, financial, or competitive pressures forced these great leaders to drive change through their organizations in an effort to remain competitive within their markets. There are others, however, where change was engineered in an effort to improve already excellent operations. These were even more difficult transformation efforts, as the tendency for most managers and employees is to leave things alone if they are working well.

Ross Operating Valve is a classic example of a small multinational organization competing in an industry of heavily engineered, one-of-a-kind products, where lead time is critical to getting and keeping business. In the 1980s, Ross' management led the organization through a unique transformation process to convert the company into a provider of "virtual" products and services. Virtual products are those that do not exist until customers call to request them to be designed and manufactured to their unique specifications.

At the time Ross began its transformation effort, the company was heavily unionized. The Detroit-area manufacturer had the same labor-management problems that plague many of the tier-one equipment suppliers even today. Its product line had remained largely unchanged for many years, and its manufacturing processes were based around large-lot production techniques. Quoted lead times were in excess of 16 weeks. Under severe competitive pressures to improve lead times and provide more custom products, the management at Ross developed a vision to transform the company into a highly agile organization that could design, build, and deliver new custom products within hours instead of weeks. While the transformation was difficult and often challenging, the management at Ross utilized the transformation model described in this chapter to successfully transform the company into one that builds virtual products to customer-defined specifications and delivers them within 24–72 hours.

Still another example is the Chamberlain Group, a manufacturer of residential and industrial garage-door openers for worldwide distribution. Chamberlain's management decided that changes were needed within the company to remain competitive. The company enjoyed a 90%+ market share in each of its main product lines and double-digit profits. Chamberlain was regularly recognized by its largest customers for quality and dependability and enjoyed world-class status. So why change something that appeared to be working so well? That was the obvious question on the minds of every manager and employee when they heard the news from management that a transformation was being planned. Chamberlain's leaders realized that prior success was no guarantee of future success. Their belief was that by constantly improving and changing operations, they could prevent complacency from setting in—in essence, keep their people sharp and competitive. It worked. Chamberlain continues to be the number-one worldwide leader in its markets and the company's profitability remains at numbers only a few organizations have ever enjoyed.

The drive for constant change is also evident at Procter & Gamble (P&G). The company has engineered continuous change into its corporate culture through its "Theory of Deliberate Change." As part of their job responsibilities, every employee and every manager is challenged to constantly improve their individual job performance to the point where their job can be eliminated altogether. They are given incentives and promotional opportunities whenever they can devise new processes, practices, and procedures that will make their job redundant. Then they are placed in new positions and challenged to do the same thing.

Turning Your Vision for Change into Action

P&G's approach has made change a natural part of the corporate climate instead of something to be feared or avoided. The managers at P&G have made employees comfortable with change. It is now institutionalized to the point where even the employees have become change agents for the company.

These examples are intended to drive home the point that transforming an organization can be done, even in today's complex business environments. It can be done by every manager at every level. In fact, it is the responsibility of all managers to find ways to make the organizations, departments, or processes they manage perform better on a continuous basis. By creating a vision for change, then engineering its implementation, every manager can maximize the contribution of his or her department to the total organization while making day-to-day activities less mundane for employees.

Changing an Organization's Culture

Successful change processes result from a manager's creation of an organizational, functional, and departmental culture in which the strategies, performance measures, and daily operating practices are consistent and compatible with internal and external customer needs and expectations. Culture, in essence, is the behavior exhibited on the job by employees and managers alike. So, for a manager to change an organization's culture, the behavior of that organization's employees must also change. To do so, often the policies and procedures, reward and appraisal systems, and at times, even some of the employees, must be changed. Consequently, a successful transformation effort considers every aspect of the organization . . . its culture, its people, and the drivers behind their behavior.

> "To change an organization's culture, the behavior of its employees must also change."

Transformation projects begin with a comprehensive situational assessment of the organization, which includes recognizing the existing problems and opportunities that create or reinforce the current culture, and a complete analysis of the alternative approaches available to address those barriers to transformation. All the while, the associated risks are balanced against the potential gains to be derived from the transformation process. If the risks outweigh the potential benefits, then the transformation timing or its compatibility with current business conditions will require further review and analysis.

Closed-loop managers typically use a simple checklist early during transformation planning to isolate potential problems before launching headlong into the change process (see Table 11-1). Negative responses require further analysis, preparation, and planning before transformation can move forward. To overlook or ignore issues of this magnitude is simply poor management. Transformation, by its very nature, breaks the rules and changes business cultures. To launch such a high-risk endeavor without a comprehensive understanding of all the issues and potential or real problems is not prudent or constructive.

> "There is a major difference between planned, controlled change and pure chaos."

Leading change within an organization, irrespective of size or discipline, is difficult even for an experienced manager. One of the first decisions a change manager makes regarding organizational transformation is how to approach the change process. Change can be forced, planned, or engineered. Each approach has its pros and cons. As such, managers should give due consideration to the existing organization or business environment before adopting an approach.

Forced Change

A forced change by management dictate is typically the approach used by managers when their organizations or departments are in crisis or at risk of imminent failure. In situations like this, the manager often has little flexibility in adopting a more participative style. With business or organizational conditions in crisis, a closed-loop manager will often take a direct, hands-on approach to designing and implementing the changes

Table 11-1. Checklist for launching a transformation process.

Considerations Before Launching a Transformation Process	Yes	No
1. Is the purpose of the transformation process consistent with organizational strategies, direction, and objectives?		
2. Does the transformation manager have the commitment and patience to see the transformation process through to completion?		
3. Are there enough change agents to lead the transformation process at all levels within the organization?		
4. Has there been an accurate assessment of the organization's capability and capacity to handle the transformation effort?		
5. Has there been an assessment of the potential impact of the change initiative on the organization's culture, employees, customers, competitors, and stakeholders?		
6. Has the current organizational culture been analyzed, along with the drivers behind it?		
7. Have the transformation goals and performance measurements been developed and communicated?		
8. Has a comprehensive strategic and tactical plan been developed to guide the transformation initiative?		
9. Have the risks associated with the launching and adoption of the transformation process been assessed and addressed?		
10. Will the organization's manager actively lead the transformation efforts?		

needed to bring the organization or department back to steady-state condition. Thereafter, one of the other two approaches is utilized to initiate further enhancements or changes.

When an organization is in crisis, the initial employee response to his manager's transformation efforts will likely be to cope with the recommended changes rather than to truly embrace them. Reaching the point of coping with the manager's plans for change, however, does not come immediately.

Coping is a natural process, often referred to by industrial psychologists as going through the stages of the *SARAH Syndrome*. It is the same psychological mechanism that individuals go through with the loss of a loved one. It begins with *shock*. The employees are in a state of shock and disbelief that things within the company or the department have degraded to such a level that radical, immediate change is necessary. When the manager continues with the transformation plans, the employees become *angry*, at times militant. This is the time when organized employees start thinking of strikes and walkouts. Outright *rejection* of the manager's transformation efforts comes next. The employees simply refuse to participate or assist the manager in any way. Over time, the employees begin to realize that something has to change to get the organization back on track and that continuing with the current operations and practices will not ensure survival. At this point, the employees transition into an *acceptance* of the change processes. They may still not like the proposed changes, but at least they are now willing to continue on to see if things do, in fact, get better. The final stage is *hope* that their manager really knows how to address the critical issues facing the organization. While the employees still have not embraced the change process, they have at least moved into passive acceptance versus active resistance of their manager's transformation efforts.

The risks with forced change are high. There must actually be a crisis that can be recognized and believed by the employees, or this approach will degrade into serious labor-management problems. Some managers successfully manufacture a crisis to drive a desired change process. It can be done. In most cases, however, such efforts lead to more, rather than fewer problems for the manager.

Planned Change

The planned approach to transformation is used by managers when the change is intended to take hold gradually throughout the organization. This evolutionary rather than revolutionary approach to transformation is based upon the belief that change will grow and expand from a small nucleus of employees until it eventually envelopes all employees within the department or organization. The manager simply creates and maintains the environment for change, then steps back and lets it happen. The problem with this approach is that it takes a significant amount of time to develop. In a transformation process, time is the equivalent of risk. The more time it takes for the transformation to be adopted into the organization's culture, the higher the risk that other factors or priorities will derail the transformation efforts. As with most business and management processes, time is of the essence.

Engineered Change

Engineered change is the most successful of the approaches. To engineer change, the manager develops a comprehensive vision of the transformed organization, department, or process. From that vision, a gap analysis is done to determine the differences in performance between the current and envisioned operations. A strategic and a tactical project plan are then developed to guide the transformation process. The plan includes project controls to ensure ongoing compliance with the transformation objectives and a post-implementation control system to make certain the changes are sustained.

THE TRANSFORMATION MODEL

Engineered change is the approach used in the transformation model (see Figure 11-1). Successful transformation efforts require a structured approach that converts the manager's

Turning Your Vision for Change into Action

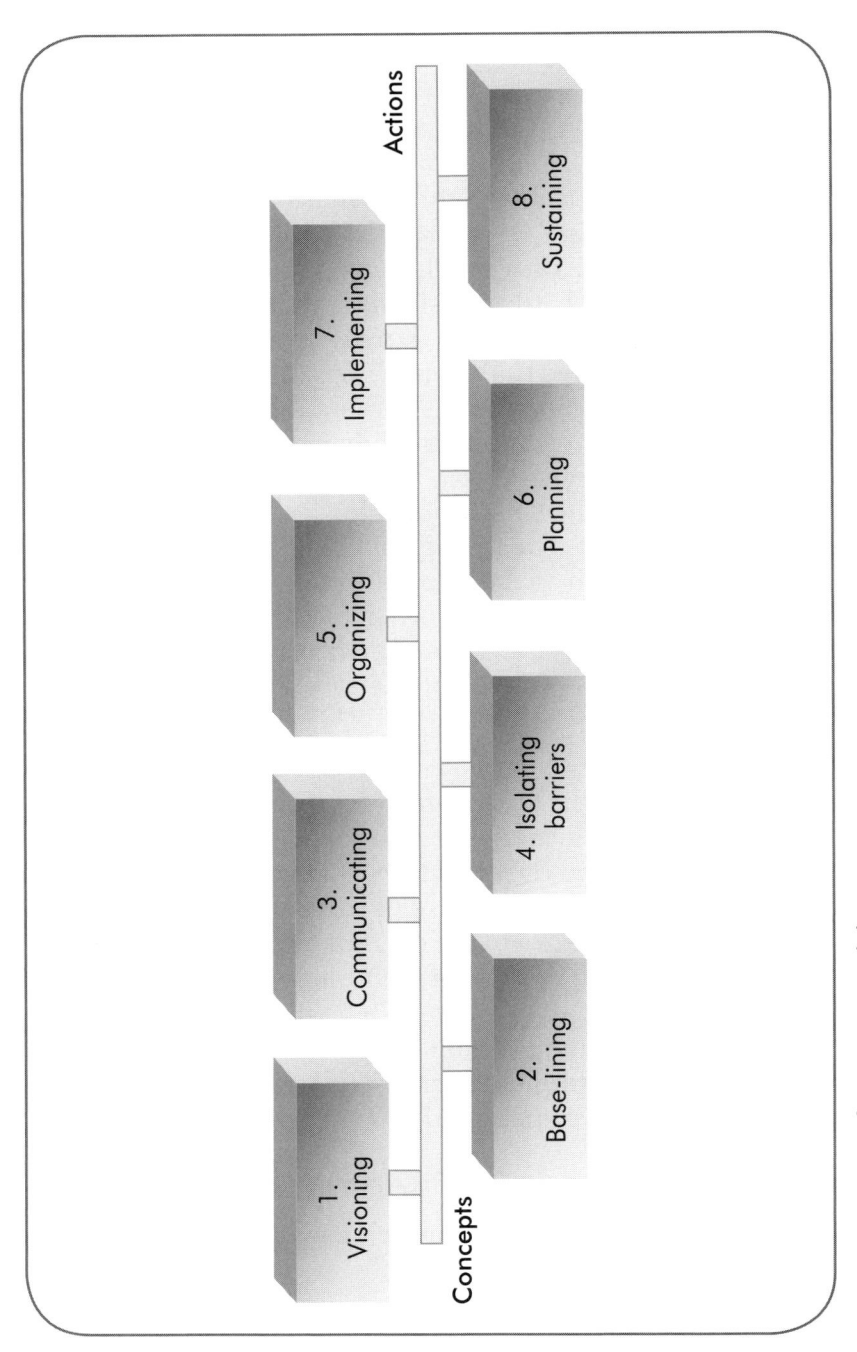

Figure 11-1. Transformation model.

vision of the transformed organization into a series of actions that lead to successful results. There are no shortcuts that allow certain steps in the process to be circumvented. Each step in the process is critical.

1. Visioning

Visioning is an essential step in the transformation process. By definition, *visioning* is defining and communicating what the business or operations are today, and what they are intended to be in the future, including how the manager intends to lead the transformation process to achieve those future objectives. For the organization, visioning establishes:

- a new direction;
- new base-lines of performance and competency;
- new priorities; and
- timelines and metrics for the cultural change processes.

In essence, visioning is used to balance the goals of the transformation initiative with the core competencies and capabilities of the organization, its support systems, financial requirements and plans, and available resources (capital, people, technologies, distribution networks, etc.). To be successful, visioning provides expectations for the transformation process in both performance and financial terms. Further, it defines the means and methodologies that will allow the organization to achieve those expectations, along with the controls required to ensure that the transformation, once achieved, is sustained.

> "Capable leaders are required at all levels of the organization to ensure that the vision does not degrade into a series of projects and tasks with no apparent purpose or linkage."

During the visioning phase of the transformation process, successful change managers define and critically assess the underlying assumptions used to guide the transformation process to ensure their validity, applicability, and sustainability. Consideration is given to:

Turning Your Vision for Change into Action

- what the manager wants to accomplish with the transformation process and why those goals are vital to the organization;
- the planning and implementation horizon that current and expected business constraints will dictate;
- the internal and external factors that could influence the timeliness and/or success of the transformation process;
- how employees and customers will react to the transformation process; and
- how market competitors will react and respond.

The transformation manager envisions all factors that will lead to success or failure, along with the risks and rewards possible throughout the life cycle of the change process.

Constraints

As Figure 11-2 depicts, visioning at the departmental or organizational level requires a comprehensive analysis of environmental constraints, operating constraints, support constraints, and resource constraints. Examples of these considerations include, but are not limited to:

- environmental constraints: organizational culture and its likely acceptance of the envisioned changes; successes or failures associated with previous change initiatives; legal or contractual obligations that dictate or limit organizational actions; internal or external compliance requirements; customer, competitor or market requirements and limitations; senior management's strategic plans and direction; organizational project portfolio status and its impact on organizational priorities; other change initiatives underway elsewhere within the organization and their potential impact on the envisioned change process; and the ability to manage and control the scope of the change initiative effectively.
- operating constraints: impact the envisioned change process will have on day-to-day operations, customer service levels, and operating costs; cash flow and budget-

Turning Your Vision for Change into Action

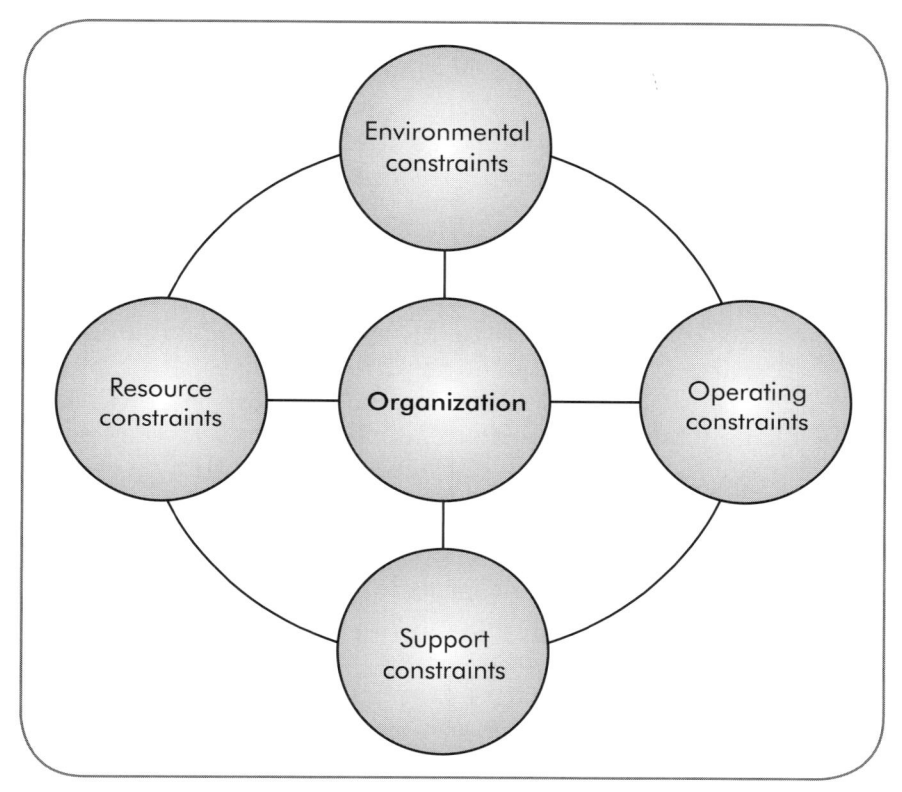

Figure 11-2. Visioning constraints.

ary impacts of the envisioned change activities; ability to effectively manage, control, and meet ongoing internal and external customer requirements and expectations during the change process; risks associated with the envisioned changes; and the ability to reverse direction should the change initiative fail.

- support constraints: ability to obtain the needed information to support the change efforts on a consistent basis; ability to obtain the required support from the supply base during and after the change process; ability to get ongoing and timely support from internal operations, management, and technical resources during the change process; ability to receive and maintain support from senior management for the change processes; and where required, the ability to receive and maintain support from external stakeholders for the envisioned changes.

- resource constraints: ability to get the necessary human and capital resources allocated and deployed to the change initiative on a timely basis; ability to retain the needed resources throughout the life cycle of the change initiative; ability to obtain the required facilities, equipment, materials, systems, and infrastructure for the project in a timely manner; ability to get the external resources required to support the project; and the ability to get the required training resources for the change initiative.

Similar visioning constraints exist for change management initiatives at the department, process, or employee levels. In all cases, it is advisable to develop and employ a series of checklists for each of the identified constraints to guide the change manager during the strategic and tactical planning and execution phases of the transformation process. These checklists are varied in content and scope to reflect the specific requirements of the transformation project under consideration by the manager. No two change projects are ever the same. While they will appear similar, they will also differ in many critical aspects. Thus, each change project requires a fresh assessment of the constraints, requirements, and risks associated with the envisioned changes. To do anything else is a recipe for disaster.

> "Each project requires a fresh assessment of the constraints, requirements, and risks associated with the envisioned changes."

2. Base-lining

The next step in the transformation model involves the establishment of a base-line for current operations. In other words, the organization's strengths and weaknesses are criti-

Turning Your Vision for Change into Action

cally assessed from a multitude of perspectives (see Figure 11-3):

- management (all levels of management and supervision),
- employee (at all levels within the organization),
- customer (internal and external),

The initial base-lining of operations includes all things that are done well and *not* well within the organization. It reflects the candid opinions of individual managers and employees alike, and not merely a regurgitation of the "party line." It is as quantifiable as possible to ensure objectivity. Base-lining considers the current performance at the level within the organization where transformation is intended to occur, along with the drivers behind that performance. Performance objectives, structure, and management at each level are used as the basis for analysis.

If change is intended to occur at the organizational level, base-lining includes an analysis of all factors that impact performance at the business or operating level. Issues of vision, structure, and management are critically assessed. Questions like those illustrated in Table 11-2 are explored and their answers analyzed for accuracy and reality. Similarly, if the

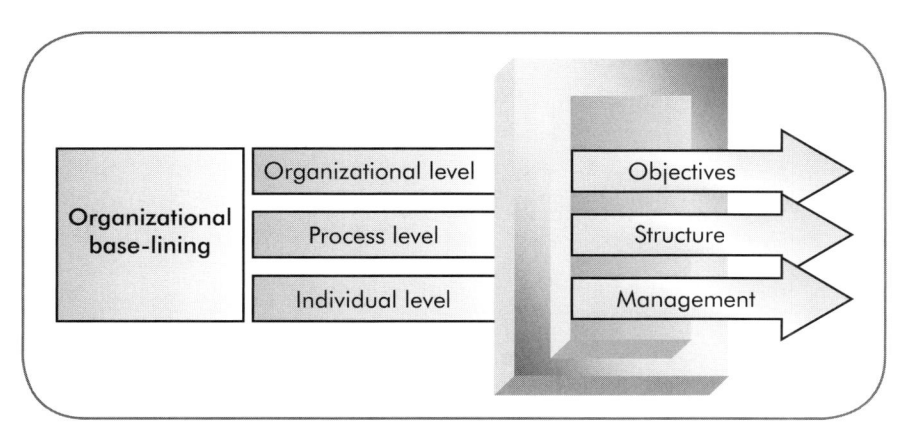

Figure 11-3. The basis for base-lining operations.

Turning Your Vision for Change into Action

transformation is intended for the process or departmental level, questions such as those in Table 11-3 are posed. Table 11-4 addresses questions at the individual level.

In addition to base-lining internal operations, it is also wise to base-line the capabilities and capacities of external support operations that have a direct impact on the performance of the

Table 11-2. Base-lining performance at the organizational level.

Base-lining Question	Response
Organizational objectives:	
Have the organization's vision and mission been communicated to all employees?	
Do the organization's vision and mission make sense given internal and external business and operating constraints?	
Have the requisite organizational deliverables been defined as part of the new vision and mission?	
Organizational structure:	
Are all required functions and processes in place to support the transformation?	
Do redundancies or conflicts exist that could impact the transformation efforts?	
Are current functional and process capabilities aligned with the new vision and mission?	
Does the organizational structure support the transformation?	
Organizational management:	
Are functional goals compatible with transformed organizational goals?	
Have the appropriate performance measures been developed for the transformed organization?	
Have the required resources been deployed to support the transformation efforts?	
Have the critical functional interfaces been defined and assigned to management personnel?	

Table 11-3. Base-lining performance at the process or departmental level.

Base-lining Question	Response
Process or departmental objectives:	
Has each process or departmental goal been linked to the organizational goals and objectives?	
Have both internal and external customer requirements been incorporated into the process or departmental objectives?	
Process or departmental structure:	
Are all process and departmental procedures well defined?	
Are all activities performed in the shortest possible cycle time?	
Are critical process or departmental interfaces defined and assigned?	
Process or departmental management:	
Are all sub-process and support process goals defined and monitored?	
Is the process or departmental performance monitored and maintained within acceptable levels?	
Is the process or department correctly staffed and supported for the transformation?	
Are critical process and departmental interfaces being effectively managed?	

organization or department under consideration for transformation. Typical examples include suppliers, information systems, external auditors, corporate staff, technology partners, and strategic alliance partners. In so doing, closed-loop managers consider:

- how each external support operation has performed over time;

Turning Your Vision for Change into Action

Table 11-4. Base-lining performance at the individual level.

Base-lining Question	Response
Employee-level objectives:	
Have all employee goals been linked to process or departmental objectives?	
Have both internal and external customer requirements been communicated to employees?	
Employee-level structure:	
Are employee job responsibilities well defined and communicated?	
Have employee job procedures and descriptions been developed and communicated?	
Have sufficient controls been employed to ensure a safe and environmentally benign workplace for employees?	
Employee-level management:	
Are employees aware of the required outputs and performance levels?	
Are said performance levels and expectations reasonable and achievable given current operating constraints?	
Are systems in place to recognize and reward individual contributions and performance?	
Do all employees possess the skill sets and capacities required to meet the new job and performance standards?	

- the capabilities, competencies, and capacities of each;
- how each aids the organization or department in meeting performance goals and objectives; and
- how each enhances or detracts from the organization's or department's core competencies, capacities, and capabilities.

Quantitative Tools

Good base-lining tools provide a quantitative analysis of the organization's strengths and weaknesses by organizing multiple inputs from personnel at all levels within the organization. A typical base-lining tool is exemplified in the questionnaires given in the Appendix of this book.

3. Communicating

To maximize the probability of change initiative success, experienced change managers create and then communicate the linkage between the envisioned changes and the day-to-day operations of the business. All impacted employees and managers fully understand how their daily activities influence and support the objectives of the change initiative. To reinforce that linkage, successful change managers redefine employee performance measurement and appraisal systems to ensure they are consistent with the transformed processes and practices.

> "Successful change managers redefine employee performance measurement and appraisal systems to ensure consistency with the transformed processes and practices."

As Figure 11-4 illustrates, employees are able to see a direct linkage between their individual performance metrics and those of each successively higher level within the revised process or organization. They clearly see how their individual contributions enhance the possibility of successfully achieving their manager's vision of the transformed organization. If that linkage cannot be seen by the employees, they will fail to understand their role in the success of the transformation efforts. Without that understanding, they will not participate.

Changing the metrics alone is not always enough. Through continuous communication with internal and external stakeholders, coupled with employee training and comprehensive process and procedural documentation, change managers ensure that employees fully understand the new performance measures,

Turning Your Vision for Change into Action

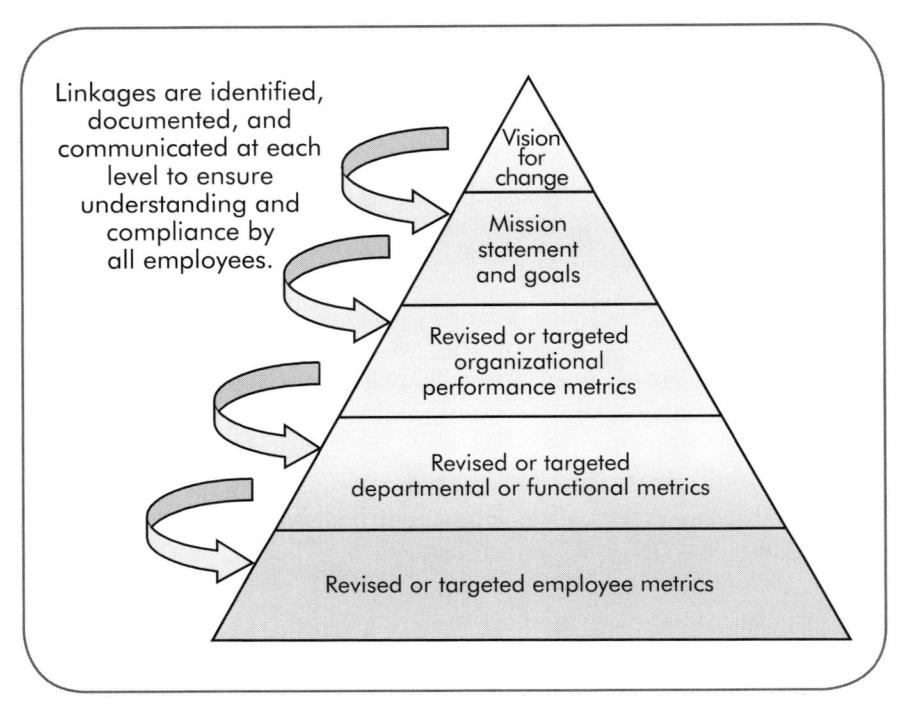

```
Linkages are identified,
documented, and
communicated at each
level to ensure
understanding and
compliance by
all employees.
```

- Vision for change
- Mission statement and goals
- Revised or targeted organizational performance metrics
- Revised or targeted departmental or functional metrics
- Revised or targeted employee metrics

Figure 11-4. Linking the vision at each level.

as well as how those new metrics link to the overall objectives of the transformed organization. Experienced change managers fully understand that organizational culture is elastic. Unless the envisioned changes are anchored to revised employee, process, and organizational performance metrics, the likelihood that employees will revert to the old methodologies and actions is great.

As Figure 11-5 illustrates, communication is particularly critical with those stakeholders whose ongoing support and approval for the chance process is paramount. They are the individuals with significant influence as either formal or informal leaders within the organization, as well as those whose influence in the assignment of required support resources is great.

Turning Your Vision for Change into Action

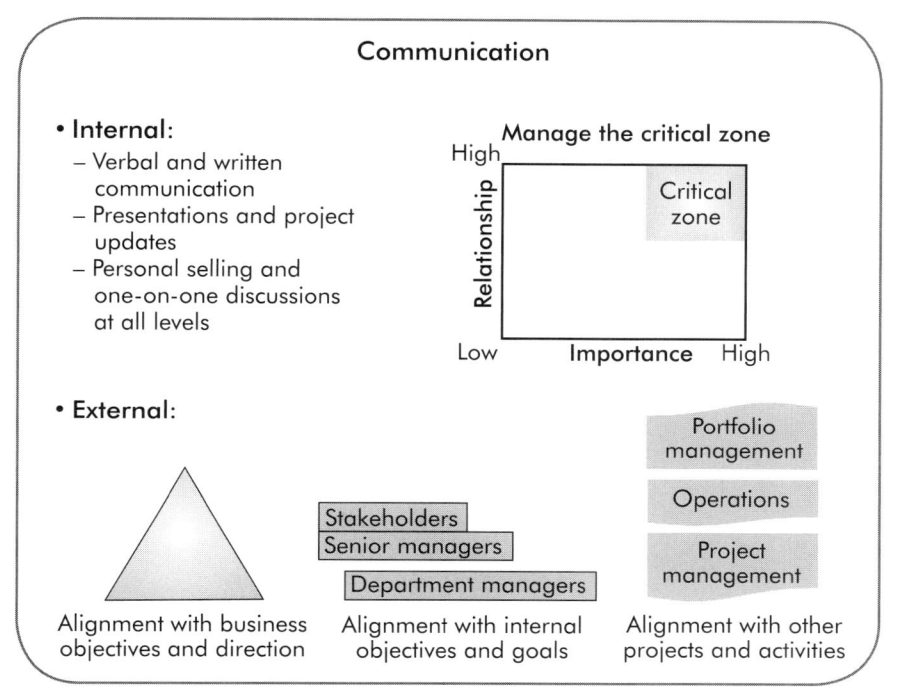

Figure 11-5. Communicating the vision internally and externally.

The Basics of Selling

There are natural barriers to transformation at every level. For example, when business is good, it is hard to sell the idea that a change is necessary ("if it isn't broken, don't change it"). When business is bad, it is hard to sell transformation processes that cost a significant amount, introduce additional business risks, or consume limited resources. In either case, the change manager is forced to do a degree of selling to get buy-in for the envisioned changes to the organization. The degree of selling required is dependent upon the extent of resistance to the proposed changes. Most of the time, this means selling upwardly to more senior management as well as downward to the employees. Often, it is even necessary to sell horizontally

Turning Your Vision for Change into Action

to peers and other support department managers to build across-the-board consensus among all critical parties.

Especially during the early stages of a transformation initiative, the basics of marketing and sales dictate that the employees be treated as customers. As such, the employee must be sold on believing that the proposed changes will yield positive, measurable benefits to the organization and to him personally. Employees must believe that the risks associated with the proposed changes are controllable and adequately offset by the benefits that will be derived from the transformed organization. They must also believe that the manager proposing and leading the transformation efforts can be trusted to make the right decisions, even if those decisions are unpopular, and then stand firmly by them in the face of opposition, politics, or resistance. In other words, employees must trust their manager or the transformation process will neither take hold nor be sustained. Without trust, employees will not take ownership of the proposed changes, nor will they take the initiative to resolve problems blocking the change processes. They will simply hand the problems over to management and walk away.

> "Employees must trust their manager or the transformation process will neither take hold nor be sustained."

It is a fact that most employees distrust or fear those who have power over them. The more levels of management, the more fear. Gaining and keeping employee trust requires:

- persistence—unrelenting commitment to the transformation process;
- promise—making only promises that the manager intends to keep; and
- example—managers walking the talk.

The question everyone will want answered is, "What's in it for me?" This deserves an honest answer. Transformation requires candid, frank dialog between the manager and his employees, peers, and supporters. All issues and opportunities are thoroughly discussed along with the possible impact transformation may have on the organization and its ability to service customers. Competitive issues and concerns, performance issues, and financial issues are all fair game. In addition, the pros and cons of doing nothing are discussed and explored relative to their impact on the organization in the present and in the future.

The change manager sells change, even if everyone knows it is needed. Employees often fear the unknown more than the daily hassles of working in a less-than-ideal business environment. So the change manager uses every selling tool at her disposal:

- employee meetings;
- employee or company newsletters;
- internal web sites, e-rooms, or intranet;
- articles about successful and unsuccessful transformation efforts;
- trips to visit organizations in which change processes have been incorporated into the organizational culture;
- posters, banners, and bulletin boards;
- company rallies, social events, and outings;
- training seminars; and
- visits or presentations by representatives of companies who have successfully implemented change of the type being proposed by the manager.

One other factor comes into play at this point: creating a sense of urgency. Effective selling creates a sense of urgency on the part of the consumer to purchase a product or service. It is the same in selling change. The change manager ensures that the purpose for and urgency in the transformation process is evident to all employees. Without a sense of urgency, transformation efforts take second place to other daily pressures and priorities. The transformation efforts are the first thing the manager wants to hear about in every meeting, formal or informal. It is reinforced as the number-one priority and then reinforced repeatedly and consistently thereafter. There is a consistent

Turning Your Vision for Change into Action

> *"Without a sense of urgency, transformation efforts take second place to other daily pressures and priorities."*

push to get results quickly. All low-hanging fruit is identified by the change manager and targeted for picking early in the transformation process. Those early successes are then used to generate enthusiasm for further changes.

Still another technique to create urgency in the process is through the use of the formal employee appraisal system. The change manager rapidly integrates the new base-line performance criteria associated with the change process into every employee's job description, performance appraisal criteria, job standards, policies and procedures, and reporting requirements. By so doing, the manager reinforces not only the urgency, but the permanence of the change process.

Example

When it comes to communicating a company's vision, consider many of the vision or mission statements written by senior managers for their organizations. Are those statements clear, easily comprehended, and measurable? In most cases, the answer to each of those questions is "No." They are simply "pie-in-the-sky" statements that sound good but have little substance. Employees, because they do not see how they can individually contribute to the mission statement, just discard them as nothing more than a tool management uses to impress customers.

The following is an example of an actual mission statement taken from a large, well-respected multinational organization. "We at XYZ, Inc. are committed to being the supplier of choice for our customers by providing only the highest quality products and services possible. Ultimately, our goal is to maximize shareholder value and employee loyalty." As an employee of this organization, could you understand how you, personally, are expected to contribute to the company's mission?

In comparison, the following mission statement is from another world-class multinational organization. "To ensure ongoing conformance with our customers' needs and expectations, XYZ, Inc. has adopted three key initiatives for each of our operating divisions. Initiative 1: 100% customer satisfaction, as measured by the customer, every year. Initiative 2: Ten times improvement in the quality of every product and service we provide, every two years. Initiative 3: A ten-fold reduction in the cycle time of every administrative and operational process every five years." The difference here is that there are dynamic metrics attached to each initiative. The leaders of this company were able to transform it into a world-class powerhouse within a decade. How did they do it? They made the initiatives outlined in the company's vision statement easily understandable and measurable by every employee at every level within the organization. As such, employees were able to see the linkage between their individual job responsibilities and the overall goals of management. There was no guessing and no misinterpretation. The vision was clearly understood by everyone at every level.

4. Isolating Barriers

In most organizations, there are both real and imagined barriers to any form of change process. Those barriers must be overcome early in the transformation initiative or failure is likely. The manager leading the transformation effort quickly isolates those barriers by addressing the way the organization is structured. Change requires frequent, open communication among employees. The change manager ensures that the organizational structure allows the informal communication channels to be kept open, even facilitated. Too often, rigid chain-of-command policies inhibit cross-functional communication and cooperation. If that structure exists, the change manager moves quickly to change it by collocating the change management teams, altering the policies that restrict informal communication, or creating informal environments in which communication can take place.

> "Rigid chain-of-command policies inhibit cross-functional communication and cooperation."

Turning Your Vision for Change into Action

If transformation is going to succeed, the change manager must take each barrier into consideration and develop plans to overcome it. Other barriers to change include: technological or financial constraints, supply-base constraints, competitive constraints, stockholder constraints, lender constraints, resource constraints, parent companies, etc. Though the list can be endless, here are some common barriers to change faced by many organizations.

- Narrow or inaccurate job descriptions for employees inhibit effectiveness and creativity.

- Compensation and reward systems foster compliance with the status quo and often penalize employees for risk-taking.

- Inconsistent direction from supervisors and managers leaves employees without a clue about what to do relative to the change process.

- Leaders of the change movement fail to take immediate and decisive action against parties actively resisting the proposed transformation. That indecisiveness leads to a loss of trust in and respect for management, as well as a propensity for employees to ride the fence rather than take the risk of joining either camp.

- Not readily apparent to change management, hidden lower-level management agendas surface early and continue actively throughout the preliminary stages of the transformation process. Employees see them clearly and quickly. If nothing is done to stop these adverse actions, employees fearing reprisal will pull back and do nothing. When that happens, the game is over.

- The organization's support systems fail to provide the required data, information, materials, etc. When this happens and it is not immediately corrected by the change manager, momentum and urgency are lost. Employees redirect their attentions to activities or projects where the needed support is available.

- Peer pressure or daily workloads inhibit transformation efforts. There are only so many hours in the day. Unless the change manager provides those responsible for implementing the desired changes with the time to do their work, the employees will quickly burn out and the transformation effort will halt.

- Contract terms are a also a common barrier to transformation efforts. In such cases, the change manager must be astute enough to either delay the transformation project until more favorable contract terms are negotiated, or pull the parties back to the bargaining table to get the restrictive contractual language changed.

Time as a Barrier

One of the most common barriers to change is *time*. As discussed in an earlier chapter, and illustrated in Table 11-5, any change process requires a significant amount of time to accomplish—years versus months. There will be resistance. The key is to be patient, dogged, and consistent.

In the initial stages of transformation, employees will simply follow the directions handed down by their manager. The change manager will essentially control every aspect of the transformation process. After about six months, the employees will begin to test the waters by making suggestions to their manager about certain problems or issues they see. They will not take ownership of the solutions, but they will begin to participate to a higher degree than earlier. When this begins to happen, the change manager takes on a less dictatorial role and adopts a participative, coaching style. By so doing, he encourages the employees to become more actively involved in the change process. Communication improves as two-way feedback begins to increase. Comfort and trust now become factors in the relationship.

> *"Getting employees to change is one thing; maintaining the change is yet another."*

Turning Your Vision for Change into Action

Table 11-5. Time-phasing transformation initiatives.

	Stage 1 Uninvolved	Stage 2 Somewhat Uninvolved	Stage 3 Somewhat Involved	Stage 4 Fully Involved
Employees	Execute facilitator's or management's directions	React, request feedback, test out concepts and ideas	Participate when requested in planning, directing, and controlling change issues	Take responsibility for planning, directing, and controlling the change process
	(0–6 months)	(6–9 months)	(9–18 months)	(18–24 months)
Management	High level of control and direction over change activities	Coaching, counseling, open communication	Involvement is typically participative in nature	Employee teams lead themselves under guidelines set mutually between employees and management

After about nine months, employees become actively involved in response to their manager's requests for assistance and input. Ideas and responsive actions become part of the employees' daily routine. Trust is enhanced by the change manager through continued mentoring, encouragement, and feedback. At this point in the transformation process, issues involving normal business routines, daily "fires," employee workloads, operating priorities, and employee skill sets become issues the change manager must address. This is a critical juncture in the transformation process. Decisions regarding which activities take priority, transformation or the business needs of the day, will make or break the momentum of the process. If the transformation efforts are allowed to take second place to every other priority, the probability of a successful conclusion is compromised. This is a difficult time for the change manager. Balancing business and transformation requirements is an arduous task that will certainly test the manager's creativity and tenacity. Employees will be watching their manager very closely. If the change manager says one thing, then does something contrary, trust will be lost. Without trust, the change processes will begin to rapidly erode back to the historical culture. Reversing that slide is almost impossible.

> "If the change manager says one thing, then does something contrary, trust is lost."

After approximately 18–24 months, employees become largely self-directed. They isolate the barriers to transformation efforts and address them, advising their manager of the actions they took and the results they achieved. At this stage in the transformation process, the change manager's role becomes that of a team member rather than a team leader. While the manager's overall responsibility for the transformation process remains, the employees now accept ownership of the process as well. The risks and the gains are shared.

Cultural Barriers

To support employees throughout the transition process, the change manager recognizes and addresses their individual and collective needs. As discussed in Chapter 7, Maslow's Hierarchy of Needs provides the basis for understanding the drivers behind the attitudes and actions of employees. Employee work groups are social structures, just like a community, church, or other social group. As such, the same behavioral issues exist.

A brief review of Maslow's theory is in order. His premise is that before an individual can be comfortable with, and thus accept, the challenges of changing to a higher behavioral level within the hierarchy, all factors within the individual's existing level must be satisfied. In the business world, this means the change manager realistically and critically assesses the work group before launching into a change process to determine at which hierarchical level the employees reside. For example, many of the early attempts to empower employees or to form quality circles failed completely. Managers attempted to encourage employees to take a larger role in day-to-day management decisions, only to find that they resisted those efforts. The harder the managers pushed, the more resistant employees became. Ultimately, management backed off and discontinued transformation efforts. What went wrong? The employees were not at a level at which they were comfortable with decision-making. Their focus was on other issues lower in the hierarchy, such as job security or salary. They were simply not ready to transition to a higher level until those lower-level issues were completely resolved.

The base-line requirement within any employee social structure is physiological needs. Simply put, this means money. At this level, employees work to pay bills and provide the essentials for their families. While the needs at this level do not dictate that employees be wealthy, they do dictate that employees be comfortable in the belief that the basics of food, shelter, clothing, etc., have been met for their families and themselves. Until these basic needs are satisfied, employees will not be interested in any change in the work environment that could jeopardize that income stream. Employees at this level of Maslow's hierarchy will often actively resist any transformation efforts. At this level, the risks to a planned transformation effort are great.

At the second level within the hierarchy, job security is of prime importance to the employee. Recent national surveys have indicated that this remains the number one concern of employees in most organizations. It is not enough that their current salary is sufficient to sustain a comfortable standard of living. Employees are more concerned that their salary will continue into the foreseeable future to allow them to sustain that standard of living. The wave of down-sizings, right-sizings, and reengineering initiatives in the 1990s and early 2000s, coupled with the economic, social, and cultural difficulties in Asia, the Middle East, and Latin America, have only intensified this concern. As before, any transformation process seen by employees as a risk to job security will be actively resisted.

At the third level within the hierarchy, employees are seeking a social structure within the workplace in which they can be viewed as an asset to the organization. Employees at this level want to be part of a recognized, respected employee team. This is an acceptable level at which to initiate a transformation effort, as the team approach is readily accepted and openly embraced by employees, so long as they believe management is sincere and will stay the course when things get tough. It will require some selling on the part of the change manager, but it is a good place to begin.

At the next level of the hierarchy, employees are looking for recognition and respect individually, as well as within the team environment. Employees at this level will openly adopt the transformation process if it allows them to earn respect and recognition. The secret is for the change manager to define the rules and guidelines for the employee, and then provide him the freedom to work independently within those work rules, rather than to attempt to micro-manage him. Mentoring, coaching, and facilitating techniques work well for managers with employees at this level.

At the pinnacle of the hierarchy, employees want to attain their full potential, explore new concepts, and learn new skills. They are willing to challenge the status quo, to press their own and the organization's limits. They seek new methodologies, new challenges, and creative approaches to daily business problems and opportunities. Because of their enthusiasm for change at this level, it is the ideal level at which to launch transformation initiatives, especially difficult ones.

Performance Barriers

Another potential barrier to transformation is performance. Early in the transformation process, the change manager determines if current performance at the employee, supervisory, and management levels is sufficient to support radical changes in the work environment, processes, or standards. Again, a critical assessment is needed to determine if the work force is capable of handling the envisioned changes while still maintaining an acceptable level of output to support the organization throughout the transformation process. In assessing these performance factors, the transformation manager considers the following key factors:

- competency of management to lead the transformation process;
- organizational performance criteria;
- political balance within the organization;
- competencies, capabilities, and capacities of the organization;
- linkage of organizational goals and objectives to process and individual level metrics;
- current organizational and functional priorities and commitments;
- availability of resources and their current deployment;
- existing communication and feedback systems; and
- organizational reward and appraisal systems.

When considering the impact of organizational appraisal and reward systems on performance, it is important for every change manager to recognize that, unless modified to correspond with the transformation objectives, the historical appraisal criteria will inhibit acceptance of change among employees. Employees, even managers, have historically been rewarded based upon compliance with those traditional measures. Unless those criteria are altered to comply with the new vision for the organization, there will be a natural tendency for those same employees and managers to adhere to the old norms that historically provided rewards and positive reinforcement. To avoid continued resistance, the transformation manager alters the system to reward only the desired behavior. When doing so, the change manager puts teeth into the system as well. That is, noncompliance is met with predictable and consistent disciplinary actions at all levels. Failure to do so will compromise the transformation process because employees will still be rewarded even if they refuse to adopt the new performance criteria.

> "Appraisal criteria must be modified to correspond with the transformation objectives so the desired behavior becomes the norm."

Here is an example taken from the automotive industry. In late 1998 at General Motors' Flint, Michigan truck plant, the employees were being paid handsomely based upon old work rules that rewarded them based on a set number of units produced daily. Achievement of that output guaranteed an individual's daily salary. Many employees found, over time, that the established output could be achieved in as little as four hours per day. That left the employee four hours daily to relax. When the managers found that competitive pressures required higher levels of output at no increase in overhead, they asked the employees to increase their individual outputs accordingly, realizing that the employees had the free time to do so. The employees refused, citing the old reward system that required only the lower output levels. The managers found themselves in a box. Because of contractual restrictions, they were unable to force the employees to work harder because they could not alter the reward system to pay employees for the higher output. Without the benefit of additional compensation, the employees were reluctant to put forth the extra effort. The end result was a costly strike that further damaged labor-management cooperation while financially hurting both sides; it was a true lose-lose situation that could have been foreseen with proper visioning and execution.

Resistance to Change

There is resistance to any significant change process. No matter how well the transformation is planned, there is always a degree of resistance. Some situations are even prone to strong resistance. It is human nature. The experienced change manager leading the transformation efforts recognizes and accepts that fact.

The greater the resistance, the greater is the risk that the transformation initiative will fail. As a result, it is vital that the change manager isolate the pockets of resistance within the organization and measure their severity through quantitative methods so appropriate proactive measures can be taken. Knowledgeable change managers first determine the reasons behind the resistance, and then develop specific action plans to eliminate or minimize it.

Table 11-6 is illustrative of the methodology used by successful change managers to quantify resistance. Employees are asked to fill out this questionnaire using the ranking scale that follows:

1 = strongly agree with statement;
2 = moderately agree with statement;
3 = neither agree nor disagree with statement;
4 = moderately disagree with statement; or
5 = strongly disagree with statement.

They are encouraged to be candid in their responses and respond to each question based upon their personal views, not those of others within the work force. Employees are asked to total their scores upon completion of all questions, note their total score in the designated location on the second page, but not to sign it. Rather, they are asked to note the general function or department they work in. The change manager then collects the questionnaires and conducts a two-step assessment.

Turning Your Vision for Change into Action

Table 11-6. Risk/resistance assessment tool.

Question	Score
1. The purpose and reasons for implementing this change are understood by all affected functions and functional managers.	
2. In the eyes of the employees, these changes are necessary to achieve the requirements of the organization and its customers.	
3. The appropriate people will be involved in or kept apprised of all aspects of the change planning and implementation.	
4. Communication regarding the change process and management's objectives will be adequate.	
5. I believe the transformation will have a low emotional and career impact on those responsible for its planning and implementation.	
6. I believe there will be tangible rewards associated with this transformation of the organization.	
7. I believe the proposed transformation will support the vision and values of the organization.	
8. I believe there is strong management commitment to this change at every level within the organization.	
9. I believe the relationships between employees, management, functions, and departments will be improved as a result of this organizational change process.	
10. I believe the required resources to implement and maintain the proposed changes will be allocated and deployed as required to ensure success.	
11. I believe the company will realize positive performance and financial results from this proposed change.	
12. I believe an appropriate amount of time will be allotted for implementation of the proposed changes.	
13. I believe the workload of the employees affected by the transformation activities will be given due consideration by management.	
14. I believe my department will be positively impacted as a result of the proposed changes.	

Turning Your Vision for Change into Action

Table 11-6. Risk/resistance assessment tool (continued).

Question	Score
15. I will actively support the proposed changes.	
16. I believe employees will not be harshly treated for making an error during implementation of the proposed changes.	
17. I believe my abilities are sufficient to support the transformation both during and after the implementation.	
18. I believe the managers responsible for the implementation of the proposed changes have the needed skills and position with which to successfully implement the transformation in my area.	
19. I trust those managers and change leaders responsible for implementing this transformation process.	
20. I trust the sponsors of the proposed transformation project.	
21. The implementation of the transformation process will neither overly stress nor overly burden me personally.	
22. I do not feel threatened in any way by this transformation project.	
23. My personal objectives and values are compatible with the stated goals and objectives of this change initiative.	
24. It will be easy to reverse the changes made during the transformation project should it not be successfully implemented.	
25. Overall, I do not believe the transformation will negatively impact me based upon my past performance on the job.	
Total score	

Directions: Rank each statement as follows and total your score:
1 = strongly agree; 2 = moderately agree; 3 = neither agree nor disagree; 4 = moderately disagree; or 5 = strongly disagree

Job Title/Department: _____

The first step is to separate the questionnaires by total score, then to look at the number of responses in each of three scoring ranges: under 35, 36 to 65, and over 65. The responses in the lower range indicate little resistance to the proposed change process. The responses in the middle range indicate a moderate level of resistance and a corresponding requirement for the manager to do additional selling and planning. Responses in the higher ranges are a warning that employees are highly resistant to the proposed transformation process. Before moving forward, it is thus imperative for the change manager to look deeper into the situation. To ignore that level of resistance is foolhardy.

The second step is a more extensive analysis of the data from the questionnaires with responses in the higher range. The change manager looks for a correlation between responses to specific questions as an indicator of where the concerns lie. For example, if the majority of employees indicated a strong disagreement with questions 10 and 13, there would be reason to believe that they were genuinely concerned about management's ability to allocate sufficient personnel to the transformation process. The net result, as seen by the employees, would be a heavier than reasonable workload on those involved.

From the manager's analysis, specific actions are taken to lessen the resistance and corresponding risk before launching the transformation activities. Then, a second resistance survey is conducted to measure the results of those actions to determine if they achieved the desired results.

Decision-making as a Barrier

Even those employees who are in total support of the transformation plan may resist taking an active role in the process. The reason is often a reluctance to make decisions. Even experienced managers will at times shun decision-making, especially when the planned changes have political overtones or if conflict is expected. Employees share those same fears. An employee often has no experience or training in making decisions. Without that experience, they are often comfortable

Turning Your Vision for Change into Action

> *"Teaching employees to make decisions allows managers to more effectively manage the 'water line' of the transformation process."*

allowing their manager to make all the decisions. The problem is that because transformation is a highly complex process, it requires multiple perspectives from every level within the organization. Managers who try to make all the decisions in this type of environment set themselves up for trouble. It is simply too complex and too large a task for any one manager to handle alone.

The secret is to create an environment in which employees feel comfortable making decisions. This will take time and training, but it can be done. Teaching employees to make decisions allows managers to more effectively manage the "water line" of the transformation process. Employees are encouraged to take ownership of the change process, and thereby become active participants instead of passive observers.

Changing Systems, Policies, and Procedures

As discussed earlier, transformation often requires a "breaking of the organization's rules." Changing business practices means doing things differently than defined in the traditional policies and procedures. Along with the identification of barriers to transformation, the change manager also envisions how operating practices, policies, and procedures will be altered to reflect the new operating base-lines after the transformation has been completed. Subsequently, the old organizational or functional policies and procedures are rewritten to reflect those transformation objectives. The same is true for many of the support-system operating policies and procedures. In today's highly complex, interrelated organizational structures, a change in one process or discipline often dictates the necessity to change numerous others. By so doing, the change manager, working in concert with his peers, forces change to take place as the transformation progresses in multiple sectors of the organization.

When changing policies and procedures, the change manager is frequently forced to employ innovative, radical, out-of-the-box thinking regarding the incorporation of new approaches, new technologies, new services, new facilities and equipment, new processes, new employee skill sets, new outputs, etc. At times, staff changes (employees or managers) are warranted when transformation requirements are found to be inconsistent with existing skill sets. This is the time for new thinking. The old paradigms must be broken if change is to be realized.

5. Organizing

Change managers, no matter how competent or experienced, recognize the requirement to surround themselves with talented change agents when undertaking a transformation effort. Thus, the organizing phase of the transformation model focuses on building a project team and a support network of individuals who share the change manager's vision. The sharing of that commmon vision and common approach to implementation greatly enhances the probability that the transformation will succeed.

> *"Change managers and sustaining managers are needed at differing times during the transformation process."*

Building a Transformation Team

Leading change is difficult enough for any manager, but to attempt to do it without the active support of a change management team is impossible. As a result, the selection of employees for the transformation team is critical to the success of any transformation initiative.

Individuals are chosen for the skill sets they possess, not necessarily the level they are at within the organization. Those selected are counted on to lead the transformation process by example, to be consistent and predictable in their actions, and to be organizationally versus politically focused. They are expected to provide *active* support and be committed to the transformation envisioned by their manager. A supportive team is comprised of the formal and informal leaders within the organization—employees with the recognized authority and

Turning Your Vision for Change into Action

ability to get things done. Each individual's mentality is one that accepts change as a natural element within the business cycle versus one that believes in maintaining the status quo.

The management style of those leading the transformation process is that of true change agents; they are individuals who embrace continuous, often revolutionary change. These are leaders who are not afraid to push the boundaries of the status quo. In contrast, sustaining managers are managers who embrace the mandate to keep current operations running with only evolutionary changes, thereby minimizing the risk associated with more radical change. Both management styles are needed at different times within the transformation process, but they cannot be used in the wrong sequence.

As Figure 11-6 illustrates, change managers are critical in the early planning stages of transformation when revolutionary thinking and actions are vital to ensure that the vision becomes reality. They set the new direction and provide the vitality needed to create and drive the new vision. As various elements of the transformation process are completed, there is a hand-off to sustaining managers who are expected to maintain

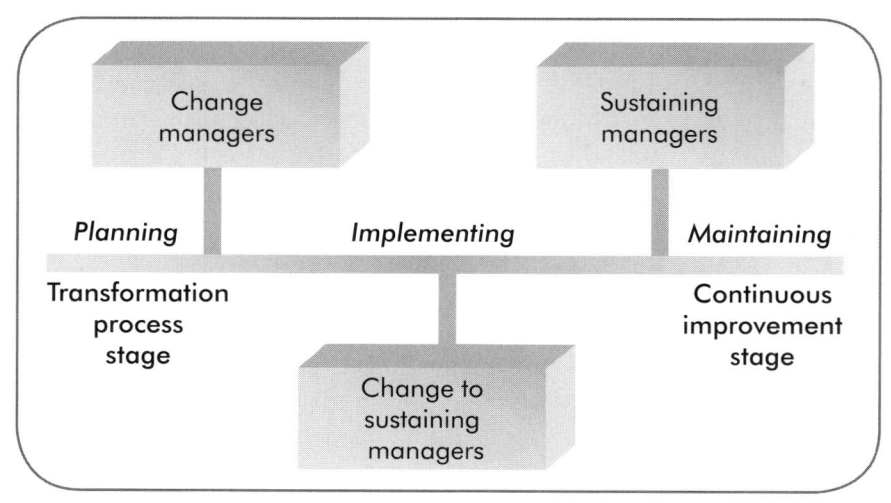

Figure 11-6. Management styles and their timing.

the new processes and procedures, as well as look for ways to further improve them through more evolutionary means. In other words, the approach of the sustaining managers is more of a continuous improvement versus a radical improvement methodology.

Building an effective change management team requires a solid base of support, as well as a solid political base to break down organizational barriers. It also requires managers and change agents who will "walk the talk" while at the same time contributing as team members. There is no room for individual superstars. Change management team members are selected for their complementary skill sets to give balance to the transformation process during critical transitional stages. In other words, the transition team members are able to both lead and follow. It is critical that the individuals selected are capable of thinking outside the box. Team members are selected from all levels within the organization and from as many different disciplines as possible. This ensures an organizational versus functional perspective while keeping hidden agendas to a minimum. The transformation manager also finds it beneficial to look outside of the organization for assistance. Excellent sources of support and creative thinking often come from key suppliers, alliance partners, technology partners, key financial or banking associates, and outside board members. Even key customers can be valuable resources.

Selecting, leading, and motivating the change management team is not always easy. There are times when certain managers or supervisors just do not fit the business environment envisioned by the change. Or, they do not have the skill sets or temperament required for a transformation process. Some will actively or passively resist the transformation efforts for either personal or political reasons. When these situations arise, it is incumbent upon the change manager to make the necessary personnel changes. If employees within the organization get mixed signals from different managers who are supposed to be leading the transformation efforts or see those same leaders push through agendas that are inconsistent with the stated transformation goals, they will move in the direction of least resistance. The transformation efforts will then grind to a halt.

The power base, or transformation leadership, is equally as important as the team. The change manager requires the assistance of senior managers, functional managers, supervisors, and informal leaders to facilitate change. Leadership is the horsepower behind the scenes when things get tough, forcing resolution to problems blocking the transformation processes, and making the necessary personnel changes required to ensure success.

6. Planning

Organizational transformation efforts require not only strong leadership but also a comprehensive plan to guide those efforts. Without a clear and measurable project plan, the essential controls and tracking capabilities will be compromised, thus diminishing the likelihood of success. There are two fundamental methodologies within project planning employed to maximize the probability of success in a project as complex as organizational transformation: a strategic project plan and a tactical project plan (Termini 1999). As noted in the referenced text, as well as in Figures 11-7 and 11-8, there is a direct linkage between the strategic and the tactical models. The strategic and tactical project plans contain several key steps, all of which are essential to defining the scope of the transformation initiative and the methodology to be utilized to address each of the transformation issues. The referenced text details these planning models (Termini 1999).

Five Phases of Transformation Planning

An overview of the transformation planning methodology is given in Figure 11-9. As depicted, an effective transformation plan contains five fundamental phases. The organizational phase includes the selection of a cross-functional management steering committee whose role is to provide counsel and a power base for the transformation manager, along with guidance in defining the scope of the transformation initiative. The steering

Turning Your Vision for Change into Action

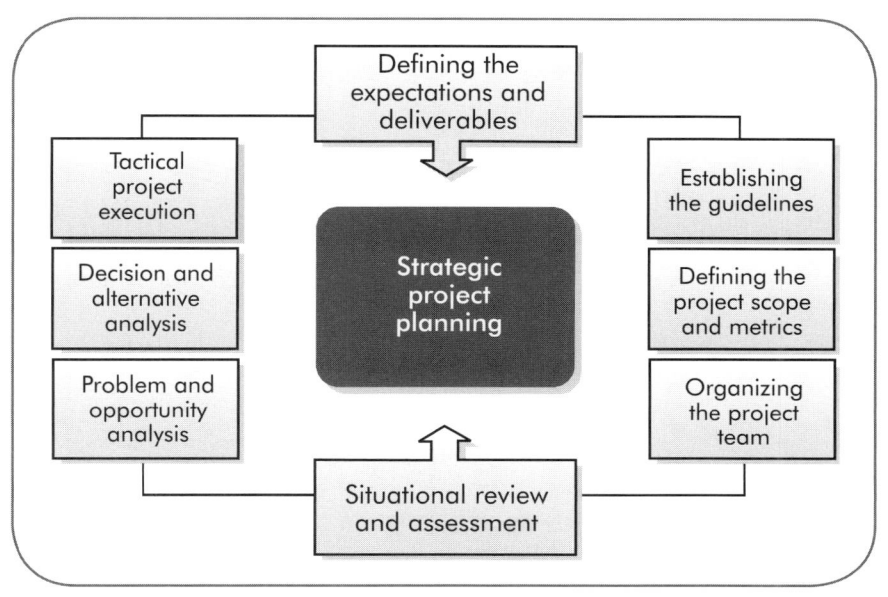

Figure 11-7. The strategic project planning model.

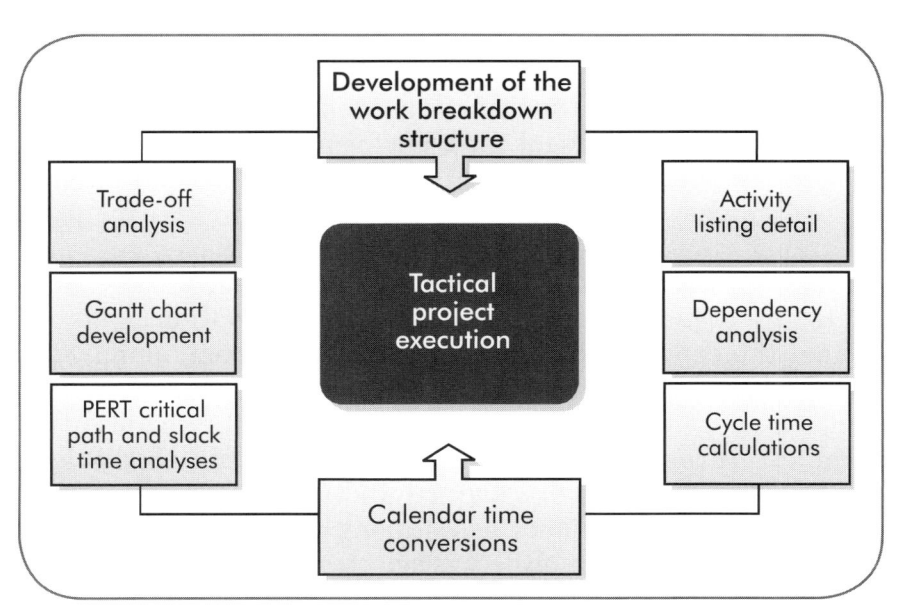

Strategic project planning:
- Defining the expectations and deliverables
- Establishing the guidelines
- Defining the project scope and metrics
- Organizing the project team
- Situational review and assessment
- Problem and opportunity analysis
- Decision and alternative analysis
- Tactical project execution

Figure 11-8. The tactical project planning model.

Tactical project execution:
- Development of the work breakdown structure
- Activity listing detail
- Dependency analysis
- Cycle time calculations
- Calendar time conversions
- PERT critical path and slack time analyses
- Gantt chart development
- Trade-off analysis

Walking the Talk: Pathways to Leadership

Turning Your Vision for Change into Action

```
→  Organizational phase
→  Formulation phase
→  Realization phase
→  Tactical phase
→  Sustaining phase
```

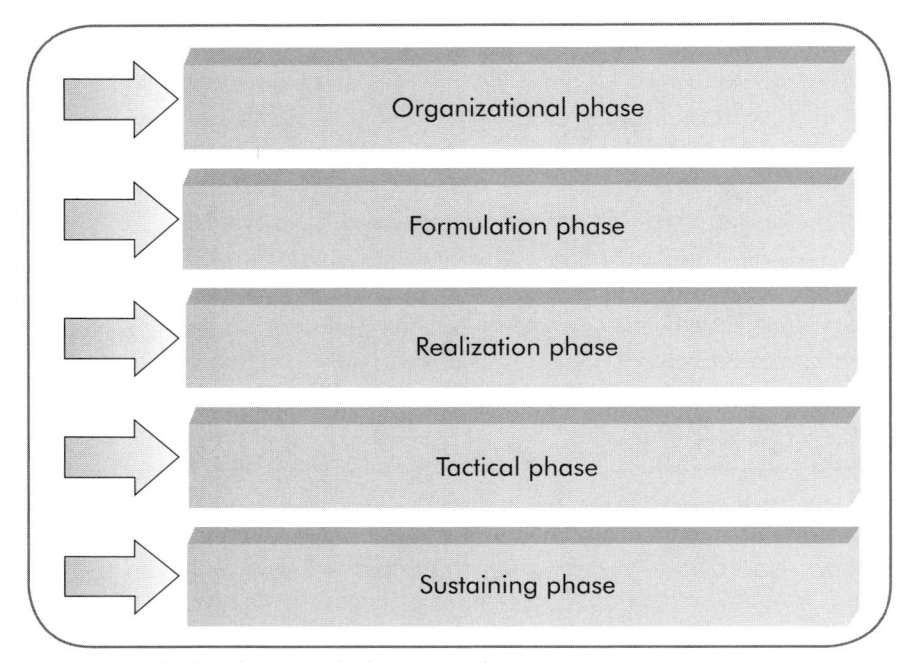

Figure 11-9. Fundamental planning phases.

committee also assists the transformation manager in establishing rules and guidelines for the transformation activities and in identifying potential pockets of resistance within and outside of the organization. In essence, the steering committee mentors the transformation manager and the change management team throughout the life of the transformation project.

In the organizational phase, the transformation manager defines the expected results of the change process, along with its schedule and budget. Like any other project sanctioned by senior management, the transformation project provides measurable returns to the organization. Also within this phase, the current base-lines are defined and measured as part of a comprehensive situational assessment. The leadership team for the transformation project is selected in this phase, with a special emphasis on chemistry and complementary skill sets. As discussed earlier, selection of this team is a critical step because it will be composed of the leaders of the change processes, for better or worse.

In the formulation phase, the transformation manager and the selected change agents carefully identify and recruit members for a series of cross-functional project teams. These teams will manage the transformation activities within different parts of the organization, along with the interfaces between those functions. The vision, scope, and objectives of the transformation initiative are explained to all team members to ensure their understanding and obtain buy-in. The level of empowerment of each of the teams is clearly outlined to ensure compliance with the rules and guidelines established in the organizational phase.

In the realization phase, the transformation teams begin to assess the organizational culture and structure, performance issues, business process designs, policies, procedures, practices, employee and management skill sets, organizational and functional competencies and capacities, support systems, etc. The drivers behind business performance problems that impact or constrain the current base-lines in each of these areas are identified, then confirmed. The purpose of this phase is to identify why the current organizational base-lines and culture exist, determine the factors that influence them, and what can be done to initiate change.

During the later stages of the realization phase, the transformation project teams analyze various alternative courses of action to redirect, redefine, or reengineer the organizational processes driving the current operating base-lines and culture. As various alternative courses of action are identified, the risks associated with each are quantified and compared against other alternatives. The alternative providing the desired outcome at the lowest cost and the least risk to the organization is selected for implementation during the tactical phase.

In the tactical phase, the implementation steps are identified, a formal schedule and budget are prepared, and control mechanisms are put into place to monitor progress. As the implementation progresses and key milestones are met, the original base-lines are redefined to ensure that the changes implemented are sustained. In some cases, the old "bridges" are "burned" to guarantee that there is no returning to the old culture and behaviors.

Throughout the tactical phase, the transformation manager constantly monitors progress, communication between and among the teams, and the cooperation the teams receive from supporting organizations and their employees using a checklist such as the one in Table 11-7. Any deviations from the tactical plan are dealt with quickly and decisively.

Once the tactical phase is completed, including all re-baselining activities and associated employee training, the project is turned over to sustaining (operational) management to oversee the sustaining phase. Here, continuous improvement actions are undertaken to ensure the sustainability of the actions taken, as well as the improvement of those actions over time.

Staff Planning

There are times when the transformation process yields radically new business processes and practices that require entirely new employee and/or management skill sets. There also may be the requirement to alter overhead expenses, resulting in a downsizing of the organization. When this situation can be reasonably foreseen during the planning stages, the transformation manager makes plans to address this difficult issue. These are not comfortable decisions for most managers. Nonetheless, they are handled for the transformation process to be successful.

In downsizing situations, the transformation manager is up-front with all personnel. The possibility of downsizing occurring because of the transformation processes is discussed candidly with those potentially impacted, along with how the organization will address those issues should they occur. History has shown that personnel will work with the transformation manager so long as the manager is candid about the situation, even if those employees know they will ultimately be displaced. It is only when employees are kept in the dark that

Table 11-7. Tactical planning checklist.

Question	Yes	No
1. Are the project teams' skill sets complementary?		
2. Is there sufficient cross-functional representation?		
3. Are there any critical skill sets missing?		
4. Is the chemistry among the teams and team members acceptable?		
5. Is the cooperation and communication within and between teams acceptable?		
6. Are the teams correctly sized?		
7. Are discussions interactive and open forum in nature?		
8. Are team roles clearly defined, understood, and accepted?		
9. Are all teams and team members actively involved?		
10. Are additional sub-teams needed for analysis work?		
11. Are the teams pursuing the critical issues aggressively?		
12. Is there consensus on the approach being recommended by the team leader?		
13. Does it appear that the teams use common goals and approaches?		
14. Is there a clear understanding of the transformation objectives?		
15. Is there belief among the teams that the transformation goals are achievable?		
16. Are controls and metrics being used effectively by the teams?		
17. Are priorities being set and maintained by the teams?		
18. Is there consistency in direction?		
19. Is there mutual accountability evident among team members?		
20. Are the team leaders and change agents effective?		
21. Are tasks being completed in a timely manner?		
22. Are there any successes to date?		

Turning Your Vision for Change into Action

Table 11-7. Tactical planning checklist *(continued)*.

Question	Yes	No
23. Are the successes being promoted at every level?		
24. Are the team members and leaders overburdened?		
25. Is a fatigue factor evident?		
26. Are other functional managers actively supporting the teams' efforts?		
27. Are senior managers actively supporting the teams' efforts?		
28. Are first-line managers actively supporting the teams' efforts?		
29. Are any hidden agendas apparent at any level?		
30. Is the transformation management team "walking the talk?"		

they become resistant. The transformation manager looks for ways to minimize the impact on personnel by finding ways to aid displaced personnel. Typical approaches include:

- outplacement,
- outside skills training for jobs within the company or jobs outside the organization,
- generous but reasonable severance packages,
- transfers, and/or
- early retirement.

As difficult and distasteful as a downsizing situation may appear on the surface, there may well be a silver lining. Often, less productive employees and managers are weaned from the organization as part of the transformation processes. Employees and managers with limited upside potential for growth are targeted for transfer or termination. But as with all aspects of the transformation process, these are planned changes based upon a realistic assessment of the organization's personnel needs both during and after the transition period. It is foolhardy to

Turning Your Vision for Change into Action

enter into this phase of the transformation process without a clear plan executed under the watchful eye of the transformation manager.

7. Implementing

The importance of early successes in the implementation process cannot be over-emphasized. The probability for success in any organizational change process is directly related to the elapsed time in implementing the desired changes. As Figure 11-10 illustrates, the longer it takes for results to be realized, the lower the likelihood that they will be realized.

In many cases, early successes are planned by the change manager and, at times, even the opportunities for those successes created in advance. The transformation manager uses the early wins to reinforce the culture of success, maintain the sense of urgency, and provide evidence that the transformation goals are achievable. Again, this is part of the selling process. It never stops. The transformation manager constantly uses

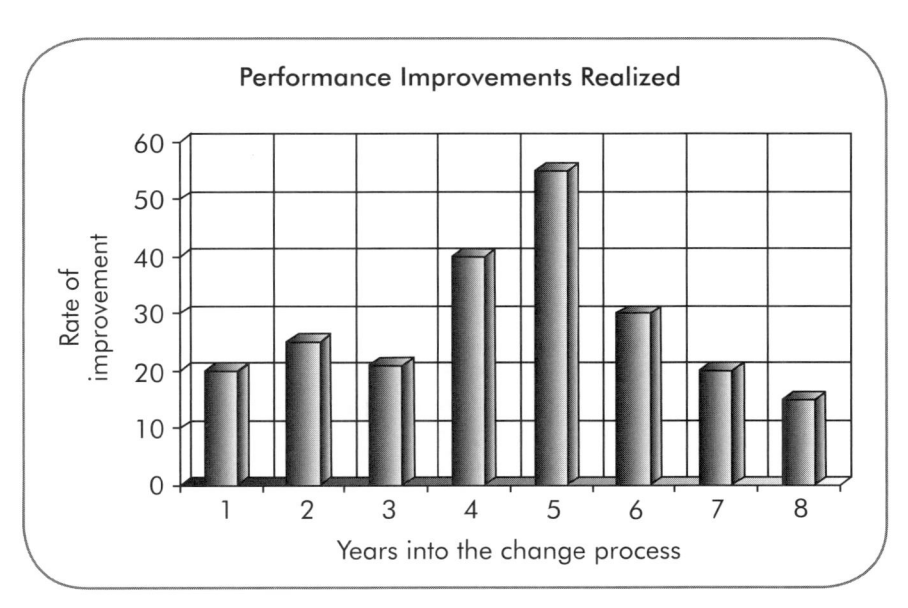

Figure 11-10. Results of change throughout the implementation cycle.

Turning Your Vision for Change into Action

every tool in his arsenal to maintain focus on the objectives and benefits of the change processes.

The first successes are targeted for realization within the first 12–18 months, with successive wins occurring no more than 12 months from the prior win. Obviously, the shorter the intervals are between successes, the higher the probability that more successes will be achieved. However, no transformation manager expects miracles overnight. In fact, the major gains achieved from typical transformation projects usually come after a sustained period of effort, commonly as many as 4–5 years after the transformation activities were initiated. It is worth restating that transforming today's complex business environments and processes will require a sustained, long-term effort. It will not happen quickly, no matter how dedicated the transformation manager.

> "Transforming today's complex business environments and processes will require a sustained, long-term effort."

8. Sustaining

Once achieved, the transformation manager makes a concentrated effort to maintain the new performance and cultural base-lines. This commonly requires a complete revamping of the operational, process, and employee performance and appraisal criteria; alteration of the reward systems to correspond with the new performance base-lines; and rewriting of all policies and procedures prior to hand-off to the sustaining managers. This "burning of the bridges" is required because, when times get tough, employees will gravitate back to old, safe practices and behaviors. Often, the only way to prevent it is to make that regression painful and difficult.

It is also imperative that the transformation manager carefully control succession planning to ensure that the sustaining managers selected or hired to maintain the new operational base-lines and culture are those that personify the transformed organization. If sustaining managers who embrace the old operating practices and cultures are allowed to take charge of the organization after the transformation is complete, the likelihood that the organization will regress is great.

Finally, the transformation manager ensures that the newly created metrics are dynamic so that continuous improvement will be realized every year.

Pitfalls

There are several common pitfalls to avoid.

The first is to never declare victory prematurely. This is a common mistake. In their enthusiasm over the first few realized changes, many transformation managers declare the transformation a success. Attention is then focused on the next business challenge, leaving the transformation projects unattended and incomplete. As priorities change, the remaining transformation projects get placed on the back burner and are ultimately forgotten altogether. Momentum is then lost and regression begins to set in. It happened with just-in-time (JIT), total quality management (TQM), quality circles, computer-integrated manufacturing (CIM), reengineering, lean, and most of the other change initiatives that took place during the last three decades of the 20th century. Unless the transformation processes are pushed through to completion, total success will be missed and regression is predictable.

Another common pitfall is to overburden the transformation teams and change agents to the point where they burn out or lose effectiveness. Transformation projects are stressful, time-consuming activities that require a high degree of personal commitment. Often, the transformation team members work on the transformation projects in addition to their normal job responsibilities. After a period, even the most dedicated change agents will tire. The experienced transformation manager is constantly aware of the fatigue factor on the project teams and frequently rotates assignments in an effort to keep fresh troops at the front line. On large transformation projects, it is a good practice to occasionally hire new change agents from the outside to bring fresh perspectives and enthusiasm to the projects.

SUMMARY

Successful transformation managers never let momentum wane. They find ways to reinforce and reward successes. They look for new challenges to keep employees sharp and constantly get more employees involved. Tough issues are tackled as they occur and are interspersed with easier challenges to level out the workload on transformation team members. Communication is frequent and widespread to ensure that every employee at every level is kept apprised of the transformation activities, their progress, and their impact on functional and operational priorities. The vision for change is continuously sold to all employees at all levels. It is backed up with a comprehensive implementation plan to ensure it remains focused and on track. Tough personnel and operational decisions are made when needed to ensure that everyone involved is following the same agenda. Successes are touted and rewarded. An overriding motto is consistently voiced: *It is not enough to think of doing things differently. Every employee must actually do those things differently. There must be action along with vision to ensure transformation success.*

In Chapter 12, the issues and challenges surrounding organizational politics will be discussed. While never openly acknowledged, politics are alive and thriving in most organizations today. It is, therefore, incumbent upon every manager, especially new ones, to understand what to expect and how to successfully interact with politicians on their turf. Failure to recognize and protect oneself from the potential impact of politics in the workplace will have devastating long-term effects on even the most stellar career.

REFERENCE

Termini, Michael J. 1999. *Strategic Project Management . . . Tools and Techniques for Planning, Decision-making, and Implementation.* Dearborn, MI: Society of Manufacturing Engineers.

12
Organizational Politics

OBJECTIVES

In this chapter, the issue of organizational politics will be discussed in detail. New and seasoned managers will gain an understanding of why politics exist within most organizations, as well as insight into how to recognize and survive political situations. Political agendas are not something that most managers find of value within an organization. In fact, most managers recoil at the thought of being political. Many seasoned managers have experienced politics first hand and have the battle scars to prove it. For them, it was an extremely unpleasant experience. Similarly, many new managers quickly find themselves the targets of politicians. Armed with little experience in the political arena, they often fall prey to professional organizational politicians who derail their management careers temporarily or even permanently.

While most managers prefer to ignore or avoid politics and politicians altogether, doing so is often a career-limiting mistake. In fact, most managers will benefit greatly from the successful application of politics to push through their agendas at all levels within the organization. Closed-loop managers recognize and use the true meaning of *politics*, which is the art of selling ideas or approaches. It is this true and positive definition that is important to a leader. In this chapter, discussions of both the true and commonly used negative definitions of politics will illustrate the dual faces of this issue and how it impacts management careers.

> "The true meaning of 'politics' is the art of selling ideas or approaches."

Organizational Politics

WHY DO POLITICS EXIST?

The answer as to why politics exist will surprise most managers ... organizational performance metrics. Whenever the performance metrics established by management are in conflict, a win-lose scenario is created. For a manager or an employee to succeed, another must lose. However, this situation is not created intentionally. Many managers simply fail to recognize the conflicts that exist because they adopt industry-standard performance measures without first assessing how those metrics complement or conflict with others within the organization.

> "Look for potential conflicts in organizational-, process-, and individual-level performance metrics whenever a political situation is at hand."

Closed-loop managers look for potential conflicts in organizational-, process-, and individual-level performance metrics whenever they find themselves in a political situation. Through analysis, they ascertain where and why discrepancies in the metrics exist and then seek a common ground that forces all parties to work cooperatively to be successful.

TEAMWORK VS. POLITICS

The theory behind the new breed of consensus managers is based upon the absence of politics within the organization. In most organizations, managers preach teamwork—a one-for-all and all-for-one view of the organizational culture exhibiting synergistic cooperation. Every decision is touted as "win-win" for all parties involved. The reality, however, is something completely different. Politics, the infusion of hidden agendas into decisions, or simply outright warfare are more the norm than the exception even in the best-managed organizations. The true risk to these managers is that employees at all levels see the differences between management's message and actions. When managers fail to walk the talk, trust is lost, leaving employees with no role models to emulate and no base-line of acceptable performance with which to judge their own actions. The net result is a "lose-lose" situation for all concerned.

Conversely, effective closed-loop managers address issues through value-added actions that benefit the entire organization. Cross-functional solutions are sought that never suboptimize any other department or process for an individual manager's personal gain. Issues are surfaced, addressed, and resolved as a management team. Acceptable compromise is always the desired outcome. If a decision is made or an action called for that negatively impacts another manager or department, the affected manager is told the reasons why no other approach provides an acceptable solution. Management decisions are not always popular, but they are always as fair as possible to all parties involved.

A TIME AND PLACE FOR POLITICS

Closed-loop managers know never to assume that they or their employees will receive credit for the work they do. In the course of any business day, senior managers are inundated with a barrage of information, suggestions, and casual comments regarding what has been done and by whom. They rarely have the time or opportunity to validate those comments; thus they accept them as fact. So, to keep the record straight, there are times when it is wise for a manager to promote the ideas, projects, and results of his employees. Although distasteful to most managers, politics can and should be used sparingly as a sales tool to gain the support of peers and senior managers. The informal discussions between managers build trust and relationships that allow a manager to get things done while at the same time working through organizational obstacles. This informal selling promotes a healthy dialogue between managers that brings disagreements and problems to the surface where they can be successfully dealt with.

The Art of War

Politicians are alive and well in many organizations today. Though most managers find politics distasteful, many often find

Organizational Politics

themselves the targets of organizational politicians. Politicians, quite frankly, seek advantage over unsuspecting managers and their organizations to maximize their own rewards or benefit their own organizations. As cold as that is, it is true. To combat this phenomenon, successful closed-loop managers have become war-like in their approach.

Most managers would not think twice about putting a competitor out of business. Senior managers develop strategic business plans accordingly and lower-level managers execute those plans without a thought or concern that success means putting another company, its managers, and employees, out of business. In business, it is about survival of the fittest. To apply that same mentality internally, however, is considered unprofessional—unless of course, a manager is placed in a political situation that is potentially career limiting. In such situations, all is fair, just like in war. Thus, there is a necessity for the closed-loop manager to be alert to the political climate of the organization and prepare for the eventuality that she may well be the next target.

Just as in the wild, predators exist in the corporate world. And as in the wild, vultures rarely attack strong prey. Their prey is either dead or very nearly so before they begin to circle. It is the same in the corporate world. Politicians, the vultures of corporate life, rarely attack a well-prepared, knowledgeable manager. Strong managers represent too much of a risk to the politician's own well-being. If the politician is unable to identify a weakness in an apparently strong, capable manager, he or she will seek easier prey. Managers who frequently make poor decisions or no decisions, who shoot from the hip, or who are unsure of what actions to take in a given situation set themselves up for the circling politicians. Their weaknesses are apparent to all, thus they are ill-prepared to defend themselves from the impending onslaught. The message is *be prepared*. Successful closed-loop managers always anticipate

> "Closed-loop managers anticipate the unexpected; they are always prepared."

the unexpected. Armed with facts and figures, they are always prepared for any question that may arise. In addition, they have cultivated a network of comrades to watch their backs.

Competition

Translations of two classic books: *The Book of the Five Rings* by Miyamoto Musashi and *Art of War* by Sun Tzu address competition from a warrior's perspective (Musashi 1994, Tzu 2006). The message of these visionaries is used today in strategic management training in many industries, as well as in many executive business programs in the Far East. Equating war to business, many of the fundamental rules of combat are transformed into management practices, providing managers with insight into dealing effectively in the political environment of today's business cultures.

Musashi states, "Never back your enemy to the sea. Always provide them with an escape route of your own design." The meaning of this statement for a manager in a business setting is straightforward. Japanese business managers use a companion phrase to this, which refers to "saving face." In the United States, the common phrase is, "Never back a jackrabbit into a corner." Each phrase delivers Musashi's message with clarity. If a manager forces a peer into a corner in which he has no escape or recourse, that peer will demonstrate incredible ferocity in his efforts to seek revenge. However, by providing his peer with a way out of his predicament, a manager can gently direct that individual to his way of thinking. This is the fundamental precept behind "saving face." It allows a manager to withdraw with respect and self-dignity. Just like elephants, people rarely forget or forgive. By allowing a peer to withdraw with his dignity intact, a manager creates lasting respect and a debt that will be repaid in the future.

An example from Tzu is equally as powerful: "The expert politician seeks victory from strategic advantage." The message for today's manager is that competitive advantage and/or business success does not come by default, but rather through strategic planning and rapid execution. Yet few of today's managers take the time to build and maintain a dynamic operational

Organizational Politics

plan supported by a series of carefully planned projects to ensure timely implementation. Rather, they gravitate to the crisis of the day, leaving their destiny to chance.

One final example from Musashi further demonstrates his wisdom. "Victory is the result of foreknowledge—that which cannot be deduced from comparisons to past events, but rather from people who know the situation." Closed-loop managers rely upon facts derived from and validated by experts on their staffs coupled with their own due diligence. To rely upon what procedures or popular opinion says "should" happen versus what actually occurs in any business setting is a recipe for disaster. This is why situational assessments (discussed in Chapter 10) are so critical. Knowing the realities of a business situation alerts a manager to the drivers behind it. Thus the closed-loop manager is better prepared to address it effectively.

Example

A television commercial aired not long ago in which an accountant is portrayed walking down a corridor with one of his friends. The accountant is complaining about a pending deadline and his inability to satisfy management's demands because he is short of staff. The accountant's friend reaches into his pocket and hands the accountant a card for Account Temps. He says to the accountant, "I've used these people in the past. They are really good."

The accountant takes the card and responds to his friend as he gets onto the elevator, "Hey, thanks, because listen, the one who pulls this off gets the next promotion." The friend reaches out, taking the card from the accountant's hand just as the elevator door closes.

Competition can bring out the best or worst in a person.

Political Security

When in a political situation, successful closed-loop managers always work from a position of strength, supported by

376   Walking the Talk: Pathways to Leadership

solid, accurate facts and data. All assumptions are validated as well. The unexpected is expected—and preparation is always comprehensive. Perception is managed to ensure the appearance of competency and confidence. Nothing is left to chance.

In the rare event that a question is presented for which the manager has no answer, he confidently replies that he is unsure, but will research the issue and respond within a few hours. Never does a closed-loop manager guess, thereby exposing himself to potential criticism and the associated political fallout that results from it. No manager is expected to have all of the answers to any conceivable question. The admission by a manager that he is unsure is often perceived as positive—he is mature and confident. Make no mistake, however. A manager who does not have an immediate answer to a question about which he is expected to be knowledgeable will be judged as ill-prepared or incapable. In a case like this, the politician wins.

SUMMARY

The game of politics is played by experts whose intent is to take no prisoners. Survival requires foreknowledge and a keen appreciation of the potential devastation that politics can bring to a career. In a political situation, closed-loop managers who are prepared and armed with knowledge demonstrate a significantly higher survival rate. Through experience, they have learned to:

- never underestimate a political situation;
- manage perception;
- validate all information;
- prepare; and
- expect the unexpected.

While there is no single recipe for success when in a political situation, these simple tips will shield a manager from many of the political maneuvers that occur within a business environment. Success comes from remaining alert and ready.

REFERENCES

Musashi, Miyamoto. 1994. Translated by Thomas Cleary. *The Book of Five Rings*. Boston: Shambhala; New York: Distributed in the United States by Random House.

Tzu, Sun. 2006. 1910 translation. *The Art of War*, 1st Edition. Fairfield, IA: 1st World Library–Literary Society.

Appendix

Competency and Capability Assessments

This appendix presents the typical questions asked in competency and capability assessments. While the questionnaires are applicable to numerous industry segments, they must be customized to the specific business, industry, and demographics of each particular organization. In short, there is no "one size fits all" tool that should be used "as is" without some modification. Existing analysis tools like the questionnaires that follow can be modified to accommodate most organizational needs.

MANUFACTURING PROCESS CAPABILITIES AND CAPACITIES

1. Can it be demonstrated that regular reviews of internal process capabilities are conducted with the objective of expanding and enhancing those capabilities?

2. Are the results of process capability studies forwarded to those in design engineering functions for use in product development activities?

3. Are recognized problem-solving and decision-making techniques used to identify, measure, and resolve internal and external process problems?

4. Are those problem-solving and decision-making techniques applied in a timely manner to minimize the impacts of problems?

5. Can it be demonstrated that those problem-solving and decision-making techniques have produced results that have systematically reduced process variability with a goal of 100% first-pass yield?

Competency and Capability Assessments

7. Are statistical techniques employed to continuously monitor process capability against product specifications?
8. Are operators provided with comprehensive procedures that clearly define the actions to be taken to prevent the process from moving out of control?
9. Are preventive techniques, such as design of experiments, employed to design out potential process variation?
10. Are process capability studies obtained from key suppliers prior to placement of orders with them?
11. Are said process capability studies utilized to determine which suppliers will be approved for critical component purchases?

MANUFACTURING PROCESS CONTROLS

1. Are all facilities kept clean and free of nonessential inventory, tools, dies, fixtures, etc.?
2. Can it be demonstrated that there is proper storage and control of hazardous materials used in the production process? Are proper procedures followed by all appropriate personnel involved with the production, handling, storage, and transportation of those products?
3. Can it be demonstrated that there is a written procedure for electrostatic discharge protection when electrical components are used? Is this procedure followed by all personnel?
4. Is a "pull" versus "push" technique used to drive production (for example, kanban or final assembly order processing)?
5. Can it be demonstrated that manufacturing lots are traceable throughout the production process?
6. Is there a written procedure defining the statistical process control (SPC) methods employed?
    a. Does it define the methods of reporting?
    b. Does it outline the frequency and timing of samples?

Competency and Capability Assessments

    c. Does it include the maintenance of statistically based control charts?

7. Have process controls been employed to address problems and are they maintained at all critical points within the process?

8. Is there evidence that process control data is prepared and distributed often enough to provide an early warning of impending process control problems?

9. Can it be demonstrated that the process control data triggers corrective action when the process is not within control limits?

    a. Is the corrective action process clearly defined along with the responsible parties?

    b. Can it be demonstrated that such actions have yielded positive, measurable results for the customer?

10. Is there concrete evidence that process changes are controlled, authorized, documented, dated, and signed?

11. Is there evidence that process and product specifications are readily accessible to all appropriate operators?

12. Is there evidence that all operators are trained and capable of interpreting customer specifications?

13. Is there a documented policy or procedure that defines the conditions under which operators and/or maintenance personnel have the authority to shut down production operations?

    a. Is it in effect for all out-of-control conditions?

    b. Is there evidence that the procedure is understood and enacted upon in the presence of an out-of-control or potentially out-of-control situation?

14. Is there evidence that process and inspection records are kept for a period that is consistent with the requirements of the industry or any unique company requirements?

Competency and Capability Assessments

15. Is there evidence that process and inspection records are accessible to all appropriate operators and quality personnel?
16. Is there evidence of a written procedure for process audits?
    a. Does it specify methods of reporting findings and recommendations?
    b. Does it define methods for corrective action and the responsible parties?
17. Can it be demonstrated that statistical process control or inspection charts are regularly reviewed by manufacturing and/or quality management?
18. Is there a documented rework procedure that is consistent with that of either customers or applicable industry standards?
19. Is there evidence of a documented setup procedure?
20. Is there evidence of setup reduction activities designed to reduce setup time and costs? Have those activities yielded measurable results for the customer?
21. Is there evidence that production equipment is consistently calibrated on a regular basis by trained personnel? Are those calibration records and dates kept?
22. Is there evidence of procedures in place to quarantine nonconforming materials?
23. Is there evidence of procedures in place to confirm the acceptability of all products prior to release to the customer?
24. Is there evidence of an official engineering or specification change system that informs customers of changes to the products in advance?
25. Can it be demonstrated that customers are surveyed for approval of any product changes that impact form, fit, or function before said changes are enacted?
26. Is there evidence of a written procedure for communication and distribution of specification and/or engineering changes?

27. Can it be demonstrated that obsolete engineering drawings and product specifications are removed from all manufacturing and quality assurance operations immediately upon implementation of a new revision?

28. Can it be demonstrated that all documents and drawings used in the manufacturing process are free of unofficial and/or handwritten changes?

29. Is there evidence of a properly documented and enforced preventive maintenance system?

    a. Is there predictive maintenance?

    b. Are documented results available for review?

30. Is there evidence that all tools and fixtures used in production are fully qualified, maintained, and identified?

31. Is there a documented tool and fixture location system in use for all production tooling?

32. Can it be demonstrated that maximum tool life is identified and monitored through formal systems and that same is communicated to all appropriate operators?

QUALITY SYSTEMS

1. Is there evidence that a formal quality system is employed?

2. Is the quality system completely and clearly documented?

3. Is there evidence that the quality system documents all applicable functions that contribute directly to the:

    a. receipt of materials?

    b. purchase of materials?

    c. design of materials?

    d. production of materials?

    e. handling of materials?

Competency and Capability Assessments

    f. storage of materials?

    g. distribution of materials?

4. Can it be demonstrated that the quality system is based upon statistical methodologies that comply with the American National Standards Institute, American Society for Testing and Materials, Underwriters Laboratories, Canadian Standards Association, ISO 9000, QS 9000, or other applicable national or international standards?

5. Does the quality system confirm through quantitative methodologies that specifications and requirements are visible throughout the production and service operations?

6. Does the quality system clearly designate who is responsible for the control and release of all nonconforming materials?

    a. Does the quality system document under what conditions nonconforming materials can be released for further processing?

    b. Is there consistent adherence to those policies and procedures?

7. Does the quality system dictate that any processed materials identified as defective must be scrapped or reworked under the guidelines approved by the organization?

8. Is there evidence that the quality system imposes a requirement for timely corrective action response to the customer when a defect is encountered? Is there demonstrated adherence to that requirement?

9. Does the quality system define the frequency of calibration for inspection and test equipment?

    a. Is that frequency consistent with recognized national standards?

    b. Is there evidence of documentation of those calibrations?

10. Is there evidence that the quality system defines the selection, control, and maintenance of all inspection and test equipment?

11. Is there evidence that the quality system includes a requirement for internal audits to ensure that all quality activities comply with the quality system and policies?

    a. Can it be demonstrated that senior management is actively involved in the review of quality system audit results?

    b. Where indicated, can it be demonstrated that management is actively involved in the corrective action processes required to bring activities into compliance with the quality system policies?

12. Can it be demonstrated that complete historical information is retained on all shipments or services provided for a period of not less than one year?

13. Is there evidence that historical quality information is used as the base-line for continuous improvement activities?

14. Is there evidence that historical information has been used as the basis for corrective action implementations? Have those corrective actions been successfully implemented and are they yielding measurable, positive results?

15. Can it be demonstrated that the quality system properly controls all applicable customer specification changes to ensure that only current revision levels are produced and shipped?

16. Can it be demonstrated that the quality system governs raw material specifications for internal use, which are consistent with those of product and/or service specifications?

17. Is there evidence that the quality system dictates an incoming inspection of raw materials and components and/or supplier test certifications prior to raw material acceptance from suppliers?

Competency and Capability Assessments

18. Does the quality system ensure that all required testing procedures and inspection capabilities are available so all of the tests or quality confirmations can be performed prior to shipment? Is there evidence that those test methods are confirmed and controlled regularly through the quality system?

19. Is there evidence that the quality system defines who has authority to stop the shipment of materials? Are the conditions under which a stop-shipment order is issued well understood by the appropriate personnel?

QUALITY MANAGEMENT

1. Can it be demonstrated that the management of the quality system clearly supports the organization's quality requirements as evidenced by:

    a. a formal written quality policy and/or quality manual?

    b. measurable quality objectives?

    c. quantified quality performance metrics?

    d. an organizational structure that clearly defines the lines of authority and responsibility relative to the quality systems and processes?

2. Can it be demonstrated that operator control versus conventional in-process inspection by independent quality inspectors is common practice? Are operators adequately trained relative to the quality and technical aspects of their position?

3. Is there evidence that inspection procedures are monitored and enforced by quality and operations management to ensure daily compliance to quality system requirements?

4. Is there evidence that test procedures and methods cover:

    a. how and when samples are to be taken?

    b. the proper equipment to be used for each test?

Competency and Capability Assessments

    c. how to compare the results obtained during testing to established acceptance criteria?

    d. the methods to be employed to record test results?

    e. to whom results are to be reported?

    f. what action to take if results are outside of acceptable limits?

    g. how the material is to be released for further processing or testing?

5. Is there evidence that senior management conducts regular quality review meetings? If so, do those quality reviews concentrate on issues like customer satisfaction, quality costs, internal audit reports, and outgoing quality levels in quantifiable terms?

6. Can it be demonstrated that there is a long-term quality system improvement plan documented as part of the company's strategic plans?

7. Can it be demonstrated that the company is striving to achieve best-in-class status as part of its quality improvement objectives?

8. Is there evidence that the quality improvement plan is incorporated into the individual departmental or functional objectives for each part of the organization with corresponding performance metrics established to monitor progress?

9. Is there evidence that the quality improvement plan is effectively communicated to and understood at all levels within the organization?

10. Is there evidence that the quality policy is a "living document" in that it is constantly updated and enhanced to reflect changes in customer requirements, process improvements, etc.?

11. Is there evidence of ongoing quality training for all levels and functions within the organization?

Competency and Capability Assessments

12. Is said quality training documented in each individual's personnel record?

13. Can it be demonstrated that the quality system has been certified by a qualified, independent third party or another customer? Are the criteria used for certification compatible with those of the organization?

14. Is there evidence that a formal follow-up system is employed to monitor customer complaints and implement corrective actions relative to those complaints?

15. Can it be demonstrated that senior management regularly monitors customer performance metrics such as on-time delivery, outgoing quality acceptance levels, and count accuracy?

16. Can it be demonstrated that senior management takes corrective action when key customer performance metrics are not met?

17. Is there evidence that operators and quality personnel utilize statistical problem-solving methods to resolve performance problems in administrative and operating areas? Are there tangible results?

18. Can it be demonstrated that statistical process control (SPC) techniques are used to ensure ongoing process control in operating and support areas?

    a. Is this data available for review?

    b. Is there evidence that SPC data has been used as the basis for corrective actions?

19. Are partnership-type relationships promoted between customers and suppliers?

20. Is there evidence that quality stamps and/or formal quality certification documentation are utilized to indicate quality acceptance of products prior to shipment? If so, are said quality stamps or certifications effectively controlled?

RAW MATERIALS COMPLIANCE

1. Can it be demonstrated that procured raw materials, finished components, and subcontracted services meet or exceed product specifications?

2. Is there evidence that suppliers confirm the incoming quality of their purchased materials through inspection methods or receipt of their suppliers' material certifications?

3. Can it be demonstrated that a documented and metrics-based supplier selection and certification process is employed to qualify suppliers? Is there evidence that those performance metrics include conformance to quality requirements, on-time delivery performance, and count accuracy?

4. Is there evidence that an evaluation of supplier performance against metrics such as quality, on-time delivery, and count accuracy, is performed on a regular basis (monthly or quarterly) to prompt corrective actions on the part of suppliers? Are those metrics actively and universally monitored for each supplier?

5. Is there evidence that timely corrective action feedback (within 30 to 60 days) is required for all defects received from suppliers?

6. Can it be demonstrated that written specifications are required from suppliers for all materials they design? Is there evidence that those specifications are verified for accuracy and the appropriate revision level?

7. If subcontractors are utilized for in-process operations, is there evidence that the necessary controls are in place to ensure that quality requirements are met?

8. Can it be demonstrated that complete records are maintained regarding approved suppliers? Is there evidence that those records are available to the suppliers' designers and engineers?

Competency and Capability Assessments

9. Can it be demonstrated that suppliers are periodically audited by a team of this company's employees or an independent auditing firm retained for this specific purpose?

10. Is there evidence that statistical data is maintained on each of the key suppliers' process capabilities?

11. Is there evidence of a written procedure covering the receipt of materials by the supplier?

    a. Is the procedure audited regularly by quality or internal audit staff?

    b. Is there consistent compliance to those receiving procedures?

12. Is there evidence that incoming materials are properly segregated from previously accepted materials until the approval process is completed?

13. Can it be demonstrated that incoming materials are properly protected from the environment upon receipt?

14. Can it be demonstrated that there is a procedure to ensure the identification and traceability of incoming lots from receiving throughout the production processes?

15. Is there evidence that raw material testing and confirmation procedures are properly documented? Are those raw material test results monitored by management-level employees?

16. Does the company possess electronic data interchange capabilities that are consistent with industry standard transaction sets?

17. Are the company's bar-coding capabilities consistent with the format(s) required by its customers?

INVENTORY MANAGEMENT AND CONTROL SYSTEMS

1. Are there written procedures outlining the storage, release, and handling of raw materials and in-process inventory items?

2. Is there evidence that those procedures ensure that only approved materials are released to and used in the production of products?

3. Can it be demonstrated that an effective inventory control procedure is employed to maximize inventory turns while controlling the incidence of inventory obsolescence?

   a. Do those procedures cover issues like shelf life and use of the first-in-first-out method to prevent deterioration of materials?

   b. Are those procedures effective in maintaining the current levels of surplus and obsolete inventory to less that 2.5% of total inventory in dollars?

4. Can it be demonstrated that either physical inventory or cycle counting is used to guarantee inventory accuracy? Does current inventory accuracy meet or exceed 99% by part count?

5. Is there evidence that a formal shop-order routing method is used to ensure that in-process materials are produced to predetermined product or customer specifications?

6. Are automated material planning techniques employed to forecast and schedule raw material needs and customer orders for finished goods?

7. Is there evidence that materials are labeled or coded to ensure their proper identification while in storage and in-process?

TECHNICAL AND PRODUCT SUPPORT

1. Can it be demonstrated that the company's scope of research and product development activities is sufficient to support the unique dynamics or technologies within the industry?

2. Is there evidence that research and new product development efforts are directed at the needs of the organization, both now and in the future?

Competency and Capability Assessments

3. Can it be demonstrated that product or process specifications are considered during the new product development process?
4. Are concurrent or simultaneous engineering methodologies utilized during the development of new products and processes?
5. Are the new product development processes clearly defined and the procedures documented?
6. Do the engineers incorporate internal manufacturing process capabilities into their product and process design rules and criteria using sound design-for-manufacturability techniques? Similarly, is there evidence of inclusion of all suppliers' process capabilities?
7. Are design changes effectively controlled throughout the organization?
   a. Does the process have documented procedures?
   b. Is there evidence that the number of design changes initiated by the organization is monitored and managed effectively?
8. Are engineering and design personnel active in industry-related professional associations and continuing education programs?
9. Can it be demonstrated that computer-based design tools are employed to support the design of new products and processes? Do those computer-based design tools include computer simulation and/or modeling, design of experiments, and failure modes and effects analyses?
10. Are designers and engineers supported in their pursuit of design patents to encourage innovation?
11. Is there a strategic long-term technology plan to guide the continued development of leading-edge technologies?
12. Is it demonstrated that there is an effective system for maintaining and storing customer and supplier documentation?

13. Is there a formal mechanism for notifying customers of documentation problems?

14. Is there evidence that new product and process development procedures adequately define the metrics employed to guarantee compliance with the design rules, cycle times, performance requirements, reliability requirements, and other customer-driven performance metrics?

15. Is there evidence of a procedure to control critical-to-function characteristics for new products, such as statistical process control characteristics and frequencies, before initiating production?

16. Are key suppliers included as part of the design team under normal circumstances? Similarly, are key customers included as part of the product and process design team?

17. Is technical support provided to employees relative to field service, installation, and application-related issues?

18. Do the installation and users manuals provided to customers clearly delineate the use and maintenance of the company's products in their applications?

COST CONTROLS

1. Is the company actively involved in product and process cost containment activities addressing:

    a. waste reduction in direct and administrative areas?

    b. supply-base-related material and service costs?

    c. production cycle time and throughput improvements?

    d. labor and equipment efficiency improvements?

    e. product development cycle-time improvements?

    f. administrative cycle-time improvements?

2. Are there established product cost standards against which operational metrics can be applied?

Competency and Capability Assessments

3. Can it be demonstrated that all appropriate operational metrics are tracked daily? Are significant variances from the standard reviewed and corrective actions implemented?

4. Are the company's product cost standards compatible with all quality, operational, and product performance metrics?

5. Are overhead and burden costs accurately applied to the products and services sold to the organization?

6. Do the accounting functions interact frequently and supportively with the operations functions?

7. Can it be demonstrated that the cost of quality or a similar quality cost metric is tracked?

    a. Are appropriate corrective action plans implemented when directed by the result of a poor cost-of-quality measurement?

    b. Is there quantifiable evidence that those implementations have yielded positive results in maintaining or reducing quality costs?

8. Is there effective control of overtime or other lead-time-associated costs?

9. Are inventory-related costs that impact raw materials, work-in-process inventories, and finished goods effectively controlled?

10. Is there evidence that labor costs are effectively controlled?

11. Is the company willing to share cost information with its key customers relative to the products and services provided to them?

12. Have cost controls been successful in reducing product or service costs during the prior 12 to 24 months?

Competency and Capability Assessments

MANAGEMENT COMMITMENT

1. Is the company's organizational structure well defined and documented?
2. Does senior management support and promote new ideas and concepts for continuous improvement?
3. Is the training provided for employees consistent with their respective job functions and levels of responsibility?
4. Is senior management actively involved in the pursuit of quality and process improvements that directly impact customers?
5. Does management support and promote the concept of employee involvement in the resolution of operational problems and the improvement of quality and process deficiencies?
6. Has senior management identified and implemented provisions for the special controls, tools, employee skills, and processes that will be required to guarantee consistent product quality improvements?
7. Has senior management established formal written objectives and initiatives aimed at reducing the cycle time of all administrative functions such as order entry, new product development, response to customer complaints and requests for information, purchasing, material planning, and production scheduling?
8. Does senior management review the customer-focused organizational performance metrics such as customer satisfaction, on-time delivery, outgoing quality levels, shipment count accuracy, quoted and requested order lead times, etc., at least weekly?
    a. Does senior management initiate corrective actions when results do not meet objectives?
    b. Is there concrete evidence that said actions have been successful?

Competency and Capability Assessments

9. Can it be demonstrated that the company is doing business with customer(s) in a partnership-type relationship as defined by their organization(s)?

10. Is senior management receptive to innovation and improvement suggestions from employees, customers, and suppliers?

11. Does senior management regularly share operational and customer performance results with the employees?

12. Does senior management use the results of internal quality system audits to implement corrective actions and quality system enhancements?

13. Is there evidence that customers are routinely notified in the event of potential nonconformance or late deliveries in advance of the scheduled due date?

14. Does senior management personally visit customers and suppliers on a regular basis (annually) to solicit input relative to product and process improvement ideas?

15. Is there evidence that senior management maintains a dynamic business plan that extends three to five years into the future?

    a. Is the business plan supported by companion product plans and integrated facility plans?

    b. Is there evidence that progress is being monitored?

16. Does senior management promote employee involvement in professional organizations such as the Instrument Society of America, American Society for Quality, Society of Manufacturing Engineers, Society of Automotive Engineers, APICS: the Association for Operations Management, or other industry-sanctioned trade or professional organizations?

17. Is the company's mission statement, which has been adopted by senior management, developed from voice-of-the-customer, quality function deployment, or similar

techniques so it takes into consideration actual customer requirements and expectations?

18. Has senior management incorporated the mission statement into all operating procedures and metrics at all levels within the organization?

19. Do said procedures and metrics include:

   a. how control is established in indirect and direct functions?

   b. how customer orders are to be controlled and processed?

   c. how product or service defects are to be addressed?

   d. how employees are to be trained?

   e. how products and processes are to be tested?

   f. how information is to be processed and controlled?

   g. who is responsible for quality?

   h. management's role in ensuring that all customer-driven quality requirements are met?

   i. management's periodic auditing of business systems to guarantee the continued suitability and effectiveness of it?

   j. what is expected from each functional area relative to customer satisfaction and how it will be measured?

   k. detailed instructions on how management's quality policies and procedures are to be implemented?

   l. the handling of technical data, specifications, and control parameters?

FINANCIAL STABILITY

1. Is the company financially stable as defined using generally accepted accounting principles (GAAP)? Is there evidence substantiating that position from an independent certified public accounting firm?

Competency and Capability Assessments

2. Is there demonstrated consistency in or a trend of continuous growth in sales and/or profitability during the past five years?
3. Is there sufficient cash flow from continuing operations to sustain normal business activities through effective utilization (versus sale) of company assets?
4. Is there evidence of an appreciable change in ownership during the past five years or is there evidence that one is anticipated?
5. Is the company highly leveraged due to its debt structure, a previous leveraged buyout, or other contributing factors or declared obligations?
6. Is there evidence that the company is likely a take-over candidate because of its cash, technological, or market position?
7. Is there a demonstrated history of frequent or unannounced price increases that cite increasing costs or recessionary business conditions as the reason?
8. Has capital been reinvested back into the business on a regular basis in an amount equal to or greater than 5–10% of annual sales revenues?

INDUSTRY KNOWLEDGE

1. Is it demonstrated that the company's representatives and employees are familiar with the industry it serves?
2. Is this company a provider of products and/or services to other companies in the industry?
3. Is the company active in industry trade groups, technical associations, or trade publications?
4. Does the company provide insight into market and industry trends, as well as industry or competitive technological developments?
5. Has the company dedicated resources and investment into servicing its markets?

Competency and Capability Assessments

6. Is the company vulnerable to forces that would interfere with its continued participation in the industry it serves?

7. Does a significant percentage of company business (greater than 30%) come from the main industry it serves?

8. Has the company been awarded patents or royalties for products developed within the last five years?

9. Is the company working toward best-in-class status or other recognizable quality standards within the industry it serves?

FACILITIES MANAGEMENT AND MAINTENANCE

1. Are general housekeeping procedures maintained and monitored for every operating department?

2. Is there evidence that comprehensive housekeeping audits are scheduled and conducted on a regular basis?

3. Is there evidence that an active preventive and predictive maintenance program is employed within all applicable operating areas and facilities?

4. Can it be demonstrated that all preventive and predictive maintenance schedules are adhered to by all areas and by all levels of management and supervision?

5. Is there evidence that written procedures for reporting deviations from the preventive maintenance standards exist and are followed?

6. Are maintenance records maintained for each piece of operating and test equipment? Are those records accessible to all appropriate operators and maintenance personnel?

7. Is the responsibility for administration and management of the preventive and predictive maintenance programs clearly defined and understood?

8. Can it be demonstrated that material storage areas, aisles, production areas, inspection areas, receiving areas, and

Competency and Capability Assessments

shipping areas are clean and free of excess materials, tools, fixtures, and packaging dunnage?

9. Can it be demonstrated that housekeeping, safety, and hygiene practices comply with industry standards and any applicable regulatory requirements?
10. Is there evidence that timely corrective actions are initiated in response to workplace injuries and lost-time accidents?
11. Is there evidence of written safety instructions (safety manuals, warnings, etc.) for all production, material handling, receiving, and shipping operations?
12. Is there evidence of written safety instructions for special processes or events such as the handling and disposal of hazardous waste, fire, emergency weather conditions, flood, earthquake, etc.?

DISTRIBUTION PROCESS CONTROL

1. Is there evidence that accurate and up-to-date packaging and labeling specifications are maintained?
2. Is the responsibility for all packaging specifications and designs clearly defined and understood by all affected employees?
3. Do written packaging and shipping procedures exist? Are they effectively deployed in the packaging and shipping departments?
4. Can it be demonstrated that packaging and shipping procedures allow package and label specifications to be defined by customers?
5. Do written procedures exist that define the methods for making shipping containers that comply with customer specifications?
6. Can it be demonstrated that proper identification labels are consistently used for each package or container in a shipment in accordance with the customer's specifications or any applicable U.S. or international regulatory requirement?

Competency and Capability Assessments

7. Are customer routing and traffic instructions always available within the shipping and packaging departments?
8. Is the bar-coding technology used consistent with the customer's labeling requirements?
9. Is the responsibility for company logistics clearly defined and documented?
10. Are agreements maintained with domestic and (when applicable) international freight carriers to ensure consistent on-time delivery performance to customers at the most advantageous rates?
11. Does the company possess electronic data interchange capabilities for tracking inbound and outbound freight?
12. Do all shipments of products to customers include a certificate of compliance to their specifications and test requirements?
13. Is there evidence that all customer requests for special marking of part numbers, work order numbers, purchase order numbers, and material codes on outgoing containers for ease in identification are honored?
14. Is control maintained over lots that are required to be kept intact throughout the packaging and shipping processes?
15. Is there evidence that all nonconforming materials found during the packaging and shipping processes are properly identified and quarantined from known good material to prevent inadvertent shipment to the customer?
16. Is there evidence that procedures exist to restrict the storage and release of materials for shipping to only authorized personnel?
17. Is there a shelf-life program for distributed products where applicable?
18. Are written agreements in place with transport companies and forwarding agents and do they include procedures to

Competency and Capability Assessments

return defective or faulty materials, as well as a process for handling those materials that were not received?

19. Is there a documented returned-goods policy and procedure?

20. Does the company support ship-direct requests from customers and are procedures for such adequately documented?

21. Is there the ability to track shipments from their point of origin to the final destination as part of normal operations and services? Are said procedures supported by on-line, real-time computer systems?

22. By procedure and practice, is material ordered for same-day shipment (via UPS, Federal Express, etc.) documented to reflect the actual date shipped?

23. Is there support for special drop shipments of "truck load" and "less than truck load" quantities to single and/or multiple locations?

ORDER-ENTRY PROCESS CONTROL

1. Are written procedures in place to govern the order-entry process? Are those procedures based upon customer-designated performance criteria?

2. Is there evidence that senior managers routinely monitor the performance of the order-entry process to ensure it complies with customer expectations of accurate and timely processing of orders?

3. Is the order-entry accuracy rate continuously measured? Does the accuracy rate consistently meet or exceed an accuracy level that ensures conformance to customer expectations?

4. Is the order-entry cycle time measurement considered one of the company's primary performance metrics? Can it be demonstrated that the targeted order-entry cycle time is consistent with customer expectations?

5. Is there evidence that customer satisfaction levels are monitored routinely? Does said monitoring include:

   a. on-time delivery performance?

   b. outgoing product quality levels?

   c. the cycle time for customer complaint resolution?

   d. the ratio of satisfactory complaint resolutions to the total number of complaints received?

   e. the ratio of invoicing or pricing errors to the total number of customer orders received?

6. Has the monitoring of customer satisfaction and order-entry metrics led to the successful implementation of measurable process performance improvements?

7. Is the receipt of customer orders via industry-standard electronic data interchange transaction sets supported?

CUSTOMER AND FIELD SERVICE

1. Is the customer-service function clearly defined within the existing organizational structure?

2. Is there evidence of a formal feedback system to ensure that customer requests and problems are expeditiously directed to the appropriate department for resolution?

   a. Is there a companion feedback system to ensure that a response from the appropriate internal department is, in turn, delivered to the customer on a timely basis?

   b. Are there performance targets governing customer response time?

   c. Are there performance targets governing the accuracy of those responses?

3. Is there evidence that senior management is actively involved with the customer-service function?

Competency and Capability Assessments

4. Can it be demonstrated that both positive and negative trends in customer satisfaction are reported directly to senior management on a timely basis?

5. Does the company maintain an emphasis on exemplary levels of customer service for all customers versus merely the large or key customers?

6. Does the company compare favorably to its direct competition relative to customer satisfaction indices?

7. Have the customer and field-service processes yielded consistent improvement in customer satisfaction throughout the last three to five years?

8. Have customer satisfaction objectives and targets been benchmarked against recognized best-in-class organizations within the industries they serve?

9. Is there evidence that senior managers take decisive action to correct performance problems when customer satisfaction levels fall short of targeted or expected goals?

10. Do senior managers personally meet with representatives of key customers on a routine basis to discuss customer satisfaction levels and requirements for improvement?

11. Is there a formal, documented procedure for handling customer complaints?

    a. Is said procedure consistently effective?

    b. Is the procedure consistently followed by all customer-service representatives?

    c. Does said procedure empower customer-service representatives to resolve routine customer complaints without seeking management approval?

12. Is there a documented procedure to inform customers of potential delivery, quality, or service problems *in advance* of the scheduled ship date?

13. Is there a documented procedure to inform customers of design, manufacturing, or process changes *in advance* of implementing those changes?
14. Is timely field support provided when operational or installation problems need to be resolved?
15. Is the company actively pursuing lead-time reduction activities? Have those activities yielded measurable results for customers?
16. Are management and employees committed to following ethical business practices?

REGULATORY COMPLIANCE

1. Is the company in full compliance with all federal, state, and local regulatory requirements applicable to its particular industry segment?
2. Is there a formal, documented procedure governing environmentally responsible and community supportive (proactive) operations? Are the company's products and operations environmentally benign?
3. Are all products in strict compliance with applicable regulations and do those that contain hazardous materials or chemicals carry appropriate labeling pursuant to applicable regulatory requirements?
4. Has the company been cited within the last three years for noncompliance with federal, state, and/or local environmental, safety, or employment regulations or is there litigation currently pending?
5. Are safety and health awareness programs documented and maintained as an integral part of normal business operations? Is there evidence of annual audits of those safety and health awareness programs to confirm their effectiveness?
6. Is there evidence that all personnel have been adequately trained relative to applicable safety, health, and other

Competency and Capability Assessments

governmentally regulated business and operating requirements?

7. Is the company's substance abuse program maintained and documented in compliance with federal and state laws?

8. Are there documented emergency procedures in place to respond to crisis situations?

9. Does the company provide material safety data sheets and other safety-related information documents to its employees?

10. Does the company maintain and promote an active recycling program in conjunction with its suppliers and customers?

LABOR RELATIONS

1. Does the company support and promote employee involvement activities such as work teams or quality improvement teams?

2. Are training and educational opportunities provided for employees at every level within the organization? Does the company maintain training records on each employee detailing the courses and education levels achieved?

3. Can it be demonstrated that the company is an equal opportunity employer?

4. Is the company in compliance with the uniform guidelines on employee selection?

5. Has the company experienced a labor-related work stoppage within the last five to six years?

6. Have labor disputes been resolved without outside intervention, arbitration, or mediation?

7. Does the company support and promote an active employee suggestion program?

   a. Is there a formal policy or procedure governing the employee suggestion program to ensure that all suggestions receive objective consideration and recognition?

Competency and Capability Assessments

b. Does the procedure ensure that the employee who submits a suggestion receives feedback as to whether or not the suggestion was accepted within a reasonable time?

8. Are employees at all levels actively involved in day-to-day decision-making activities?

9. Is there evidence that senior management keeps employees apprised on a regular basis of the financial and market conditions impacting the company?

10. Is the company equal to or better than industry averages relative to:

    a. employee turnover rate?

    b. employee absenteeism?

    c. employee productivity?

    d. employee advancement?

11. Is the company involved in either pending or active litigation relative to labor disputes, sexual harassment, discrimination, or unfair labor practices?

12. Is there evidence that the average length of service of employees is reasonably consistent with other companies within the same industry, given the age of the company?

DOCUMENT CONTROL

1. Does the company maintain a document control procedure to guarantee that the specifications, bills-of-materials, engineering change notices, and drawing revision levels of both customer and internal documents are current and readily available to all appropriate operating personnel?

    a. Have all appropriate employees been trained on the application and scope of the document control procedures?

    b. Are those procedures routinely audited to ensure accuracy?

Competency and Capability Assessments

2. Is there evidence that the appropriate employees review and confirm all applicable documentation (customer and internal) prior to the processing of each customer order?

3. Is the internal and customer design and process documentation regularly monitored to ensure a high level of accuracy?

4. Is there evidence of a written procedure that defines and monitors the retention period for key documents?

5. Is there evidence of an effective storage and retrieval process and procedure for all key documents maintained?

6. Is an off-site or secured storage location maintained for key documents or back-up copies?

7. Is there restricted and/or controlled access to key documents?

8. Does the company comply with applicable ISO 9000 document control requirements?

9. Is the company registered under the applicable ISO guideline?

PRODUCT RELIABILITY AND WARRANTY

1. Can it be demonstrated that product reliability and life-cycle costs have been confirmed through failure mode and effects analysis, design of experiments, or other statistically based methodologies?

2. Can it be demonstrated that design for manufacturability, assembly, and maintainability methodologies are routinely utilized?

3. Are there documented design rules encompassing those methodologies that have been adopted in day-to-day operations?

4. Is there evidence of routine tracking of product life cycles and life-cycle costs?

5. Is there evidence that products routinely perform to advertised specifications, performance levels, and life-cycle costs under typical applications and environments?

6. Can it be demonstrated that product warranties cover all applications, conditions, and environments normally experienced by the respective products and systems?

7. Is there evidence to substantiate that warranty periods, terms, and conditions are comparable to normal industry standards?

8. Is there evidence that a formal policy and procedure for handling warranty claims is maintained? Is there evidence of adherence to those policies and procedures in normal situations?

Index

A

above-the-water-line decision-making, 173, 180-181
absenteeism, 110-115, 291
ACEG case study, (Tables 10-3 to 10-5) 302-314
affirmative action, 92
Age Discrimination in Employment Act, 90
American employees (Figure 7-4), 194-195
American Federation of Labor, 84
Americans with Disabilities Act, 91
antagonism, 107-108
appraisal criteria, 350-351
arbitration, 152-153
assess, analyze, decide, and act, 269-271
assignment card, (Figure 1-2), 14
assumptions, (Table 9-1) 266-268, 329-330
attack dog, 55-56
Auerbach, Red, 183-184, 205, 207

B

Baby Boomers, 210-214
balancing the organization, 21, 30, 140-141, 165-166, (Figure 8-1), 225-257, 329-330
barriers to transformation, (Tables 11-5, 11-6) 343-357
base-lining, 227-229, 232, 270-275, 329-330
   capabilities, 259-276
   infrastructure questions, (Table 8-1) 231
   performance, (Tables 11-2 to 11-4) 332-337
   quantitative tools, 337
   redefining, 363-364
   situational analysis, 57-58, 253, 262-275
benchmarking, 246-247
best practices, 287
bias in management, 17, 74
blame, 40
Boeing, 281-282
bottlenecks, 138-139
brainstorming, 282-283

C

capability assessment, 128, 197, 225-227, 379-409
capacity analysis, 139, (Eq. 9-1) 259-262
challenger, 55
Chamberlain Group, 322
change, 32-33, 356-357
   agent, 29, 37-38, 320
   barriers, (Tables 11-5, 11-6) 343-357
   communicating, (Figures 11-4, 11-5) 337-343
   constraints, (Figure 11-2) 330-332
   culture, 290-291, 323-327, 347-350
   engineered, 327
   failure, 16, 39-41, 169, 317-320, 352
   forced, 324, 326-327
   implementing, (Figure 11-10) 367-368
   in thinking, 179
   leadership, 318-319, (Figure 11-6) 357-360
   manager, (Figure 11-6) 358-360
   metrics, 337-338
   model, (Figure 11-1) 327-369
   momentum, 370
   not chaos, 32-33
   notices, 285-286
   organizing, (Figure 11-6) 357-360
   performance, barriers to, (Table 11-6) 350-355
   pitfalls, 369

Index

change (cont.),
  planned, 33, 327
  planning, (Figures 11-7 to 11-9, Table 11-7) 360-367
  policies, 356-357
  processes, 317
  resistance, 318, 339, (Table 11-6) 352-355
  selling, 339-343
  sense of urgency, 66, 201, 319, 341-342
  success, (Table 11-1) 320-327, 368
  sustaining, 342, (Figure 11-6) 358-360, 368-369
  team, 357-360
  technological, 166-168
  time, 327, (Table 11-5) 345-347, (Figure 11-10) 367
  unrealistic goal, 320
  vision, 37, 319, 327, 329-332, 342-343
chaos, 32-33
cheerleaders, 76-77
child labor regulations, 92-93
Civil Rights Act, 84-85
closed-loop management, 166, (Figures 7-3 to 7-5, Table 7-1) 182-208, 218, 376-377
  aligning capability and competency with vision, 225-227
  assess, analyze, decide, and act, 269-271
  assumptions (Table 9-1), 266-268, 377
  Auerbach, Red, 183-184
  communication, 64, 114, 208-216, 250-256, 343
  decision-making, 300-302
  listening, 218
  mapping processes, 287-288
  model, 184-207
  planned spontaneous recognition, 52, 220-221
  politics, 371, 376-377
  prepared, 377
  risk management, 20, 41-42, 261-262, (Table 9-1) 266-268, (Table 10-3) 302-303
  situational analysis, 57-58, 253, 262-275
  visioning, 225, 229-231
coaching, 47-48
collective bargaining, 94
communication, 12-15, 45-51, 114, 208-216
  argument, 215
  barriers, 75-76
  closed-loop, 64, 208-216
  consensus, 250-256
  cross-functional, 343
  cybercommunication, 48-49
  disagreements, 49, 215, 251-252
  expectations, 15-16
  failure, 141, 208
  flip chart, 61
  gender difference, 14
  generational challenges, 210-214
  Hawthorne Effect, 61, 65
  manager as a clearinghouse, 215-216
  of change, (Figures 11-4, 11-5) 337-343
  selling, 339-343
competency analysis, 228-229, 379-409
competition, 375-376
complementary skill sets, 30-31, 188-190, 359
conflict, 7-8, 17, 49, 213-214, 215, 252
conflicting metrics, 23-25, 115-118, 372
confrontation, 17, 143
consensus vs. consensus management, 250-256
Consolidation Omnibus Budget Reconciliation Act (COBRA), 95
constraints, 42, 280-282, 330-332
controversy, 7-8
corrective action, 64-65, 150-151, 233, 302, 311
cost controls assessment, 393-394
culture, 16, 290-292, 323-327, 338

412 *Walking the Talk: Pathways to Leadership*

barriers, 347-350
change, 317-318, 323-327
norms, 290-291
of failure, 16
of success, 16
current condition, 262-275
customer and field service assessment, 403-405
customer service deficiencies, 288-290

D

decision-making, 7-8, 77-78, 167-168, 171-181, 253, 293-302
authority, 178
avoiding, 274, 293-294
brainstorming, 282-283, 297-298
comfort level, 348, 356
consequences, 298
"desired" objectives, (Table 10-1, Table 10-2) 296-300
employee, 77-78, 167-168, 173-175, 178, 222-223, 253, 348, 355-356
empowered teams, 174-175
fear, 355
governing law, 175
instruction, 221-223
matrix, (Table 10-1, Table 10-2), 296-299, (Table 10-4) 310
"must" objectives, (Table 10-1, Table 10-2) 296-300
politics, 294
process, (Table 10-2) 296-302
quantitative analysis, 253
pro/con analysis, (Table 10-2), 302-303
reality check, 300-302
reluctance, 355-356
risk, 20, 41-42, 261-262, (Table 9-1) 266-268, 293, 295-296, 302
union vs. non-union environments, 175
unorthodox, 216-218
validating data, 264
delegation, 173

Deming, Ed, 39
disciplinary action, 126-127, 143-163
burden of proof, 148-149
documentation, 149
due diligence, 148
steps, 149-151
distribution process control assessment, 400-402
document control assessment, 407-408
documentation error, 287-288
downsizing, 364-365
DuPont, 174

E

Echo Boomers, 210-214
Electromation, 174
employee,
above-the-water-line decisions, 173
absenteeism, 110-115, 125-127, 132-135, 291
American vs. European (Figure 7-4), 194-195
antagonism, 107-108, 130-131
assignments, 78
attitudes, 74, 107, 130-131, 290-291
behavior, 65, 107-108, 144-147, (Figure 7-4, Table 7-1) 195-196
boredom, 100-101, 246
challenge, 80, 101, 255, 349-350
compensation, 344
competency, 119-121, 131-132, 157
confidence, 219
creativity, 79, 246-249
decision-making, 77-78, 167-168, 173-175, 178, 222-223, 253, 348, 355-356
dependency problems, 102-103, 110-111, 133
development, 132
disagreement, 49, 215, 251-252
disciplinary action, 126-127, 143-163
empowerment, 109-110, 169, 171-181

Walking the Talk: Pathways to Leadership

Index

employee (cont.),
  enthusiasm, 109-110
  error, 106-107
  expectations, 15-16, 100, 132
  favoritism, 122
  fear, 39-41, 178-179
  flex-time, 112
  fundamental needs, 168-169
  generational challenges (Table 7-2), 210-214
  growth, 196-197
  harassment, 138
  hiring, 18-22
  ideas, 41, 80
  involvement, 33-34, 43
  job classification, 124
  job description, 147-148, 155, 261-262, 287, 344
  job security, 170, 195, 349
  mentor, 197-198
  morale, 74, 110, 290-291
  motivation, 155, (Figure 7-4, Table 7-1) 194-203, 210-214, 216-218, 246-249
  needs, 75, 77, (Figure 7-1) 168-171, 202, 245, 348
  no-smoking policy, 135-138
  pay, 123-124
  peer pressure, 206, 345
  perception, 122, 376-377
  performance, 102-104, 125-127, 132, 143-149, 155-163, 265-266
  performance metrics, 219
  personal water line, 174
  potential, 101-102
  preparing for management position, 69-70
  productivity, 118-119, 128, (Eq. 9-1) 260-262
  quiet, 256
  red-lining, 123-125, 155
  relationships, 248-249
  reverse discrimination, 135
  review, 146-147, 150-151, 154
  revitalization, 216-218, 246-249
  reward and recognition, 52-53, 77, 120-121, 220-221, 245-246, 344, 349
  risk-taking, 80
  security needs, 170, 195
  selection, 185-194
  self-esteem, 170
  self-fulfillment, 170
  shielding from outside influence, 202-203
  skill sets, 178, 197, 231-241
  social needs, 170-171
  succession planning (Figure 8-4), 241-242
  tardiness, 110-115
  termination, 18-22, 126, 131, 133, 144, 155-163, 266
  thinking outside the box, 79, 235, 246-249
  training, 70, (Table 8-3) 238-241
  triggers, 200-202, 211-214
  turnover, 289, 291
  workload, 118-121, 128-130, 139, 260-262, 345
  wrong job, 100, 157, 159-163
employee selection, 185-194
  complementary skills, 188-190
  creative thinkers, 191-193
  hire a replacement, 190-191
  role players, 187-188
  superstars, 186-187
  teachers and students, 193-194
  tenacity, 190
employment laws, 83-98
empowerment, 109-110, 169, 171-181
  caution, 181
  teams, 174-176
  time frame, 179-181
  vs. involvement, 181
engineered change, 327
entrepreneur, 54
environmental constraints, 330
Equal Employment Opportunity Act, 84-85
Equal Pay Act, 89
errors, 106-107, (Eq. 10-1) 285-288
external metrics, 60-61

414   *Walking the Talk: Pathways to Leadership*

Index

F

facilities management and maintenance assessment, 399-400
failure analysis, (Figure 2-4) 43
Fair Labor Standards Act, 92-93
Family and Medical Leave Act, 93
far-sighted management, 38, 229
favoritism, 122
fear of failure, 39-41, 178-179
federal labor laws, 84-97
   affirmative action, 92
   Age Discrimination in Employment Act, 90
   Americans with Disabilities Act, 91
   Civil Rights Act, 84-85
   Consolidation Omnibus Budget Reconciliation Act (COBRA), 95
   discrimination against the handicapped, 90
   Equal Employment Opportunity Act, 84-85
   Equal Pay Act, 89
   Fair Labor Standards Act, 92-93
   Family and Medical Leave Act, 93
   Immigration Reform and Control Act, 96
   National Labor Relations Act, 94
   Occupational Health and Safety Act, 96
   Plant Closing Act, 95
   Pregnancy Discrimination Act, 86
   Rehabilitation Act, 90-91
   religious discrimination, 89
   sexual discrimination, 85-86
   sexual harassment, 86-89
   Taft-Hartley Act, 94, 97
   Worker Adjustment and Retraining Notification Act, 95
financial constraint, 280
financial stability assessment, 397-398
firefighting, 54, 261, 276
firing, 18-22
flavor-of-the-month program, 169, 180

flex-time, 112
flip chart, 61
forced change, 324, 326-327
fundamental needs, 168-169

G

Gen X and Gen Y, 210-214
General Motors, (Figure 2-2) 39, 351
generational challenges, (Table 7-2) 210-214
goals, 34-35, 151

H

Hawthorne Effect, 61, 65
Hay System, 124
hiring, 18-22
Honda, 249
horizontal management, (Figure 1-1) 11

I

Iacocca, Lee, 31
Immigration Reform and Control Act, 96
indecision, 35, 294
industry knowledge assessment, 398-399
informal leaders, 53-56
inherited problems, 21-23, 56-57, 130-132
innovative ideas, 80, 246-249
inventory management and control systems assessment, 390-391

J

job classification, 124
job description, 147-148, 155, 261-262, 287, 344
job security, 170, 195, 349
Jordan, James F., xiii-xv

L

labor laws, 83-98
labor relations assessment, 406-407

Walking the Talk: Pathways to Leadership

Index

leader,
  attitude, 49-51, 74
  honesty, 51-52
  informal, 53-56
  mentor, 54-55, 121, 197-198
  visibility, 51, 73
leadership, 27-67
  blame, 40-41
  by example, 5-7
  change agent, 29, 37-38, 320
  change processes, 318-319, (Figure 11-6) 357-360
  coaching, 47-48
  credibility, 44, 51-52, 56, 104, 157
  employee involvement, 33-34, 43
  facilitating, 208
  fear of failure, 39-41
  history, 27-31, 56-58
  honesty, 51-52
  listening, 42-45, 209-210, 218
  mature organizations, 241-249
  mentoring, 47-48, 119, 125, 240-241
  of transformation effort, 318-319, (Figure 11-6) 357-360
  organizational alignment, (Figure 8-1) 225-257
  organizational momentum, 35-38
  people issues, 5, 9
  performance goals, 34-35
  pressures, 31
  pros and cons, 32
  respect, 45
  situation driven (Figure 2-1), 30
  sustaining manager, 29
  techniques, 33-45
  Theory X, Y, and Z management, 27
  time, 42-45
  tradition, 207
  trust, 45, 340, 347, 372
  walking the talk, 47, 52, 108, 207, 209, 340, 372
listening, 42-45, 209-210, 218

M

Malcolm Baldrige National Quality Award, 230
management,
  and decisions, 8, 294
  and perception, 122, 376-377
  bias, 17, 74
  building consensus, 250-256
  building organizational depth, 197-198, 241
  candidates, 69-70
  capabilities, 3
  closed loop, 166, (Figures 7-3 to 7-5, Tables 7-1) 182-208, 218, 376-377
  commitment assessment, 395-397
  credibility, 44, 51-52, 56, 104, 157
  cultural norms, 291-291
  decision-making, 77-78, 221-223, 274-275, (Table 10-1, Table 10-2) 293-302
  employee disciplinary action, 126-127, 143-163
  employee equality, 205-206
  employee error, 106-107
  employee growth, 196-197
  employee morale, 74, 110, 290-291
  employee selection, 18-22, 185-194
  employee skill sets, 30-31, 178, 188-190, 197, 231-241
  employee termination, 18-22, 126, 131, 133, 144, 155-163, 266
  employee training, 70, (Table 8-3) 238-241
  far-sighted, 38, 229
  flexibility, 115
  honesty, 51-52
  generational challenges, (Table 7-2) 210-214
  horizontal, (Figure 1-1) 11
  indecision, 35, 294
  motivating employees, 155, (Figure 7-4, Table 7-1) 194-203, 210-214, 216-218, 246-249
  nearsighted, 38-39, 229

of creative thinkers, 192-193
people issues, 5, 9
policy enforcement, 135-137, 203, 244
predictability, 13, 205
problem transference, 221-223
respect, 332
setting precedent, 137
shielding the organization, 202-203
skill-building, 99-142
staff planning (Table 8-1, Table 8-2), 231-238, 241
strategy, 196-198
styles, 210-211, (Figure 11-6) 358-360
succession planning, (Figure 8-4) 241-242
Theory X, Y, and Z, 27
tools, 219-223
visibility, 51-52
walking the talk, 47, 52, 108, 207, 209, 340, 372
manager,
 avoiding conflict, 252,
 avoiding decisions, 274, 293-294
 behavior, 74
 beneath-the-water-line decisions, 172
 cheerleader, 76-77
 clearinghouse for communication, 215-216
 consistency, 179
 credibility, 44, 51-52, 56, 104, 157
 delegation, 173
 employee favoritism, 122
 employee morale, 74, 110, 290-291
 enforcement of rules and guidelines, 135-137, 203, 244
 honesty, 51-52
 ignoring issues, 156
 indecision, 35, 294
 listening, 42-45, 209-210, 218
 new, 21-23, 56-66, 81, 121-122, 130-132, 269-275

peer support, 234
prepared, 377
radical decisions, 216-218
respect, 332
role and responsibility, 70-73, 172, 207-208
setting precedent, 137
shooting the messenger, 108
span of control, 167
success, 206-208
vision, 229-231
walking the talk, 47, 52, 108, 207, 209, 340, 372
managing,
 assignment rotation, 199-200
 building consensus, 250-256
 cultivating skill sets, 231-241
 employee morale, 74, 110, 290-291
 employee turnover, 289, 291
 enforcement of rules and guidelines, 135-137, 203, 244
 generational challenges, (Table 7-2) 210-214
 group dynamics, 205
 identifying employee triggers, 200-202, 211-214
 mature organizations, 241-249, 254
 people issues, 5, 9
 performance issues, 23, 38, 56-57, 100-111, 125-127, 132-133, 143-163, 233, 264, 284-293
 perimeter of organization, (Figure 7-5) 204
 politicians, 198-199, 373-375
 revitalizing employees, 216-218, 246-249
 reward and recognition, 52-53, 77, 120-121, 220-221, 245-246, 344, 349
 risk, 20, 41-42, 261-262, (Table 9-1) 266-268, 293, 295-296, 302, 326-327
 setting priorities, 58, 233
 shielding organization, 202-203

Walking the Talk: Pathways to Leadership 417

Index

managing (cont.),
  skill set requirements, (Table 8-2) 236-238
  technical professionals, 208
  water lines, (Figure 7-2) 171-174, 356
  workload, 118-121, 128-130, 139, 260-262, 345
manufacturing process capabilities and capacities assessment, 379-380
manufacturing process controls assessment, 380-382
market dynamics, 166-168
Maslow's Hierarchy of Needs, 77, (Figure 7-1) 168-171, 202, 245, 348
  fundamental needs, 168-169, 348
  security needs, 170, 349
  self-esteem, 170, 349
  self-fulfillment, 170, 249, 349
  social needs, 170-171, 349-350
mature organizations, 241-249
  benchmarking, 246-247
  challenges, 246-249
  complacency, 248
  continuous improvement, 249
  employee relationships, 248-249
  enforcing rules and guidelines, 135-137, 203, 244
  like thinking, 254
  peer challenge, 255
  reward and recognition, 52-53, 77, 120-121, 220-221, 245-246, 344, 349
  Theory of Deliberate Change, 248
mentor, 54-55, 121, 197-198
mentoring, 47-48, 119, 125, 240-241
metrics, 60-61, 219
  conflicting, 372
  corrective action, 64-65
  external, 60-61
  linking to vision, 62-63, (Figure 11-4) 337-338
  monitoring, (Figure 2-6) 66, 219
  organizational, 244-245, 372

performance, 23-25, 59-61, 66, 115-118, 150, 219, 338, 372
  progress review, 64
mission statement, 62, 208, 342-343
mistakes, (Figure 2-3) 40, (Eq. 10-1) 285-286
morale, 74, 110, 290-291
motivating employees, 155, (Figure 7-4, Table 7-1) 194-203, 210-214, 216-218, 246-249
Motorola, 63-64
Musashi, Miyamoto, 239, 375-376

N

National Labor Relations Act, 94, 174
National Labor Relations Board, 22, 148-149, 152, 174
natural instincts, 3
nearsighted management, 38-39, 229
new manager, 56-66
  assess, analyze, decide, and act, 269-271
  base-lining the organization, 270-275
  decision-making, 270-275
  employee favoritism, 121-122
  inherited problems, 21-23, 56-57, 130-132
  internal customers, 60
  nuisance issues, 274-275
  performance measures, 60-61
  prioritizing issues, 58, 270, 273-275
  situational analysis, 271-273
  success, 81
  validating data, 270-275
non-value-added activities, 289-290
no-smoking policy, 135-138

O

Occupational Health and Safety Act, 96
operating constraints, 330-331
order-entry process control assessment, 402-403

Index

organizational, 10-12
　alignment, (Figure 8-1) 225-257
　balance, 21, 140-141, 165-166, 227
　base-lining, 57-58, 227-229, (Table 8-1) 231-232, 253, 259-276, 329-330, (Tables 11-2 to 11-4) 332-337, 363-364
　bottlenecks, 138-139
　capability, 128, 197, 225-227
　capacity, 139, 259-262
　communication, 12-15, 45-51, 114, 208-216
　competency analysis, 228-229, 379-409
　complacency, 37-38, 248
　culture, 16, 290-292, 317-318, 323-327, 338, 347-350
　depth, 197-198, 241
　discipline, 203-206
　dynamics, 205
　enforcement of rules and guidelines, 135-137, 203, 244
　history, 56-68
　metrics, 244-245, 372
　mission statement, 62, 208
　momentum, 35-38
　needs, 77, (Figure 7-1) 168-171, 202, 234-236, 245, 348
　opportunity gap, (Figure 8-1) 226-228
　politics, 23-25, 115-118, 294, 320-321, 371-378
　rebalancing, 21
　recognition, 52-53, 77, 120-121, 220-221, 245-246, 344, 349
　self-management, 243, 347
　skill sets, 231-241
　succession planning, (Figure 8-4) 241-242
　teamwork, 219-220
　Theory of Deliberate Change, 248
　unilateral actions, 105-106
　vision, 229-231
　workload, 118-121, 128-130, 139, 260-262, 345
outsourcing, 238

P

people issues, 5, 9-10
performance,
　appraisal criteria, 350-351
　barriers, (Table 11-6) 350-355
　corrective action, 64-65, 150-151, 233, 302, 311
　documentation, 154-155, 287
　drivers, 144
　expectations, 100, 149
　gap, (Figure 8-2) 225-227
　goals, 34-35, 151
　improvement, 23, 38, 100-111, 125-127, 132, 149-155, 264
　issues, 143-163, 233, 264
　measures, 60-61
　metrics, 23-25, 59-61, 66, 115-118, 150, 219, 338, 372
　monitoring, (Figure 2-6) 66
　problems, 21-23, 56-57, 133, 143-163, 284-293
　review, 146-147, 150-151, 154
　variations, 286-288
Peter Principle, 155-156
planned change, 33, 327
planned spontaneous recognition, 52, 220-221
planning a transformation, (Figures 11-7 to 11-9, Table 11-7) 360-367
Plant Closing Act, 95
policy enforcement, 135-137, 203, 244
politicians, 198-199, 373-375
politics, 23-25, 115-118, 294, 320-321, 371-378
　art of war, 373-375
　competition, 375-376
　Musashi, Miyamoto, 375-376
　security, 376-377
　time and place for, 373
　Tzu, Sun, 375-376
　vs. teamwork, 372-373
positive anxiety, 201
practical capacity analysis, (Eq. 9-1) 259-262
Pregnancy Discrimination Act, 86

Index

prejudice, 17, 74
preliminary failure analysis, (Figure 2-4) 43
preparing employees for management, 69-70
priority setting, 58, 233, 264, 273-275
pro/con analysis, (Table 10-2), 302-303
problem,
　analysis, 222-223, 277-284
　assessment clues, 284-293
　brainstorming, 282-283
　collecting data, 283-284
　inherited, 21-23, 56-57, 130-132
　performance, 56-57, 133, 143-163, 284-293
　prioritizing, 58, 233, 264, 273-275
　root cause, 114, 253, 259, 263, (Figure 10-1) 278-279
　solver, 54
　solving, 34, 264, 277, (Figure 10-2) 282-284
　transference, 221-223
　types, 285-293
　unresolved, 263
process capability, 106
process control, 106, 285
process issues, 9, (Eq. 10-1) 285-286
process thinking vs. silo, (Figure 1-1) 11
Procter & Gamble, 322-323
product reliability and warranty assessment, 408-409
productivity factor, (Eq. 9-1) 260-262
progress review, 64, 146-147, 150-151, 154
promotion into management, 1-25, 69-82

Q

quality circles, 176, 348
quality management assessment, 386-388
quality systems assessment, 383-386
quantitative tools, 337

R

raw materials compliance assessment, 389-390
rebalancing the organization, 21
regulatory compliance assessment, 405-406
rejection and rework, 285-286
religious discrimination, 89
resistance to change, 339, (Table 11-6) 352-355
resource constraints, 332
respect, 45
reward and recognition, 52-53, 77, 120-121, 220-221, 245-246, 344, 349
right-to-work laws, 97
risk criticality analysis, (Figure 2-5) 42, 44
risk management, 20, 41-42, 261-262, (Table 9-1) 266-268, 293, 295-296, 302, 326-327
risk-taking, 41-42, 280, 296
root cause, 114, 253, 259, 263, (Figure 10-1) 278-279
　constraints, 280-281
　problem-solving tools, 282-284
Ross Operating Valve, 321

S

SARAH syndrome, 326
security needs, 170
self-discipline, 203-205
self-esteem, 170
self-fulfillment, 170
self-managed organizations, 243, 347
sense of urgency, 66, 201, 319, 341-342
sexual discrimination, 85-86
sexual harassment, 86-89
shooting the messenger, 108
silo vs. process thinking, (Figure 1-1) 11
situational analysis, 57-58, 114, 233, 253, 259, (Table 9-1) 262-275, (Figure 10-1) 278-284, 323-324

Index

ACEG case study, (Tables 10-3 to 10-5) 302-314
   assumptions, (Table 9-1) 266-268
   prioritizing issues, 58, 233, 264, 273-275
   root cause, 114, 253, 259, 263-267, (Figure 10-1) 278-284
   validating data, 264, 266-267
skill sets, 30-31, 178, 188-190, 197, 231-241
social needs, 170-171
spontaneous recognition, 52, 220-221
squeaky wheel syndrome, 274
staff planning, (Table 8-1, Table 8-2) 231-238, 364-367
STAR rule, 144
state labor laws, 97-98
   right-to-work, 97
   workers' compensation, 97-98
status quo, 36, 344, 349-350
stop, think, assess, and react, 144
strategic project planning model, (Figure 11-7) 361
success, 16, 38, 81, 195-196
   reward and recognition, 52-53, 77, 120-121, 220-221, 245-246, 350
   tools for, 219-223
   tradition of, 206-208
succession planning, 368-369
superstars, 186-187, 198
supply chain problems, 292-293
support constraints, 331-332
sustaining manager, 29, (Figure 11-6) 358-360

T

tactical project planning model, (Figure 11-8) 361
Taft-Hartley Act, 94, 97
tardiness, 110-115
team leader, 55
teams, 170-171, 174-176, 186, 219-220, 349, (Figure 11-6) 357-360
teamwork vs. politics, 372-373
technical and product support assessment, 391-393
technical professionals, 208
technological change, 166-168
technology constraint, 281
Termini, Michael J., xvii, 42
Theory of Constraints, 139
Theory of Deliberate Change, 248, 322
theory of horizontal management, (Figure 1-1) 11
Theory X management, 27, 207
Theory Y and Theory Z management, 27
thinking outside the box, 79, 235, 246-249
time barrier, (Table 11-5) 345-347
time constraint, 280
Title VII, 84-89, 92
training, 70, (Table 8-3) 238-241
transformation,
   and cultural norms, 291-291
   barriers, (Tables 11-5, 11-6) 343-357
   base-lining, (Figure 11-3, Tables 11-2 to 11-4) 332-337, 364, 368
   Chamberlain Group, 322
   change manager, (Figure 11-6) 358-360
   change processes, 317
   changing policies, 356-357
   checklist, (Table 11-1) 324-325
   communicating, (Figures 11-4, 11-5) 337-343
   constraints, (Figure 11-2) 330-332
   culture, 290-291, 323-327, 347-350
   decision-making reluctance, 355-356
   engineered change, 327
   environmental constraints, 330
   failure, 16, 39-41, 169, 317-320, 352
   forced change, 324, 326-327
   formulation phase, (Figure 11-9) 363
   implementing, (Figure 11-10) 367-368
   leadership, 318-319, (Figure 11-6) 357-360

Index

transformation (cont.),
  linking metrics, 337
  Maslow's Hierarchy of Needs, 348-350
  model, (Figure 11-1) 327-369
  momentum, 370
  not chaos, 32-33
  operating constraints, 330-331
  organizational phase, (Figure 11-9) 362
  organizing, (Figure 11-6) 357-360
  patience, 319
  pitfalls, 369
  planned change, 33, 327
  planning, (Figures 11-7 to 11-9, Table 11-7) 360-367
  politics, 320-321
  Procter & Gamble, 322-323
  project plan, 320-321
  quantitative tools, 337
  realization phase, (Figure 11-9) 363
  resistance, 318, 339, (Table 11-6) 352-355
  resource constraints, 332
  risk/resistance assessment tool, (Table 11-6), 353-354
  Ross Operating Valve, 321
  SARAH syndrome, 326
  selling, 339-343
  sense of urgency, 66, 201, 319, 341-342
  situational assessment, 57-58, 114, 233, 253, 259, (Table 9-1) 262-275, (Figure 10-1) 278-284, 323-324
  staff planning, (Table 8-1, Table 8-2) 231-238, 364-367
  strategic project planning model, (Figure 11-7) 361
  success, (Table 11-1) 320-327, 368
  succession planning, 368-369
  support constraints, 331-332
  sustaining, 342, (Figure 11-6) 358-360, 368-369
  tactical phase, (Figure 11-9, Table 11-7) 363-366
  tactical project planning model, (Figure 11-8) 361
  team, (Figure 11-6) 357-360
  time, 327, (Table 11-5) 345-347, (Figure 11-10) 367
  unrealistic goal, 320
  vision, 37, 319, 327, 329-332, 342-343
transition into management, 1-25, 69-82
trust, 45, 108, 121, 340, 347
Tzu, Sun, 375-376

U

under-performer, 155
urgency, 66, 201, 319, 341-342

V

vision, 37-38, 229-231
  aligning capability and competency with, 225-227
  for change, 37, 319, 327, 329-332, 342-343
  linking to metrics, 62-63
  Motorola example, 63-64
  statement, 62, 208, 342-343

W

walking the talk, 47, 52, 108, 207, 209, 340, 372
Worker Adjustment and Retraining Notification Act, 95
workers' compensation, 97-98
workload, 118-121, 128-130, 139, 260-262, 345
wrong job, 100, 157, 159-163